THE FUNDAMENTAL RIGHT TO DATA PROTECTION

Since the entry into force of the Lisbon Treaty, data protection has been elevated to the status of a fundamental right in the European Union and is now enshrined in the EU Charter of Fundamental Rights alongside the right to privacy. This timely book investigates the normative significance of data protection as a fundamental right in the EU. The first part of the book examines the scope, the content and the capabilities of data protection as a fundamental right to resolve problems and to provide for an effective protection. It discusses the current approaches to this right in the legal scholarship and the case-law and identifies the limitations that prevent it from having an added value of its own. It suggests a theory of data protection that reconstructs the understanding of this right and could guide courts and legislators on data protection issues. The second part of the book goes on to empirically test the reconstructed right to data protection in four case-studies of counterterrorism surveillance: communications metadata, travel data, financial data and Internet data surveillance. The book will be of interest to academics, students, policy-makers and practitioners in EU law, privacy, data protection, counter-terrorism and human rights law.

Volume 71 in the Series Modern Studies in European Law

Modern Studies in European Law
Recent titles in this series:

**For the complete list of titles in this series, see
'Modern Studies in European Law' link at
www.bloomsburyprofessional.com/uk/series/modern-studies-in-european-law**

The Fundamental Right to Data Protection

Normative Value in the Context of Counter-Terrorism Surveillance

Maria Tzanou

·HART·

OXFORD · LONDON · NEW YORK · NEW DELHI · SYDNEY

HART PUBLISHING
Bloomsbury Publishing Plc
Kemp House, Chawley Park, Cumnor Hill, Oxford, OX2 9PH, UK

HART PUBLISHING, the Hart/Stag logo, BLOOMSBURY and the Diana logo are
trademarks of Bloomsbury Publishing Plc
First published in Great Britain 2017

First published in hardback, 2017
Paperback edition, 2019

A catalogue record for this book is available from the British Library.

Library of Congress Cataloging-in-Publication Data

Names: Tzanou, Maria, author.

Title: The fundamental right to data protection : normative value in the context of
counter-terrorism surveillance / Maria Tzanou.

Description: Oxford [UK] ; Portland, Oregon : Hart Publishing, 2017. | Series: Modern studies in
European law ; v. 71 | Includes bibliographical references and index.

Identifiers: LCCN 2016057792 (print) | LCCN 2016058889 (ebook) |
ISBN 9781509901678 (hardback) | ISBN 9781509901692 (Epub)

Subjects: LCSH: Data protection—Law and legislation. | Terrorism—Prevention—Law and legislation.

Classification: LCC K3264.C65 T93 2017 (print) | LCC K3264.C65 (ebook) | DDC 342/.0662—dc23

LC record available at https://lccn.loc.gov/2016057792

ISBN: HB: 978-1-50990-167-8
PB: 978-1-50993-307-5
ePDF: 978-1-50990-168-5
ePub: 978-1-50990-169-2

Typeset by Compuscript Ltd, Shannon

To find out more about our authors and books visit www.hartpublishing.co.uk. Here you will find
extracts, author information, details of forthcoming events and the option to sign up for our
newsletters.

Acknowledgements

This book is a revised and updated version of my doctoral research. I would like to thank my supervisor, Martin Scheinin for introducing me to the fascinating topic of data protection, as well as the other members of the jury of my Phd thesis defence, Valsamis Mitsilegas, Tuomas Ojanen and Giovanni Sartor, for guiding and stimulating my research. I concluded this book at Keele Law School and I wish to thank that institution and my colleagues Andrew Francis, Tsachi Keren-Paz, Eliza Varney, Marie-Andree Jacob and Sharon Thompson, for giving me ideas, enthusiasm, encouragement, as well as generous research leave. Many thanks also to Stephanie Worton for research assistance. This book would not have been possible if it were not for stimulating discussions and advice from friends and colleagues. In particular, I would like to thank Marise Cremona, Bruno de Witte, Federico Fabbrini, Joris Larik, Lorenzo Casini, Paul de Hert and Elaine Fahey. I am also indebted to Hart, and in particular, Sinead Moloney, Emily Braggins and Roberta Bassi for their patience and support throughout the drafting of this book. I am glad to acknowledge that an earlier version of sections of Chapter 1 was published as 'Data protection as a fundamental right next to privacy? "Reconstructing" a not so new right' (2013) 3 (2) *International Data Privacy Law* 88.

I wish to thank my parents and my brother for their love and unconditional support throughout this journey. This book is dedicated to Raul and Alexis, who have been incredibly patient.

Maria Tzanou
Keele Law School
September 2016

Contents

Table of Cases

European Union

European Court of Human Rights

European Commission on Human Rights

EU Member States

Belgium

Bulgaria

Cyprus

Czech Republic

Germany

Romania

Table of Legislation

Council Framework Decisions

Council Regulations

Council Decisions

Commission Decisions

Other

Agreements

International

National Legislation

Austria

Bulgaria

Czech Republic

Denmark

France

Germany

Hungary

Norway

Romania

United States

Introduction

Καὶ μὴν καὶ τῶν πόνων πλείστας ἀναπαύλας τῇ γνώμῃ ἐπορισάμεθα, ἀγῶσι μέν γε καὶ θυσίαις διετησίοις νομίζοντες, ἰδίαις δὲ κατασκευαῖς εὐπρεπέσιν, ὧν καθ'ἡμέραν ἡ τέρψις τὸ λυπηρὸν ἐκπλήσσει.[1]

THIS BOOK INVESTIGATES the normative significance of data protection as a fundamental right in the European Union (EU). The Lisbon Treaty, which entered into force on 1 December 2009, elevated data protection to the status of a fundamental right as this was recognised in Article 8 of the European Union Charter of Fundamental Rights (EUCFR) alongside the right to privacy (Article 7 EUCFR). A substantial body of laws in the European Union—either general or sector-specific—pertains to data protection; however, the constitutional entrenchment of this as a fundamental right next to privacy, albeit welcomed in general with enthusiasm, raised the question of whether something had actually changed. In this context, the question normally goes: what is the added value of a right to personal data protection? Or to put it more simply, does it add anything to the right to privacy?

To answer these questions, the book explores the scope, the content and the capabilities of data protection as a fundamental right to resolve problems and to provide for effective protection. It identifies the limitations currently affecting this right that prevent it from having an added value of its own. Using a number of normative and structural arguments, the book reconceptualises our understanding of data protection so that it can operate as a fully fledged fundamental right.

It goes on to empirically test the reconstructed right to data protection in four case-studies of counter-terrorism surveillance. Surveillance is one of the main tools in the fight against terrorism, fundamental to the apprehension of terrorist networks and the prevention of terrorist attacks.[2] Surveillance is facilitated through the rapid advancement of new technologies and is often based on the co-operation of private actors compelled by law. Surveillance often targets personal information. This trend, also known as 'dataveillance', refers to the 'systematic monitoring

---

[1] Thoukidides: Pericles' Funeral Oration from the Peloponnesian War (Book 2.34–46), para 38. English translation available at http://hrlibrary.umn.edu/education/thucydides.html: 'Further, we provide plenty of means for the mind to refresh itself from business. We celebrate games and sacrifices all the year round, and the elegance of our private establishments forms a daily source of pleasure and helps to banish the spleen.'

[2] D Lyon, *Surveillance Society—Monitoring Everyday Life* (Celtic Court, Open University Press, 2001); M Tzanou, 'The EU as an Emerging "Surveillance Society": The Function Creep Case Study and Challenges to Privacy and Data Protection' (2010) 4 *Vienna Online Journal of International Constitutional Law* 407.

of people's actions or communications through the application of information technology.[3] The main purpose of dataveillance is to identify proactively 'risky groups'.[4] Dataveillance involves different aspects of individuals' everyday lives: their communications, their travel information, their financial information, their activities on the Internet.

This book analyses the normative significance of the reconstructed right to data protection in the context of four instances of EU counter-terrorism data surveillance: electronic communications metadata surveillance, travel data surveillance, financial data surveillance and Internet data surveillance. The surveillance case studies were selected for two main reasons. The first relates to the scope of application of the rights enshrined in the Charter. According to Article 51(1) EUCFR, the provisions of the Charter are addressed to the EU institutions, bodies, offices and agencies and to the Member States only when they are implementing EU law. While it has been generally accepted that Article 8 EUCFR can be applied horizontally,[5] it appears crucial to test the capabilities of this fundamental right, first and above all, in its vertical application to EU institutions and Member States' actions when they implement EU law. In this respect, data surveillance represents 'the broadest of the EU's actions to counter terrorism.'[6] Indeed, EU counter-terrorism law largely concerns the collection and exchange of personal data[7] that affect in an indiscriminate manner almost every person in the EU. This leads to the second reason: the effects of EU data surveillance measures are particularly significant, thus, making it imperative to investigate the normative significance of the fundamental right to data protection in this context. In essence, the study of data surveillance measures in the light of the fundamental right to data protection aims to test the legal bite of this right in the most difficult context. The empirical chapters of the book follow a common structure that both reflects a discussion of the normative value of the fundamental right to data protection in each particular context of data surveillance, and provides a substantive counter-terrorism analysis of the specific measures examined against the fundamental rights to privacy and data protection.

The book, which bridges the gap between EU constitutional data protection law and counter-terrorism law, is divided into two parts. Part I reflects on the extent to which data protection can operate as a fully fledged fundamental right. Part II

---

[3] R Clarke, 'Introduction to Dataveillance and Information Privacy, and Definitions of Terms' (1988) 31(5) *Communications of the ACM* 498.

[4] M Levi and D Wall, 'Technologies, Security and Privacy in the post 9/11 European Information Society' (2004) 31 *Journal of Law and Society* 194, 200.

[5] E Frantziou, 'The Horizontal Effect of the Charter of Fundamental Rights of the EU: Rediscovering the Reasons for Horizontality' (2015) 21(5) *European Law Journal* 657, 660; E Spaventa, 'The horizontal application of fundamental rights as general principles of Union Law', in A Arnull et al (eds) *A constitutional order of states: essays in honour of Alan Dashwood* (Oxford, Hart Publishing, 2011) 199.

[6] C Murphy, *EU Counter-Terrorism Law: Pre-Emption and the Rule of Law* (Oxford, Hart Publishing, 2012) 147.

[7] See V Mitsilegas, *EU Criminal Law* (Oxford, Hart Publishing, 2009) ch 5; V Mitsilegas and A Baldaccini, 'Interdependence of the various initiatives and legislative proposals in the fields of Counter-terrorism and police co-operation at the European level', Briefing Note requested by the European Parliament's LIBE Committee, October 2007, 11.

informs the theoretical discussion on the added value of the fundamental right to data protection by empirically examining, in the light of this right, four case studies of EU counter-terrorism data surveillance. '*Ratione temporis*' the study presents the legal framework until the end of September 2016.

Part I lays down the theoretical and analytical framework of the analysis and consists of the first two chapters. Chapter 1 brings clarity to the concepts of privacy and data protection and considers the differences between them. It situates data protection in the context of EU constitutionalism and human rights law by paying special attention to its initial conception as a factor that would permit the free movement of data rather than a fundamental human right. It examines the foundational values and aims of the fundamental right to data protection and argues that these transcend privacy. It discusses the current approaches in the legal scholarship and the case law on data protection, and identifies their shortcomings. It then develops a theory on data protection that reconstructs this right and shapes its understanding in a clear and comprehensive manner that can guide courts and legislators on data protection issues.

Chapter 2 examines the jurisprudence of the European Court of Human Rights (ECtHR) and the Court of Justice of the European Union (CJEU or ECJ, used interchangeably) on the right to data protection. The ECtHR in a series of judgments has recognised data protection as an aspect of the right to private and family life found in Article 8 ECHR. Data protection has been the subject-matter of a rich case law of the CJEU even before its constitutional entrenchment as a fundamental right by the Lisbon Treaty. However, the Court's jurisprudence regarding data protection has significantly developed since that point. In the initial years after the inclusion of this right in the Charter, the Court, while aware of its existence, could not disassociate it from privacy. Subsequently, it reluctantly started to distinguish the two rights, and recent decisions illuminate that it has reached its maturity regarding the assessment of data protection. However, it is argued that there are still outstanding issues in the Court's analysis of this fundamental right that raise confusion as to its content and impede its functionality.

Part II examines the normative significance of the reconstructed fundamental right to data protection in different instances of counter-terrorism data surveillance. Chapter 3 considers the case of communications metadata surveillance. Communications metadata refers to information that can reveal the equipment, the location, the time and the participants of a communication, but not its content. The analysis examines the EU Data Retention Directive that imposed an obligation on electronic communications service providers to retain such data in order to fight terrorism and serious crime. The Directive was invalidated by the Court of Justice in its landmark decision in *Digital Rights Ireland*,[8] but the issue of metadata retention has not been resolved, since Member States have maintained or reintroduced such legislation at the domestic level.

---

[8] Joined Cases C-293/12 and C-594/12 *Digital Rights Ireland Ltd v Minister for Communications, Marine and Natural Resources* [2014] ECR I-238.

Chapter 4 focuses on travel data surveillance and examines the Passenger Name Record (PNR) case. This has both an international aspect, as the EU has entered into several bilateral international agreements on the transfer of PNR data, and a domestic one, as the EU has recently adopted its own PNR system. The chapter discusses the EU-US PNR saga and the EU PNR system. It analyses the context and content of these measures as well as the institutional actors involved in their adoption. It provides an overview of US privacy law and highlights its major shortcomings. It assesses the EU-US 'Umbrella' Agreement in the field of law enforcement and the recently adopted Judicial Redress Act of 2015, and finds that these do not provide robust protection of personal data on the other side of the Atlantic. It argues that the PNR case study is a prime example of the normative added value of a reconstructed fundamental right to data protection and demonstrates why the conceptual confusions of privacy and data protection often committed by the European judiciary are not merely theoretically erroneous, but also dangerous in practice. The chapter also reflects on the issues raised by terrorist profiling and concludes with a substantive fundamental rights assessment of the PNR.

Chapter 5 discusses financial data surveillance by considering the Terrorist Finance Tracking Programme (TFTP). It analyses how the programme became the subject of an international agreement between the EU and the US after its initial secret operation. It investigates the problematic role of Europol in the context of the EU-US TFTP Agreement and discusses the implications of the programme in the light of the fundamental rights to privacy and data protection.

Chapter 6 focuses on the Internet data surveillance undertaken by the US intelligence authorities as revealed by Edward Snowden. It examines the US foreign intelligence surveillance measures carried out with the compulsory assistance of leading US-based Internet companies such as Facebook, Skype, Google, Microsoft and Apple, and analyses the CJEU's seminal decision in *Schrems*[9] that invalidated the Safe Harbour scheme. It assesses the recently adopted Privacy Shield in the light of fundamental rights and concludes that this does not comply with the Court's pronouncements regarding the permissibility of mass surveillance targeting the content of electronic communications.

Chapter 7, Conclusions, draws together the discussion and addresses the core questions of whether and how the fundamental right to data protection can have a normative significance in the context of counter-terrorism data surveillance. While it is argued that the reconstructed right to data protection has an added value in the substantive assessment of counter-terrorism measures, the case studies suggest that modern surveillance techniques can empty essential aspects of the content of this right to the detriment of the data subjects. The book submits that it is in these cases that the essence of the fundamental right to data protection should be able to play a role and calls for the Court of Justice to develop its case law in this direction.

---

[9] Case C-362/14 *Maximillian Schrems v Data Protection Commissioner* (Judgment of the Court (Grand Chamber), 6 October 2015).

Part I

The Theoretical Framework

1

Data Protection as a Fundamental Right

I. CONCEPTUALISING PRIVACY

P RIVACY IS ENSHRINED in a number of international legal documents. The Universal Declaration of Human Rights (UDHR)[1] recognises in Article 12 that 'no one shall be subjected to arbitrary interference with his privacy, family, home or correspondence, nor to attacks upon his honour and reputation.' Article 17 of the International Covenant on Civil and Political Rights (ICCPR)[2] contains an almost identical provision. Article 8(1) of the European Convention on Human Rights (ECHR)[3] provides that 'everyone has the right to respect for his private and family life, his home and his correspondence', while Article 11(2) of the American Convention on Human Rights[4] holds that 'no one may be the object of arbitrary or abusive interference with his private life, his family, his home, or his correspondence…'. However, neither of these documents provides a definition of privacy.

Defining privacy is no easy task.[5] 'What is privacy?' is a question that has bothered numerous legal scholars, philosophers, sociologists and psychologists.[6] Many of them have despaired of arriving at a satisfactory definition of the concept of privacy.[7] As a concept, privacy has been accused of being 'exasperatingly vague and evanescent',[8] 'notoriously elastic and equivocal',[9] 'engorged with various and distinct meanings',[10] 'highly subjective',[11] 'culturally relative',[12] and operating 'in a

---

[1] The UNDHR was proclaimed by the General Assembly of the United Nations in 1948.

[2] Adopted and opened for signature, ratification and accession by General Assembly Resolution 2200A (XXI) of 16 December 1966.

[3] Signed on 4 November 1950.

[4] Signed on 22 November 1969 by the Organisation of American States.

[5] See W Beaney, 'The Right to Privacy and American Law' (1996) 31 *Law & Contemporary Problems* 253, 255.

[6] AD Moore, *Privacy Rights: Moral and Legal Foundations* (University Park PA, The Pennsylvania State University Press, 2010) 11.

[7] See C Raab and CJ Bennett, 'Taking the Measure of Privacy: Can Data Protection Be Evaluated?' (1996) 62 *International Review of Administrative Sciences* 535, 537.

[8] AR Miller, *The Assault on Privacy: Computer, Data Banks, and Dossier* (Ann Arbor, University of Michigan Press, 1973).

[9] H Delany and E Carolan, *The Right to Privacy: A Doctrinal and Comparative Analysis* (Dublin, Thompson Round Hall, 2008) 4.

[10] RC Post, 'Three Concepts of Privacy' (2000) 89 *Georgetown Law Journal* 2087.

[11] CJ Bennett and C Raab, *The Governance of Privacy: Policy Instruments in a Global Perspective*, 2nd edn (Cambridge MA, MIT Press, 2006) 8.

[12] Moore, n 6 above, p 11.

plethora of unrelated contexts'.[13] Nevertheless, the conceptual difficulty in defining privacy 'does not undermine its importance'.[14] Privacy has been described as 'the right most valued by civilized men'[15] and its value has rarely been questioned.[16] The value of privacy has been defended in academic literature by deontological and consequentialist theories.[17] Deontological theories argue that privacy has an intrinsic value 'as a right inherent to an individual's existence as a "human person"'.[18] In this respect, privacy is linked to human dignity, autonomy and personhood, and invasions of privacy are deemed to offend these values.[19] Consequentialist theories focus on the utility of privacy for 'the promotion of various goods (both for the individual and for society) that flow from its protection or are undermined by its violation'.[20] For instance, privacy is viewed as standing 'as a bulwark against governmental oppression and totalitarian regimes'.[21] In this vein, the argument normally goes that privacy has a value because it 'limits the forces of oppression' of 'despotic regimes'.[22]

A number of different methodologies have been suggested over time in order to approach the concept of privacy. It has been argued that one can identify different levels[23] or different contexts[24] of privacy: the 'descriptive level', which comprises the neutral definition of privacy that can be found in dictionaries;[25] the 'value level' that entails value considerations;[26] the 'legal level' which refers to the particular area of privacy that is protected by law;[27] and, the 'interest' level that

---

[13] JT McCarthy, *The Rights of Publicity and Privacy* (St Paul, Thomson West, 1987) 5.59; L BeVier, 'Information About Individuals in the Hands of Government: Some Reflections on Mechanisms for Privacy Protection', (1995) 4 *William and Mary Bill of Rights Journal* 455, 458.

[14] Delany and Carolan, n 9 above, p 4.

[15] *Olmstead v United States* 277 US 438, 478 (1928) (Brandeis J, dissenting). See also D Solove, *Understanding Privacy* (Cambridge MA, Harvard University Press, 2008) 3; J Rachels, 'Why Privacy is Important' (1975) 4 (4) *Philosophy & Public Affairs* 323.

[16] Some scholars have questioned the inherent value of privacy. See for instance A Etzioni, *The Limits of Privacy* (New York, Basic Books, 1999); RA Posner, *The Economics of Justice* (Boston MA Harvard University Press, 1983) 229; G Sartor, 'Privacy, Reputation, and Trust: Some Implications for Data Protection', European University Institute, EUI Working Papers, Law No 2006/04, 7.

[17] C Hunt, 'Conceptualizing Privacy and Elucidating its Importance: Foundational Considerations for the Development of Canada's Fledgling Privacy Tort' (2011) 37 (1) *Queen's Law Journal* 167, 202; C Hunt, 'From Right to Wrong: Grounding a "Right" to Privacy in the "Wrongs" of Tort' (2015) 52(3) *Alberta Law Review* 635, 639.

[18] ibid, p 639.

[19] ibid.

[20] ibid, p 640.

[21] AD Moore, 'Privacy, speech, and values: what we have no business knowing' (2016) 18 *Ethics & Information Technology* 41, 43.

[22] ibid.

[23] B Rodriguez-Ruiz, 'Protecting the secrecy of telecommunications: a comparative study of the European Convention on Human Rights, Germany and United States' (PhD thesis, European University Institute 1995) 35.

[24] R Gavison, 'Privacy and the Limits of Law' (1979) 89 *Yale Law Journal* 421, 423.

[25] Rodriguez-Ruiz, n 23 above, p 37.

[26] ibid, p 40.

[27] ibid, p 42.

expresses the reasons ('interests') justifying the protection granted to the right.[28] Definitions of privacy can be couched in descriptive or normative terms, depending on whether privacy is seen as a 'mere condition' or a 'moral claim' on others to refrain from certain activities.[29] Some commentators argue that privacy should be conceived as instrumental to other rights or values,[30] or as a 'derivative notion' that rests upon more basic rights such as liberty,[31] autonomy[32] and human dignity.[33] Finally, Solove suggests that privacy should be conceptualised by focusing on 'the different kinds of activities which impinge upon it'.[34]

Furthermore, privacy is often understood as protecting what falls within the 'private' as opposed to the 'public' sphere.[35] In this respect, a distinction is frequently made between the 'private' and the 'public' spheres,[36] 'privacy' and 'publicity'.[37] Following this distinction, privacy is sometimes regarded as 'suspicious'[38] and 'socially detrimental',[39] because it advocates a form of 'retreat from society'.[40] The origins of this approach to privacy are traced by philosophers and legal scholars[41] to ancient Greece and Rome, where privacy had a negative connotation, since a citizen's life meant active participation in the *polis*. This theory was further taken up by republican philosophers such as Rousseau, who saw private concerns as a threat to the functioning of good government and the end of the state.[42] More recently, Hannah Arendt heavily criticised a private life,[43] relying on the idea that privacy in ancient Greece meant 'literally a state of being deprived of something'.[44] This distinction between private and public life, between the 'self' and the

---

[28] ibid, p 44.

[29] Moore, n 6 above, p 11.

[30] A Rouvroy and Y Poullet, 'The Right to Informational Self-Determination and the Value of Self-Development: Reassessing the Importance of Privacy for Democracy?', in S Gutwirth and others (eds), *Reinventing Data Protection?* (New York, Springer, 2009) 45.

[31] S Gutwirth, *Privacy and the Information Age* (Oxford, Rowman & Littlefield, 2002) 2.

[32] L Bygrave, *Data Protection Law: approaching its rationale logic and limits* (The Hague, Kluwer Law International, 2002) 133; P Bernal, *Internet Privacy Rights—Rights to Protect Autonomy* (Cambridge, Cambridge University Press, 2014).

[33] See G González Fuster, *The Emergence of Personal Data Protection as a Fundamental Right of the EU* (Cham, Springer, 2014), 23 and references therein.

[34] Solove, n 15 above, p 9.

[35] P de Hert, 'The Case of Anonymity In Western Political Philosophy—Benjamin Constant's Refutation of Republican And Utilitarian Arguments Against Anonymity' in C Nicoll et al (eds), *Digital Anonymity And The Law: Tensions And Dimensions* (The Hague, T.M.C Asser Press, 2003) 47, 52.

[36] See also J Habermas, *The Structural Transformation of the Public Sphere—An Inquiry into a Category of Bourgeois Society*, new edition (Cambridge, Polity Press, 1992).

[37] ibid.

[38] ibid.

[39] Solove, n 15 above, p 80.

[40] ibid.

[41] For an analysis of the historical development of the public–private debate, see J Bailey, 'From Public to Private: The Development of the Concept of the "Private"' (2002) 69 *Social Research: An International Quarterly* 15.

[42] JJ Rousseau, 'Du contrat social' (1762), in *Oeuvres completes de Jean-Jacques Rousseau* (eds B Gagnebin and M Raymond) (Paris, Gallimard (Pleiade), 1964) Book 1, ch VIII, 365.

[43] H Arendt, *The Human Condition* (Chicago, University of Chicago Press, 1998) 38.

[44] ibid.

'society',[45] sees privacy as an individual right in juxtaposition with the larger community.[46] This perception, however, fails to recognise the 'broader social importance of privacy',[47] since it understands it as a right that solely serves the individual. Such understanding is very problematic, because, as Priscilla Regan explains, when privacy is defined as an individual right, policy formulation often entails a balancing of this individual right against a competing interest or right, such as for instance, the police interest in law enforcement, which is recognised as a societal interest. In this regard, privacy has to be on the defensive, 'with those alleging a privacy invasion bearing the burden of proving that a certain activity does indeed invade privacy and that the "social" benefit to be gained from the privacy invasion is less important than the individual harm incurred'.[48] According to Regan, it should, therefore, be accepted that privacy has 'value beyond its usefulness in helping the individual to maintain his or her dignity or develop personal relationships'. In fact, privacy serves 'not just individual interests but also common, public and collective purposes.'[49] Privacy, thus, has a public value,[50] because it protects the individual 'for the good of society'.[51]

Numerous definitions of the notion of privacy have been suggested. Among the most influential, is the conception of privacy as 'the right to be let alone', based on the famous article 'The Right to Privacy' by Samuel Warren and Louis Brandeis.[52] In this path-breaking work,[53] Warren and Brandeis contended that 'the common law secures to each individual the right of determining, ordinarily, to what extent his thoughts, sentiments, and emotions shall be communicated to others'.[54] Privacy has also been defined as the 'right to decide how much knowledge of [a person's] personal thought and feeling … private doings and affairs … the public at large shall have.'[55] Variations of this definition, which has been called the 'limited access to the self' conception of privacy,[56] have been developed by a number of scholars.[57] Moreover, privacy has been seen as 'concealment of

---

[45] RF Hixson, *Privacy in a Public Society: Human Rights in Conflict* (New York, Oxford University Press, 1987) 212.

[46] Solove, n 15 above, p 89.

[47] PM Regan, *Legislating Privacy: Technology, Social Values, and Public Policy* (Chapel Hill, University of North Carolina Press, 1995) 213. See also NA Moreham, 'Privacy in Public Places' (2006) 65(3) *Cambridge Law Journal* 606.

[48] ibid.

[49] ibid, p 321.

[50] S Simitis, 'Reviewing Privacy in an Information Society' (1987) 135 *University of Pennsylvania Law Review* 707, 709.

[51] Solove, n 15 above, pp 92–93.

[52] SD Warren and LD Brandeis, 'Right to Privacy' (1890) 4 *Harvard Law Review* 193.

[53] The article has been characterised as the 'most influential law review article of all'. See H Kalven, 'Privacy in Tort Law—Were Warren and Brandeis Wrong?' (1966) 31 *Law and Contemporary Problems* 326, 327.

[54] Warren and Brandeis, n 52 above, p 205.

[55] E Godkin, 'The Rights of the Citizen To His Own Reputation' (1890) 8 *Scribner's Magazine* 58, 65.

[56] Solove, n 15 above, p 18.

[57] See S Bok, *Secrets: On the Ethics of Concealment and Revelation* (New York, Vintage Books, 1989) 10; Gavison, n 24 above, p 423.

information'[58] from others. Another theory views privacy as a form of protecting 'the individual's interest in becoming, being, and remaining a person.'[59] Furthermore, privacy has been conceived as a form of intimacy. In this sense, privacy is 'the state of the agent having control over decisions concerning matters that draw their meaning and value from the agent's love, caring, or liking.'[60]

A number of authors conceive privacy as control over personal information. According to Alan Westin, privacy is 'the claim of individuals, groups, or institutions to determine for when, how, and to what extent information about them is communicated to others.'[61] Charles Fried argues that

> privacy is not simply an absence of information about what is in the minds of others; rather it is the *control* we have over information about ourselves … The person who enjoys privacy is able to grant or deny access to others … Privacy, thus, is control over knowledge about oneself. But it is not simply control over the quantity of information abroad; there are modulations in the quality of the knowledge as well. We may not mind that a person knows a general fact about us, and yet feel our privacy invaded if he knows the details.[62]

As a theory of privacy, the control over personal information conception has been criticised for being both too narrow and too vague.[63] On the one hand, it is too narrow because it excludes the non-informational aspects of privacy, also known as 'decisional privacy', which under the USA's constitutional protection of privacy refers to the individual's entitlement to make his own decisions.[64] The distinction between 'informational' and 'decisional' privacy in US constitutional law has been recognised by Justice Stevens, who, in his Opinion in *United States Department of Justice v Reporters Committee for Freedom of the Press*,[65] noted that privacy cases before the Supreme Court 'in fact involved at least two different kinds of interests. One is the individual interest in avoiding disclosure of personal matters, and another is the interest in independence in making certain kinds of important

---

[58] R Posner, *Economic Analysis of Law* 5th edn (New York, Aspen, 1998) 46.

[59] JH Reiman, 'Privacy, Intimacy, and Personhood' (1976) 6 *Philosophy and Public Affairs* 26.

[60] JC Inness, *Privacy, Intimacy and Isolation* (Oxford, Oxford University Press, 1996) 56; C Fried, *An Anatomy of Values Problems of Personal and Social Choice* (Boston MA, Harvard University Press, 1970) 142.

[61] A Westin, *Privacy and Freedom* (London, The Bodley Head, 1970) 142. See also AC Breckenridge, *The Right to Privacy* (Lincoln, University of Nebraska Press, 1970) 1; RP Bezanson, 'The Right to Privacy Revisited: Privacy, News, and Social Change, 1890–1990' (1992) 80 *California Law Review* 1133, 1133.

[62] C Fried, 'Privacy' (1968) 77 *Yale Law Journal* 475, 482–83.

[63] Solove, n 15 above, p 24.

[64] As Solove and Schwartz explain, 'decisional privacy involves matters such as contraception, procreation, abortion, and child rearing, and is at the centre of a series of Supreme Court cases often referred to as "substantive due process" or "the constitutional right to privacy". Non-informational aspects of privacy are inherent also in the right to private and family life as protected in Art 8 ECHR. See D Solove and P Schwartz, *Information Privacy Law* (New York, Wolters Kluwer Law & Business, 2009) 1.

[65] *United States Department of Justice v Reporters Committee for Freedom of the Press* 489 US 749 (1989).

decisions.'[66] In this respect, the control over personal information conception of privacy is narrow because it fails to take the second interest into account. On the other hand, it is too vague because it does not provide a clear definition of the notion of personal information, over which the individual is entitled to control.[67] For instance, while one definition of personal information as 'control over who can see us, hear us, touch us, smell us, and taste us, in sum, control over who can sense us',[68] is considered unduly broad; another, that sees personal information as 'any data about an individual that is identifiable to that individual'[69] does not fit well in a privacy theory, because 'there is a significant amount of information identifiable to us that we do not deem as private'.[70]

II. CONCEPTUALISING DATA PROTECTION

Writing on the concept of data protection, Paul de Hert and Serge Gutwirth comment that 'it is impossible to summarise data protection in two or three lines. Data protection is a catch-all term for a series of ideas with regard to the processing of personal data'.[71] Directive 95/46/EC (the 'European Data Protection Directive' or 'Data Protection Directive')[72] considers data protection as the protection of 'the fundamental rights and freedoms of natural persons, and in particular their right to privacy with respect to the processing of personal data.'[73] The General Data Protection Regulation (GDPR),[74] which repeals the Data Protection Directive and which will apply from 25 May 2018, states that it 'protects fundamental rights and freedoms of natural persons and in particular their right to the protection of personal data.'[75] The notions of 'processing' and 'personal data' are central to understanding the concept of data protection. In general terms, 'processing' can be

---

[66] ibid, 762. *See* also *Whalen v Roe* 429 US 589 (1977), 598–600.

[67] Solove, n 15 above, p 24.

[68] RB Parker, 'A Definition of Privacy' (1974) 27 *Rutgers Law Review* 275, 280.

[69] RS Murphy, 'Property Rights in Personal Information: An Economic Defence of Privacy' (1996) 84 *Georgetown Law Journal* 2381, 2383.

[70] Solove, n 15 above, p 25.

[71] P de Hert and S Gutwirth, 'Data Protection in the Case Law of Strasbourg and Luxembourg: Constitutionalisation in Action' in S Gutwirth and others (eds), *Reinventing Data Protection?* (New York, Springer, 2009) 3.

[72] Directive 95/46/EC of the European Parliament and of the Council of 24 October 1995 on the protection of individuals with regard to the processing of personal data and on the free movement of such data [1995] OJ L281/3, (Data Protection Directive).

[73] Data Protection Directive, Art 1(1). Similarly, Convention No 108 of the Council of Europe defines data protection as 'the respect of the rights and freedoms [of the individual], and in particular his right to privacy, with regard to automated processing of personal data relating to him'. Convention for the Protection of Individuals with regard to Automatic Processing of Personal Data, Strasbourg, 28 January 1981, European Treaty Series No 108.

[74] Regulation 2016/679 of the European Parliament and of the Council of 27 April 2016 on the protection of natural persons with regard to the processing of personal data and on the free movement of such data, and repealing Directive 95/46/EC (General Data Protection Regulation, GDPR) [2016] OJ L119/1.

[75] GDPR, Art 1(2). See also Art 1(1).

seen as any operation performed upon the data, from their collection, recording, storage, use, to their disclosure, dissemination, erasure and destruction.[76] The data are considered personal, when they can be linked to a certain individual, normally referred to as the 'data subject'.[77] Data protection can be conceived, thus, as referring to this set of legal rules that aim to protect the rights, freedoms and interests of individuals, whose personal data are collected, stored, processed, disseminated, destroyed, etc.[78] The rights granted to the 'data subjects' correspond to relevant responsibilities of the 'controllers'. 'Controllers' are the natural or legal persons who 'determine the purposes and means of the processing of personal data'.[79]

The ultimate objective of data protection is to ensure 'fairness in the processing of data and, to some extent, fairness in the outcomes of such processing'.[80] The fairness of processing is safeguarded by a set of principles (also known as 'fair information principles' or 'data protection principles'), which, in general terms, can be couched as follows:[81]

1) personal information should be collected and processed fairly and lawfully;
2) it should be collected for specified, explicit and legitimate purposes and not further processed in a way incompatible with those purposes;
3) it should be adequate, accurate, relevant and not excessive with regard to the purposes for which it is collected and processed;
4) it should not be kept for longer than is necessary for the purposes for which it was collected and processed;
5) the consent of the person to whom the information relates is necessary for some categories of processing;
6) security measures should be taken in order to protect the data from accidental loss or unauthorised disclosure and use;
7) the individual should be informed that his/her data are held by others; should be given access to them and the possibility to correct them and delete them in certain cases;
8) the processors of personal information should be accountable for complying with the fair information principles;
9) compliance with these requirements should be controlled by an independent authority.

---

[76] See Data Protection Directive, Art 2(b); Art 4(1) GDPR and Art 2(c) of Convention 108.

[77] Data Protection Directive Art 2(a) provides that 'personal data' denotes 'any information relating to an identified or identifiable natural person'. See also Art 4(1) GDPR and Art 2(c) of Convention 108.

[78] F Hondius, *Emerging Data Protection in Europe* (New York, American Elsevier, 1975) 1.

[79] Data Protection Directive, Art 2(d) and Art 4(7) GDPR. Art 2(d) of Convention 108 uses the concept 'controller of the file'.

[80] Bygrave, n 32 above, p 168.

[81] The list presents indicatively only a core of fair information principles. The exact formulation of the principles differs in the various texts, for instance, the EU Data Protection Directive, the GDPR, the CoE Convention No 108, the OECD and the APEC privacy guidelines. See also Art 29 WP, Transfers of personal data to third countries: Applying Arts 25 and 26 of the EU Data Protection Directive, 24 July 1998, 5.

While defining data protection does not seem to involve the philosophical controversies and difficulties that the concept of privacy faces, nevertheless, it is not a notion without problems itself. Its meaning is not very clear from the outset,[82] all the more because its definition appears to be quite technical and confusing, as it is based on further concepts, such as 'personal data' and 'processing' that seek definition themselves.[83] The term 'data protection', which is derived from the German *Datenschutz*, is most commonly used in (continental) European jurisdictions; in the USA, Canada and Australia, other terms such as 'informational privacy', 'data privacy' or simply 'privacy protection' are used.[84]

A. Approaches to Data Protection

There is often a confusion at to how data protection should be perceived. Is data protection a factor of economic growth? Is it a fundamental human right? Is it a consumer right?[85] Or can it be simply seen as a 'problem of trust' over the security of personal information?[86] There are different ways of approaching data protection[87] and the debate is not without practical consequences for the concept of the notion. Below, the two main approaches to data protection, the economic approach and the fundamental rights' approach are discussed. The OECD privacy regulatory framework is used as an example of the former, and that of the EU as an example of the latter.[88]

i. The Economic Approach

An example of the economic approach to data protection can be found in the OECD Privacy Guidelines. The Organisation for Economic Co-operation and

---

[82] *Contra* Hondius who argues that 'Etymologically, … the term [data protection] is not quite correct, but its meaning is clear.' Hondius, n 78 above, p 1.

[83] The term data protection has also been criticised for concentrating disproportionately on the data rather than the person as the object of protection. See Bennett and Raab, n 11 above, p 11; L Bygrave, *Data Privacy Law—An International Perspective* (Oxford, Oxford University Press, 2013) 23.

[84] Bygrave, n 32 above, p 1.

[85] This approach is followed in the APEC Privacy Framework, www.dpmc.gov.au/privacy/apec/apec_privacy_framework.cfm. The Framework contains nine Privacy Principles: 1) Preventing Harm; 2) Notice; 3) Collection Limitations; 4) Uses of Personal Information; 5) Choice; 6) Integrity of Personal Information; 7) Security Safeguards; 8) Access and Correction; and 9) Accountability. See also, CD Terwangne, 'Is a Global Data Protection Regulatory Model Possible?' in S Gutwirth and others (eds), *Reinventing Data Protection?* (New York, Springer, 2009) 175, 181, 183–85.

[86] This was the approach adopted by the World Summit on the Information Society in its Declaration of Principles (Declaration of Principles—Building the Information Society: a global challenge in the new Millennium, Document WSIS-03/GENEVA/DOC/4-E, Geneva, 12 December 2003). According to this approach, data protection coincides with data security, and security breaches are the problems to be dealt with.

[87] For an analysis of the different regulatory regimes worldwide see AL Newman, *Protectors of Privacy: Regulating Personal Data in the Global Economy* (Ithaca, Cornell University Press, 2008).

[88] It should be noted that the two approaches are not mutually exclusive; on the contrary, they are often both present at the same time in legal documents.

Development (OECD) is an international organisation established in 1961, whose aim is to promote policies to improve economic and social well-being. It is an economic organisation that measures productivity and global flows of trade and investment, carries out analysis mainly in economic matters, and is not involved in human rights activities. It attempts to promote rules and set international standards in many areas, such as, for instance, development, education, employment, energy, environment, finance, investments, science and technology, taxation and trade.

In a symposium organised by the OECD in 1977 on Transborder Data Flows and the Protection of Privacy, the economic value and national interest of transborder data flows was discussed by the participants. In a comment made by Louis Joinet,[89] who participated later in the drafting of the OECD Guidelines, it was noted:

> Information is power, and economic information is economic power. Information has an economic value and the ability to store and process certain types of data may well give one country political and technological advantage over other countries. This in turn may lead to a loss of national sovereignty through supranational data flows.[90]

Following the symposium, an Expert Group[91] was created to begin work on the privacy guidelines. The main aim was to tackle concerns about the growing use of personal data and computerised processing. But, given the OECD's mandate to promote economic growth and contribute to the expansion of world trade, a further aim was to prevent national laws from creating barriers to the free flow of information[92] and to the development of economic and social relations among member countries.[93] The Guidelines, adopted on 23 September 1980,[94] place an emphasis on ensuring that the measures introduced to protect personal data would not result in restricting transborder data flows. Thus, data protection is

---

[89] Louis Joinet was at the time the President of the French *Commission nationale de l'informatique et des libertés* (CNIL) (National Commission on Informatics and Liberty).

[90] Louis Joinet as quoted in J Eger, 'Emerging Restrictions on Transnational Data Flows: Privacy Protections or Non- Tariff Barriers?' (1978) 10 *Law and Policy in International Business* 1065, 1066.

[91] Expert Group on Drafting Guidelines Governing the Protection of Privacy and Transborder Data Flows of Personal Data.

[92] See Working Party on Information Security and Privacy, 'The Evolving Privacy Landscape: 30 Years after the OECD Privacy Guidelines', OECD Digital Economy Paper, 30 April 2011, www.oecd.org/officialdocuments/displaydocumentpdf/?cote=dsti/iccp/reg(2010)6/final&doclanguage=en.

[93] See OECD Recommendation of the Council Concerning Guidelines Governing the Protection of Privacy and Transborder Flows of Personal Data (23 September 1980), available at www.oecd.org/document/18/0,3746,en_2649_34255_1815186_1_1_1_1,00.html.

[94] OECD Guidelines on the Protection of Privacy and Transborder Flows of Personal Data, available at www.oecd.org/document/18/0,3746,en_2649_34255_1815186_1_1_1_1,00.html. The OECD Privacy Guidelines are not legally binding. The Guidelines contain eight fair information principles: 1) the Collection Limitation Principle; 2) the Data Quality Principle; 3) the Purpose Specification Principle; 4) the Use Limitation Principle; 5) the Security Safeguards Principle; 6) the Openness Principle; 7) the Individual Participation Principle; and 8) the Accountability Principle.

seen mainly as a factor fostering international economic aims through the facilitation of free and unimpeded transfers of personal information.[95]

ii. The Fundamental Rights' Approach

The European Union constitutes the prime example of the fundamental rights approach to data protection.[96] Unlike the Council of Europe, the EU is not a human rights organisation. It was created as an economic community, and while it has gone a long way from that, still, many of its competences are of an economic nature.

Data protection, hence, at its birth in the EU, was an internal market concern, similar to the economic approach of the OECD Guidelines analysed above. Directive 95/46/EC, the 'Data Protection Directive', was the first piece of legislation adopted in the EU on the protection of personal data.[97] The Directive had two objectives: to harmonise the different national rules on data protection, and to ensure simultaneously the free movement of such data.[98] Fundamental rights and market freedoms were placed on the same footing under the Directive.[99] According to Recital 3, the establishment and functioning of the internal market in which goods, persons, services and capital can move freely requires 'not only that personal data should be able to flow freely from one Member State to another, but also that the fundamental rights of individuals should be safeguarded.' This was because divergent levels of protection of fundamental rights, and in particular of the right to privacy with regard to the processing of personal data, would create obstacles to the pursuit of a number of economic activities at Community level.[100] In order to remove these obstacles, the level of protection of individual rights had to be made equivalent in all Member States.[101] The equivalent protection of fundamental rights was expected to render free movement of data possible because

---

[95] See S Nouwt, 'Towards a Common European Approach to Data Protection: A Critical Analysis of Data Protection Perspectives of the Council of Europe and the European Union' in S Gutwirth and others (eds), *Reinventing Data Protection?* (New York, Springer, 2009) 275, 278.

[96] Data protection is recognised as a fundamental right at the constitutional level in several European countries, such as Portugal, Austria, Spain, Greece, Hungary, Slovakia, the Czech Republic, Poland and Estonia.

[97] For an analysis of the EU legal framework see M Tzanou, 'Data Protection in EU Law: An Analysis of the EU Legal Framework and the ECJ Jurisprudence' in C Akrivopoulou and A Psygkas (eds), *Personal Data Privacy and Protection in a Surveillance Era: Technologies and Practices* (Hershey, IGI Global, 2011) 273; M Tzanou, 'Data Protection in EU Law after Lisbon: Challenges, Developments, and Limitations' in M Gupta (ed) *Handbook of Research on Emerging Developments in Data Privacy* (Hershey, IGI Global, 2014) 24.

[98] Data Protection Directive, Art 1.

[99] This is also evident in the title of the directive: 'Directive 95/46/EC on the protection of individuals with regard to the processing of personal data and on the free movement of such data.' See S Gutwirth, *Privacy and the Information Age* (Oxford, Rowman & Littlefield Publishers, 2002) 91–92; L Bergkamp, 'EU Data Protection Policy—The Privacy Fallacy: Adverse Effects of Europe's Data Protection Policy in an Information-Driven Economy' (2002) 18 *Computer Law and Security* 31, 33 and 37.

[100] Data Protection Directive, Recital 7.

[101] Data Protection Directive, Recital 8.

Member States would 'no longer be able to inhibit the free movement between them of personal data on grounds relating to the protection of the rights and freedoms of individuals, and in particular the right to privacy.'[102] The Directive was, thus, intended as a harmonisation instrument and was adopted under the legal base of Article 95 of the EC Treaty (now Article 114 TFEU), which concerns the approximation of legislation relating to the internal market.

Data protection was not only born out of internal market concerns; its concept was also recognised as a dimension of privacy and its protection was dependent on it. According to the Data Protection Directive:

> the object of the … laws on the processing of personal data is to protect fundamental rights and freedoms, notably the right to privacy, which is recognised both in Article 8 of the ECHR and the general principles of Community law.[103]

Data protection was included as a fundamental right in the EUCFR, which enjoys the status of EU primary law pursuant to Article 6(1) TEU,[104] since the Lisbon Treaty entered into force as from 1 December 2009. The relevant provision is Article 8 EUCFR. The right to privacy is enshrined in the Charter in Article 7 EUCFR, which reads:

Article 7—Respect for private and family life

Everyone has the right to respect for his or her private and family life, home and communications.

Article 8 of the Charter provides:

Article 8—Protection of personal data

1. Everyone has the right to the protection of personal data concerning him or her.
2. Such data must be processed fairly for specified purposes and on the basis of the consent of the person concerned or some other legitimate basis laid down by law. Everyone has the right of access to data which has been collected concerning him or her, and the right to have it rectified.
3. Compliance with these rules shall be subject to control by an independent authority.

The fundamental right to personal data protection is set out in three paragraphs in Article 8 EUCFR. The first contains the general recognition of the right: everyone has the right to the protection of personal data concerning him or her. The second and the third paragraphs describe the content of the right and lay down six requirements applicable to the processing of personal data.[105] Personal data:

---

[102] Data Protection Directive, Recital 9.

[103] Data Protection Directive, Recital 10. Art 1 of the Directive stipulates: 'Member States shall protect the fundamental rights and freedoms of natural persons, and in particular their right to privacy with respect to the processing of personal data.'

[104] Consolidated Version of the Treaty on European Union [2008] C326/15 (TEU), Art 6(1) TEU provides: 'The Union recognises the rights, freedoms and principles set out in the Charter of Fundamental Rights of the European Union of 7 December 2000, as adapted at Strasbourg, on 12 December 2007, which shall have the same legal value as the Treaties.'

[105] González Fuster, n 33 above, p 4.

1) must be processed fairly; 2) for specified purposes; 3) on the basis of the consent of the person concerned or some other legitimate basis laid down by law; 4) individuals must have a right to access data concerning them; 5) a right to rectify it; and 6) compliance with these rules must be subject to control by an independent authority. All six requirements correspond to respective data protection principles: 1) the principle of fair processing; 2) the principle of purpose specification; 3) the need of a legitimate basis for processing; 4) the right of access; 5) the right of rectification; and 6) the principle of independent supervision.

The inclusion of data protection in the EUCFR signals the EU's departure from an economic approach to data protection to a fundamental rights' one for two reasons: first, data protection is formally recognised as a fundamental right in primary EU constitutional law,[106] and second, for the first time at the international level, data protection is disassociated from the right to privacy, in that it is no longer regarded as a fundamental right, insofar as it can be seen as an aspect of privacy.

B. Data Protection as a Fundamental (Human?) Right

Human rights scholars normally agree that 'there are no inherent reasons' explaining why new human rights should not be recognised in international law.[107] Nonetheless, the recognition of new human rights must be able to achieve a balance between, on the one hand, 'the need to maintain the integrity and credibility of the human rights tradition', and on the other hand, 'the need to adopt a dynamic approach that fully reflects changing needs and perspectives and responds to the emergence of new threats to human dignity and well-being.'[108] In this sense, it has been suggested that a certain claim should satisfy a number of criteria in order to qualify as a human right in terms of international law. There is not a unique, authoritative list of criteria, but most commonly these have been set out in the following way.[109] The new human right should: a) 'reflect a fundamentally social value'; b) be relevant in diverse value systems; c) be eligible for recognition on the basis that it is an interpretation of international law obligations or a formulation that is declaratory of general principles of law; d) 'be consistent with, but not merely repetitive of, the existing body of international human rights law'; e) be

---

[106] Data protection is also enshrined in Arts 16 TFEU and 39 TEU. See H Hijmans, *The European Union as Guardian of Internet Privacy: The Story of Art 16 TFEU* (Switzerland, Springer International Publishing, 2016).

[107] P Alston, 'Making Space for New Human Rights: The Case of the Right to Development', (1988) 1 *Harvard Human Rights Year Book* 3, 39.

[108] P Alston, 'Conjuring up New Human Rights: A Proposal for Quality Control' (1984) 78 *American Journal of International Law* 607, 609.

[109] The list of criteria is adapted from the relevant list provided by Alston regarding the recognition of new human rights in international law. Alston, n 108 above, p 615.

capable of achieving a very high degree of consensus; and f) 'be sufficiently precise as to give rise to identifiable rights and obligations'.[110]

While international law instruments normally use the term 'human rights', the EU (and national legal orders) speak of 'fundamental rights'. Fundamental rights are defined as 'rights contained in a constitution or in a certain part of it, or if the rights in question are classified by a constitution as fundamental rights'.[111] The explicit recognition of an EU bill of rights, the EU Charter of Fundamental Rights has its own history. Although fundamental rights were recognised and protected as general principles of EU law by the ECJ, the EU did not have a written text of rights. Discussions for the adoption of an EU list of fundamental rights started in the 1980s. Following the adoption of the Amsterdam Treaty, the Commission appointed a 'Group of Experts' to assess the opportunities and constraints of an explicit recognition of fundamental rights, including the introduction of new rights mirroring the 'challenges of an information society'.[112] The Group of Experts concluded that 'a text enabling individuals to ascertain their rights' was 'imperative for *affirming* fundamental rights in the European Union'.[113] In June 1999, the Cologne European Council decided that a 'Charter of Fundamental Rights' should be established in the EU in order to make the overriding importance and relevance of fundamental rights 'more visible to the Union's citizens'.[114] The elaboration of the drafting of the Charter was assigned to a body composed of representatives of the Heads of State and Government, the President of the Commission, Members of the European Parliament and national parliaments.[115] The body, which named itself 'the Convention', officially concluded the draft of the Charter on 2 October 2000. The Charter of Fundamental Rights of the EU was formally proclaimed by the EU institutions on 7 December 2000[116] and became legally binding with the entry into force of the Lisbon Treaty on 1 December 2009.

The Charter's preamble states that 'it is necessary to *strengthen* the protection of fundamental rights in the light of changes in society, social progress and scientific and *technological developments* by making those rights *more visible*.'[117] In fact, according to the preamble, the Charter 'reaffirms' fundamental rights as they result from 'the constitutional traditions and international obligations common to the Member States', the EU Treaties, the ECHR, the Social Charters adopted by the Community and by the Council of Europe and the case law of the Court of Justice

---

[110] ibid.

[111] R Alexy, 'Discourse Theory and Fundamental Rights' in Agustín José Menéndez and Erik Oddvar Eriksen (eds), *Arguing Fundamental Rights* (Dordrecht, Springer, 2006) 15.

[112] Expert Group on Fundamental Rights, *Affirming Fundamental Rights in the European Union: Time to Act* (Brussels: European Commission, 1999) 6.

[113] ibid, p 13. Emphasis added.

[114] Cologne European Council, 3–4 June 1999, Conclusions of the Presidency, Annex IV—European Council Decision on the drawing up of a Charter of Fundamental Rights of the European Union.

[115] ibid.

[116] Charter of Fundamental Rights of the European Union proclaimed on 7 December 2000 in Nice ([2000] OJ C364/1). For a commentary on the Articles of the Charter, see EU Network of Independent Experts on Fundamental Rights, 'Commentary of the EU Charter of Fundamental Rights', 2006.

[117] Preamble to the Charter of Fundamental Rights. Emphasis added.

of the European Communities and of the European Court of Human Rights.[118] The Explanations to the Charter[119] state that the right to the protection of personal data is based on Article 286 EC, Directive 95/46/EC, Article 8 ECHR and Convention 108 of the Council of Europe for the Protection of Individuals with regard to Automatic Processing of Personal Data. This pronouncement appears confusing for several reasons. First, Article 8 ECHR establishes the right to respect for private and family life, but does not mention data protection. Second, Directive 95/46/EC constitutes secondary EU law and does not fall within any of the fundamental rights sources mentioned in the Charter's preamble. Thirdly, Convention 108 refers to data protection as safeguarding respect for 'the rights and fundamental freedoms of the individual, and in particular his right to privacy, with regard to automatic processing of personal data relating to him'.[120] Data protection is, therefore, associated with privacy in that instrument, and is not recognised as a fundamental right as such.[121] Finally, Article 286 EC (now replaced by Article 16 TFEU) was the Treaty legal basis ensuring that Community institutions and bodies were bound by data protection legislation under the supervision of an independent body. Article 286 EC, while primary law, did not establish a fundamental right to the protection of personal data as the one recognised by Article 8 EUCFR. It seems, therefore, that the Charter has done much more than simply 'reaffirming' data protection as a right found in other sources; the Charter has introduced a new fundamental right, albeit with an already familiar content. The recognition of data protection as a fundamental right in the EU seems to broadly satisfy the criteria employed by international human rights scholars for the introduction of new human rights: data protection reflects fundamental social values in the era of the rapid advancement of new technologies; it has been relevant for some time in national, international and transnational systems; it is consistent with the existing body of laws in the field; it achieved a high degree of consensus at least in the EU; and it gives rise to 'identifiable rights and obligations'.

As to why data protection was recognised as a fundamental right in the EU, academic literature has identified three possible explanations. First, the European Union, 15 years after the Data Protection Directive, is more than an economic union, as its name implies. Its competences extend to Common Foreign and Security Policy (CFSP)—the former Second Pillar, and Police and Judicial Cooperation in Criminal Matters (PJC)—the former Third Pillar.[122] Data protection had, therefore, to be distanced somehow from internal market freedoms in order

---

[118] ibid.

[119] On the interpretative value of the explanations of the Charter, see K Lenaerts, 'Exploring the Limits of the EU Charter of Fundamental Rights' (2012) 8 *European Constitutional Law Review*, 375, 401–02.

[120] Art 1 Convention No 108.

[121] See D Flaherty, *Protecting Privacy in Surveillance Societies: The Federal Republic of Germany, Sweden, France, Canada and the United States* (Chapel Hill, University of North Carolina Press, 1989) xiv.

[122] The shortcomings of fundamental rights protection in the second and third pillars were identified by the Group of Experts also as reasons for the elaboration of a written text of fundamental rights in the EU.

to cover those areas.[123] Data protection as a fundamental right applies to further areas of processing, besides the common market and the commercial flows of personal data. Data protection is made, thus, 'a legal requirement throughout the Union'[124] and covers processing for law enforcement purposes.[125] Second, the time seemed ripe for the 'independence' of data protection from privacy.[126] A fundamental right to data protection expresses values that go beyond privacy.[127] In this respect, some authors have also pointed out that the recognition of a separate right to data protection, next to privacy, is 'more respectful of the different European constitutional traditions',[128] because it takes into account that certain EU Member States, for instance, Germany and France, do not link data protection to privacy, but base it on different constitutional values, such as liberty (France) or dignity and personality (Germany).[129] Finally, there is a pragmatic reason for the elevation of data protection to the status of a fundamental right: individuals must be aware of its existence and conscious of the ability to enforce it in the light of the new challenges arising from the rapid development of information and communication technologies.[130]

C. A Complicated Relationship: Data Protection and Privacy

Following the constitutional entrenchment at the EU level of a right to data protection, the exact nature of the relationship between privacy and data protection has been the subject of a vivid academic debate. In particular, legal scholars have been concerned with the question whether data protection can be conceived as a 'separate'[131] or an 'autonomous'[132] fundamental right, 'distinct'[133] from the right

---

[123] In its First Report on the Implementation of the Data Protection Directive, the Commission notes that Art 8 EUCFR 'has given added emphasis to the fundamental rights dimension of the Directive.' See Commission, 'First report on the implementation of the Data Protection Directive (95/46/EC) (Data Protection)', COM(2003) 265.

[124] Art 29 WP on the Protection of Individuals with Regard to the Processing of Personal Data, Recommendation 4/99 on the inclusion of the fundamental right to data protection in the European catalogue of fundamental rights.

[125] Nouwt, n 95 above, p 286.

[126] De Hert and Gutwirth note that the recognition of a constitutional right to data protection in the EU Charter 'allows for a sensible constitutional division of labour.' P De Hert and S Gutwirth, 'Privacy, Data Protection and Law Enforcement. Opacity of the Individual and Transparency of Power', in Erik Claes et al (eds), *Privacy and the Criminal Law* (Antwerpen, Intersentia, 2006) 61, 81.

[127] Art 29 WP, Opinion 4/2007 on the concept of personal data. For an overview of the values see below.

[128] De Hert and Gutwirth, n 126 above, p 82.

[129] See P Schwartz and KN Peifer, 'Prosser's Privacy and the German Right of Personality: Are Four Torts Better than One Unitary Concept?' (2010) 98 *California Law Review* 1925, 1946.

[130] See EU Network of Independent Experts on Fundamental Rights, n 116 above, p 11.

[131] N Scandamis, F Sigalas and S Stratakis, 'Rival Freedoms in Terms of Security: The Case of Data Protection and the Criterion of Connexity', (2007) CEPS, CHALLENGE, Research Paper No 7, 15.

[132] S Rodotà, 'Data Protection as a Fundamental Right' in S Gutwirth et al (eds), *Reinventing Data Protection?* (New York, Springer, 2009) 79.

[133] G González Fuster, P De Hert and S Gutwirth, 'The Law-Security Nexus in Europe: State-of-the-Art report' (INEX, 2008) 10.

to privacy, or whether it should be regarded as an aspect of privacy. The confusion is further exacerbated by the fact that data protection is often referred to as 'informational privacy', 'data privacy' or simply 'privacy', especially on the other side of the Atlantic. Furthermore, it has been argued that it is not clear whether privacy and data protection 'overlap'[134] in certain aspects, so that they can be seen as 'similar' rights.[135]

A number of points can be advanced here. First, one cannot lose sight of the EU constitutional reality: data protection has been recognised as a fundamental right, alongside privacy in the EU Charter of Fundamental Rights, which constitutes primary EU law. This means that, in the European constitutional landscape at least, data protection is considered (or expected) to add something to privacy. Whether this is the case, in the context of counter-terrorism surveillance, is a question that the present book explores.

Second, one cannot lose sight of the historical reality: data protection legislation is a relative newcomer; it only appeared in Member States' legislation in the 1970s as a response to the concerns raised about the increasingly centralised processing of personal data and the establishment of huge data banks.[136] The first piece of data protection legislation was enacted in 1970 by the German state of Hesse.[137] It was followed by Sweden in 1973[138] and, subsequently, by other European countries.[139] In most cases, legislators opted to legitimise the data protection regulation by simply referring to traditional privacy concepts.[140] As has been pointed out, 'provisions proclaiming the right to privacy or private life constitute the most direct inspiration for the principles of data protection laws.'[141] On the other hand,

---

[134] R Wacks, *Privacy: A Very Short Introduction* (Oxford: Oxford University Press, 2010) 122.

[135] G González Fuster, n 33 above, p 271 and references therein. It is not clear, however, what the meaning of 'similar' rights is and what is the normative significance of such characterisation.

[136] For a detailed account on the history of the emergence of data protection laws in national and international legal orders, see G González Fuster, n 33 above; O Lynskey, *The Foundations of EU Data Protection Law* (Oxford, Oxford University Press, 2016); Bygrave, n 32 above, p 93; S Simitis, 'New Developments in National and International Data Protection Law in Recent Developments' in J Dumortier (ed), *Data Privacy Law: Belgium's Data Protection Bill and the European Draft Directive* (Leuven, Leuven University Press, 1992) 1, 22.

[137] *Datenschutzgesetz*, 7 Oct 1970, § 6, 1 *Gesetz- und Verordnungsblatt für das Land Hessen* 625 (1970). For the history and development of the law, see S Simitis, 'Datenschutzrecht' in Hans Meyer and Michael Stolleis (eds) *Hessisches Staats- und Verwaltungsrecht (HESSSTVWR)* (2nd edn) (Baden-Baden, Nomos, 1986) 111, 114.

[138] *Datalagen* (Swedish Data Act) of 11 May 1973, entered into force 1 July 1973.

[139] Austria (Federal Act of 18 October 1978 on the protection of personal data, *Bundesgesetzblatt* No 565/1968); Denmark (Public Authorities Registers Act, No 294 (1978), and Private Registers Act No 293 (1978)); France (Act 78-17 of 6 January 1978 on Data Processing, Data Files and Individual Liberties, [1978] JO 227); West Germany (Federal Data Protection Act [1977] BGB1 I 201); Norway (Act of 9 June 1978 relating to Personal Data Registers).

[140] Simitis, n 50 above, p 730.

[141] Bygrave, n 32 above, p 116. However, González Fuster contends that it is a 'misconception' to argue that data protection derives from privacy, because 'there are a number of Member States that historically have not envisaged the protection of personal data from the perspective of the right to privacy.' See G González Fuster, n 33 above, p 268.

to rephrase Spiros Simitis, privacy is 'an old and venerable'[142] right, entrenched for many years as a fundamental right in national constitutions and international texts.

Nevertheless, privacy and data protection are not identical rights. On the one hand, data protection seems to fall in this aspect of privacy that is known, as seen above, as control over personal information. However, 'what privacy protects is irreducible to personal information'.[143] Privacy is a much broader concept that embodies a range of rights and values, such as non-interference or the right to be let alone, limited access to oneself, intimacy, seclusion, personhood, and so on according to the various definitions.[144]

On the other hand, not all personal data are necessarily 'private'. As the Court of First Instance (CFI) (now: General Court) rightly observed in *Bavarian Lager*:[145]

> It should be emphasised that the fact that the concept of 'private life' is a broad one, in accordance with the case-law of the European Court of Human Rights, and that the right to the protection of personal data may constitute one of the aspects of the right to respect for private life, *does not mean that all personal data necessarily fall within the concept of 'private life'*. A fortiori, *not all personal data are by their nature capable of undermining the private life of the person concerned.*[146]

This was confirmed by the Court of Justice that stated categorically in *Client Earth* that 'the concepts of "personal data"… and of "data relating to private life" are not to be confused.'[147] A different approach is very problematic, as the UK case *Durant v Financial Services Authority*[148] demonstrates. This case concerned an individual's request to access certain files containing information about some litigation he had with his bank. The Court of Appeal rejected his request on the basis that such information did not constitute personal data because personal data is only information which is

> biographical in a significant sense; has to have the individual as its focus; and has to affect an individual's privacy whether in his personal family life, business or professional activity.[149]

So restrictive a view of personal data cannot be accepted. Personal data is information relating to an identified or identifiable individual, and not information that

---

[142] Simitis comments: 'Privacy is an old and venerable subject.' Simitis, n 50 above, p 730.

[143] Rouvroy and Poullet, n 30 above, p 70.

[144] C Kuner, 'An International Legal Framework for Data Protection: Issues and Prospects' (2009) 25 *Computer Law and Security Review* 307, 309.

[145] Case T-194/04 *Bavarian Lager* (CFI, 8 November 2007).

[146] ibid, paras 118–19. Emphasis added.

[147] See Case C-615/13 P *Client Earth* (CJEU, 16 July 2015), para 32.

[148] *Durant v FSA* [2003] EWCA Civ 1746, Court of Appeal (Civil Division). For a comment see among others L Edwards, 'Taking the "Personal" Out of Personal Data: Durant v FSA and Its Impact on the Legal Regulation of CCTV' (2004) 1 *SCRIPT-ED* 341, 341.

[149] ibid. See also M Viola de Azevedo Cunha et al, 'Peer-to-Peer Privacy Violations and ISP Liability: Privacy Violations in the User-Generated Web' (2012) 2 *International Data Privacy Law* 50.

might affect 'in a significant sense' an individual's private life. This means that data protection and privacy are not exactly the same rights.[150]

Furthermore, unlike privacy's elusive and subjective nature, that makes this right different across different contexts and jurisdictions, data protection does not display any subjective elements in determining its limits and the grounds for remedies.[151] On the contrary, it has in many respects a procedural nature that makes it more 'objective' as a right.[152] Finally, data protection transcends informational privacy itself because, as is demonstrated in the section below, it serves other, further fundamental rights and values besides privacy.[153]

D. The Foundational Values of Data Protection

i. Privacy

It should be accepted that privacy is 'one—if not the—major'[154] value that data protection laws aim to safeguard.[155] Article 1 of both Convention No 108 and the Data Protection Directive states that their purpose is the protection of the fundamental rights and freedoms of the individual and in particular his right to *privacy*, with respect to the processing of personal data. Other international data protection instruments, such as the UN and the OECD Guidelines, also stress the link between data protection and privacy, but remain unclear about the exact nature of this link.[156] Moreover, national data protection texts, or their *travaux préparatoires*, often refer to privacy as one of the main aims[157] of their data protection legislation.[158] Privacy is, however, not defined in those data protection laws and, therefore, its meaning must be further sought 'partly in the substance of the principles laid down in the laws themselves, partly in the way those principles have been applied, and partly in general, societal notions of what privacy is.'[159] The fact that

---

[150] G González Fuster, n 33 above, p 271.

[151] R Polcak, 'Aims, Methods and Achievements in European Data Protection' (2009) 23 *International Review of Law Computers and Technology* 179, 181.

[152] See Bennett and Raab, n 11 above, p 8.

[153] S Gutwirth and M Hilderbrandt, 'Some Caveats on Profiling' in S Gutwirth, Y Roullet and PD Hert (eds), *Data Protection in a Profiled World* (Dordrecht, Springer, 2010) 31, 36; UK Information Commissioner, 'The Legal Framework: An Analysis of the "Constitutional" European Approach to Issues of data protection law', Study Project, 6.

[154] Bygrave, n 32 above, p 125.

[155] EJ Bloustein, 'Privacy as an Aspect of Human Dignity: An Answer to Dean Prosser' (1964) 39 *New York Law Review* 962, 1003; Fried, n 60 above, pp 477–78; Reiman, n 59 above, p 26; Westin, n 61 above, p 39.

[156] UK Information Commissioner, n 153 above, p 4.

[157] Writing on national data protection rules in Europe, Hondius contends that 'Privacy plays a certain role in all the laws, but never a dominating one.' See FW Hondius, 'Data Law in Europe' (1980) 16 *Stanford Journal of International Law* 87, 94–95.

[158] ibid, pp 92–93; Bygrave, n 32 above, p 116.

[159] L Bygrave, 'The Place of Privacy in Data Protection Law' (2001) 24 *University of New South Wales Law Journal* 277, 278.

the concept of privacy is somewhat elusive is not regarded as necessarily negative; on the contrary, it has been argued that this elusiveness enables data protection rules 'to assimilate and express in a relatively comprehensive, economic manner the ... fears attached to increasingly intrusive data-processing practices.'[160]

Among the different conceptualisations of privacy, informational control is the one regarded as the closest to data protection. As mentioned above, the control over personal information theory is not without problems. What is 'control', and where is control to be derived from? A number of authors argue that control should be understood as 'ownership of information' in the sense of the existence of proprietary rights over the personal data.[161] However, justifying data protection on property theories is problematic, for several reasons. First, ownership theories argue in favour of a commodification of personal data in the sense that personal data can be viewed as a commodity and become tradable. From the moment that such data are placed on the market, the market is supposed to achieve the ideal amount of privacy protection by balancing the value of personal information to the potential buyers against the value of the information to the individual.[162] The market solution, however, has serious deficiencies: not only is it difficult to ascribe a value to personal data,[163] but a market approach can also lead to inequalities.[164] Furthermore, it cannot be accepted that data controllers enjoy property rights on information systems or the data contained therein because they have invested in compiling the databases and developing algorithms to process the information.[165] Second, the utility of an ownership approach is also dubious because property rights do not enjoy any kind of elevated protection, and are not considered absolute in any case.[166]

Although control over personal information is viewed as the conception of privacy predominantly advanced by data protection rules,[167] it is not the sole privacy concept behind data protection. Data protection principles often embody further privacy concerns, such as 'the right to be let alone' or privacy as non-interference, limited access to oneself, and even conceptions of privacy such as intimacy (for instance in the context of the processing of sensitive personal data).[168]

---

[160] Bygrave, n 32 above, p 127.
[161] Westin, n 61 above, p 324. For a more recent analysis on why privacy is better protected by property rights see L Lessig, 'Privacy As Property' (2002) 69 *Social Research: An International Quarterly* 247. Theories of ownership have been also proposed in the context of personal data too. See Bygrave, n 32 above.
[162] D Solove, 'Privacy and Power: Computer Databases and Metaphors for Information Privacy' (2001) 53 *Stanford Law Review* 1393, 1446–47.
[163] ibid, pp 1452–53.
[164] Cohen notes that '[p]ersonally-identified data is the wedge that enables "scientific," market-driven, and increasingly precise separation of "haves" from "have-nots".' J Cohen, 'Examined Lives: Informational Privacy and the Subject as Object' (2000) 52 *Stanford Law Review* 1373, 1378.
[165] ibid.
[166] Bygrave, n 32, p 120.
[167] ibid, 130.
[168] ibid, 132–33.

ii. Transparency, Accountability and Due Process

The processing of personal data bears inherent imbalances. These are manifest in the asymmetries between the two main actors of information processing: the data subject, on the one hand, and data controllers, on the other hand. It has been argued that data subjects are facing a situation where 'a) there is virtually no limit to the amount of information that can be recorded, b) there is virtually no limit to the scope of analysis that can be done—bounded only by human ingenuity and c) the information may be stored virtually for ever.'[169] Data protection rules attempt to address this problem[170] by embodying the values of transparency, foreseeability in data processing, accountability of data controllers, and—to the extent that it is possible—participation of the data subject in the processing of his information. These values are voiced in a number of fair information principles; above all, in the principle of fair and lawful processing, in the purpose specification principle, and in the individual participation principle.

The principle of 'fair and lawful' processing[171] strives for transparency[172] in data processing and establishes a respective level of accountability of data controllers.[173] The processing should be lawful in that it should be carried out in accordance with the law. Processing should also be fair. Fairness in processing denotes that data controllers must ensure that the collection and processing of personal data is undertaken in accordance with the reasonable expectations of the data subjects. Seen from the point of view of the data subject, this means that the data subject should be able to know the purposes of the collection and processing of his personal data.[174] The interests of foreseeability and predictability of processing are echoed in the 'purpose specification principle'. 'Purpose specification' requires that personal data must be collected for specified, explicit and legitimate purposes and should not be further processed in a way incompatible with the initial purposes.[175]

Further to the above principles, in order to address the asymmetries and power imbalances between data subject and data controller, data protection regulations attempt to grant the former some form of participation in the processing of his personal data. The 'due process' concerns in the processing of personal data normally find their expression in the so-called 'individual participation' principle.[176] The principle is manifested in a variety of data protection rules: certain processing operations cannot be undertaken without the consent of the data subject;[177] the

---

[169] H Nissenbaum, 'Protecting Privacy in an Information Age: The Problem of Privacy in Public' (1998) 17 *Law and Philosophy* 559, 576.

[170] See H Burkert, 'Towards a New Generation of Data Protection Legislation' in S Gutwirth and others (ed), *Reinventing Data Protection?* (New York, Springer, 2009) 335, 339.

[171] See Data Protection Directive, Art 6(1)(a); GDPR, Art 5(1)(a); Art 5(a) Convention No 108.

[172] See GDPR, Recital 39.

[173] See GDPR, Art 5(2).

[174] Bygrave, n 32, pp 58–59.

[175] See Data Protection Directive, Art 6(1)(b); GDPR, Art 5(1)(b); and, Art 5(b) Convention No 108.

[176] See for instance OECD Guidelines, para 13.

[177] See Data Protection Directive, Arts 7(a) and 8(2)(a); GDPR, Arts 6(1)(a) and 7.

data subject has the right to know that information is held on him by the controller or others;[178] he has the right to access it,[179] correct, erase and block it if the processing is not in accordance with data protection rules, or the data is inaccurate or incomplete;[180] he has a right to object to the processing of his personal data;[181] and—recently—a right to obtain the de-listing of links to web pages published by third parties containing information relating to him from the list of results displayed following a search made on the basis of his name.[182]

iii. Data Security and Data Quality

Privacy may well be the main value behind data protection rules, but data protection legislation advances further interests.[183] A set of interests that data protection laws aim to safeguard, further to privacy, concerns the security of the information systems ('data security') and the quality of data contained therein ('data quality'). 'Data security' pertains to keeping the data secure against certain risks, such as the risks of data being lost or accessed by unauthorised persons. In this regard, the Data Protection Directive requires data controllers to implement appropriate technical and organisational measures to protect personal data against accidental or unlawful destruction, accidental loss, unauthorised disclosure or access, in particular where the processing involves the transmission of data over a network. The measures should ensure a level of security appropriate to the risks represented by the processing and the nature of the data.[184] Roger Clarke points out that 'data security' is often confounded with data protection, as security specialists and computer scientists, especially in the United States, tend to understand data protection as referring solely to the security of personal data against unauthorised disclosure and accidental losses.[185] The general public often follows the same misconception, with concerns about data protection violations normally being raised when a case of unwarranted access or loss of personal data is brought into light by the media.[186]

---

[178] See Data Protection Directive, Art 10; GDPR, Arts 12, 13 and 14; and Art 8(a) Convention No 108.

[179] See Data Protection Directive, Art 12(a); GDPR, Art 15; and, Art 8(b) Convention No 108.

[180] See Data Protection Directive, Art 12(b); GDPR, Arts 16 and 17; and, Art 8(c) Convention No 108.

[181] See Data Protection Directive, Art 14(a); GDPR, Art 21.

[182] GDPR, Art 17; Case C-131/12 *Google Spain SL, Google Inc v Agencia Española de Protección de Datos and Mario Costeja González* [2014] ECR I-000 (nyr), para 88.

[183] Raab and Bennett note that data protection achieves 'other purposes that may or may not be compatible with the protection of privacy'. Raab and Bennett, n 7 above, 537. See also L Bygrave, 'Privacy and data protection in an international perspective' (2010) 56 *Scandinavian Studies in Law* 165, 172.

[184] Data Protection Directive, Art 17(1); GDPR, Arts 5(1)(f) and 32. A similar provision is found in Art 7 of the Council of Europe Convention No 108.

[185] R Clarke, 'Introduction to Dataveillance and Information Privacy, and Definitions of Terms' (1988) 31 (5) *Communications of the ACM* 498. See also P Schwartz and J Reidenberg, *Data Privacy Law: A Study of United States Data Protection* (Charlottesville, Michie Law Publishers, 1996) 5.

[186] ibid.

'Data security', however, is only an interest safeguarded by data protection laws, and should not be confused with data protection itself.[187]

'Data quality' refers to the accuracy, adequacy, relevance and up-to-dateness of the personal information.[188] Personal information that is accurate, adequate and up-to-date does not safeguard solely the interests of data controllers that in principle would be able to make more accurate decisions based on valid, adequate and relevant data. It equally promotes the interests of the data subjects, as inaccurate information held on them concomitantly means inaccuracy in the sketching of their 'digital persona'.[189] For this reason, data protection laws normally stipulate that every reasonable step should be taken to ensure that inaccurate or incomplete data should be rectified or erased.[190]

iv. Non-Discrimination

There is a further value safeguarded by data protection rules that goes beyond the above categories of interests: the principle of non-discrimination. This principle, which prohibits the different or unequal treatment of individuals based on their personal characteristics, is particularly pertinent for data protection regulations that aim to grapple with certain processes, such as profiling, which can be discriminatory. The concern of data protection legislation for the principle of non-discrimination is, above all, manifest in the rules that require the additional protection of the processing of special categories of data that are normally described as 'sensitive'. Personal data that reveal racial or ethnic origin, political opinions, religious beliefs, sexual orientation and health, as well as genetic and biometric data are made subject to enhanced protection, and their processing is in principle prohibited as a default rule in the European data protection context.[191] This is because the processing of such data can lead to illegal discrimination.[192] Concerns about discriminatory processes are also manifest in provisions, such as Article 15 of the European Data Protection Directive, aimed at protecting individuals against fully automated decision-making.[193]

v. Proportionality

While it might be wrong to regard the proportionality principle as an autonomous value pursued by data protection laws, proportionality concerns run through data

---

[187] Bennett and Raab, n 11 above, p 11.

[188] Data Protection Directive, Art 6(1)(c) and (d); GDPR, Art 5(1)(d).

[189] 'Digital persona' is a term used by Roger Clarke to describe 'a model of an individual's public personality based on data and maintained by transactions, and intended for use as a proxy for the individual.' See R Clarke, 'The Digital Persona and Its Application to Surveillance' (1994) 10 *The Information Society* 77.

[190] Data Protection Directive, Art 6(1)(d); GDPR, Art 5(1)(d).

[191] See Data Protection Directive, Art 8(1); GDPR, Art 9(1). Art 6 of Convention No 108 refers to this type of data as 'special categories of data'.

[192] Rouvroy and Poullet, n 30 above, p 70.

[193] Data Protection Directive, Art 15(1); GDPR, Art 22(1).

protection legislation and 'underpin' the operation of most of the fair information principles.[194] Direct references to the principle of proportionality can be found in the rules that require that personal data should be 'relevant' and 'not excessive' in relation to the purposes for which they are collected and further processed;[195] that they are 'necessary';[196] and that they are kept for no longer than is necessary for the purposes for which the data were collected or further processed.[197] The proportionality principle, albeit not directly mentioned, is also manifest in the criterion of 'fairness' of processing.[198] This requires that proportionality should be taken into account when balancing the respective interests of data subjects and controllers.[199]

vi. Dignity

The ultimate foundation of data protection is to safeguard the dignity of the data subject. Human dignity is enshrined in Article 2 TEU as the first foundational value of the European Union, and in Article 1 EUCFR,[200] and has been recognised by the Court of Justice of the EU as a general principle of EU law.[201] Dignity is considered one of the 'ethical cornerstones of European constitutionalism' and the 'overall general goal of fundamental rights' protection'.[202] The concept of dignity is closely related to humanity which is understood as an expression of the values of individualism, equality and freedom.[203]

With human dignity as an underpinning value, data protection can be seen as informational autonomy rather than a mere claim for information management.[204] Data protection as informational autonomy finds its legal description in the right to 'informational self-determination' (*informationelle Selbstbestimmung*), as pronounced by the German Constitutional Court (*Bundesverfassungsgericht*) in its landmark Census decision (*Volkszählungsurteil*).[205] According to the Court, the right to 'informational self-determination' guarantees, in principle, the power

---

[194] L Bygrave and D Schartum, 'Consent, Proportionality and Collective Power' in S Gutwirth and others (eds), *Reinventing Data Protection?* (New York, Springer, 2009) 157, 162.

[195] See Data Protection Directive, Art 6(1)(c); GDPR, Art 5(1)(c).

[196] See Data Protection Directive, Art 6(1)(d).

[197] See Data Protection Directive, Art 6(1)(e); GDPR, Art 5(1)(e).

[198] Bygrave and Schartum, n 194 above, p 162.

[199] ibid, 163.

[200] See also Art 25 EUCFR that recognises the right of the elderly 'to lead a life of dignity and independence' and Art 31 EUCFR which provides that 'every worker has the right to working conditions which respect his or her health, safety and dignity.'

[201] See Case C-36/02 *Omega Spielhallen-und Automatenaufstellungs-GmbH v Oberbürgermeisterin der Bundestadt Bonn* [2004] ECR I-9609.

[202] See O Gstrein, 'The cascade of decaying information: putting the "right to be forgotten" in perspective', (2015) 21 (2) *Computer and Telecommunications Law Review* 40, 43 and references therein.

[203] C Dupré, 'Human Dignity in Europe: A Foundational Constitutional Principle' (2013) 19(2) *European Public Law* 319.

[204] Gstrein, n 202 above, p 43.

[205] *Volkszählungsurteil*, 65 BVerfGE 1, 68–69 (1983).

of the individual to determine for himself the disclosure and use of his data. The right is based on Articles 1(1) (human dignity)[206] and 2(1) (personality right)[207] of the German Constitution. These require 'clearly defined conditions of processing', which ensure 'that under the conditions of automatic collection and processing of personal data the individual is not reduced to a mere object of information.'[208]

In its judgment, the German Court couched its concerns regarding modern methods of data processing that can result in treating the individuals as objects. It noted that in order to reach a decision, one can rely today on the technical means of storing information about personal or factual situations of an individual with the aid of automatic data processing. Furthermore, these data can be pieced together with other data collections—particularly when integrated information systems are built up—to add up to a partial or virtually complete personality profile (*Persönlichkeitsbild*), the accuracy and application of which normally the person concerned has no sufficient means of control over. According to the Court, these possibilities of inspection may influence the individual's behaviour by the psychological pressure exerted by public interest. Under conditions of modern information processing technology, individual self-determination presupposes that the person is left with the freedom of decision about actions that he should take or avoid, including the possibility to follow that decision in practice. According to the Court, if the individual cannot predict with sufficient certainty what information about himself in certain areas is known in his social milieu, and cannot accurately estimate the parties to whom communication may possibly be made, he is crucially inhibited in his freedom to plan and decide freely, without being subject to any pressure or influence. The exercise of individual freedoms, such as freedom of speech or freedom of association and assembly, is rendered excessively difficult when it is uncertain whether, under what circumstances, and for what purposes, personal information is collected and processed.[209] The right to informational self-determination, therefore, precludes a social order, in which the citizens can no longer know who knows what, when and on what occasion about them, as such would not only impair their chances of development, 'but it would also impair the common good, because self-determination is an elementary functional condition of a free democratic community based on its citizens' capacity to act and to cooperate.'[210]

The understanding of data protection as 'informational self-determination' rooted in the concept of dignity has found support in academic legal scholarship. Julie Cohen contends that

> informational autonomy comports with important values concerning the fair and just treatment of individuals within society ... these principles have clear and very specific

---

[206] Art 1(1) of the German Basic Law proclaims: 'Human dignity is inviolable. To respect and protect it is the duty of all State authority.'

[207] Art 2(1) provides: 'Everyone has the right to the free development of his personality insofar as he does not violate the rights of others or offend against the constitutional order or against morality.'

[208] *Volkszählungsurteil*, n 205 above.

[209] See Simitis, n 50 above, p 732.

[210] *Volkszählungsurteil*, n 205 above.

implications for the treatment of personally-identified data: They require that we forbid data-processing practices that treat individuals as mere conglomerations of transactional data, or that rank people... based on their financial or genetic desirability.[211]

This has been termed 'new humanism', namely the assertion 'that people are special, in the sense that people are something more than machines or algorithms'[212] and the processing of their personal data should be 'designed to serve mankind'.[213] Furthermore, it has been argued that 'the rush to capture ever-greater amounts of personally-identified information is premised on the assumption that this information will yield the ability to understand, and ultimately predict, individual behaviour ... The view of human nature reinforced by data processing algorithms is both unforgiving and ungenerous.'[214] The 'digital persona'[215] that emerges out of data processing presents such a powerful image of the individual, that it can be used as a 'proxy for the real person'.[216] Data processing may hold individuals accountable for whatever the combination of their information with powerful algorithms will reveal. In terms of commercial processing of data (eg consumer profiling, behavioural advertising, etc), it has been argued that the evaluation of knowledge raises concerns about 'behaviour modification and free will'.[217] In terms of processing of personal data for law enforcement and counter-terrorism purposes, it could be about much more: discrimination, reversal of the presumption of innocence principle, ultimately individual liberty.[218] In this respect, the values pursued by data protection, such as privacy, transparency of processing, accountability, due process, non-discrimination and proportionality all aim ultimately to safeguard the dignity of the data subject.

III. THEORIES OF DATA PROTECTION AND THEIR SHORTCOMINGS

Data protection has been studied by legal scholars, political scientists, public administration and public policy[219] researchers and informational scientists. The debate is joined by data protection authorities and information commissioners, civil society organisations, companies and individuals that assume the role of data controllers, and finally by (national or supranational) administrations and law enforcement authorities. Despite extensive writing by scholars and practitioners on various data protection issues, the research could pinpoint two theories on

---

[211] Cohen, n 164 above, p 1408.
[212] Gstrein, n 202 above, p 47 and references therein.
[213] See GDPR, Recital 4.
[214] Cohen, n 164 above, p 1408.
[215] See Clarke, n 189 above.
[216] ibid.
[217] Cohen, n 164 above, p 1408.
[218] For the risks that may result from the processing of see GDPR, Recital 75.
[219] W van de Donke and others, 'The Politics and Policy of Data Protection: Experiences, Lessons, Reflections and Perspective' (1996) 62 *International Review of Administrative Science* 459, 460.

data protection, which will be approached critically below, before I turn, to the submission of a new understanding of the fundamental right to data protection.

Until now, the most comprehensive theory on data protection has been developed by Paul de Hert and Serge Gutwirth.[220] Their theory discusses the respective roles that privacy and data protection can play in a democratic constitutional state. It is based on the premise that privacy and data protection can be seen as two distinct legal tools of power control that perform different, but complementary functions (an approach I call the 'separatist model'). According to the two authors, 'much can ... be learned from making and ascertaining the *difference* in scope, rationale and logic between privacy on the one hand, and data protection on the other.'[221] In this respect, privacy is conceived as a tool of *opacity*, while data protection as a tool of *transparency*. Their function is different: opacity tools 'embody normative choices about the limits of power';[222] transparency tools 'come into play after these normative choices have been made in order still to channel the normatively accepted exercise of power.'[223] Hence privacy, on the one hand, as a tool of opacity, aims to protect individuals against illegitimate and excessive use of power (non-interference); data protection, on the other hand, as a tool of transparency, is directed towards the control and channelling of legitimate use of power. Pursuant to this approach, while data protection can be seen as offering a regulated acceptance,[224] privacy is presenting a prohibition rule,[225] which is, however, in general subject to exceptions, since privacy is not an absolute right itself.[226] In terms of 'how much of which tool is necessary when?', de Hert and Gutwirth explain that data protection transparency tools should be considered as the default rules;[227] 'only in rare cases or after due consideration of actual risks will prohibitive opacity measures be taken to protect rights and freedoms and to promote trust in the Information Society.'[228]

It cannot be denied that the 'separatist model' has many obvious merits. It attempts to understand and ascertain the role of data protection in a legal system through the very content of its principles: they are designed to promote procedural justice, rather than normative (or substantive) justice.[229] Therefore, according to de Hert and Gutwirth, data protection does not operate in a prohibitive manner,

---

[220] De Hert and Gutwirth, n 126 above.

[221] ibid, p 62.

[222] ibid, p 70.

[223] ibid.

[224] De Hert and Gutwirth note: 'Data protection is not prohibitive ... The main aims of data protection consist in providing various specific procedural safeguards to protect individuals' privacy and in promoting accountability by government and private record-holders. Data protection laws were precisely enacted not to prohibit, but to channel power, viz to promote meaningful public accountability, and provide data subjects with an opportunity to contest inaccurate or abusive record holding practices.' Ibid, p 77.

[225] ibid.

[226] ibid.

[227] ibid.

[228] ibid, p 96.

[229] ibid, p 78.

but it 'ruptures' the common legal logic: it replaces the traditional prohibition-ary rule 'thou shall not kill' with 'thou can process personal data under certain circumstances'.[230] The prohibitive role is found by these authors in the function of privacy. Due to these different functions, de Hert and Gutwirth explain, for the first time, why data protection is needed alongside privacy in a democratic constitutional state. Its added value in a democratic constitutional framework can be seen, according to these authors, in the clear separation of the two rights,[231] which implies a distinction between the legal tools of opacity, on the one hand, and transparency, on the other.

There is, however, a fundamental problem with de Hert's and Gutwirth's approach that undermines the basic core of their argument altogether. The theory of these two authors seeks to establish, above all, the added value of the constitu-tional entrenchment of a separate right to data protection, next to the right to pri-vacy. The enthusiasm of the two scholars could not be more evident: 'Apparently, something new is happening at constitutional level';[232] 'very recently, the proper role of data protection has received constitutional recognition in Article 8 of the 2000 Charter of Fundamental Rights of the EU';[233] 'this recognition of a consti-tutional right should be welcomed';[234] and so on. There is, however, a paradox in their line of thinking: their theory, while it aims to be a theory on data protection, does not focus on data protection itself. Rather, the added value of data protec-tion is demonstrated through its distinction from privacy. By preaching separa-tion, they strive to show the indispensability of data protection. But, their very argument proves them wrong. In the end, according to de Hert and Gutwirth, everything will be judged on the basis of privacy, as the tool of opacity[235] will be the benchmark for establishing prohibited interferences. Data protection, as a transparency tool, merely describes the permitted processing; the limits will then be set on the basis of privacy. This, however, means that data protection is not indispensable: we could live well without it. Certainly we are better off with it, as it has some utility as a useful transparency tool, but still we could live without it, since every possible interference will be judged against privacy. De Hert and Gutwirth fail to prove why data protection is so fundamental that it explains its constitutional entrenchment.

Despite its problems, the 'separatist' approach is the most comprehensive the-ory of data protection elaborated so far. The research could identify in the litera-ture a further approach to data protection, with the essential caveat, however, that this has been developed mainly as a response-criticism to the 'separatist' model

---

[230] ibid, p 77.

[231] ibid.

[232] De Hert and Gutwirth, n 71 above, p 7.

[233] De Hert and Gutwirth, n 126 above, p 81.

[234] ibid.

[235] Opacity as a notion for describing privacy is also problematic because it appears to conceive of privacy as secrecy, or as having something to hide.

analysed above, and thus, cannot be viewed as a stand-alone, comprehensive theory on data protection. Replying essentially to de Hert and Gutwirth, Antoinette Rouvroy and Yves Poullet argue that privacy and data protection have 'an "intermediate" rather than a "final" value, because they are "tools" through which more fundamental values, or more "basic" rights—namely human dignity and individual personality right—are pursued.'[236] For this reason, they should be conceived as *instruments* for fostering the autonomic capabilities of individuals that are necessary for sustaining a vivid democracy[237] (an approach I call the 'instrumentalist' model). The two authors explain that the emergence of a right to data protection is due to the technological evolutions that 'may require legal protections of privacy to evolve, simply because those technological evolutions threaten, in new ways, the fundamental value of personal autonomy.'[238] They support this argument by invoking the German Constitutional Court's Census decision, according to which, 'the development of the data processing technologies obliged the State to revise and adapt the guarantees it provides to individuals in order to protect and foster the capabilities needed to implement their right to freely self-determine their personality.'[239]

Rouvroy and Poullet contend, however, that privacy and data protection 'are not to be put on the same footing',[240] because they are different tools for enabling individual reflexive autonomy. They criticise, therefore, the acknowledgement of the right to data protection as a fundamental right, distinct to the traditional fundamental right to privacy, in the EUCFR, because

> by placing the right to data protection on the same level as privacy, the European text carries the risk that the fundamental anchoring of data protection regimes in the fundamental values of dignity and autonomy will soon be forgotten by lawyers and that legislators will soon forget to refer to these fundamental values in order to continuously assess data protection legislation taking into account the evolution of the Information Society.[241]

In this regard, they explain, in a rather confusing way, that making data protection a distinct and fundamental right

> risks obscuring the essential relation existing between privacy and data protection and further estrange data protection from the fundamental values of human dignity and individual autonomy, foundational to the concept of privacy in which data protection regimes have their roots.[242]

Besides the fact that the 'instrumentalist' approach fails to provide a robust analysis of the right to data protection, it is fraught with fears that remain unsubstantiated.

---

[236] Rouvroy and Poullet, n 30 above, p 53.
[237] ibid, p 46.
[238] ibid, p 54.
[239] ibid, p 55.
[240] ibid, p 70.
[241] ibid, p 71.
[242] ibid, p 74.

It is not clear why data protection cannot have an instrumental value, while at the same time being at an equal footing with privacy. The two authors seem to negate any value of data protection, because this might allegedly end up in trumping the instrumental value of privacy, and thus undermine privacy as a fundamental right. Rouvroy and Poullet make a valid point about the uniqueness of the final goals of the two rights (be that autonomy or dignity or the right to individual personality), but they do not provide convincing reasons why the constitutional entrenchment of data protection is so harmful.

IV. A NEW THEORY FOR DATA PROTECTION[243]

A. Method: How Should We Approach Data Protection?

Despite the differences in the conclusions of the two approaches analysed above—the 'separatist' recognising an added value to data protection; the 'instrumentalist' negating it—the two theories share a common insightful point: they both view data protection through privacy. They attempt, therefore, to formulate a data protection theory by looking into its relationship with privacy.

Starting from the premise that data protection is a fundamental right, at least within the EU legal framework,[244] I argue that an approach to understanding the added value—if there be any—of this right must have a focus. Its focus should be data protection, not its possible interactions with privacy. This does not mean, however, that I deny that the two rights are closely related. Privacy is an umbrella notion for a plurality of things[245] that covers aspects of data protection in any case. This does not imply, necessarily, that data protection has no added value. My argument, therefore, is that if we want to approach this value, we should try to see data protection in isolation for a moment.

B. Is Data Protection 'Mature' to Stand Alone? Problems and Limitations

i. Data Protection and Privacy

Why is it that the two theoretical attempts to approach data protection, that exist so far, find it necessary to view data protection through the lens of privacy? Certainly, data protection pursues, above all, privacy objectives, but is this the real reason? Or is there something missing from data protection rules that makes the right unable to stand alone? De Hert and Gutwirth view data protection as a tool of transparency, aimed to channel or regulate—but not prohibit—power. Data

---

[243] An earlier version of this theory appears in M Tzanou, 'Data protection as a fundamental right next to privacy? "Reconstructing" a not so new right' (2013) 3 (2) *International Data Privacy Law* 88.

[244] See UK Information Commissioner, n 153 above, p 8.

[245] Solove, n 15 above, p 45.

protection operates, thus, only as an affirmative liberty. As will be demonstrated below, the same approach was adopted until recently by the ECJ that found it necessary to fall back on privacy and examine the two rights together in order to determine if certain forms of processing are illegitimate.

Indeed, taking a closer look at Article 8 of the EUCFR, one can agree that data protection is depicted in affirmative terms, as a transparency tool. The first paragraph of Article 8 introduces the general right—everyone has the right to the protection of personal data concerning him or her—while the second paragraph goes on to set the rules of the permissible processing—fair processing, for specified purposes, on the basis of the consent of the person concerned or some other legitimate basis, granting the data subject the rights of access and rectification. The right to privacy in Article 7 is also formulated in an affirmative way. One should not be confused though. Pursuant to Article 52(3) EUCFR, in so far as the Charter contains rights which correspond to rights guaranteed by the ECHR, the meaning and scope of those rights shall be the same as those laid down by the Convention.[246] The right to privacy is found in Article 8 of the ECHR.[247] The second paragraph stipulates that:

> There shall be no interference by a public authority with the exercise of this right except such as is in accordance with the law and is necessary in a democratic society in the interests of national security, public safety or the economic well-being of the country, for the prevention of disorder or crime, for the protection of health or morals, or for the protection of the rights and freedoms of others.

It is clear, therefore, that the right to privacy in the EUCFR has the function of the opacity, non-interference tool.

Viewing data protection merely in affirmative terms is, however, problematic. The problem is not only theoretical. As Cohen astutely points out, 'the conventional wisdom is that ... affirmative liberty claims are weaker and less principled than negative liberty claims.'[248] This explains why data protection cannot stand alone as a fundamental right. The right to privacy is needed in the end to determine the prohibitive instances of non-interference.

I argue that this approach to data protection obstructs the right itself to operate independently from privacy. Contrary to what de Hert and Gutwirth contend, the value, of a fundamental right to data protection, thus interpreted, is limited: it can operate only as a transparency tool, but illegitimate interferences will have to be determined on the basis of privacy.[249] These limitations, whether they are

---

[246] The same article clarifies, however, that 'this provision shall not prevent Union law providing more extensive protection'. See Lenaerts, n 119 above, p 394.

[247] The Explanations relating to the Charter confirm that 'Article 7 corresponds to Article 8 ECHR'. See the explanations relating to the Charter of Fundamental Rights, [2007] OJ C303/17.

[248] Cohen, n 164 above, p 1400. See also D Currie, 'Positive and Negative Constitutional Rights' (1996) 53 *University of Chicago Law Review* 864, 887.

[249] See also Martin Scheinin and Mathias Vermeulen who contend that '[a]ddressing issues related to the protection of personal data will not suffice to determine the limits of the use of detection

attributed to the drafters of the right,[250] or the particularities of its genesis, initial drafting[251] and interpretation to take into account economic concerns, demonstrate that data protection is not 'mature' enough, as it is currently perceived by the academic literature, to operate alone.[252]

ii. Data Protection and Secondary Legislation

Privacy and its confusing relationship with data protection is not the only limitation that the fundamental right to data protection faces. This is also limited by its relationship with secondary legislation. Historically, data protection appeared in the EU in different pieces of secondary legislation, such as the Data Protection Directive, the central EU data protection instrument adopted in 1995, and other documents, including Directive 2002/58/EC concerning the processing of personal data and the protection of privacy in the electronic communications sector (the 'ePrivacy Directive'),[253] Regulation 45/2001/EC on the protection of individuals with regard to the processing of personal data by the EU institutions and bodies[254] and the Council Framework Decision 2008/977/JHA on the protection of personal data processed in the framework of police and judicial cooperation in criminal matters,[255] long before it was elevated to the status of a fundamental right. The Data Protection Directive was repealed on 24 May 2016 by the General Data Protection Regulation, and the Framework Decision 2008/977/JHA by Directive 2016/680.[256] Therefore, it cannot be denied that data protection has been

technologies. Data protection rules formulate the conditions under which the processing of data is legitimate. The right to data protection will therefore come into play only *secondarily, in order to minimize the negative impact of the use of technology on the right to privacy*. The right to protect personal data is a procedural right in this context: it informs the right to privacy and provides important parameters of *control* over some aspects of the private life of a person.' M Scheinin and M Vermeulen, 'DETECTER, Detection Technologies, Terrorism, Ethics and Human Rights', European Commission, Seventh Framework Programme, 7. Emphasis added.

[250] C Kuner and others, 'Let's not kill all the privacy laws (and lawyers)' (2011) 1 *International Data Privacy Law* 209.

[251] Simitis eloquently observes: 'Data protection laws have always been marked by the uneasiness in dealing with constantly advancing technology. Legislators deliberately chose a distinctly abstract language in order to improve the chances to address unknown aspects and new developments of technology.' S Simitis, 'Privacy—An Endless Debate?' (2010) 98 *California Law Review* 1989, 1999.

[252] D Rowland, 'Data Retention and the War Against Terrorism—A Considered and Proportionate Response?' (2004) 3 *The Journal of Information, Law and Technology* 10.

[253] Directive 2002/58/EC of the European Parliament and of the Council of 12 July 2002 concerning the processing of personal data and the protection of privacy in the electronic communications sector, [2002] OJ L201/37.

[254] Regulation (EC) 45/2001/EC of the European Parliament and of the Council of 18 December 2000 on the protection of individuals with regard to the processing of personal data by the Community institutions and bodies and on the free movement of such data, [2001] OJ L8/1.

[255] Council Framework Decision 2008/977/JHA of 27 November 2008 on the protection of personal data processed in the framework of police and judicial cooperation in criminal matters, [2008] OJ L350/60.

[256] Directive 2016/680 of the European Parliament and of the Council of 27 April 2016 on the protection of natural persons with regard to the processing of personal data by competent authorities

for a considerable time the subject-matter of an extensive legal framework before and after its inclusion in the Charter.

In fact, as mentioned above, the Explanations to the Charter refer to the Data Protection Directive as one of the sources of inspiration of this fundamental right.[257] Moreover, Article 52(7) EUCFR states that the explanations drawn up as a way of providing guidance in the interpretation of the Charter must be given 'due regard by the courts of the Union and of the Member States'. This raises pertinent questions regarding the relationship of the fundamental right to data protection with secondary legislation. These concern the content and the interpretation of this right. Besides the six constitutive principles of data protection expressly listed in paragraphs 2 and 3 of Article 8 EUCFR, can the content of the right to data protection be ascertained also with reference to secondary EU legislation? And, what if secondary legislation changes over time the level of protection offered? Would amendments resulting from subsequent secondary law affect the interpretation of Article 8 EUCFR?[258]

C. Reconstructing Data Protection: The Conditions

If the right to data protection is to be a bona fide fundamental right with a value of its own, it needs to be reconstructed, in order to satisfy three conditions. The first is that it should be recognised that the fundamental right to data protection has an 'autonomous content' of its own, which is independent from secondary legislation. The second condition that data protection needs to satisfy in order to be a fully-functional fundamental right is that it should be balanced against opposing rights or other interests as such, not through the proxy of privacy. The third condition is that data protection as a fundamental right should be able to function both positively and negatively. It should be able, on the one hand, to regulate, channel and control power, and on the other hand, to prohibit power.

i. The Fundamental Right to Data Protection Should Have an 'Autonomous' Content

Data protection may well have been regulated in a number of secondary law instruments in the EU legal order, but its inclusion in the Charter has a normative significance, only if this is disassociated from secondary legislation and it is recognised that as a fundamental right it has an 'autonomous' content of its own. This fundamental requirement derives from EU constitutional law and in particular,

---

for the purposes of the prevention, investigation, detection or prosecution of criminal offences or the execution of criminal penalties, and on the free movement of such data, and repealing Council Framework Decision 2008/977/JHA, [2016] OJ L119/89.

[257] See above.
[258] The Austrian Supreme Court referred this question to the CJEU in the *Digital Rights Ireland* case.

Article 6(1) TEU, which stipulates that the rights, freedoms and principles set out in the EU Charter of Fundamental Rights have the same legal value as the Treaties. Since data protection is listed as a fundamental right in the Charter, the content of Article 8 EUCFR cannot be dependent on secondary legislation. In fact, the validity of secondary legislation, including secondary data protection laws and their subsequent amendments, should be reviewable in the light of the fundamental rights enshrined in the Charter, such as the fundamental right to data protection. Indeed, the CJEU in its seminal judgment in *Digital Rights Ireland*, reviewed (and annulled) the Data Retention Directive, which was listed as modification of secondary data protection legislation on the basis of Article 8 EUCFR.

It is accepted that there are some difficulties disassociating the fundamental right to data protection from relevant secondary legislation because certain concepts crucial for the right to the data protection, such as 'personal data' and 'processing' are defined in secondary legislation. This, however, does not mean that data protection as a fundamental right cannot have an 'autonomous' content. Such autonomous content does not require that the definition of these concepts should be necessarily different from the one provided in secondary legislation. It requires merely that this should be *independent* from secondary law. A similar argument can be made regarding the data protection principles listed in Article 8 EUCFR. The autonomous nature of the fundamental right to data protection does not prohibit the interpretation of these to draw inspiration from a broader list of data protection principles found in other international or European legal instruments. Indeed, this is confirmed by Article 52(7) EUCFR, which states that the Explanations of the Charter can provide guidance in its interpretation and should be given due regard by the courts of the Union and of the Member States.[259] The Explanations of the Charter refer to the Data Protection Directive and Convention No 108, and these could be taken into consideration when assessing and interpreting the data protection principles listed in Article 8 EUCFR. Nevertheless, the content of these principles remains autonomous and does not depend on secondary legislation. Thus, changes to the level of protection of personal data in subsequent amendments of secondary legislation do not affect the autonomous concept of the fundamental right to data protection enshrined in the Charter and are subject to review in the light of this.

Before turning to the second condition, it is necessary at this point to make a clarification about the content of the fundamental right to data protection. In particular, it should be considered what exactly constitutes this right, on the basis of which we should be able to assess any interferences with this. Article 8 EUCFR consists of three paragraphs: the first states that 'everyone has the right to the protection of personal data concerning him or her'; the second provides that such data must be processed fairly for specified purposes on a legitimate basis laid down by law and guarantees a right of access to the data and a right to rectification;

---

[259] See also Art 6(1) TEU.

the third paragraph makes compliance with these rules subject to control by an independent authority. In this respect, is the right to data protection enshrined in Article 8 (1) EUCFR or is it found in Article 8 EUCFR taken as a whole? The answer to this question is important because it will determine how an interference to this fundamental right is to be established. If we consider that the fundamental right to data protection is found in Article 8(1) solely, which stipulates that every-one has a right to the protection of his personal data, then any processing of such data will necessarily mean that it interferes with this fundamental right. If, on the other hand, we accept that the right is not confined only in the first paragraph of Article 8 but it is enshrined in all the three paragraphs of this Article, an interfer-ence with this will be established only when the processing in question interferes with one or more data protection principles. The case law of the CJEU has so far followed the former approach.[260] Nevertheless, I submit that the latter approach that sees the right to data protection in all the three paragraphs of Article 8 EUCFR is more correct and should, therefore, be adopted. This is for two reasons. First, the view that any type of processing of personal data interferes with the right to data protection, besides introducing a cyclical argument, is counter-intuitive because it also includes lawful processing that complies with all the requirements of Article 8 EUCFR. Secondly and more importantly, determining with accuracy the actual interference of a certain type of processing with the right to data protection is fun-damental in order to be able to undertake a robust analysis of the permissibility of such interference on the basis of Article 52(1) EUCFR. Instead of merely assessing that the measure in question entails processing of personal data and, therefore, interferes with the right to data protection in general, it is important to determine the specific data protection principles the processing at issue interferes with. This makes the scope of the analysis clearer from the start and allows for a solid further examination of the justifiability of the established interference.

ii. A Balancing Mechanism for Data Protection

Data protection—as privacy—is not an absolute right.[261] On the contrary, it should be weighed against contrasting values and rights in a democratic society.[262] This means, furthermore, that data protection can legitimately be subjected to restrictions. These restrictions, however, will be permissible, insofar as they meet the following conditions: i) they are provided by law, ii) they pursue objectives

---

[260] For a detailed analysis see Chs 2, 3 and 6.

[261] The Court of Justice has repeatedly held that 'the right to the protection of personal data is not an absolute right, but must be considered in relation to its function in society'. See Joined Cases C-92/09 and C-93/09 *Volker und Markus Schecke GbR* (C-92/09), *Hartmut Eifert* (C-93/09) *v Land Hessen* (ECJ (GC), 9 November 2010), para 48 and Case C-543/09 *Deutsche Telekom* (ECJ, 5 May 2011), para 51. See also GDPR, Recital 4.

[262] As the Court of Justice has held, human rights are 'far from constituting unfettered prerogatives' and they are subject 'to limitations laid down in accordance with the public interest.' See Case 4/73 *Nold v Commission* [1974] ECR 491, para 14.

of general interest recognised by the Union or the need to protect the rights and freedoms of others, iii) they are necessary, iv) they conform with the principle of proportionality, and v) they respect the 'essence' of the right to data protection.[263]

This is the second condition that data protection needs to satisfy in order to be a fully functional fundamental right. It should be balanced against opposing interests as such, not through the proxy of privacy. This means that infringements of the right to data protection should be determined on the basis of the data protection principles themselves, with the application of the principle of proportionality,[264] without the need to recourse to the right to privacy. The processing, thus, of personal data should be deemed proportionate or disproportionate, on the basis of the specific fair information principle or principles, with which it interferes. Determining disproportionate processing on the basis of the right to privacy and not of the specific data protection principle that this goes against, is not only an unnecessary circumvention of the existing law that renders data protection virtually useless. It is also dangerous, because there could be instances of disproportionate processing of personal data that hardly, however, constitute disproportionate interferences with the right to privacy. The problem posed in the US Supreme Court case of *United States v Miller*[265] could be a useful example here. In this case, federal law enforcement officials issued subpoenas to two banks to produce a customer's financial records. The banks complied with the subpoenas, but the customer was not notified of the disclosure of the records until later in the course of prosecution. He argued that the subpoenas violated his Fourth Amendment rights,[266] but the Court concluded that he lacked a reasonable expectation of privacy in the financial records maintained by his bank,[267] because 'the Fourth Amendment does not prohibit the obtaining of information revealed to a third party and conveyed by him to Government authorities.'[268] According to the Court, '[a]ll of the documents obtained, including financial statements and deposit slips, contain only information voluntarily conveyed to the banks and exposed to their employees in the ordinary course of business.'[269] Leaving aside the problems of the US constitutional protection of privacy through the 'legitimate expectations' doctrine, this example is also illuminating in the EU fundamental rights context.[270] The further use by the government of personal financial data is specifically

---

[263] Art 52 (1) EUCFR.

[264] On the relationship between the 'principle of proportionality' and the 'essential core' doctrine see the very interesting analysis of R Schutze, 'Three "Bills of Rights" for the European Union' (2011) 30 *Yearbook of European Law* 131, 140. See also R Alexy, *A Theory of Constitutional Rights* (Oxford, Oxford University Press, 2009) 51; L Zucca, *Constitutional Dilemmas: Conflicts of Fundamental Legal Rights in Europe and the USA* (Oxford, Oxford University Press, 2008).

[265] *United States v Miller* 425 US 435, 437 (1976).

[266] ibid, 438.

[267] ibid, 442.

[268] ibid, 443.

[269] ibid, 442.

[270] For a discussion on how the ECtHR has applied a 'reasonable expectations' test, see T Gómez-Arostegui, 'Defining Private Life Under the European Convention on Human Rights by Referring to Reasonable Expectations' (2005) 35 *California Western International Law Journal* 153.

addressed by the purpose/use limitation principle, a keystone principle of data protection laws. It is not so evident, however, whether an interference with the right to privacy can be established here, without recourse to other fundamental rights and principles, such as, for instance, procedural rights of the individual to know if his personal information is further disseminated, or in certain cases, the principle of non-discrimination. Moreover, any potential claim of the customer against his bank would have to be established not on the basis of his right to privacy, but on breach of contractual obligations.

Taking data protection principles seriously is, therefore, a necessity. Data protection principles should not be seen as mere proclamations, void of any coercive meaning. Viewing fair information principles as coercive principles is not merely a theoretical issue emanating of the debate on the added value of data protection. It can have serious practical consequences in the drafting of legislation. This is because data protection principles are more specific and they can provide for prescriptive guidance better than the general privacy concept. They can be, thus, very informative for legislators, when they seek to adopt measures that clearly go against specific fair information principles. In these cases, stricter scrutiny against the test of proportionality should be applied, on the basis not only of privacy, but also of the specific data protection principle at stake. The problem remains the same, when the measure should be judged *ex post*, by courts: if a certain data protection principle is at issue, then it would be clearer if the court focused on that in order to perform the proportionality analysis, instead of seeking recourse to a general notion of privacy.

iii. The Essence of the Right to Data Protection: 'Hard Core' Data Protection Principles

In order for data protection to be able to function both positively and negatively, I argue that it should be recognised that this has an essential core that cannot be submitted to further restrictions. This follows from Article 52(1) EUCFR, that provides that 'any limitation of the exercise of the rights and freedoms recognized by this Charter must ... respect the essence of those rights and freedoms.' This provision, which draws inspiration from national constitutions' pronouncements[271] and the ECtHR case law,[272] aims to guarantee that no limitation will deprive the rights and freedoms of the Charter of their substance.[273] Along the same lines, the ECJ has consistently held that restrictions to fundamental rights are justified when they 'do not constitute disproportionate and intolerable interference, impairing *the very substance* of the rights guaranteed'.[274] However, the Court has not clarified

---

[271] For instance, Art 19(2) of the German Basic Law provides that '[i]n no case may the essence of a basic right be affected.'

[272] *See Sporrong and Lönnroth v Sweden* (1982) Series A no 52, paras 58 and 60.

[273] Lenaerts, n 119 above, p 391.

[274] This pronouncement is often used with regard to the right to property. See Case 44/79 *Hauer* [1979] ECR 3727, para 23; Case 265/87 *Schräder HS Kraftfutter* [1989] ECR 2237, para 15; Case

whether the essence of a fundamental right refers to some kind of common and universal core of this right or whether this has a different meaning dependent on the circumstances of each particular case.[275]

Determining what constitutes the essence of the right to data protection is not an easy task. The Court referred to the essence of the right to data protection[276] in its judgment in *Digital Rights Ireland*,[277] asserting that this had not been adversely affected in that case because the Data Retention Directive contained certain principles of data protection and data security.[278] This pronouncement indeed confirms that the CJEU has recognised that data protection is a fully fledged fundamental right that operates both positively and negatively, and has an inviolable core. However, it is concerning that 'certain data protection and data security principles' may dangerously confine the essence of the fundamental right to data protection only to 'minimum safeguards'.

It should be noted, at the outset, that the essence of fundamental rights is necessarily a vague notion and should to an extent remain so. As is seen in detail below, the CJEU in *Digital Rights Ireland* and *Schrems* pinpointed in a dangerously accurate manner the essence of the right to privacy to the access to content of communications as opposed to metadata. Such an approach opened up criticisms concerning the artificiality of this division, but in my view, it is also risky because it ends up prescribing in definitive terms the essence of privacy. I disagree with such a prescriptive definition and, therefore, my attempt to approach the essence of data protection, is based on the premise that this should remain to an extent vague. Nevertheless, a number of points could be advanced here. The starting point for determining the essence of the right to data protection should be, of course, Article 8 of the Charter and the six data protection principles contained therein (the fair processing principle, the purpose specification principle, legitimate basis for processing, rights of access and rectification and the independent supervision principle). The fair processing principle includes further concerns and principles that should be considered even if not expressly listed in Article 8 EUCFR. Furthermore, there are certain types of processing that go against several, *cumulative* data protection principles. For instance, sensitive data should be shielded from certain categories of processing that can lead to profiling, especially if such processing is undertaken for different purposes from the ones that the data were initially collected for. Such processing that goes against a number of different data protection principles could be seen as an *aggravated* interference with the

---

C-293/97 *Standley and Others* [1999] ECR I-2603, para 54; Joined Cases C-402/05 P and C-415/05 P *Kadi and Al Barakaat International Foundation v Council and Commission* [2008] ECR I-6351, para 355; and, C-380/08 *ERG* [2010] ECR I-2007, para 80 (emphasis added).

[275] See Dirk Ehlers et al (eds), *European Fundamental Rights and Freedoms* (Berlin, De Gruyter, 2007) 393.

[276] The Court also discussed the essence of the right to privacy. See Case C-362/13 *Maximillian Schrems v Data Protection Commissioner* (ECJ, 6 October 2015), para 39.

[277] Joined Cases C-293/12 and 594/12 *Digital Rights Ireland and Seitlinger* [2014] ECR I-238, para 40.

[278] ibid.

fundamental right to data protection. The purpose specification and limitation principle should also have a 'hard core', which should prohibit the secondary use of personal data, even if those are not necessarily sensitive. This 'essence' of the purpose limitation principle should apply when the further processing of personal data threatens the principle of non-discrimination or the core of the right to 'informational self-determination' of the individual. In essence, the 'hard core' of data protection would be what needs to be protected, so that the final values that data protection pursues such as dignity, informational self-determination and individual autonomy are safeguarded. This might require a recognition that the essence of one or more data protection principles has been touched upon in certain particular instances of processing.

2

The Judicial Assessment of the Right to Data Protection

I. THE EUROPEAN COURT OF HUMAN RIGHTS (ECtHR) CASE LAW

ATTEMPTING TO FIND a mention of data protection as a fundamental right in the case law of the Strasbourg Court is a somewhat quaint exercise. This is because no right to personal data is recognised, as such, in the European Convention of Human Rights (ECHR). Data protection, which is recognised as a right by the Council of Europe Convention No 108[1] is not, however, unknown to the Strasbourg Court. The European Court of Human Rights finds it encompassed in the right to respect for private and family life enshrined in Article 8 ECHR, the notion of which the Court has kept open and broad on purpose.[2]

The Strasbourg Court has recognised in a series of judgments some elements of data protection law and data protection principles as deriving from Article 8 ECHR. In *Leander,* the Court held that the storing by the police of 'information relating to an individual's private life' in a secret register and the release of such information amounted to an interference with his right to privacy as guaranteed by Article 8(1) ECHR.[3] It is not entire clear, however, what the exact meaning of 'information relating to an individual's private life' is and whether it corresponds to the notion of 'personal data' as defined in Convention 108. Interpretation is further complicated by the fact that the Commission of Human Rights and the ECtHR had in certain cases drawn a line of distinction between the 'private' and the 'public'. For instance, in *Friedl,* a case where the police took and stored pictures of an individual participating in a demonstration, the Commission found no violation of Article 8 ECHR because there had been no intrusion of the 'inner circle' of the applicant's private life, since he was not at home but at a public event when the pictures were taken.[4] In *Amann* the Court mentioned Convention 108

---

[1] Council of Europe Convention for the Protection of Individuals with regard to Automatic Processing of Personal Data, European Treaty Series No 108; adopted 28 January 1981.

[2] The ECtHR has held that 'private life should be considered as broad term which is not susceptible to an exhaustive definition'. See *PG and JH v UK* App no 44787/98 (25 September 2001). See also E Brouwer, *Digital Borders and Real Rights: Effective Remedies for Third-Country Nationals in the Schengen Information System* (The Netherlands, Brill, 2008) 153.

[3] *Leander v Sweden* App no 9248/81, para 48.

[4] *Friedl v Austria* [1994] RJD 31, paras 49–51.

and held that the broad interpretation of the notion of 'private life' that it had adopted corresponded with the purpose of the Convention 'to secure … for every individual … respect for his rights and fundamental freedoms, and in particular his right to privacy, with regard to automatic processing of personal data relating to him.'[5] The ECtHR concluded that a card filled in on the applicant on which it was stated that he was a 'contact with the Russian embassy' and did 'business of various kinds' amounted to data relating to the applicant's private life.[6] In *Rotaru*, the Court seemed to slowly depart from the 'private/public' distinction as it established that 'public information can fall within the scope of private life where it is systematically collected and stored in files held by the authorities.'[7] The ECtHR also stated in the same case that the refusal to allow an opportunity for the personal data to be refuted constitutes an interference with the right to privacy.[8] In *Gaskin*, the Court had to consider the right of an individual to have access to his personal social services files and the data held therein.[9] The applicant in this case, who had been taken into care as a child, wished to obtain details of where he had been kept and by whom and in what conditions, in order to be able to overcome his problems and learn about his past.[10] The Court distinguished the case from *Leander*, where information was compiled about an individual and used to his detriment, because Mr Gaskin had not challenged the information compiled about him, but rather the failure to grant him unimpeded access to that information.[11] In this respect, the ECtHR opined that this was not a case of 'interference' with Article 8 ECHR, but one of breach of the positive obligation arising from the same Article requiring that 'everyone should be able to establish details of *their identity as individual human beings* and that in principle they should not be obstructed by the authorities from obtaining such very basic information without specific justification.'[12] Granted, the Strasbourg Court's analysis took place on the basis of Article 8 ECHR, but the Court could have used the right of access to personal data guaranteed in Article 8(a) and (b) of Convention 108, instead of having to emphasise the 'vital interest' of persons in the situation of the applicant 'in receiving the information necessary to know and to understand their childhood and early development.'[13] In *S and Marper*, it was established that the blanket and indiscriminate nature of the powers of retention of the fingerprints, cellular samples and DNA profiles of persons suspected but not convicted of offences constituted a disproportionate interference with the right to private life and, therefore, a violation of Article 8 ECHR.[14] Finally, in *Khelili* the Court mentioned processing

---

[5] *Amann v Switzerland* App no 27798/95 (ECtHR, 16 February 2000), para 65.
[6] ibid, para 70.
[7] *Rotaru v Romania* App no 28341/95 (ECtHR, 4 May 2000,) para 43.
[8] ibid, para 46.
[9] *Gaskin v UK* App no 10454/83 (ECtHR, 7 July 1989).
[10] ibid, para 11.
[11] ibid, para 41.
[12] ibid, paras 31, 41 and 49. Emphasis added.
[13] ibid, para 49.
[14] *S and Marper v UK* App nos 30562/04 and 30566/04 (ECtHR, 4 December 2008).

of personal data expressly to note that personal data subject to automatic process-ing can considerably facilitate access to and the distribution of such data by public authorities.[15] The Court, however, did not delve further into these concepts as the rest of the analysis was confined to Article 8 ECHR.

The Court has also given particular importance to the protection of health data in its case law. In *Z v Finland*, it held that 'the protection of personal data, particularly medical data, is of fundamental importance to a person's enjoyment of his or her right to respect for private and family life as guaranteed by Article 8 of the Convention.'[16] In *I v Finland*, having reiterated that the processing of information relating to an individual's private life comes within the scope of Article 8(1) ECHR,[17] the Strasbourg Court ruled that Article 8 ECHR, in addi-tion to protecting the individual against arbitrary interference by the state, also entails 'positive obligations', which require 'the adoption of measures designed to secure respect for private life even in the sphere of the relations of individuals between themselves.'[18] In this respect, it found that the safeguarding of personal data from unauthorised access—essentially the data security principle—consti-tutes a positive obligation of the state under Article 8 ECHR.[19]

The cases discussed[20] demonstrate that the Strasbourg Court is aware of Convention 108 and data protection, but when it comes to the application of this right in practice, it adopts a very cautious approach. This is not surprising, given that data protection is not one of the rights of the Convention. It is, thus, viewed as an aspect of the very broad notion of private life.[21] This approach, while under-standable, is not without shortcomings: not all personal data are deemed to form part of the right to private and family life, and the recognition of specific data protection principles, such as the right to access to personal data, the right to rec-tification and data security appears quite complicated since the Court has to find a way to read these principles within Article 8 ECHR,[22] instead of looking directly at Convention 108.

---

[15] *Khelili v Switzerland* App no 16188/07 (ECtHR, 18 October 2011).

[16] *Z v Finland* App no 22009/93 (ECtHR, 25 February 1997), Rep. 1997-I, para 95. See also *MS v Sweden* App no 20837/92 (ECtHR, 27 August 1997), para 41.

[17] *I v Finland* App no 20511/03 (ECtHR, 17 July 2008), para 35.

[18] ibid, para 36.

[19] ibid, paras 37 and 46.

[20] A further particularity of the ECtHR's case law is that it concerns, in most cases, data processing in rather special contexts, such as secret surveillance activities by the police or intelligence agencies. See L Bygrave, 'Where Have All the Judges Gone? Reflections on Judicial Involvement in Developing Data Protection Law' (2000) *Privacy Law & Policy Reporter*, 11, 12.

[21] As the Court put it in *Rotaru*: its case law 'emphasise[s] the correspondence of this broad interpretation [of Art 8 ECHR with that of the Convention 108].' *Rotaru*, n 7 above, para 43.

[22] P de Hert and S Gutwirth, 'Data Protection in the Case Law of Strasbourg and Luxemburg: Con-stitutionalisation in Action' in S Gutwirth and others (eds), *Reinventing Data Protection?* (New York, Springer, 2009) 3, 27. See also J Kokott and C Sobotta, 'The distinction between privacy and data pro-tection in the jurisprudence of the CJEU and the ECtHR' (2013) *International Data Privacy Law*, 222.

II. DATA PROTECTION IN THE CASE LAW OF THE COURT
OF JUSTICE OF THE EU

Unlike the European Convention of Human Rights that enshrines the right to privacy, but makes no mention of a right to data protection, the EU explicitly recognises a fundamental right to personal data protection in Article 8 EUCFR. It is worth investigating, therefore, how the ECJ has perceived this fundamental right in its jurisprudence. The analysis below is divided into two parts: first, it focuses on the Court's judgments delivered before the entry into force of the Lisbon Treaty, which rendered the Charter of Fundamental Rights legally binding. Subsequently, it discusses the evolution of the ECJ's case law on the nature of the fundamental right to data protection after the Charter had become primary EU law.

A. The Court's Approach Before the EU Charter of Fundamental Rights Became Legally Binding

Before the entry into force of the Lisbon Treaty, several judgments had been pronounced by the Court of Justice of the EU concerning data protection issues.[23] Most often, they concerned preliminary rulings on questions of interpretation of the Data Protection Directive.[24] If we attempt a general comment on this case law, this would be that 'the Court, in essence, has interpreted an internal market harmonisation instrument (the Directive) in a manner that fosters the protection of a fundamental right.'[25] This notwithstanding, the Court was accused of viewing 'data protection as privacy, no more no less.'[26] According to this argument, the Court's approach was straightforward: A breach of the right to privacy signified an unlawful processing in the sense of the Directive; no breach of privacy implied no breach of the Directive.[27]

The first significant judgment concerning the nature of data protection was the *Österreichischer Rundfunk*[28] case, delivered in May 2003. *Österreichischer Rundfunk* was a preliminary ruling case on the compatibility with Community law of an Austrian provision requiring entities which were subject to control by the

---

[23] For an analysis of the ECJ case law on data protection, see M Tzanou, 'Data Protection in EU Law after Lisbon: Challenges, Developments, and Limitations' in M Gupta (ed), *Handbook of Research on Emerging Developments in Data Privacy* (Hershey, IGI Global, 2014) 24.

[24] Directive 95/46/EC of the European Parliament and of the Council of 24 October 1995 on the protection of individuals with regard to the processing of personal data and on the free movement of such data [1995] OJ L281/3 (Data Protection Directive).

[25] M Tzanou, 'Balancing Fundamental Rights: United in Diversity? Some Reflections on the Recent Case Law of the European Court of Justice on Data Protection' (2010) 6 *Croatian Yearbook of European Law and Policy* 53, 59.

[26] De Hert and Gutwirth, n 22 above, p 33.

[27] ibid, 32.

[28] Joined Cases C-465/00, C-138/01 & C-139/01 *Österreichischer Rundfunk* [2003] ECR I-4989 (Full Court).

Rechnungshof (Austrian Court of Audit), to inform the latter about the salaries of their employees when they exceeded a certain level. This information was subsequently published by the Rechnungshof in a report which contained the names of the persons and the level of their respective salaries. In this respect, the Court was asked to rule whether the Data Protection Directive was applicable at all to this control activity exercised by the Rechnungshof. Unlike Advocate General Tizzano, who pleaded against the applicability of the Directive,[29] the ECJ found that it was applicable. According to the Court, 'since any personal data can move between Member States, Directive 95/46 requires in principle compliance with the rules for protection of such data with respect to any processing of data as defined by Article 3'.[30] The ECJ rejected the argument that the Data Protection Directive applies only to activities which have a sufficient connection with the common market, by holding that recourse to Article 95 EC (now Article 114 TFEU) as a legal basis 'does not presuppose the existence of an *actual link* with free movement between Member States *in every situation* referred to by the measure founded on that basis.'[31] If a contrary interpretation were to be adopted, it would make the limits of the field of application of the Data Protection Directive particularly unsure and uncertain, which would be contrary to its essential objective that is the harmonisation of the data protection rules of the Member States, in order to eliminate obstacles and ensure the free movement of personal data within the internal market.[32]

The same wide interpretation of the scope of the Data Protection Directive was reiterated in *Lindqvist*.[33] Before moving to the reasoning of the Court, it is worth taking a closer look at the Opinion of the Advocate General. Advocate General Tizzano reasoned against the applicability of the Data Protection Directive to the processing of personal data which consisted of setting up an Internet page as an ancillary activity to Mrs Lindqvist's voluntary work as a catechist in a parish of the Swedish Protestant Church. To refute the Commission's argument that Mrs Lindqvist's activity fell within the scope of the Directive because this was not confined to pursuing economic objectives but also had objectives connected with social imperatives and the protection of fundamental rights, the Advocate General observed that the need to safeguard the fundamental rights of individuals in order to ensure a high level of protection of those rights 'was conceived in the course

---

[29] Opinion of Advocate General Tizzano, Joined Cases C-465/00, C-138/01 & C-139/01 *Österreichischer Rundfunk*, delivered on 14 November 2002.

[30] *Österreichischer Rundfunk*, n 28 above, para 40.

[31] ibid, para 41 (emphasis added). Classen argued that that the ECJ has shown an increasing interest in human rights questions, 'but this does not exonerate the Court from the obligation to examine the applicability of Community law.' CD Classen, 'Joined Cases C-465/00, C-138/01 & C-139/01, *Österreichischer Rundfunk*, Judgment of 20 May 2003, Full Court, [2003] ECR I-4989' (2004) 41 *Common Market Law Review* 1377, 1382.

[32] ibid, para 42.

[33] Case C-101/01 *Bodil Lindqvist* [2003] ECR I-12971; L Coudray, '*Bodil Lindqvist* case note' (2004) 41 *Common Market Law Review*, 1361.

of and with a view to achieving the *main objective* of the Directive, namely the *free movement* of personal data inasmuch as it is held to be "vital to the internal market".[34] According to the Advocate General, contributing to economic and social progress and safeguarding fundamental rights represent important values and imperatives which the Community legislature took into account in framing the harmonised rules required for the establishment and functioning of the internal market but they were not *independent* objectives of the Directive.[35] In accordance with its legal basis, Directive 95/46 had, in the view of the Advocate General, as its *principal* objective the guaranteeing of the free movement of data within the internal market. Thus, the harmonisation of national legislation on the protection of personal data was only a *means* of guaranteeing free movement of personal data. This meant that, although it called upon the Member States to adopt a harmonised system of protection of personal data, the Directive was not a norm for the protection of fundamental rights. To support this analysis, Advocate General Tizzano adopted a strict reading of the principle of 'attributed competences' and recalled that the European Community did not have any general competence to design provisions protecting fundamental rights. On the basis of Article 95 EC, the Community legislature did not have competence to design an act guaranteeing, in all cases, the protection of fundamental rights. Thus, far from offering general protection to individuals, the Directive, according to the Advocate General, applied only to the activities within the scope of Community law.

The ECJ did not agree with this approach. It stressed once more that a distinction should be made between the general objective of an act adopted on the basis of Article 95 EC and the specific situations where this act can be applied even if those are not directly linked to the internal market. It clarified that the exception of Article 3(2)[36] applies only to the activities which are expressly listed there or which can be classified in the same category. As a result, the Directive applies to all the other activities regardless of their connection with the internal market. Thus, it applied to the charitable and religious activities carried out by Mrs Lindqvist.

Having established that the applicability of the Data Protection Directive was not based on the 'connection' of the processing activity with the internal market, on the substantive issue of the nature of data protection, the Court seemed to think that this should be interpreted on the basis of the right to privacy:

> It should also be noted that the provisions of Directive 95/46, in so far as they govern the processing of personal data liable to infringe *fundamental freedoms*, in particular the right to *privacy*, must necessarily be interpreted in the light of fundamental rights, which,

---

[34] Opinion of Advocate General Tizzano, *Lindqvist* Case C-101/01, para 40.

[35] ibid, para 41.

[36] Data Protection Directive, Art 3(2) excludes from the scope of application of the Directive processing operations concerning public security, defence, state security and the activities of the state in areas of criminal law that fall outside the scope of Community law and the processing of personal data by a person in the course of a purely personal or household activity.

according to settled case-law, form an integral part of the general principles of law whose observance the Court ensures.[37]

This pronouncement seems to suggest that the Court did not consider data protection as a fundamental right, but was only concerned over certain forms of processing that might infringe fundamental rights, and in particular the right to privacy; in this case, the protection afforded to fundamental rights as general principles of EU law would apply. Having stated this, the ECJ went on to examine in *Österreichischer Rundfunk* whether the activities of the Rechnungshof constituted interference with the right to privacy. It concluded that:

> while the mere recording by an employer of data by name relating to the remuneration paid to his employees cannot as such constitute an interference with private life, the communication of that data to third parties, in the present case a public authority, infringes the right of the persons concerned to respect for private life, whatever the subsequent use of the information thus communicated, and constitutes an interference within the meaning of Article 8 of the Convention.[38]

This approach of the Court, albeit understandable, was quite problematic, because by failing to recognise data protection as a fundamental right, all possible interferences had to be assessed on the basis of the right to privacy. Thus, activities that would constitute, without doubt, interferences with data protection, such as the recording of remuneration, are not deemed to interfere with the right to privacy, unless the recorded data are communicated to third parties. This lessens the scope of protection, especially since data protection was recognised as a fundamental right, next to privacy, in the EU legal order.

While the ECJ in *Österreichischer Rundfunk* and *Lindqvist* focused solely on the Data Protection Directive, in *Promusicae*[39] it recognised for the first time data protection as a fundamental right enshrined in the Charter. *Promusicae* concerned the refusal of Telefónica, a commercial company in Spain which provides internet access services, to disclose to Promusicae—a non-profit-making organisation of producers and publishers of musical and audiovisual recordings, acting on behalf of its members who were holders of intellectual property rights—the personal data of certain persons to whom it provided internet access services. Promusicae sought disclosure of this information before the Commercial Court of Madrid in order to be able to bring civil proceedings against those persons, who, according to it, used the KaZaA peer-to-peer file exchange program and provided access in shared files of personal computers to recordings in which the members of Promusicae held the exploitation rights. The Spanish Court referred the issue to the ECJ by asking it essentially whether Community law, in particular Directives

---

[37] *Österreichischer Rundfunk*, n 28 above, para 68.
[38] *Österreichischer Rundfunk*, n 28 above, para 74.
[39] Case C-275/06 *Productores de Música de España (Promusicae) v Telefónica de España SAU* (29 January 2008); X Groussot, 'Music Production in Spain (Promusicae) v Telefónica de España SAU—Rock the KaZaA: Another Clash of Fundamental Rights' (2008) 45 *Common Market Law Review* 1745.

2000/31,[40] 2001/29[41] and 2004/48,[42] read in the light of Articles 17 and 47 of the EUCFR, require Member States to lay down, in order to ensure effective protection of copyright, an obligation to communicate personal data in the context of civil proceedings.

Having established that the secondary Community legislation did not provide a clear answer on the issue at stake, the Court turned its attention to primary EU constitutional law, namely fundamental rights. In this part of its analysis, it noted from the outset that while the fundamental right to property, which includes intellectual property rights such as copyright, and the fundamental right to effective judicial protection, constitute general principles of Community law,[43] the situation in respect of which the national court put the question at issue involves, in addition to those two rights, a further fundamental right, namely the right that 'guarantees protection of personal data and *hence of private life*'.[44] This was the first time that the Court expressly recognised that the right to data protection enjoys the status of a fundamental right within the EU. It did so by looking at Article 8 of the EUCFR—even though the Charter was not legally binding at that point—which expressly proclaims the right to data protection.[45] It seems, though that the ECJ in this case went one step forward from its existing case law concerning the Charter: until *Promusicae*, if a right was contained in the Charter, this created a presumption that it was protected under the general principles of Community law.[46] In *Promusicae* however, the fact that the protection of personal data was enshrined in the Charter was enough for the ECJ to identify it as an autonomous fundamental right.[47]

Promusicae is remarkable from this point of view; in terms of substance, however, it marked no real difference from the ECJ's understanding of data protection in *Österreichischer Rundfunk* and *Lindqvist*. The Court seemed to think that data protection is a fundamental right that guarantees protection of personal data and *hence of private life*. The balancing of fundamental rights, therefore, in this

---

[40]   Directive 2000/31/EC of the European Parliament and of the Council of 8 June 2000 on certain legal aspects of information society services, in particular electronic commerce, in the Internal Market (Directive on electronic commerce) [2000] OJ L178/1.

[41]   Directive 2001/29 of the European Parliament and of the Council of 22 May 2001 on the harmonisation of certain aspects of copyright and related rights in the information society [2001] OJ L167/19.

[42]   Directive 2004/48 of the European Parliament and of the Council of 29 April 2004 on the enforcement of intellectual property rights [2004] OJ L157/32.

[43]   *Promusicae*, n 39 above, para 62.

[44]   ibid, para 63 (emphasis added).

[45]   ibid, para 64.

[46]   See M Dougan, 'The Treaty of Lisbon 2007: Winning Minds, Not Hearts' (2008) 45 *Common Market Law Review* 617, 662.

[47]   M Tzanou, 'Data Protection in EU Law: An Analysis of the EU Legal Framework and the ECJ Jurisprudence' in C Akrivopoulou and A Psygkas (eds), *Personal Data Privacy and Protection in a Surveillance Era: Technologies and Practices* (Hershey, IGI Global, 2011) 273, 275; F Bignami, 'The Case for Tolerant Constitutional Patriotism: The Right to Privacy Before the European Courts' (2008) 41 *Cornell International Law Journal* 211.

case took place between 'the right to respect for *private life* on the one hand and the rights to protection of property and to an effective remedy on the other.'[48] Data protection was not mentioned by the Court, since apparently it was a part of privacy.

There was no mention of the fundamental right to data protection in the judgments delivered by the Court after *Promusicae*. In *Satamedia*[49] the Court after reiterating that the objective of the Data Protection Directive was to ensure the free flow of personal data, while protecting 'the fundamental rights and freedoms of natural persons and, *in particular, their right to privacy*, with respect to the processing of personal data',[50] it went on to explain that the object of Article 9 of the Data Protection Directive was 'to reconcile two fundamental rights: the protection of privacy and freedom of expression'.[51] In *Rijkeboer*[52] the ECJ noted that certain fair information principles and the data subject's rights included in the Data Protection Directive, such as the principle of fair and lawful processing of personal data, the data quality principle, the right of the data subject to rectification, erasure and blocking of his data as well as the right to object to the processing of his personal data formed part of the right to privacy.[53]

B. The Court's Approach after the EU Charter of Fundamental Rights Became Legally Binding

i. The Initial Years: Data Protection as an Aspect of Privacy

Schecke[54] was the first case where the Court had to judge the validity of EU law in the light of the provisions of the—by now—legally binding Charter.[55] In this case the Court was presented with a unique opportunity to clarify its position regarding the nature of data protection as a fundamental right. The case concerned the questions raised in the course of proceedings between two German nationals, a natural and a legal person, and the *Land* Hessen concerning the publication on the Internet site of the *Bundesanstalt für Landwirtschaft und Ernährung* (Federal Office for

---

[48] *Promusicae*, n 39 above, para 65 (emphasis added).
[49] Case C-73/07 *Satakunnan Markkinapörssi and Satamedia* [2008] ECR I-9831; W Hins, 'Case C-73/07 Satakunnan Markkinapörssi and Satamedia, Judgment of 16 December 2008, not yet reported' (2010) 47 *Common Market Law Review* 215.
[50] ibid, para 52.
[51] ibid, para 54.
[52] Case C-553/07 *Rijkeboer* ECR I-3889.
[53] ibid, paras 49 and 64.
[54] Joined Cases C-92/09 and C-93/09 *Volker und Markus Schecke GbR* (C-92/09), *Hartmut Eifert* (C-93/09) *v Land Hessen* (CJEU (GC), 9 November 2010); M Bobek, 'Joined Cases C-92 & 93/09, Volker und Markus Schecke GbR and Hartmut Eifert, Judgment of the Court of Justice (Grand Chamber) of 9 November 2010' (2011) 48 (6) *Common Market Law Review*, 2005.
[55] S Iglesias Sánchez, 'The Court and the Charter: The impact of the entry into force of the Lisbon Treaty on the ECJ's approach to fundamental rights' (2012) 49 *Common Market Law Review* 1565, 1581.

Agriculture and Food) of personal data relating to them as recipients of funds from the European Agricultural Guarantee Fund (EAGF) or the European Agricultural Fund for Rural Development (EAFRD). The publication was mandatory pursuant to Article 44a of Regulation No 1290/2005,[56] which obliges Member States to ensure annual *ex-post* publication of the beneficiaries of the EAGF and the EAFRD and the amounts received per beneficiary under each of these funds.

Before turning to the reasoning of the Court of Justice, it is worth taking a look at the national court's position. This was that the obligation to publish under Article 44a of Regulation No 1290/2005 constituted an unjustified interference with the fundamental right to the protection of personal data.[57] In particular, it considered that that provision, which pursues the aim of increasing the transparency of the use of European funds, does not improve the prevention of irregularities, since extensive control mechanisms exist for that purpose. In any event, according to the German court, that obligation to publish was not proportionate to the aim pursued, because the Regulation did not limit access to the Internet site concerned to 'Internet Protocol' (IP) addresses situated in the European Union, and it was not possible to withdraw the data from the Internet after the expiry of the two-year period laid down in Article 3(3) of Regulation No 259/2008.[58] The German court's pronouncement on the case is very important, because it essentially invited the Court of Justice of the EU to recognise data protection as a self-standing fundamental right: the court suggested that any possible interference had to be determined on the basis of the fundamental right to data protection without any recourse to privacy.

The Court, however, did not follow that path. It started by pointing out that the relevant provision on publication of the Regulation should be assessed in the light of the EU Charter of Fundamental Rights, which at the time of the delivery of the decision constituted binding EU law. The Court mentioned that Article 8 EUCFR was the relevant Charter provision at this case, but with the necessary clarification that 'that fundamental right is *closely connected* with the right to respect of private life expressed in Article 7 of the Charter.'[59] Having said that, the Court proceeded with its analysis on the permissible limitations that can be imposed to the right to data protection by confounding, however, data protection and privacy, in what it called 'the right to respect for private life with regard to the processing of personal data, recognised by Articles 7 and 8 of the Charter.'[60] The *Schecke* formula of seeing one right recognised by two Charter Articles instead of two different rights was repeated in the Court's decision in *ASNEF*.[61]

---

[56] Council Regulation (EC) No 1290/2005 of 21 June 2005 on the financing of the common agricultural policy, [2005] OJ L209/1.

[57] *Schecke*, n 54 above, para 30.

[58] ibid, para 31.

[59] ibid, para 47 (emphasis added).

[60] ibid, para 52.

[61] Joined Cases C-468/10 and C-469/10 *Asociación Nacional de Establecimientos Financieros de Crédito (ASNEF) and Federación de Comercio Electrónico y Marketing Directo (FECEMD) (C-469/10) v Administración del Estado* (CJEU (Third Chamber), 24 November 2011), para 42.

The approach of the Court of Justice toward data protection in its initial judgments after the Charter became legally binding seemed to be rooted in the perception that the right to data protection cannot operate alone without privacy on its side.[62] The only solution, therefore, for the Court was to consider them together as 'the right to respect for private life with regard to the processing of personal data'. Privacy appeared necessary in the equation, because on the basis of this, the possible interferences would be determined, according to Article 8(2) ECHR. Had the Court followed, however, the way shown by the national court in *Schecke*, it would have demonstrated that data protection can operate independently as a fundamental right. This reading could have been possible through a direct application of the conditions of Article 52(1) EUCFR to the right to data protection in Article 8 EUCFR without the need to go through Article 52(3) to the relevant provision of Article 8(2) ECHR on the permissible limitations to the right to privacy.

ii. The Intermediate Phase: The Recognition

In *Scarlet*,[63] a judgment which was delivered on the same day as *ASNEF*, the ECJ seemed to be making a step forward as it referred directly to the right to protection of personal data safeguarded by Article 8 EUCFR without mentioning Article 7 and privacy. In that case, the Court had to consider a preliminary reference question from the Belgian Cour d'appel asking it whether national courts were authorised by EU law to issue an injunction requiring an Internet Service Provider (ISP) to install a filtering system that actively monitors, without any limitation in time, all the electronic communications data made through its network and relating to each of its customers in order to prevent infringements of intellectual property rights. According to the Court, such a filtering system may infringe the fundamental rights of that ISP's customers, 'namely their *right to protection of their personal data* and their freedom to receive or impart information, which are rights safeguarded by Articles 8 and 11 of the Charter respectively.'[64] In this respect, the Court of Justice held that a fair balance should be struck 'between the right to intellectual property, on the one hand, and the freedom to conduct business, *the right to protection of personal data* and the freedom to receive or impart information, on the other.'[65] In *Netlog*,[66] a similar case, the Court had to consider a national court injunction, this time against an online social networking platform, Netlog, requiring it to install a filtering system capable of identifying electronic

---

[62] Compare F Boehm, *Information Sharing and Data Protection in the Area of Freedom, Security and Justice: Towards Harmonised Data Protection Principles for Information Exchange at EU-level* (Berlin/Heidelberg, Springer, 2012) 126.

[63] Case C-70/10 *Scarlet Extended SA v Société belge des auteurs, compositeurs et éditeurs SCRL (SABAM)* (CJEU (Third Chamber), 24 November 2011).

[64] ibid, para 50. Emphasis added.

[65] ibid, para 53. Emphasis added.

[66] Case C-360/10 *Belgische Vereniging van Auteurs, Componisten en Uitgevers CVBA (SABAM) v Netlog NV* (CJEU (Third Chamber), 16 February 2012).

files containing musical, cinematographic or audio-visual work shared by its users, with a view to preventing those works from being made available to the public in breach of copyright. The ECJ repeated its pronouncement in *Scarlet* that such an injunction was liable to infringe the fundamental rights of the network users to protection of personal data and freedom of expression, recognised in Articles 8 and 11 EUCFR respectively.[67] This pronouncement distinguishes *Scarlet* and *Netlog* from *Promusicae*, where solely the right to privacy was mentioned in the balancing exercise between fundamental rights.

It was in *Deutsche Telekom*[68] that the Court acknowledged for the first time that the aim of the Data Protection Directive was to ensure the observance of the right to data protection.[69] It, thus, abandoned its hitherto frequently used mantra that the objective of the Data Protection Directive was to safeguard the 'the fundamental rights and freedoms of natural persons and, in particular, their right to privacy, with respect to the processing of personal data'.[70] *Deutsche Telekom* concerned the refusal of a telecommunications network operator in Germany, Deutsche Telekom to make available to two undertakings, GoYellow GmbH ('GoYellow') and Telix AG ('Telix') operating an internet enquiry service and a telephone directory enquiry service respectively, data contained in the nationwide telephone directory enquiry service that relate not only to its own customers, but also to subscribers of other telecommunications networks undertakings. The dispute, which was between Deutsche Telekom and GoYellow and Telix, concerned the passing on, to an undertaking whose activity consists in providing publicly available directory enquiry services and directories, by an undertaking which assigns telephone numbers, of data in its possession relating to subscribers of a third-party undertaking. The dispute reached the Bundesverwaltungsgericht (Federal Administrative Court), which decided to stay the proceedings and refer the issue to the ECJ. In its preliminary reference, the Bundesverwaltungsgericht asked the ECJ whether Article 12 of Directive 2002/58/EC[71] (the 'e-Privacy' Directive) made the passing on of data relating to subscribers of a third-party undertaking conditional on the consent of that undertaking or its subscribers. In its reply, the ECJ commenced its analysis by taking a look at Article 8(1) EUCFR that guarantees everyone the right to protection of personal data.[72] It clarified, however, that this right is 'not an absolute right, but must be considered in relation to its function in society'.[73] The second paragraph of this Article authorises the processing of personal data if

---

[67] ibid, para 48.
[68] Case C-543/09 *Deutsche Telekom AG v Bundesrepublik Deutschland* (CJEU (Third Chamber), 5 May 2011).
[69] ibid, para 50.
[70] See for instance *Satamedia*, n 49 above, para 52.
[71] Directive 2002/58/EC of the European Parliament and of the Council of 12 July 2002 concerning the processing of personal data and the protection of privacy in the electronic communications sector [2002] OJ L201/37.
[72] *Deutsche Telekom*, n 68 above, para 49.
[73] ibid, para 51.

certain conditions (fair and lawful processing for specified purposes on the basis of the consent of the data subject or some other legitimate basis provided by the law) are satisfied.[74] In this respect, the Court observed that while the passing of subscribers' personal data to a third-party undertaking which intends to provide publicly available directory enquiry services and directories constitutes processing of personal data for the purposes of Article 8(2) EUCFR,[75] such processing is not capable of 'substantively impairing the right to protection of personal data, as recognised in Article 8 of the Charter.'[76]

It is interesting to see that only two years after the entry into force of the Lisbon Treaty the Court's approach toward the right to data protection had already evolved substantially. The Court referred in *Scarlet*, *Deutsche Telekom* and *Netlog* directly to Article 8 EUCFR without mentioning privacy[77] or repeating the *Schecke* formula and recognised this right as the aim of the Data Protection Directive. But the ECJ did not restrict itself to mentioning the right to data protection, it also sought to apply it even when considering questions of interpretation of secondary EU law, such as the ePrivacy Directive in *Deutsche Telekom*. In this regard, it used the fundamental right to data protection as the starting point of its analysis, but also as some kind of benchmark—if this was not 'substantially impaired', then the particular kind of processing at issue could take place. It remains unclear, however, how this benchmark works as to when the right to data protection is considered to be 'substantially impaired'. Was the Court alluding to a proportionality analysis and the essence of the right to data protection according to the criteria of Article 52(1) EUCFR, or did the 'substantially impaired' test mean something else? No guidance is provided on this issue in *Deutsche Telekom*. This case also raised questions as to the exact content of the right to data protection. The Court's analysis seemed to suggest that the right is enshrined only in the first paragraph of Article 8, and not in the whole Article, with paragraph 2 laying down the conditions for permissible processing. This issue is not without practical implications, especially when considering whether an interference with the right to data protection exists. Following the Court's position in *Deutsche Telekom*, if the right to data protection is only found in Article 8(1) EUCFR ('Everyone has the right to the protection of personal data concerning him or her'), the processing of this personal data—any processing—would imply interference with Article 8(1) EUCFR. If the right is to be found in the whole Article 8, however, and not only in the first paragraph, this might mean that processing of personal data in accordance with paragraphs 2 and 3 does not constitute an interference with this fundamental right.[78]

---

[74] ibid, para 52.

[75] ibid, para 53.

[76] ibid, para 66.

[77] The Court referred to the fundamental right to data protection also in *Patrick Kelly*. See Case C-104/10 *Patrick Kelly v National University of Ireland (University College, Dublin)* (CJEU (Second Chamber), 21 July 2011), para 55.

[78] G González Fuster, 'Balancing intellectual property against data protection: a new right's wavering weight' (2012) *Revista de Internet, Derecho y Política* 34. For further analysis, see below.

In subsequent judgments on data protection questions, the Court appeared to struggle slightly with the data protection/privacy terminology. In *IPI*,[79] a preliminary reference case that concerned the activities of private detectives acting for a professional body in order to investigate breaches of ethics of a regulated profession, in that case that of estate agents, the ECJ noted, citing *Satamedia* and *Schecke*, that 'the protection of the fundamental right to *privacy* requires that derogations and limitations in relation to the *protection of personal data* must apply only in so far as is strictly necessary.'[80] In *X*[81] the terminology diffulties of the Court appeared even more severe, as here the Court stated that privacy was enshrined in Article 8 EUCFR.[82]

iii. The Age of Maturity: Application and Interpretation of the Fundamental Right to Data Protection

After the uncertainties of the intermediate phase of the Court's jurisprudence concerning the fundamental right to data protection, the Court reached its maturity in 2014 and 2015 in three groundbreaking decisions: *Digital Rights Ireland*,[83] *Google Spain*[84] and *Schrems*.[85] *Digital Rights Ireland* was probably the most important judgment concerning the fundamental rights to privacy and data protection delivered by the Court of Justice. This seminal decision, a Grand Chamber judgment issued on 8 April 2014 concerning the validity of the Data Retention Directive, has significant ramifications for metadata retention, which will be considered in the second Part of the book.[86] As far as the ECJ's approach to the two fundamental rights is concerned, the Court started its analysis in *Digital Rights Ireland* by observing that Article 3 of Directive 2006/24 (the 'Data Retention Directive'),[87]

---

[79] Case C-473/12 *Institut professionnel des agents immobiliers (IPI) v Geoffrey Englebert, Immo 9 SPRL, Grégory Francotte)* (CJEU (Third Chamber), 7 November 2013).

[80] ibid, para 39. Emphasis added.

[81] Case C-486/12 *X* (CJEU (Eighth Chamber), 12 December 2013).

[82] ibid, para 29. In particular, the ECJ noted: 'In view of the importance—highlighted in recitals 2 and 10 in the preamble to Directive 95/46—of protecting *privacy*, emphasised in the case-law of the Court (see *Rijkeboer*, paragraph 47 and the case-law cited) and *enshrined in Article 8 of the Charter*, the fees which may be levied under Article 12(a) of the directive may not be fixed at a level likely to constitute an obstacle to the exercise of the right of access guaranteed by that provision.' Emphasis added.

[83] Joined Cases C-293/12 and C-594/12 *Digital Rights Ireland Ltd v Minister for Communications, Marine and Natural Resources* [2014] ECR I-238.

[84] Case C-131/12 *Google Spain SL, Google Inc v Agencia Española de Protección de Datos and Mario Costeja González* [2014] ECR I-000 (nyr) (CJEU (Grand Chamber), 13 May 2014).

[85] Case C-362/14 *Maximillian Schrems v Data Protection Commissioner* (CJEU (Grand Chamber), 6 October 2015).

[86] See Ch 3.

[87] Directive 2006/24/EC of the European Parliament and of the Council of 15 March 2006 on the retention of data generated or processed in connection with the provision of publicly available electronic communications services or of public communications networks and amending Directive 2002/58/EC [2006] OJ L105/54.

which obliged the providers of publicly available electronic communications services or of public communications networks to retain certain types of data in order to make them available to national authorities for the purposes of fighting serious crime raised questions relating to three fundamental rights recognised in the EUCFR: the right to respect for private life and communications (Article 7 EUCFR), the right to protection of personal data (Article 8 EUCFR) and freedom of expression (Article 11 EUCFR).[88] It then went on to explain why the retention of traffic and location data under the Directive affected these three rights. With regard to the right to respect for private life and communications the Court noted that the traffic and location data retained under the Directive may allow very precise conclusions to be drawn concerning the private lives of the persons whose data have been retained, such as their everyday habits, their permanent or temporary places of residence, their daily or other movements, the activities they carry out, their social relationships and the social environments they frequent.[89] The retention of such data might also affect the exercise of the freedom of expression of these persons.[90] Finally, according to the ECJ, such a retention of data also 'falls under Article 8 of the Charter because it constitutes the processing of personal data within the meaning of that article and, therefore, necessarily has to satisfy the data protection requirements arising from that article'.[91] In this respect, the Court explicitly noted that while the preliminary references in the case raised questions as to the compatibility of the Data Retention Directive with Article 7 EUCFR, they also concerned the question of principle as to whether that Directive met 'the requirements for the protection of personal data arising from Article 8 of the Charter'.[92] It, therefore, proceeded to examine the validity of the Directive in the light of both Articles 7 and 8 EUCFR.[93] It is noteworthy that the Court left behind it the *Schecke* formula of viewing one right in two Charter Articles and carried out its examination separately on each fundamental right, thus acknowledging that data protection enshrined in Article 8 EUCFR is a distinct, autonomous right and not a subset of privacy. In terms of substance, however, its analysis regarding what constitutes an interference with the right to data protection seemed to be lacking in depth. The ECJ simply stated that the Data Retention Directive interfered with the fundamental right to the protection of personal data 'because it provide[d] for the processing of personal data',[94] without further clarifying which fair information principles in particular were affected by this.

Having found that the Directive interfered with both the fundamental rights to privacy and data protection, the Court turned to examine whether such interference was justified according to the requirements of Article 52(1) EUCFR. It first

---

[88] *Digital Rights Ireland,* n 83 above, para 25.
[89] ibid, paras 27 and 29.
[90] ibid, para 28.
[91] ibid, para 29.
[92] ibid, para 30.
[93] ibid, para 31.
[94] ibid, para 36.

assessed whether the Data Retention Directive adversely affected the essence of these fundamental rights. With regard to the essence of the right to data protection, the ECJ concluded that this had not been affected because the Data Retention Directive required Member States to ensure that appropriate technical and organisational measures were adopted against accidental or unlawful destruction, accidental loss or alteration of the data.[95] It thus appeared to perceive the notion of the right to data protection in excessively narrow terms, confined to the data security principle, without any mention of other fair information principles that form part of the essence of the fundamental right to data protection. Nevertheless, the ECJ alluded in its judgment to further data protection principles besides data security that should have been safeguarded by the Data Protection Directive. In particular, it pointed out that the Directive did not contain any rules regarding data minimisation, protection of sensitive data[96] and provisions ensuring the control by an independent supervisory authority of compliance with the requirements of data protection, according to Article 8(3) EUCFR.[97] The Court also reiterated that the right to data protection enshrined in Article 8 EUCFR aims to serve the right to privacy, holding that the protection of personal data resulting from the explicit obligation laid down in Article 8(1) EUCFR is 'especially important' for the right to respect for private life enshrined in Article 7 EUCFR.[98] A similar understanding of the foundational purposes of the right to data protection appeared also in *Ryneš*,[99] where the ECJ noted that the protection of '*the fundamental right to private life* guaranteed under Article 7 EUCFR requires that derogations and limitations *in relation to the protection of personal data* must apply only in so far as is strictly necessary.'[100]

Google Spain was another landmark decision concerning the fundamental rights to data protection and privacy. In that case, the ECJ was asked to decide whether search engines have an obligation under the Data Protection Directive to remove links to web pages containing information relating to an individual from the list of results displayed following a search made on the basis of that person's name. This has been referred to as 'the right to be forgotten' or—more accurately—the right to erasure. The Court confirmed indeed that data subjects have a right to

---

[95] *Digital Rights Ireland*, n 83 above, para 40. See also para 54.

[96] ibid, para 66.

[97] ibid, para 66. *See* also *Commission v Hungary*, where the Court held that 'the requirement that compliance with the EU rules on the protection of individuals with regard to the processing of personal data is subject to control by an independent authority derives from the primary law of the European Union and, in particular, from Article 8 (3) of the Charter of Fundamental Rights of the European Union and Article 16(2) TFEU'; and that 'the establishment in Member States of independent supervisory authorities is ... an essential component of the protection of individuals with regard to the processing of personal data.' Case C-288/12 *Commission v Hungary* (CJEU (Grand Chamber), 8 April 2014), paras 47 and 48.

[98] ibid, para 53. Emphasis added.

[99] Case C 212/13 *František Ryneš v Úřad pro ochranu osobních údajů* (CJEU (Fourth Chamber), 11 December 2014).

[100] ibid, para 28. Emphasis added.

erasure on the basis of a teleological interpretation of Articles 12 and 14 of the Data Protection Directive.[101] In its analysis, it reiterated that the provisions of Directive 95/46, 'in so far as they govern the processing of personal data liable to infringe fundamental freedoms, in particular the right to privacy, must *necessarily be interpreted in the light of fundamental rights*, which form an integral part of the general principles of law … and … are now set out in the Charter'.[102] These two fundamental rights are found in Article 7 EUCFR that guarantees the right to respect for private life and Article 8 EUCFR, which expressly proclaims the right to the protection of personal data.[103] According to the ECJ, processing of personal data carried out by a search engine is 'liable to *affect significantly* the fundamental rights to privacy and to the protection of personal data when the search by means of that engine is carried out on the basis of an individual's name'.[104] The Court accepted, however, that the removal of links from the list of results could have effects upon the interest of Internet users in having access to that information.[105] In such cases, it called for a fair balance to be struck between the interest of the internet users and the data subject's fundamental rights under Articles 7 and 8 EUCFR,[106] without mentioning, however, that this balancing has also to take into account the fundamental right to freedom of expression found in Article 11 EUCFR. Regarding the balancing exercise, the Court held that 'as a general rule', the data subject's rights to privacy and data protection *override* the interest of internet users in having access to information.[107] This presumption established in favour of privacy and data protection can only be rebutted in certain cases, for instance when the data subject plays a role in public life.[108]

In *Schrems* the Court had to decide whether the transfer of personal data to the US under the Safe Harbour complied with the EU law requirement of adequate protection given that the US authorities were able to access the personal data of EU citizens held by leading Internet companies, such as Facebook in order to fight terrorism.[109] In its analysis, the ECJ stressed the importance of both the fundamental right to privacy, guaranteed by Article 7 EUCFR, and the fundamental right to the protection of personal data, under Article 8 EUCFR.[110] In this respect, it held that the adequacy requirement under Article 25(6) of the Data Protection Directive concerning the transfer of personal data to third countries 'implements

---

[101] *Google Spain*, n 84 above, paras 70–76.
[102] ibid, para 68. Emphasis added. See also Joined Cases C-141/12 and C-372/12 *YS (C-141/12) v Minister voor Immigratie, Integratie en Asiel,* and *Minister voor Immigratie, Integratie en Asiel (C 372/12) v M, S* (CJEU (Third Chamber), 17 May 2014), para 54.
[103] *Google Spain*, n 84 above, para 69.
[104] ibid, para 80. Emphasis added.
[105] ibid, para 81.
[106] ibid.
[107] ibid. Emphasis added.
[108] ibid.
[109] For a detailed analysis of the case see Ch 6.
[110] *Schrems*, above n 85, para 39.

the express obligation laid down in Article 8(1) of the Charter to protect personal data.'[111] The Court reiterated that privacy is at the core of data protection, repeating its pronouncement in *Digital Rights Ireland* that the protection of the fundamental right to privacy at EU level requires derogations and limitations in relation to the protection of personal data to apply only in so far as is strictly necessary.[112] However, unlike *Digital Rights Ireland,* the substantive analysis of the Court in *Schrems* took place only on the basis of Articles 7 and 47 EUCFR, without any further mention of the right to data protection. In particular, the ECJ found that the essence of both the Article 7 EUCFR right to privacy and the Article 47 EUCFR right to effective judicial protection had been violated in that case as the US public authorities have access on a generalised basis to the content of electronic communications[113] without any legislative provision of legal remedies to individuals that wish to access their personal data or exercise their rights to rectification and erasure.[114]

The judgments in *Digital Rights Ireland, Google Spain* and *Schrems* demonstrate that the Court's data protection jurisprudence has reached its maturity. In *Digital Rights Ireland* and *Schrems* the ECJ invalidated, for the first time, EU secondary legislation in the light of the fundamental rights enshrined in the Charter. In fact, in *Digital Rights Ireland* the Court not only approached the fundamental right to data protection independently from the right to privacy, but it carried separate analysis regarding the interference with these two fundamental rights and the potential justifications, discussing for the first time the essence of both these rights. While *Digital Rights Ireland* and *Schrems* concerned the legality of secondary legislation in the light of the Charter, *Google Spain* was about the interpretation of the Data Protection Directive in order to ascertain whether a right to erasure could be derived from this. After confirming that such a right indeed exists under the Directive, the Court went on to assess the permissible limitations to it. It is to be noted that the Court carried out the analysis on the permissible limitations to this right, which is not a fundamental right itself, on the basis of EU primary law, at the level of the fundamental rights to privacy and data protection enshrined in Articles 7 and 8 EUCFR, and not on the basis of secondary legislation. *Google Spain* is remarkable for another reason as well. In that case, the Court established a privacy- prevalence rule when the right to erasure is balanced with opposing interests or rights. In this respect, the ECJ could be seen as engaging

---

[111]   ibid, para 72. In *Weltimo,* however, the Court stated that the Data Protection Directive's objective was to ensure an effective and complete protection of the right to privacy. See Case C-230/14 *Weltimmo sro v Nemzeti Adatvédelmi és Információszabadság Hatóság* (CJEU (Third Chamber), 1 October 2015), para 30.

[112]   *Schrems,* above n 85, para 92.

[113]   ibid, para 94.

[114]   ibid, para 95.

in what I call 'data protection activism':[115] data privacy rights are favoured with regard to opposing rights as a general, a priori rule.

The data protection jurisprudence of the Court may well have reached its peak in these three cases,[116] but the scope of the fundamental right to data protection still remains uncertain. In *Digital Rights Ireland* the Court asserted that there was an interference with the fundamental right to data protection because the Data Retention Directive provided for the processing of personal data. Such pronouncement seems to imply, first, that any processing of personal data triggers the application of Article 8 EUCFR and constitutes automatically an interference with this Article, even if this is undertaken in accordance with the principles established in paragraphs 2 and 3 of Article 8 EUCFR. Such an approach should be criticised because, to paraphrase Floridi, it ends up inflating the concept of data protection in ways that turn out to be unrealistic and then vacuous (nothing counts as data protection-unrelated).[117] In addition, this approach wrongly suggests that the fundamental right to data protection is enshrined only in paragraph 1 of Article 8 EUCFR, and not in the whole of Article 8 EUCFR.

Furthermore, the ECJ did not clarify in *Digital Rights Ireland* which fair information principles exactly were affected by the processing of personal data under the Data Retention Directive. This makes it difficult to assess the permissible limitations to this right and their justifications. Finally, while the Court mentioned for the first time the essence of the fundamental right to data protection under Article 52(1) EUCFR, it did not clarify what determines this. In *Digital Rights Ireland* the Court found that this essence had not been impaired because the Data Retention Directive made provision for data security measures. While, as mentioned above, data protection is not to be limited to data security, it is certainly interesting that the Court referred to the data security information principle, which is not even listed among the principles mentioned in Article 8(2) EUCFR. This suggests that the essence of the fundamental right to data protection could include fair information principles that are not found in paragraphs 2 and 3 of Article 8 EUCFR.

---

[115] Giovanni Sartor has spoken of 'data protection exceptionalism', referring to the failure to apply the e-commerce immunities granted to Internet providers regarding liability for user-generated content to user-generated violations of data protection. See G Sartor, 'Providers' liabilities in the new EU Data Protection Regulation: A threat to Internet freedoms?' (2013) 3(1) *International Data Privacy Law* 3, 5.

[116] Kuner has argued that data protection has emerged as a 'super right' in the recent case law of the CJEU. See C Kuner, 'A "Super-right" to Data Protection? The Irish Facebook Case & the Future of EU Data Transfer Regulation' LSE Media Policy Project Blog, http://blogs.lse.ac.uk/mediapolicyproject/2014/06/24/a-super-right-to-data-protection-the-irish-facebook-case-the-future-of-eu-data-transfer-regulation/.

[117] Floridi noted: 'others may end up inflating the concept of informational privacy in ways that turn out to be unrealistic (things stand differently) and then vacuous (nothing counts as privacy-unrelated). This is the case when any informational process concerning a person becomes a breach of that person's informational privacy.' L Floridi, 'Four challenges for a theory of informational privacy' (2006) 8 *Ethics and Information Technology* 109, 116.

Part II

Case Studies

3

Metadata Surveillance

I. THE EU DATA RETENTION DIRECTIVE

ON 25 MARCH 2004, in the aftermath of the Madrid train bombings, the European Council adopted a Declaration on Combating Terrorism,[1] in which it instructed the Council, among others, to examine measures for establishing rules on the retention of communications traffic data by service providers.[2] One month later, on 28 April 2004, France, Ireland, Sweden and the UK presented a proposal for a Draft Framework Decision on the Retention of Data[3] to be adopted by the Council under the framework of police and judicial cooperation in criminal matters (the former third pillar).[4] The Draft Framework Decision covered data processed and stored by providers of a public communications network or publicly available electronic communications services and provided that these would be retained for a period of at least 12 months and no more than 36 months following their generation.[5] The Article 29 Working Party criticised this proposal,[6] noting that the mandatory retention of all types of data on every use of telecommunication services for public order purposes under the conditions provided in the Draft Framework Decision was not acceptable within the legal framework set out in Article 8 ECHR.[7] Concerns regarding the Draft Framework Decision were also voiced within the European Parliament, arguing that the proposal contained measures that came under both the first and the third pillars.[8]

---

[1] European Council, Declaration on Combating Terrorism, 25 March 2004.

[2] ibid, 4.

[3] Draft Framework Decision on the Retention of Data Processed and Stored in Connection with the Provision of Publicly Available Electronic Communications Services or Data on Public Communications Networks for the Purpose of Prevention, Investigation, Detection and Prosecution of Crime and Criminal Offences Including Terrorism, Council Doc 8958/04 (28 April 2004).

[4] The legal basis for the draft framework decision were Arts 31(1)(c) TEU and 34(2)(b) TEU.

[5] C Walker and Y Akdeniz, 'Anti-terrorism Laws and Data Retention: War Is Over?' (2003) 54 *Northern Ireland Legal Quarterly* 159, 169.

[6] Art 29 WP, Opinion 9/2004 on a Draft Framework Decision on the storage of data processed and retained for the purpose of providing electronic public communications services or data available in public communications networks with a view to the prevention, investigation, detection and prosecution of criminal acts, including terrorism. (Proposal presented by France, Ireland, Sweden and Great Britain (Council Doc 8958/04—28 April 2004)), 5.

[7] ibid.

[8] Committee on Civil Liberties, Justice and Home Affairs, Report of the European Parliament on the initiative by the French Republic, Ireland, the Kingdom of Sweden and the United Kingdom for a Draft Framework Decision on the retention of data processed and stored in connection with the

Almost a year later, and after numerous debates about the correct legal basis of the measure,[9] on 21 September 2005 the Commission presented a proposal for a directive on the retention of data processed in connection with the provision of public electronic communication services.[10] The proposal was again criticised by the Working Party[11] and the European Data Protection Supervisor (EDPS), who noted that he was not convinced of 'the necessity of the retention of traffic and location data for law enforcement purposes'.[12] After long negotiations among the Commission, the European Parliament and the Council, the Directive was finally passed on 15 March 2006.

A. Aim and Scope

Directive 2006/24/EC[13] (the 'Data Retention Directive') aimed to harmonise Member States' provisions concerning the obligations of the providers of publicly available electronic communications services or of public communications networks with respect to the retention of certain data generated or processed by them, in order to ensure that the data were available for the purpose of the investigation, detection and prosecution of serious crime, as this was defined by each Member State in its national law.[14] It applied to traffic and location data on both legal entities and natural persons and to the related data necessary to identify the subscriber or registered user, but did not apply to the content of electronic communications.[15]

---

provision of publicly available electronic communications services or data on public communications networks for the purpose of prevention, investigation, detection and prosecution of crime and criminal offences including terrorism (8958/2004–C6-0198/2004–2004/0813(CNS)) (31 May 2005), Rapporteur: Alexander Nuno Alvaro, A6-0174/2005 final.

[9] E Kosta and P Valcke, 'Retaining the Data Retention Directive' (2006) 22 *Computer Law & Security Report* 370, 373; M Taylor, 'The EU Data Retention Directive' (2006) 22 *Computer Law & Security Review* 309.

[10] Proposal for a directive on the retention of data processed in connection with the provision of public electronic communication services and amending Directive 2002/58/ EC, 21 September 2005).

[11] Art 29 Data Protection Working Party, Opinion 113/2005 on the Proposal for a Directive of the European Parliament and of the Council on the Retention of Data Processed in Connection with the Provision of Public Electronic Communication Services and Amending Directive 2002/58/EC (COM(2005)438 final of 21.09.2005), 21 October 2005.

[12] Opinion of the European Data Protection Supervisor on the proposal for a Directive of the European Parliament and of the Council on the retention of data processed in connection with the provision of public electronic communication services and amending Directive 2002/58/EC (COM(2005) 438 final) [2005] OJ 298/1.

[13] Directive 2006/24/EC of the European Parliament and of the Council of 15 March 2006 on the retention of data generated or processed in connection with the provision of publicly available electronic communications services or of public communications networks and amending Directive 2002/58/EC [2006] OJ L105/54 (Data Retention Directive).

[14] ibid, Art 1(1).

[15] ibid, Art 1(2).

The Directive required the retention of data only for the purpose of the 'investigation, detection and prosecution of serious crime' and did not include within its regulatory framework the prevention of crimes, which had been an objective of the abandoned framework decision. Member States were obliged to ensure that the data retained and any other necessary information relating to such data could be transmitted upon request to the competent authorities without 'undue delay'.[16]

The lack of a definition of what constituted 'serious crime' under the Directive was very problematic as it opened the door to a broadening of its scope, and therefore the retention of data, for any crime that was deemed 'serious' by each Member State.[17] To avoid such a risk, the Council urged[18] Member States to have 'due regard' to the crimes listed in Article 2(2) of the Framework Decision on the European Arrest Warrant[19] and crime involving telecommunications when they implemented the Directive into national law. Nevertheless, the Commission's Evaluation Report of the Data Protection Directive[20] found that 10 Member States[21] had defined 'serious crime' in their national legislation with reference to a minimum prison sentence, to the possibility of a custodial sentence being imposed, or to a list of criminal offences defined elsewhere in national legislation; eight Member States[22] required data to be retained not only in relation to serious crime, but also in relation to 'all criminal offences and for crime prevention, or on general grounds of national or state and/or public security'; and finally, four Member States[23] had not provided any definition of 'serious crime' at all.[24]

B. Content

The Directive obliged Member States to retain 'traffic' and 'location' data as well as any other related data necessary to identify the subscriber or user of telecommunications. The definition of 'traffic' and 'location' data was not provided in the Data Retention Directive itself, but was to be found in the e-Privacy Directive.[25] 'Traffic data' referred to any data processed for the purpose of the conveyance of a

---

[16] ibid, Art 8.

[17] See House of Lords European Union Committee, 'After Madrid: The EU's response to terrorism', 5th Report of Session 2004–05, 18.

[18] Council of the European Union, Statements, Council Doc 5777/06 ADD 1 (10 February 2006).

[19] Council Framework Decision on the European arrest warrant and the surrender procedures between Member States (2002/584/JHA).

[20] Report from the Commission to the Council and the European Parliament, Evaluation report on the Data Retention Directive (Directive 2006/24/EC) COM(2011) 225 final, 18.4.2011.

[21] Bulgaria, Estonia, Ireland, Greece, Spain, Lithuania, Luxembourg, Hungary, Netherlands and Finland.

[22] Belgium, Denmark, France, Italy, Latvia, Poland, Slovakia and Slovenia.

[23] Cyprus, Malta, Portugal and United Kingdom.

[24] Evaluation report on the Data Retention Directive, n 20 above, p 6.

[25] C Goemans and J Dumortier, 'Enforcement Issues—Mandatory Retention of Traffic Data in the EU: Possible Impact on Privacy and On-line Anonymity' in C Nicoll et al (eds), *Digital Anonymity and the Law* (The Hague, Asser Press ITeR, 2003) 161.

communication on an electronic communications network or for the billing thereof;[26] and 'location data' was understood as any data processed in an electronic communications network, indicating the geographic position of the terminal equipment of a user of a publicly available electronic communications service.[27] Traffic data may, *inter alia*, consist of data referring to the routing, duration, time or volume of a communication, to the protocol used, to the location of the terminal equipment of the sender or recipient, to the network on which the communication originates or terminates, to the beginning, end or duration of a connection and to the format in which the communication is conveyed by the network.[28] Location data may refer to the latitude, longitude and altitude of the user's terminal equipment, to the direction of travel, to the level of accuracy of the location information, to the identification of the network cell in which the terminal equipment is located at a certain point in time, and to the time the location information was recorded.[29]

The Directive explicitly excluded, however, the retention of data revealing the content of the communication.[30] The categories of data retained were laid down in Article 5. They included data necessary a) to trace and identify the source of a communication; b) to identify the destination of a communication; c) to identify the date, time and duration of a communication; d) to identify the type of communication; e) to identify users' communication equipment; and f) to identify the location of mobile communication equipment.

The Directive stipulated that the data had to be retained for a period of between six months and two years starting from the date of the communication.[31] Member States facing particular circumstances were allowed to request an extension of the maximum retention period.[32] The variation of the retention periods raised questions as to the level of harmonisation the Directive intended to achieve.[33] Indeed, the Commission found in its Evaluation that retention periods varied in national laws from two years (one Member State), 1.5 years (one Member State), one year (10 Member States) six months (three Member States), to different retention periods for different categories of data (six Member States).[34] In this respect, the Commission admitted that the Directive provided 'only limited legal certainty and foreseeability across the EU for operators operating in more than one Member

---

[26] Directive 2002/58/EC of the European Parliament and of the Council of 12 July 2002 concerning the processing of personal data and the protection of privacy in the electronic communications sector [2002] OJ L201/37 (ePrivacy Directive), Art 2(b).

[27] ibid, Art 2 (c).

[28] ibid, Recital 15.

[29] ibid, Recital 14.

[30] Data Retention Directive, Arts 1(2) and 5(2).

[31] ibid, Art 6.

[32] ibid, Art 12.

[33] House of Lords European Union Committee, n 17 above, p 18; Kosta and Valcke, n 9 above, p 376.

[34] Evaluation Report on the Data Retention Directive, n 20 above, p 14.

State and for citizens whose communications data may be stored in different Member States.'[35]

The Directive stipulated that data retained were to be provided only to the competent national authorities in specific cases and in accordance with national law.[36] Member States were allowed to define in their national law the procedures to be followed and the conditions to be fulfilled in order to gain access to retained data in accordance with necessity and proportionality requirements and subject to the relevant provisions of European Union law or public international law, and in particular the ECHR as interpreted by the European Court of Human Rights.[37] The failure of the Directive to define the competent national authorities resulted in a wide list of different authorities being given access to the retained data in the different Member States. This included the police (in all Member States, except in Ireland and the United Kingdom), security or intelligence services or even the military (in 14 Member States) and tax and border authorities.[38] Only 11 Member States required judicial authorisation for each request for access to retained data, and another four required authorisation from a senior authority but not a judge.[39] According to the Commission's Report, overall over 2 million data requests were submitted each year, with significant variation between Member States, from less than 100 per year (Cyprus) to over 1 million (Poland).[40]

Providers of electronic communication services were required by the Directive to ensure four fundamental requirements with respect to the retained data. First, retained data had to be of the same quality and subject to the same security and protection as those data on the network.[41] Second, the data had to be subject to appropriate technical and organisational measures to protect them against accidental or unlawful destruction, accidental loss or alteration, or unauthorised or unlawful storage, processing, access or disclosure.[42] Third, the data had to be subject to appropriate technical and organisational measures to ensure that they were accessed by specially authorised personnel only.[43] Fourth, the data, except those that had been accessed and preserved, had to be destroyed at the end of the retention period.[44] It should be noted that the retention, storage and data security requirements of the Directive were liable to impose a 'considerable financial

---

[35] ibid, 15.
[36] Data Retention Directive, Art 4.
[37] ibid.
[38] Evaluation Report on the Data Retention Directive, n 20 above, p 9.
[39] ibid.
[40] ibid, 21. See also Commission, 'Statistics on requests for data under the directive for 2008–2012', 7–8, http://ec.europa.eu/dgs/home-affairs/what-we-do/policies/police-cooperation/data-retention/docs/statistics_on_requests_for_data_under_the_data_retention_directive_en.pdf.
[41] Data Retention Directive, Art 7(a).
[42] ibid, Art 7(b).
[43] ibid, Art 7(c).
[44] ibid, Art 7(d).

burden'[45] on the service providers. This was indeed confirmed in the Evaluation Report, according to which, five major industry associations had reported that the economic impact of the Directive was 'substantial' or 'enormous' for smaller service providers.[46] The question of who was responsible to bear that cost was certainly important and in this context some commentators have pointed out that it was at least ironic that EU citizens were possibly called upon to 'pay for their own surveillance.'[47]

II. DATA RETENTION BEFORE THE COURTS

A. The EU Inter-Pillar Litigation

There were vigorous debates among the EU institutions and the Member States at the time of the negotiation of the Data Retention Directive regarding its legal basis, and in particular whether it fell under the Community competence or was a measure that came under the framework of police and judicial cooperation in criminal matters. The case was not resolved even after the adoption of the Directive as a first pillar measure. Ireland, supported by Slovakia, challenged it before the ECJ, on the ground that Article 95 EC (now Article 114 TFEU), which has as its object the establishment and the functioning of the internal market was not the appropriate legal basis. Indeed, Ireland argued that the main aim of the Data Retention Directive was to facilitate the investigation, detection and prosecution of serious crime, including terrorism, and thus it should have been adopted under the (former) third pillar.

The Court in its judgment disagreed and held that the Directive was adopted on the appropriate legal basis, since both its aim and its content fell under Article 95 EC.[48] It started by noting that after the Madrid and London terrorist attacks, several Member States, 'realising that data relating to electronic communications

---

[45] See A Tsiftsoglou and S Flogaitis, 'Transposing the Data Retention Directive in Greece: Lessons from Karlsruhe' in *Values and Freedoms in Modern Information Law & Ethics*, paper presented at the 4th International Conference of Information Law, Thessaloniki, 21 May 2011.

[46] Evaluation report on the Data Retention Directive, n 20 above, p 26. See www.gsmeurope.org/documents/Joint_Industry_Statement_on_DRD.PDF.

[47] M Kaifa-Gbanti, 'Surveillance Models in the Security State & Fair Criminal Trial', (2010) *Nomiki Vivliothiki* 43 (in Greek). The Commission in its Evaluation Report noted that there was no evidence of any 'quantifiable or substantial effect of the Directive on consumer prices for electronic communications services' and that 'there were no contributions to the 2009 public consultation from consumer representatives'. See Evaluation report on the Data Retention Directive, n 20 above, p 26.

[48] C-301/06 *Ireland v European Parliament and European Council* [2009] ECR I-593, para 93. For an analysis see See E Herlin-Karnell, 'Annotation of Ireland v. Parliament and Council' (2009) 46 *Common Market Law Review* 1667; T Konstadinides, 'Wavering between Centres of Gravity: Comment on Ireland v. Parliament and Council' (2010) 35 *European Law Review* 88; C Murphy, 'Fundamental rights and security: the difficult position of the European judiciary' (2010) 16 *European Public Law* 289; T Konstadinides, 'Destroying democracy on the ground of defending it? The Data Retention Directive, the surveillance state and our constitutional ecosystem' (2011) 36 *European Law Review* 722.

constitute an effective means for the detection and prevention of crimes, including terrorism' adopted measures imposing obligations on service providers to retain such data.[49] These measures, according to the Court, had significant economic implications for service providers in so far as they might involve substantial investment and operating costs[50] and 'differed substantially particularly in respect of the nature of the data retained and the periods of data retention.'[51] These legislative and technical disparities between the national provisions governing the retention of data by service providers, were liable to have 'a direct impact on the functioning of the internal market',[52] and, thus, justified the adoption of harmonised rules by the Community legislature. The Court clarified that Article 95 EC was, therefore, the correct legal basis for the adoption of these rules, since the provisions of the Data Retention Directive were 'essentially limited to the activities of service providers' and did 'not govern access to data or the use thereof by the police or judicial authorities of the Member States.'[53] The Court concluded, therefore, that the Data Retention Directive did not fall under the framework of police cooperation in criminal matters (former third pillar),[54] but had to be adopted on the basis of Article 95 EC under the Community (former first pillar), and dismissed Ireland's action.

The Court of Justice did not refer in its judgment to the human rights dimension of the Directive.[55] The examination of this was dismissed with a short statement that

> the action brought by Ireland relate[d] solely to the choice of legal basis and not to any possible infringement of fundamental rights arising from interference with the exercise of the right to privacy contained in Directive 2006/24.[56]

Further to the inter-pillar litigation, the Court had also to consider infringement proceedings brought under Article 258 TFEU by the Commission against several Member States for their failure to implement the Data Retention Directive.[57]

---

[49] *Ireland v European Parliament and Council*, para 67.

[50] ibid, para 68.

[51] ibid, para 69.

[52] ibid, para 71.

[53] ibid, para 80.

[54] ibid, para 83.

[55] An amicus curiae brief was submitted to the Court by the *Arbeitskreis Vorratsdatenspeicherung* (Working Group on Data Retention) acting on behalf of 43 privacy organisations, asking the Court to invalidate the Data Retention Directive on the basis of Art 8 ECHR. See www.vorratsdatenspeicherung. de/images/data_retention_brief_08-04-2008.pdf.

[56] *Ireland v European Parliament and Council*, para 57.

[57] See, for example, Cases C-202/09 *Commission v Ireland* [2009] ECR I-00203*; C-211/09 *Commission v Greece* [2009] ECR I-00204*; C-189/09 *Commission v Austria* [2010] ECR 2010 I-00099; C-394/10 *Commission v Luxembourg*, 4 August 2010; C-185/09 *Commission v Sweden* [2010] ECR I-00014*. Sweden was ordered by the ECJ to pay a lump sum of €3 million for its delay in implementing the legislation in accordance with the Court's earlier ruling: C-270/11 *Commission v Sweden* [2013] ECR I-0000.

B. Data Retention Before National Courts

A second line of litigation relating to the Data Retention Directive took place before national courts. These cases concerned the challenge of national measures transposing the Directive into domestic law. The national law implementing the Data Retention Directive had been the subject of litigation in Bulgaria, Hungary,[58] Romania, Germany, the Czech Republic, Cyprus and Slovakia.[59] The national courts in these cases[60] did not make any request to the CJEU for a preliminary reference on the validity of the Directive on the basis of EU fundamental rights. Such requests were eventually made by the Irish High Court and the Austrian Constitutional Court and resulted in the invalidation of the Data Retention Directive in the CJEU's landmark decision in *Digital Rights Ireland*.[61]

i. The Bulgarian Administrative Court Decision

The Bulgarian transposing law of the Data Retention Directive[62] stipulated that a directorate within the Ministry of Interior would have direct access to the data retained by the providers via a computer terminal and that 'security services and other law enforcement bodies' would have access 'to all retained data by Internet and mobile communication providers' without needing court permission.[63] The Supreme Administrative Court held that these very broad rules of access to the data violated the right to private life enshrined in Article 32(1) of the

---

[58]   In 2008 the Hungarian Civil Liberties Union (HCLU or TASZ, Társaság a Szabadságjogkért) filed a complaint before the Hungarian Constitutional Court requesting the ex-post examination of the constitutionality of certain provisions of the Hungarian Act C of 2003 on electronic communications that were amended in order to implement the Data Retention Directive into Hungarian law. Hungary's new constitution that entered into force on 1 January 2012 imposed restrictions on submitting cases to the Constitutional Court. As a result, pending cases that were submitted by persons or organisations that did not enjoy the right to submit a complaint under the new constitutional rules were terminated. See C Jones and B Hayes, 'The EU Data Retention Directive: a case study in the legitimacy and effectiveness of EU counter-terrorism policy', SECILE—Securing Europe through Counter-Terrorism—Impact, Legitimacy & Effectiveness, D2.4 available at www.statewatch.org/news/2013/dec/secile-data-retention-directive-in-europe-a-case-study.pdf, 23.

[59]   A complaint against the national implementation of the Data Retention Directive was brought in 2012 before the Slovak Constitutional Court. See Statewatch, Slovakian data retention law faces challenge before Constitutional Court available at http://database.statewatch.org/article.asp?aid=31892. The Constitutional Court decided to suspend the provisions of national law only a few days after the CJEU invalidated the Data Retention Directive. See Press Information by European Information Society Institute, available in Slovak at www.eisionline.org/index.php/sk/projekty%E2%80%90m/ochrana%E2%80%90sukromia/75%E2%80%90ussr%E2%80%90pozastavil%E2%80%90sledovanie.

[60]   For an overview see E Kosta, 'The Way to Luxembourg: National Court Decisions on the Compatibility of the Data Retention Directive with the Rights to Privacy and Data Protection' (2013) 10(3) *SCRIPTed* 339.

[61]   Joined Cases C-293/12 and 594/12 *Digital Rights Ireland ltd and Seitlinger and others* [2014] ECR I-238.

[62]   Regulation No 40 of the Ministry of Interior of 7 January 2000, available in Bulgarian at http://lex.bg/laws/ldoc/2135577924.

[63]   Art 5 of Regulation No 40.

Bulgarian Constitution and Article 8 ECHR, and annulled the relevant Article of the Regulation.[64] In particular, the Supreme Administrative Court found that the national transposing law did not provide citizens with the necessary safeguards against the violation of their constitutional rights and did not determine the conditions under which an interference with the right to privacy would be permitted.[65]

The Bulgarian Court did not discuss in its decision the Data Retention Directive or the issue of the retention of metadata, but focused on the very problematic national implementing rule regarding the conditions of access to the data by public authorities. Nevertheless, it highlighted an important problem of the EU's metadata retention legal framework, namely its inability to harmonise divergent practices concerning the access and use of the data that posed serious challenges to the fundamental rights to privacy and data protection. Indeed, the Commission recognised in its Evaluation Report that the Directive did 'not in itself guarantee that retained data are being stored, retrieved and used in full compliance with the right to privacy and protection of personal data.'[66] The responsibility for ensuring these rights lay with Member States. According to the Commission, the Directive only sought 'partial harmonisation of approaches to data retention'; therefore, it was unsurprising that there was 'no common approach' with respect to both the national implementation of specific provisions of the Directive itself, such as purpose limitation or retention periods, and the regulation of aspects outside its scope, such as public authorities' access to the retained data or cost reimbursement.[67] The EDPS had also warned about these consequences of the Data Retention Directive that could lead to the use of the data by national authorities for all kinds of unrelated purposes. In particular, the EDPS had noted that the introduction of the obligation to retain data might lead to 'substantial databases and has particular risks for the data subject. One could think of the commercial use of the data, as well as of the use of the data for "fishing operations" and/or data mining by law enforcement authorities or national security services.'[68] This risk, while related *stricto sensu* to the access and use of the data, and not their retention—which was a matter of EU law—was far from being hypothetical. Granted, the Member States had responsibilities with regard to fundamental rights when implementing the Directive. But the fact that the Directive provided for the availability of telecommunications data for law enforcement purposes opened up the way for their abuse and misuse at the national level,[69] as the Bulgarian case demonstrated.

---

[64] Bulgarian Supreme Administrative Court, No 13627, 11 December 2008, available in Bulgarian at www.capital.bg/getatt.php?filename=o_598746.pdf.

[65] ibid.

[66] Evaluation report on the Data Retention Directive, n 20 above, p 31.

[67] ibid.

[68] Opinion of the EDPS on the proposal for a Directive on the retention of data processed in connection with the provision of public electronic communication services, n 12 above, p 11.

[69] Giovanni Buttarelli characterised the Directive as 'the most privacy invasive instrument ever adopted by the EU in terms of scale and the number of people it affects.' See G Buttarelli, 'What Future for the Data Retention Directive', EU Council Working Party on data protection and information exchange (DAPIX—DATA PROTECTION), Discussion on the Commission Evaluation report, 4 May 2011.

ii. *The Romanian Constitutional Court Decision*

The Romanian Constitutional Court[70] identified several problems in the Romanian law transposing the Data Retention Directive.[71] First, it criticised this for requiring the retention of traffic and location data as well as 'the related data necessary for the identification of the subscriber or registered user', without explicitly defining what it meant by 'related data'. According to the Court, this lack of a precise legal provision that determines with accuracy the sphere of the data necessary to identify physical and legal users, opened up the possibility for abuses in the activity of retaining, processing and using the data stored by the electronic communication services and public networks providers.[72] The Court also criticised the legislator for the 'ambiguous manner of drafting' with regard to the term 'threats to national security', the prevention of which justified access to the retained data.[73]

Beyond these linguistic problems of the national transposition law, the Constitutional Court noted that the continuous retention of personal data transformed 'the exception from the principle of effective protection of privacy right and freedom of expression, into an absolute rule.'[74] In this respect, the users of electronic communication services or networks were made 'permanent subjects to intrusions into their exercise of their private rights to correspondence and freedom of expression, without the possibility of a free, uncensored manifestation, except for direct communication, thus excluding the main communication means used nowadays.'[75]

Moreover, the Romanian Court focused on a further aspect of the data retention regime: the fact that it had an effect not only on the person that made the communication, by sending for instance a text message, but also on the receiver of that information. The recipient was thus exposed as well as the sender, according to the

---

[70] Decision No 1258 of Romanian Constitutional Court, 8 October 2009. The decision is available in Romanian at www.legi-internet.ro/fileadmin/editor_folder/pdf/Decizie_curtea_constitutionala_pastrarea_datelor_de_trafic.pdf. Unofficial translation by Bogdan Manolea and Anca Argesiu at www.legi-internet.ro/fileadmin/editor_folder/pdf/decision-constitutional-court-romania-data-retention.pdf. The present analysis is based on this. See C Murphy, 'Romanian Constitutional Court, Decision No. 1258 of 8 October 2009 Regarding the Unconstitutionality Exception of the Provisions of Law No. 298/2008 Regarding the Retention of the Data Generated or Processed by the Public Electronic Communications Service Providers, as Well as for the Modification of Law No. 506/2004 Regarding the Personal Data Processing and Protection of Private Life in the Field of Electronic Communication Area' (2010) 47 *Common Market Law Review* 933; A Bannon, 'Romania retrenches on data retention' (2010) 24(2) *International Review of Law, Computers and Technology* 145.

[71] Law no 298/2008 regarding the retention of the data generated or processed by the public electronic communications service providers or public network providers, as well as the modification of law 506/2004 regarding the personal data processing and protection of private life in the field of electronic communication area, Official Monitor of Romania, Pt I, no 780, 21 November 2008.

[72] Decision No 1258 of Romanian Constitutional Court, n 70 above.

[73] ibid.

[74] ibid.

[75] ibid.

Court, to the retention of the data connected to his private life, irrespective of his own act or any manifestation of will, but only based on the behaviour of another person—the caller—whose actions he could not control to protect himself against bad faith or intent of blackmail, harassment etc. Even though he is a passive subject in the intercommunication relationship, the recipient can become, despite his will, a suspect before the law enforcement authorities. This intrusion into the private life of third parties was deemed excessive by the Romanian Court.[76]

The Romanian Constitutional Court found the legal obligation of data retention with its continuous character and general applicability more problematic than the data's 'justified use' by law enforcement authorities. This is because, according to the Court, data retention concerns equally

> all the law subjects, regardless of whether they have committed penal crimes or not or whether they are the subject of a penal investigation or not, which is likely to overturn the presumption of innocence and to transform *a priori* all users of electronic communication services or public communication networks into people susceptible of committing terrorism crimes or other serious crimes.[77]

This pronouncement incorporated necessarily a criticism of the overall system established by the Data Retention Directive that clearly went beyond the problems of the national transposing law.[78] Indeed, a similar argument regarding the indiscriminate retention of personal data was also used by the CJEU in *Digital Rights Ireland*. However, the Romanian Constitutional Court did not make a preliminary reference request to the CJEU, thus raising questions about its position on the issue of the supremacy of EU law over national law.[79]

iii. The German Constitutional Court Decision

In a seminal decision,[80] the German Constitutional Court declared unconstitutional the law transposing the Data Retention Directive into Germany, because it did not guarantee adequate data security or an adequate restriction of the purposes of use of the data, and it did not satisfy, in every respect, the constitutional requirements of transparency and legal protection.[81]

---

[76] ibid.
[77] ibid.
[78] Murphy, n 70 above, p 939; Kosta, n 60 above, pp 348–49.
[79] Murphy, n 70 above, p 941.
[80] 1 BvR 256/08 of 2 March 2010, www.bverfg.de/entscheidungen/rs20100302_1bvr025608.html.
[81] For an analysis see C DeSimone, 'Pitting Karlsruhe Against Luxembourg? German Data Protection and the Contested Implementation of the EU Data Retention Directive' (2010) 11 *German Law Journal* 291; W Abel and B Schafer, 'The German Constitutional Court on the Right in Confidentiality and Integrity of Information Technology Systems—a Case Report on BVerfG, NJW 2008 822' (2009) 6 *SCRIPT-ed* 106; K de Vries, R Bellanova, P De Hert and S Gutwirth, 'The German Constitutional Court judgment on data retention: Proportionality overrides unlimited surveillance (Doesn't it?)' in Serge Gutwirth et al (eds), *Computers, Privacy and Data Protection: an Element of Choice* (Dordrecht, Springer Science+Business Media, 2011), 3; AB Kaiser, 'German Federal Constitutional Court: German data retention provisions unconstitutional in their present form, Decision of 2 March 2010, NJW 2010, p. 833' (2010) 6(3) *European Constitutional Law Review* 503.

The Constitutional Court started its analysis by rejecting the need to submit a referral to the Court of Justice, since 'a potential priority of Community law' was not relevant in this case. After this—not unquestionable—assertion, the Court went on to discuss the possible constitutional problems that the transposing law—not the Directive—raised in the Federal Republic of Germany. The Court rightly based its analysis on the right to secrecy of telecommunications, enshrined in Article 10(1) of the German Constitution. In this respect, it distinguished between the storage of telecommunications by service providers and their subsequent access and use by law enforcement authorities. The Court opined that the storage of telecommunications traffic data for six months as required by German law for strictly limited uses in the course of prosecution, the warding off of danger and intelligence service duties was not in itself incompatible with Article 10 of the Basic Law.[82] Nevertheless, such storage constituted 'a particularly serious encroachment with an effect broader than anything in the legal system to date.'[83] This was because, according to the Court, even though the storage did not extend to the contents of the communications, these data could be used to draw content-related conclusions extending into the user's private sphere. In combination, the recipients, dates, time and place of telephone conversations, if they are observed over a long period of time, permit detailed information to be obtained on social or political affiliations and on personal preferences, inclinations and weaknesses. Depending on the use of the telecommunication, such storage could make it possible to create 'meaningful personality profiles of virtually all citizens and track their movements.'[84] It also increased the risk of citizens being exposed to further investigations without themselves having given occasion for this. In addition, the possibility of abuse associated with such collection of data aggravated its burdensome effects. In particular, according to the Court, since the storage and use of data were not noticed, they were capable of creating a 'diffusely threatening feeling of being watched which can impair a free exercise of fundamental rights in many areas.'[85]

However, the German Constitutional Court recognised that there were certain factors that made such a data retention acceptable under the Constitution. The first was that the storage was not realised directly by the state, but by imposing a duty on the private service providers. In this way, the data were not yet combined at the point of storage itself, but remain distributed over many individual enterprises and were not 'directly available to the state as a conglomerate.'[86] The second, and more dubious one had to do with the fact that the 'precautionary storage of telecommunications traffic data' considerably reduced 'the latitude for further

---

[82] 1 BvR 256/08, n 80 above.
[83] ibid.
[84] ibid.
[85] ibid.
[86] ibid.

data collections without occasion, including collections by way of European Union law'.[87]

In any case, such storage, according to the Court, could be deemed compatible with Article 10(1) of the Basic Law only if its formulation satisfied particular constitutional requirements on data security, purpose limitation, transparency and legal protection. The Court provided detailed guidance on all these issues to the legislator. Concerning the pro-active use of data, in order to prevent criminal activity, the Court accepted that this may only be permitted, according to the principle of proportionality, 'if there is a sufficiently evidenced concrete danger to the life, limb or freedom of a person, to the existence or the security of the Federal Government or of a *Land* or to ward off a common danger.' The principle of proportionality also requires that there should be a fundamental prohibition of transmission of data for certain types of telecommunications connections which rely on 'particular confidentiality'. In this respect, the Constitutional Court gave the example of authorities or organisations in the social or ecclesiastical fields which offer advice in situations of emotional or social need, completely or predominantly by telephone, to callers who normally remain anonymous and where these organisations and their staff are subject to obligations of confidentiality.

Leaving aside the Court's refusal to submit a preliminary reference to the European Court of Justice, the judgment is important for two reasons. First, it demonstrates why the retention of metadata that exclude the content of communications constitutes a serious interference with the fundamental right to privacy. Metadata retention can easily reveal detailed personal information about the individual and the feeling of being watched can create a chilling effect upon the way they exercise their fundamental rights.[88] For this reason, the Court rejected the argument that traffic and content data are not the same, therefore the interference was not as grave in the case at issue.[89] Second, the Court's analysis on the principle of proportionality provides extremely useful guidance for legislators and courts and shows that data surveillance that satisfies certain conditions can be constitutional and permissible under the law.

iv. The Decision of the Supreme Court of Cyprus

The Supreme Court of Cyprus had to consider a number of civil applications requesting the annulment of orders[90] issued by district courts 'ordering the disclosure of telecommunication data concerning several persons who were

---

[87] ibid.

[88] See M Tzanou, 'Is Data Protection the Same as Privacy? An Analysis of Telecommunications Metadata Retention Measures' (2013) *Journal of Internet Law* 21.

[89] See dissenting opinion of Judge Schluckebier on the issue.

[90] Supreme Court of Cyprus, Decision of civil applications 65/2009, 78/2009, 82/2009 & 15/2010-22/2010, 1 February 2011, available in Greek at www.supremecourt.gov.cy/judicial/sc.nsf/0/5B67A764B86AA78EC225782F004F6D28/$file/65-09.pdf.

relevant to criminal investigations to the Cyprus police'[91] on the basis of the fundamental right to private and family life (Article 15(1) of the Constitution of Cyprus) and the right to protection of secrecy of correspondence (Article 17(1) of the Constitution of Cyprus).

The Court observed that the Data Retention Directive did not regulate the access to the retained data by law enforcement authorities, but this was left to the Member States.[92] It therefore concluded that it could examine the constitutionality of Articles 4 and 5 of Law 183(1)/2007 on the retention of telecommunications data for the investigation of serious penal crimes because these referred to the access of the retained data by the police and fell outside the scope of the Directive. The Supreme Court of Cyprus found that the limitations of the fundamental rights of three out of the four applicants were not permissible under the Constitution of Cyprus and annulled the relevant orders for access to the retained data.

The decision is interesting for its deference to EU law. This is in accordance to the Constitution of Cyprus that provides in Article 1A:

> No provision of the Constitution shall be deemed as overriding any legislation, acts or measures enacted or taken by the Republic that are deemed necessary due to its obligations as a Member State of the European Union, neither does it prevent Regulations, Directives or other Acts or binding measures of a legislative character, adopted by the European Union or the European Communities or by their institutions or competent bodies thereof on the basis of the Treaties establishing the European Communities or the Treaty of the European Union, from having legal effect in the Republic.

v. The Czech Constitutional Court Decision

On 22 March 2011 the Czech Constitutional Court delivered its decision on the national law implementing the Data Retention Directive in the Czech Republic.[93] Following the judgments of other national courts, it declared the implementing law unconstitutional.

The Court had, first, to decide whether it should submit a preliminary reference question to the ECJ on the validity of the Directive. Employing a similar argument to the German Court, it rejected this possibility on the basis that the content of the Data Retention Directive provided the Czech Republic with sufficient space to implement it in conformity with the constitutional order, since its individual

---

[91]   ibid. See also C Markou, 'The Cyprus and other EU court rulings on data retention: The Directive as a privacy bomb' (2012) 28 *Computer Law & Security Review* 468; Kosta, n 60 above, p 352.

[92]   ibid.

[93]   Czech Constitutional Court, Decision of 22 March 2011 on petition Pl. ÚS 24/10, available online in Czech at www.usoud.cz/fileadmin/user_upload/ustavni_soud_www/Aktualne_prilohy/2011_03_31b. pdf. Translation in English, available online at www.usoud.cz/en/decisions/?tx_ttnews%5Btt_news%5 D=40&cHash=bbaa1c5b1a7d6704af6370. For an analysis see P Molek, 'Czech Constitutional Court—Unconstitutionality of the Czech implementation of the Data Retention Directive; Decision of 22 March 2011, Pl. ÚS 24/10' (2012) 8 *European Constitutional Law Review* 338; Jan Kudrna, 'Human rights—real or just formal rights? Example of the (un)constitutionality of data retention in the Czech Republic' (2012) 19 (4) *Jurisprudence* 1289.

provisions in fact only defined the obligation to retain data. The legislator had certainly to respect the objective of the Directive when transposing it in national law, but the challenged provisions concerned 'an expression of the will of the Czech legislator, which may vary to some extent as far as the choice of relevant means is concerned, while observing the Directive's objective, yet when making such choice, the legislator was at the same time bound to the constitutional order'.[94]

The Czech Constitutional Court assessed the law implementing the Directive on the basis of 'the individual's fundamental right to privacy in the form of the right to informational self-determination'.[95] The Court noted that although the obligation to retain traffic and location data did not apply to the content of individual messages,

> the data on the users, addresses, precise time, dates, places, and forms of telecommunication connection, provided that monitoring takes place over an extended period of time and when combined together, allows compiling detailed information on social or political membership, as well as personal interests, inclinations or weaknesses of individual persons.[96]

As *obiter dictum* the Constitutional Court expressed its doubts on whether an instrument of global and preventive retention of location and traffic data on almost all electronic communications could be deemed 'necessary and adequate from the perspective of the intensity of the intervention to the private sphere of an indefinite number of participants to electronic communications',[97] and whether it was at all desirable that private persons (service providers in the area of the Internet, telephone and mobile communication, in particular, mobile operators and commercial enterprises providing Internet access) should be required to retain all data on the communication provided by them.[98]

C. The Invalidation of the Data Retention Directive by the CJEU

The different challenges presented by national laws transposing the Data Retention Directive before national courts demonstrate that the Directive was not a popular measure in many Member States. However, its fate was meant to be decided by the ultimate judicial adjudicator in Europe: the Court of Justice of the EU. The case was brought before the CJEU by two requests for preliminary reference made by the Irish High Court (Case C-293/12) and the Austrian Constitutional Court, the Verfassungsgerichtshof (Case C-594/12).

The litigation before the High Court commenced on 11 August 2006 when Digital Rights Ireland brought an action before it, challenging the legality of

---

[94] Czech Constitutional Court decision, para 25.
[95] ibid, para 37. Art 10 para 3 and Art 13 of the Czech Constitutional Charter.
[96] ibid, para 44.
[97] ibid, para 55.
[98] ibid, para 57.

national legislative and administrative measures concerning the retention of data relating to electronic communications. In particular, Digital Rights asked the High Court to declare invalid the Data Retention Directive and Part 7 of the Criminal Justice (Terrorist Offences) Act 2005, which required telephone communications service providers to retain traffic and location data in order to prevent, detect, investigate and prosecute crime and safeguard the security of the state. The High Court, considering that it was not able to resolve the questions raised relating to national law unless the validity of the Data Retention Directive had first been examined, stayed the proceedings and referred to the CJEU a number of questions for a preliminary ruling regarding the compatibility of the Directive with Article 5(4) TEU and a number of fundamental rights enshrined in the Charter.

The case before the Verfassungsgerichtshof arose when the Kärntner *Landesregierung* and Mr Seitlinger, Mr Tschohl and 11,128 other applicants brought an action seeking the annulment of paragraph 102a of the 2003 Austrian Law on Telecommunications (*Telekommunikationsgesetz* 2003), which was inserted in order to transpose the Data Retention Directive into Austrian national law on the basis that this infringed the fundamental right to data protection. In this respect, the Austrian Constitutional Court also referred several questions regarding the compatibility of the Directive with fundamental rights to the CJEU requesting a preliminary ruling. By decision of the President of the Court, the two cases were joined for the purposes of the oral procedure and the judgment.

i. The Opinion of the Advocate General

In his Opinion delivered on 12 December 2013,[99] Advocate General Cruz Villalón discussed two sets of issues: whether the Data Retention Directive was proportionate within the meaning of Article 5(4) TEU, and whether it was compatible with the EUCFR and in particular with Articles 7, 8 and their permissible limitations under Article 52(1) EUCFR. He commenced his analysis by making a number of preliminary remarks. First, he noted that the Data Retention Directive had altered 'profoundly' the EU law applicable to electronic communications data as this stood following the adoption of the Data Protection Directive and the ePrivacy Directive by providing for the collection and retention of traffic and location data.[100] Second, he observed that the Data Retention Directive was characterised by a dual functionality: on the one hand, it harmonised Member States' rules on the retention of traffic and location data relating to electronic communications; on the other hand, however, that objective required the simultaneous imposition, on Member States which did not have such legislation, of an obligation to collect

---

[99] Opinion of AG Cruz Villalón in Joined Cases C-293/12 and C-594/12 *Digital Rights Ireland Ltd v Minister for Communications, Marine and Natural Resources, Minister for Justice, Equality and Law Reform, Commissioner of the Garda Síochána, Ireland, The Attorney General and Kärntner Landesregierung, Michael Seitlinger, Christof Tschohl and others*, delivered on 12 September 2013.

[100] ibid, para 36.

and retain such data[101] (the AG called this second function of the Directive the '"creating" effect of the obligation that data be retained').[102] Third, he clarified that the fundamental right affected 'primarily' in that case was the right to privacy under Article 7 EUCFR with the right to data protection under Article 8 raising only issues that needed to be assessed 'secondarily'.[103] In this respect, he provided an interesting discussion on the relationship between the two rights which will be addressed below.

The AG then turned to show why such an interference with the fundamental right to privacy was 'particularly serious'.[104] He noted that the retention in huge databases of large quantities of data generated in connection with most of the everyday electronic communications of citizens of the Union established conditions for surveillance which constituted 'a permanent threat throughout the data retention period to the right of citizens of the Union to confidentiality in their private lives.'[105] The AG emphasised that the data in question, were 'special' personal data, the use of which made it possible to 'create a both faithful and exhaustive map of a large portion of a person's conduct strictly forming part of his private life, or even a complete and accurate picture of his private identity.'[106] He also observed that the intensity of the interference was exacerbated by the 'outsourcing' of data retention to the providers of electronic communications services which distanced the data from the direct grip and control of the public authorities of the Member States.[107]

Following his preliminary remarks, the AG turned to answer the Irish High Court's question regarding the proportionality of the Data Retention Directive in the light of Article 5(4) TEU. In this respect, he clarified that while proportionality in the context of Article 5(4) TEU is aimed, in conjunction with the principle of subsidiarity, to channel action by the European Union with due respect for Member State competence, proportionality within the meaning of Article 52(1) EUCFR is a requirement for the legitimacy of any limitation on the exercise of fundamental rights.[108] Since the Data Retention Directive limited the exercise of fundamental rights and had therefore to be examined under the proportionality requirement of Article 52(1) EUCFR, the AG took the view that it was not necessary to settle definitively the matter of its proportionality in the light of Article 5(4) TEU in that case.[109]

Regarding the Directive's compatibility with fundamental rights, the AG discussed, first, the 'provided for by law' requirement under Article 52(1) EUCFR.

---

[101] ibid, paras 37 and 46.
[102] ibid, para 47.
[103] ibid, paras 66 and 67.
[104] ibid, para 70.
[105] ibid, para 72.
[106] ibid, para 74.
[107] ibid, paras 75–79.
[108] ibid, para 89.
[109] ibid, para 105.

Recalling the relevant case law of the ECtHR, the AG noted that this must go beyond a purely formal requirement and cover also the lack of precision of the law ('quality of the law') to express it in the simplest terms possible.[110] In this respect, he observed that where the limitation on fundamental rights stems from the legislation of the European Union itself and is therefore attributable to it, as in the case of the Directive, the European Union legislature has a responsibility to define and set out in detail the guarantees necessary to regulate the limitation on fundamental rights.[111] Therefore, according to the AG, the Data Retention Directive was as a whole incompatible with Article 52(1) EUCFR, since the obligation to retain data which it imposed was not accompanied by 'the necessary principles for governing the guarantees needed to regulate access to the data and their use'.[112]

Regarding the proportionality of the Data Retention Directive, the AG recognised that this pursued a perfectly legitimate objective, namely the investigation, detection and prosecution of serious crime.[113] Regarding the proportionality of the retention period, the AG pointed out that 'an accumulation of data at indeterminate locations in cyberspace such as the accumulation at issue, which always concerns actual and particular persons, tends, whatever its duration, to be perceived as an anomaly.'[114] According to the AG, such a state of retention of data relating to the private lives of individuals should only be exceptional and cannot extend in time beyond the period necessary.[115] The AG concluded that he had not found any sufficient justification for not limiting the data retention period to less than one year.[116] The retention period of up to two years prescribed in the Article 6 of the Directive was not necessary and, therefore, incompatible with the requirements under Articles 7 and 52(1) EUCFR.[117] On the basis of these reasons, he invited the Court to invalidate the Data Retention Directive.[118]

ii. The Judgment of the Court

The CJEU delivered its seminal judgment[119] in a Grand Chamber formation on 8 April 2014.[120] The Court commenced its analysis by noting that the obligation

---

[110] ibid, para 109.
[111] ibid, para 117.
[112] ibid, para 131.
[113] ibid, para 136.
[114] ibid, para 144.
[115] ibid, para 144.
[116] ibid, para 149.
[117] ibid, paras 151–52.
[118] ibid, para 159.
[119] Joined Cases C-293/12 and C-594/12 *Digital Rights Ireland Ltd v Minister for Communications, Marine and Natural Resources* [2014] ECR I-238.
[120] For a commentary see F Boehm and MD Cole, 'Data Retention after the Judgement of the Court of Justice of the European Union. Munster/Luxembourg, 30 June 2014', www.janalbrecht.eu/fileadmin/material/Dokumente/Boehm_Cole_-_Data_Retention_Study_-_June_2014.pdf.; F Fabbrini, 'Human Rights in the Digital Age: The European Court of Justice Ruling in the Data Retention Case and its Lessons for Privacy and Surveillance in the US' (2015) 28 *Harvard Human Rights Journal* 65; MP Granger

to retain electronic communications data for the purpose of making them accessible to the competent national authorities raised questions relating to respect for private life and communications under Article 7 EUCFR, the protection of personal data under Article 8 EUCFR and respect for freedom of expression under Article 11 EUCFR. According to the Court, those data that make it possible to know the identity of the person with whom a subscriber has communicated, the means, the time, the place and the frequency of the communications[121] taken as a whole, may allow 'very precise conclusions to be drawn concerning the private lives of the persons whose data has been retained, such as the habits of everyday life, permanent or temporary places of residence, daily or other movements, the activities carried out, the social relationships of those persons and the social environments frequented by them.'[122] In this respect, the Court acknowledged that the Data Retention Directive might have an effect on the use by subscribers of the means of communication covered by that Directive and, consequently, on their exercise of the freedom of expression guaranteed by Article 11 EUCFR.[123] However, it observed that the Directive directly and specifically affected private life under Article 7 EUCFR and fell under Article 8 EUCFR because it entailed the processing of personal data and, therefore, decided to examine its validity in the light of these two fundamental rights.[124]

Starting from the fundamental right to privacy, the Court recalled its established case law, according to which, to establish an interference with this, it does not matter whether the information on the private lives concerned is sensitive

---

and K Irion, 'The Court of Justice and the Data Retention Directive in Digital Rights Ireland: telling off the EU legislator and teaching a lesson in privacy and data protection' (2014) 39(6) *European Law Review* 835; E Guild and S Carrera, 'The Political and Judicial Life of Metadata: Digital Rights Ireland and the Trail of the Data Retention Directive', CEPS Paper in Liberty and Security No 65 (May 2014); O Lynskey, 'The Data Retention Directive is incompatible with the rights to privacy and data protection and is invalid in its entirety: *Digital Rights Ireland*. Joined Cases C-293 & 594/12, Digital Rights Ireland Ltd and Seitlinger and others, Judgment of the Court of Justice (Grand Chamber) of 8 April 2014' (2014) 51 (6) *Common Market Law Review* 1789; T Ojanen, 'Privacy Is More Than Just a Seven-Letter Word: The Court of Justice of the European Union Sets Constitutional Limits on Mass Surveillance. Court of Justice of the European Union, Decision of 8 April 2014 in Joined Cases C-293/12 and C-594/12, Digital Rights Ireland and Seitlinger and Others' (2014) 10 *European Constitutional Law Review* 528; J Rauhofer and D MacSithigh, 'The data retention directive never existed' (2014) 11 *Scripted* 122; A Roberts, 'Privacy, Data Retention and Domination: *Digital Rights Ireland Ltd v Minister for Communications*' (2015) 78(3) *Modern Law Review* 522; A Spina, 'Risk Regulation of Big Data: Has the Time Arrived for a Paradigm Shift in EU Data Protection Law? (2014) 5(2) *European Journal of Risk Regulation* 248; X Tracol, 'Legislative genesis and judicial death of a directive: The European Court of Justice invalidated the data retention directive (2006/24/EC) thereby creating a sustained period of legal uncertainty about the validity of national laws which enacted it' (2014) 30(6) *Computer Law & Security Review* 736.

[121] *Digital Rights Ireland*, n 119 above, para 26.
[122] ibid, para 27.
[123] ibid, para 28.
[124] ibid, paras 29–31.

or whether the persons concerned have been inconvenienced in any way.[125] As a result, the CJEU found that the obligation imposed on providers of electronic communications services to retain, for a certain period, data relating to a person's private life and to his communications, constituted an interference with Article 7 EUCFR.[126] Furthermore, the access of the competent national authorities to the data constituted, according to the Court, a further interference with Article 7 EUCFR.[127] Insofar as the right to data protection was concerned, the CJEU found that the Directive constituted an interference with this fundamental right because it provided for the processing of personal data.[128]

Having established an interference with both fundamental rights, the Court moved then to discuss the relevant justification under Article 52(1) EUCFR. It, first, considered the essence of the two rights and held that the essence of Article 7 EUCFR had not been adversely affected by the Data Retention Directive because this did not permit the access to the content of the electronic communications.[129] Similarly, the essence of Article 8 EUCFR had also not been touched because Article 7 of the Directive provided certain principles of data protection and data security that had to be respected by providers of publicly available electronic communications services. According to those principles, Member States were required to ensure that appropriate technical and organisational measures were adopted against accidental or unlawful destruction, accidental loss or alteration of the data.[130]

The CJEU accepted that the fight against international terrorism and serious crime pursued by the Directive were objectives of general interest,[131] and went on to discuss the proportionality of the interference. In this respect, it clarified that 'in view of the important role played by the protection of personal data in the light of the fundamental right to respect for private life and the extent and seriousness of the interference with that right caused by Directive 2006/24', the EU legislature's discretion was reduced and, therefore, the judicial review of that discretion should be strict.[132] The CJEU accepted that data retention was an appropriate measure for attaining the objective of fighting serious crime.[133] It then turned its attention to the fundamental right to data protection under Article 8 EUCFR and having pointed out that this 'is especially important for the right to respect for private life enshrined in Article 7 of the Charter',[134] it held that EU legislation interfering

---

[125] ibid, para 33. See Cases C-465/00, C-138/01 and C-139/01 *Österreichischer Rundfunk and Others* [2003] ECR I-4989, para 75.
[126] *Digital Rights Ireland*, n 119 above, para 34.
[127] ibid, para 35.
[128] ibid, para 36.
[129] ibid, para 39.
[130] ibid, para 40.
[131] ibid, paras 41–44.
[132] ibid, para 48.
[133] ibid, para 49.
[134] ibid, para 53.

with this right 'must lay down clear and precise rules governing the scope and application of the measure in question and imposing minimum safeguards' so that the persons whose data had been retained have 'sufficient guarantees to effectively protect their personal data against the risk of abuse and against any unlawful access and use of that data'.[135] The need for such safeguards is all the greater, according to the Court, where personal data are subjected to automatic processing and where there is a significant risk of unlawful access to those data.[136]

The Court found that the Directive's interference with the fundamental rights enshrined in Articles 7 and 8 EUCFR was not limited to what was strictly necessary for three reasons.[137] Firstly, the Directive covered 'in a generalised manner, all persons and all means of electronic communication as well as all traffic data without any differentiation, limitation or exception being made in the light of the objective of fighting against serious crime.'[138] In fact, according to the CJEU, the Directive affected in a comprehensive manner, all persons using electronic communications services, 'but without the persons whose data are retained being, even indirectly, in a situation which is liable to give rise to criminal prosecutions.' It therefore applied even to persons for whom there was no evidence suggesting that their conduct might have a link with serious crime and did not provide for any exception, with the result that it applied even to persons whose communications are subject, according to rules of national law, to the obligation of professional secrecy.[139] Secondly, it did not determine the limits of the access of the competent national authorities to the data and their subsequent use[140] by imposing substantive and procedural conditions relating to this.[141] In particular, the Court noted that the Directive did not lay down any objective criterion limiting the number of persons authorised to access and subsequently use the data; the access by the competent national authorities to the data retained was not made dependent on a prior review carried out by a court or by an independent administrative body; and it did not oblige Member States to establish such limits.[142] Thirdly, the data retention period did not make any distinction between the different categories of data retained under Article 5 on the basis of their possible usefulness[143] and was not determined on objective criteria in order to ensure that it was limited to what was strictly necessary.[144]

Moreover, the Court found that the Directive did not provide for sufficient data protection safeguards, as required by Article 8 EUCFR, to ensure effective

---

[135] ibid, para 54.
[136] ibid, para 55.
[137] ibid, para 65.
[138] ibid, para 57.
[139] ibid, para 58.
[140] ibid, para 60.
[141] ibid, para 61.
[142] ibid, para 62.
[143] ibid, para 63.
[144] ibid, para 64.

protection of the data retained against the risk of abuse and against any unlawful access and use of that data. In particular, the Directive did not lay down rules
regarding: the vast quantity of data whose retention is required; the sensitive
nature of that data; the risk of unlawful access to that data;[145] and the irreversible
destruction of the data at the end of the data retention period.[146] Furthermore,
the Court observed that the Directive did not require the data in question to be
retained within the European Union, with the result of making difficult its control
by an independent authority, as required by Article 8(3) EUCFR.[147]

On the basis of these considerations, the Court concluded that the Data Retention Directive did not comply with the principle of proportionality in the light of
Articles 7, 8 and 52(1) EUCFR and declared it invalid.[148] Unlike the AG's opinion
that the effects of the invalidity of the Directive should be suspended 'pending
adoption by the EU legislature of the measures necessary to remedy the invalidity
found to exist', the Court did not limit the temporal effects of its ruling.

III. DATA RETENTION AND THE RIGHTS TO PRIVACY AND DATA PROTECTION

A. The Conceptual Difficulties

The Data Retention Directive raised concerns about its compliance with the fundamental rights to privacy, data protection, freedom of expression and the right
to property.[149] Privacy and data protection were the two rights on which the
CJEU based its reasoning to invalidate the Directive in *Digital Rights Ireland*. In
this respect, the Court should be praised for abandoning in this case its *Schecke*
formula of seeing Articles 7 and 8 EUCFR in combination and examining the
interference of the Data Retention Directive with these two rights and the permissible limitations under Article 52(1) EUCFR separately. There are still some problematic aspects with the CJEU's fundamental rights analysis, in particular with
regard to the right to data protection, but these will be discussed below. For the
moment, the analysis will focus on the conceptual difficulties regarding the two
fundamental rights that surround the Data Retention Directive. The debate on
whether communications' metadata retention raises privacy or data protection
issues or both is not merely theoretical. It has serious implications on the question
of the compatibility of such retention with fundamental rights. Only by posing the

---

[145] ibid, para 66.
[146] ibid, para 67.
[147] ibid, para 67.
[148] ibid, paras 69 and 71.
[149] P Breyer, 'Telecommunications Data Retention and Human Rights: The Compatibility of Blanket Traffic Data Retention with the ECHR', (2005) 11 *European Law Journal* 365, 375. See also I Brown,
'Communications Data Retention in an Evolving Internet', (2010) 19 *International Journal of Law and
Information Technology* 95.

question of which fundamental right is at stake correctly, can we reach a concrete answer on the human rights assessment of the measures. Privacy and data protection raise different issues and this is the way they should be approached, as the CJEU's analysis in *Digital Rights Ireland* demonstrated.

A first conceptual difficulty arises from the nature of the Data Retention Directive. This was listed as a modification of EU data protection legislation,[150] but, as Advocate General Cruz Villalón rightly noted in his Opinion, it altered profoundly the EU data protection legal framework law and posed serious interferences to fundamental rights. A second cause of confusion comes from the dichotomy that the Directive established in terms of the types of processing: on the one hand, there was the information retention—including data collection and storage—and on the other hand, information access and use. These were dealt with differently with the Data Retention Directive regulating solely the harmonisation of the obligations of the service providers to retain communications' data and not the conditions of access to such data by the Member States' competent authorities.[151] In these terms, it made the obligations of service providers an issue of EU law, while the conditions for access to the data in order to fight terrorism and serious crime a matter of national law. These dichotomies did not only raise inter-pillar litigation issues; they also had serious implications on the fundamental rights' compliance of the Directive.

While the Court in *Digital Rights Ireland* avoided the misconceptions between the rights to privacy and data protection and provided a robust analysis, the Opinion of AG Cruz Villalón contains a number of confusions regarding the two rights that need to be addressed. As seen above, the AG considered that the Data Retention Directive interfered 'primarily' with the right to privacy, and only 'secondarily' with the right to data protection. In this respect, he explained that although data protection is enshrined in Article 8 EUCFR as a right distinct from the right to privacy, it seeks to ensure respect for privacy, but it is subject to an autonomous regime, primarily determined by the secondary law found in Directive 95/46, Directive 2002/58, Regulation No 45/2001 and Directive 2006/24 and, in the field of police and judicial cooperation in criminal matters, by Framework Decision 2008/977/JHA.[152] He recognised that the Data Retention Directive significantly affected the right to the protection of personal data, since it imposed the obligation to retain data which allow identification of a person as the source or the destination of a communication, and of his position in space and time, by reference to his telephone number or any another information specific to him such as an IP address.[153] According to the AG, those data 'fall within the category of

---

[150] See Data Retention Directive, Art 11 of which essentially amends Art 15(1) of the ePrivacy Directive by adding a paragraph stipulating that Art 15(1) of the latter does not apply to data retained under the Data Retention Directive. See also Murphy, n 48 above, p 300.

[151] Data Retention Directive, Art 1.

[152] Opinion of AG Cruz Villalón, n 99 above, para 55.

[153] ibid, para 56.

data whose disclosure is subject to the express authorisation of each individual, in respect of which he has a "right to informational self-determination".[154] The AG noted, however, that it was not the processing of the data retained, whether in terms of the manner in which they were collected by the providers of electronic communications services or the manner in which they were used by the competent authorities which required the utmost vigilance, but the actual collection and retention of the data at issue, as well as the data's impact on the right to privacy.[155] In fact, according to the AG, even if the Data Retention Directive satisfied fully the requirements of Article 8(2) and (3) EUCFR and was, therefore, deemed to be compatible with Article 8 EUCFR, in no way would that mean that this would be also compatible with the right to privacy guaranteed by Article 7 EUCFR.[156] The AG explained that this is because the 'private sphere' forms the core of the 'personal sphere' and, therefore, it cannot be ruled out that legislation limiting the right to the protection of personal data in compliance with Article 8 EUCFR may nevertheless be regarded as constituting a disproportionate interference with Article 7 EUCFR.[157] In this regard, the AG recalled[158] the ECJ's formulation in *Schecke* that Articles 7 and 8 EUCFR are so closely linked that they may be regarded as establishing a 'right to respect for private life with regard to the processing of personal data.'[159] He observed, however, that the link which unites those two rights cannot apply systematically, but depends on the nature of the data at issue.[160] The AG's analysis on the nature of the data is slightly confusing. According to him, personal data, namely data that individually identify a person, 'frequently have a certain permanence and are frequently somewhat neutral too. They are personal but no more than that and, in general, it could be said that they are those for which the structure and guarantees of Article 8 of the Charter are best suited.'[161] The AG continued that there are, however, data 'which are in a sense more than personal'. These relate essentially to private life, to the confidentiality of private life, including intimacy. In such cases, the AG held that the issue raised by such data

> commences further 'upstream'. The issue which arises in such cases is not yet that of the guarantees relating to data processing but, at an earlier stage, that of the data as such, that is to say, the fact that it has been possible to record the circumstances of a person's private life in the form of data, data which can consequently be subject to information processing.[162]

---

[154] ibid, para 57.
[155] ibid, para 59.
[156] ibid, para 60.
[157] ibid, para 61.
[158] ibid, para 62.
[159] Joined Cases C-92/09 and C-93/09, *Volker und Markus Schecke GbR* (C-92/09), *Hartmut Eifert* (C-93/09) *v Land Hessen* (CJEU (Grand Chamber), 9 November 2010), para 52.
[160] Opinion of AG Cruz Villalón, n 99 above, para 63.
[161] ibid, para 64.
[162] ibid, para 65.

There are a number of problems with this analysis. First, the AG acknowledged that data protection is recognised as a distinct fundamental right to privacy in the EUCFR, but nevertheless, according to him, it seeks to ensure privacy. Data protection, however, pursues values that include, but go beyond, the right to privacy. Secondly and more importantly, according to the AG, the fundamental right to data protection under Article 8 EUCFR is subject to an autonomous regime determined by secondary law. This view of data protection might help to differentiate it from the right to privacy, but it is risky and erroneous because it ends up negating data protection of its fundamental right's status. In other words, it seems to suggest that there is no point in the existence of Article 8 EUCFR, since this reflects a regime established in any case in secondary legislation. Data protection, however, is a fundamental right with a content of its own laid down in the three paragraphs of Article 8 EUCFR. Thirdly, the AG's explanation as to how the Data Retention Directive affected the right to the protection of personal data is unclear. Was this because the Directive required the retention of personal data? What is the meaning of personal data? The AG defined these as requiring the express authorisation for their disclosure. However, 'express authorisation' or 'consent', in the words of Article 8(2) EUCFR, is just one of the requirements of processing: it does not define on its own the meaning of personal data or the right to data protection. Moreover, the AG seemed to link the 'express authorisation' requirement for the disclosure of the personal data with the 'right to informational self-determination'.[163] Informational self-determination describes the core of the right to data protection and is certainly not reduced only to the requirement of consent for the disclosure of personal data. Fourthly, the AG went to great lengths to explain that even though Articles 7 and 8 EUCFR are so closely linked that they may be regarded as establishing a 'right to respect for private life with regard to the processing of personal data', this link cannot apply systematically, and a measure that complies with Article 8 may interfere disproportionately with Article 7 EUCFR. The recognition of data protection as a fully-fledged fundamental right next to privacy is enough to render such an explanation redundant. Data protection and privacy operate separately and, therefore, a measure that complies with the one right may breach the other, and vice-versa, or a measure may violate both rights for different reasons. Overall, the AG's explanation seems to imply a hierarchy between the two rights. On the one hand, the personal data that individually identify a person are 'somewhat neutral', they 'are personal but no more than that and, in general, they are those for which the structure and guarantees of Article 8 are best suited.' On the other hand, there are data 'which are in a sense more than personal' and relate to the confidentiality of private life, including intimacy. In such cases, the issue commences further 'upstream' and is not about the guarantees relating to data processing. However, there is no legal basis for distinguishing data in different categories,[164] and this approach ignores the fact that the

---

[163] See E Kosta, *Consent in European Data Protection Law* (Leiden-Boston, Martinus Nijhoff, 2013).
[164] Tracol, n 120 above, p 740.

danger arises from the aggregation of apparently 'neutral' personal information, that data protection also covers sensitive data, which are personal data relating to the private life of a person, and that the right to data protection goes beyond the safeguarding of certain guarantees relating to data processing. Indeed, the significance of the data depends on the context in which it is used, rather than on subjective characterisations of certain forms of data as special and, therefore, more important than others.[165]

B. Metadata Retention and the Rights to Privacy and Data Protection

The Data Retention Directive required the retention of data revealing the source, the destination, the date, time, duration, the type and the location of the communication, along with any other related data necessary to identify the subscriber or user of electronic telecommunication services. As pointed out by the CJEU, 'traffic' and 'location' data interfere with the confidentiality of the communications, as they can reveal very precise details concerning the private lives of the persons whose data has been retained, such as the habits of everyday life, permanent or temporary places of residence, daily or other movements, the activities carried out, the persons to whom they talk and their social relationships, the social environments frequented by them, the websites that they visit, and information on the e-mails they sent, such as the time, the addressee and the size of possible attached files.[166] Metadata retention, therefore, as prescribed in the Data Retention Directive, raises a privacy issue. The right to privacy enshrined in Article 7 EUCFR provides that '[e]veryone has the right to respect for his or her private and family life, home and communications'. In the case of metadata retention, it is the privacy of individuals' communications that is at stake (communications privacy). The fact that 'traffic' and 'location' data are merely 'envelope' data and do not touch upon the content of the communications is not crucial. 'Envelope' data can reveal an extensive amount of information about individuals, concerning, for instance, political activities, medical conditions, ideological, religious and philosophical beliefs, and sexual preferences. Therefore, they interfere with the confidentiality of personal communications, even if they do not apply to their exact content. It would be mistaken, hence, to restrict the protection of confidentiality of communications merely in the content of these communications and exclude 'envelope' data. Such an approach, besides disregarding the fact that 'envelope' data already reveal a lot about individuals, introduces a very narrow understanding of the concept of personal privacy as secrecy.

---

[165] Boehm and Cole, n 120 above, p 31.

[166] See J Rauhofer, 'Just Because You're Paranoid, Doesn't Mean They're Not After You: Legislative Developments in Relation to the Mandatory Retention of Communications Data in the European Union' (2006) *Script-ED* 322, 323; I Brown and D Korff, 'Terrorism and the Proportionality of Internet Surveillance' (2009) 6 *European Journal of Criminology* 119, 124.

Moreover, whereas in the context of the traditional telephone communications it is rather easy to separate content from metadata, in the context of the Internet, such a distinction does not always work.[167] This is because, in practice, in the Internet environment content and traffic data are generated simultaneously. The example frequently used is that of a request operated with a search engine, such as Google. For instance, if one makes a search on 'postnatal depression', the request will give the following result: 'https://www.google.co.uk/webhp?sourceid=chrome-instant&ion=1&espv=2&ie=UTF-8#q=postnatal+depression'. This data can reveal sensitive health information and combined with the IP address, whether dynamic or static, allocated by the Internet access service provider to a communication, and the user ID of the subscriber or registered user IP as required by Article 5(1)(c) of the Data Retention Directive as well as 'the related data necessary to identify the subscriber or registered user' under Article 1(2) of the Data Retention Directive, will constitute information 'relating to an identified or an identifiable natural person' and, thus, personal data.[168]

Regarding IP addresses,[169] there is an issue whether these constitute personal data. In this respect, the Article 29 Working Party noted that

> unless the Internet Service Provider is in a position to distinguish with absolute certainty that the data correspond to users that cannot be identified, it will have to treat all IP information as personal data, to be on the safe side.[170]

This broad interpretation could prove problematic in particular with regard to 'dynamic' IP addresses, namely those which are allocated on a temporary basis for each connection to the network and are changed when subsequent connections are made.[171] The Article 29 Working Party has stated that even dynamic IP addresses can be considered as data relating to an identifiable person because:

> Internet access providers and managers of local area networks can, using reasonable means, identify Internet users to whom they have attributed IP addresses as they normally systematically 'log' in a file the date, time, duration and dynamic IP address given to the Internet user. The same can be said about Internet Service Providers that keep a logbook on the HTTP server. In these cases there is no doubt about the fact that one can talk about personal data in the sense of Article 2(a) of the Directive …[172]

---

[167] Goemans and Dumortier, n 25 above, p 4.

[168] See Art 29 WP

[169] An Internet Protocol address ('IP address') is a sequence of binary numbers which, when allocated to a device (a computer, a tablet or a smartphone), identifies it and allows it to access that electronic communications network. The device, in order to connect to the Internet, must use the number sequence provided by Internet service providers. The IP address is transmitted to the server on which the accessed web page is stored. See Opinion of Advocate General Manuel Campos Sánchez-Bordona in Case C-582/14 *Patrick Breyer v Bundesrepublik Deutschland*, delivered on 12 May 2016, p 1.

[170] Art 29WP, Opinion 4/2007 on the Concept of Personal Data, 17.

[171] 'Fixed' or 'static' IP addresses are invariable and allow continuous identification of the device connected to the network.

[172] Art 29W, Working Document 'Privacy on the Internet—An Integrated EU Approach to On-line Data Protection', 5063/00/EN/FINAL, 21 November, 2000.

The Court of Justice held in *Scarlet Extended* that IP addresses 'are protected personal data because they allow those users to be precisely identified' in cases where the collection and identification of IP addresses is carried out by the Internet service provider.[173] Advocate General Campos Sánchez-Bordona opined in *Breyer* that a dynamic 'IP address stored by a service provider in connection with access to its web page constitutes personal data for that service provider, insofar as an Internet service provider has available additional data which make it possible to identify the data subject.'[174] This is interesting because it suggests that dynamic IP data are always to be considered personal data. The CJEU has not delivered its judgment on this case at the time of the writing, but nevertheless, in the context of metadata surveillance where electronic communications data are retained by the Internet service providers that also have 'the related data necessary to identify the subscriber or registered user', IP addresses—including dynamic IP addresses—should be considered personal data.

Insofar as the right to data protection is concerned, the CJEU found that the Data Retention Directive interfered with this right because it provided for the processing of personal data.[175] This is a straightforward but superficial approach that does not demonstrate why the Directive interferes with the fundamental right to data protection.[176] Such an approach can be followed with respect to secondary law, for instance in order to confirm that a certain type of processing of personal data falls within the scope of the Data Protection Directive, but it is not enough to determine an interference of a certain measure with the fundamental right to data protection. It is submitted that in order to establish an interference with the fundamental right to data protection, it should be considered whether the processing of personal data affects one or more data protection principles. In this regard, the Data Retention Directive mandated the retention of 'traffic' and 'location' data, as well as 'the related data necessary to identify the subscriber or user'[177] of the electronic communications network or service. The combination of these data relates to an identified and identifiable person and can, therefore, be considered as personal data. The retention and further use of such data constitutes 'processing', which interferes with a number of data protection principles. In particular, the fair information principles affected by metadata retention are purpose limitation, data security, data minimisation, proportionality with regard to the duration of the data retention period and the requirement for an independent supervision under Article 8(3) EUCFR.

---

[173] Case C-70/10 *Scarlet Extended* EU:C:2011:771, para 51.
[174] Opinion of Advocate General Manuel Campos Sánchez-Bordona, n 169 above, paras 74 and 77.
[175] *Digital Rights Ireland*, n 119 above, para 36.
[176] See Tracol, n 120 above, p 743; Lynskey, n 120 above, p 1809.
[177] Data Retention Directive, Art 2(2)(a).

IV. A SUBSTANTIVE ASSESSMENT OF METADATA RETENTION ON
THE BASIS OF THE FUNDAMENTAL RIGHTS TO PRIVACY
AND DATA PROTECTION

The CJEU in *Digital Rights Ireland* assessed the justification of the interference with Article 7 EUCFR not on the basis of paragraph 3 of Article 52 EUCFR,[178] but on the basis of paragraph 1 of this Article. The permissible limitations to Article 8 were also examined under Article 52(1) EUCFR. According to this, limitations on the exercise of the rights and freedoms laid down by the Charter must be provided for by law, respect their essence and, subject to the principle of proportionality, limitations may be made to those rights and freedoms only if they are necessary and genuinely meet objectives of general interest recognised by the Union or the need to protect the rights and freedoms of others. The discussion below follows the CJEU's analysis in *Digital Rights Ireland*.

A. The Essence of the Fundamental Rights to Privacy and Data Protection

The Court commenced its analysis from the essence of the rights to privacy and data protection because in the event that it found that this had been compromised, the discussion on the permissibility of the interference would have stopped there. This is because the essence of fundamental rights represents an inviolable core that cannot be affected under any circumstances and determines definitely the outcome of a case barring any balancing of legitimate interests.[179]

The CJEU concluded that the essence of the right to privacy had not been affected because the Data Retention Directive did not permit access to the content of the electronic communications. It seems that the content of communications represents in fact, for the CJEU, the essence of the fundamental right to privacy as this was confirmed in *Schrems*, where access to the content of the data was indeed deemed to violate the essence of this right.[180] However, this dichotomy between 'content' and 'metadata' is not immune from criticism, given that metadata can in

---

[178] Art 52(3) EUCFR provides: 'In so far as this Charter contains rights which correspond to rights guaranteed by the Convention for the Protection of Human Rights and Fundamental Freedoms, the meaning and scope of those rights shall be the same as those laid down by the said Convention. This provision shall not prevent Union law providing more extensive protection.' Art 7 EUCFR corresponds to Art 8 ECHR and, therefore, the justification of the interference with this could have been assessed under the conditions of Art 8(2) ECHR.

[179] T Ojanen, 'Making the Essence of Fundamental Rights Real: The Court of Justice of the European Union Clarifies the Structure of Fundamental Rights under the Charter' (2016) 12(2) *European Constitutional Law Review* 318, 322.

[180] Case C-362/14 *Maximillian Schrems v Data Protection Commissioner* (CJEU (Grand Chamber), 6 October 2015), para 94.

certain cases reveal information that goes beyond content[181] and the distinction between the two is unclear and often blurred, especially in the Internet context, as explained above.[182]

The CJEU's analysis on the essence of the right to data protection is ground-breaking because it confirms that this can operate as a fully fledged fundamental right. That being said, it is still not clear what constitutes the essence of the fundamental right to data protection. The Court held that this was not affected in the context of the Data Retention Directive because this required that certain principles of data protection and data security were to be respected by providers of publicly available electronic communications services or of public communications networks and, in particular provided for appropriate technical and organisational measures to be adopted against accidental or unlawful destruction, accidental loss or alteration of the data. The Court did not clarify which are these data protection principles that should be included in the legislation, but only referred to the data security measures enshrined in the Directive. Data security is not mentioned as such in Article 8(2) and (3) EUCFR and this raises further issues with regard to the essence of the right to data protection. First, it cannot be accepted that the notion of data protection, and indeed its very essence, is restricted to data security only. The protection of personal data from unauthorised access and accidental loss is certainly important, but the right to informational self-determination should require more than data security, if it is to be accepted that this can have a normative value in the protection of individuals in the age of Big Data aggregations. The statement of the CJEU also appears to be confounding data protection with data security as it seems to suggest that if certain data security principles exist, the relevant measure will not affect the essence of the right to data protection. Nevertheless, the Court's analysis is so ambiguous that it opens up the door to an ambitious interpretation as well. Since data security is not mentioned in Article 8 EUCFR, it could be assumed that the Court is not limited by the wording of this Article, but can search the essence of the right to data protection in further data protection principles not explicitly included in this. An alternative and more plausible explanation could be that data security comes under 'fair processing', which constitutes one of the six requirements listed in Article 8 and applicable to the processing of personal data. If this is indeed the case, the Court could have been clearer on this point by mentioning in its judgment in *Digital Rights Ireland* the 'fair processing' requirement with regard to the essence of the fundamental right to data protection.

---

[181] See the Report of the United Nations High Commissioner for Human Rights (Human Rights Council) on the right to privacy in the digital age, 30 June 2014, A/HRC/27/37, para 19: 'The aggregation of information commonly referred to as "metadata" may give an insight into an individual's behaviour, social relationships, private preferences and identity that go beyond even that conveyed by accessing the content of a private communication.'

[182] M Scheinin, 'Towards evidence-based discussion on surveillance: A Rejoinder to Richard A. Epstein' (2016) 12(2) *European Constitutional Law Review* 341, 342; M Tzanou, 'European Union Regulation of Transatlantic Data Transfers and Online Surveillance', *Human Rights Law Review* (*forthcoming*).

B. Provided for by Law

According to the relevant case law of the ECtHR, the requirement that an interference with a fundamental right must be 'in accordance with the law' covers two aspects. First, there must be a legal basis for the interference; secondly, the measure should be compatible with the 'rule of law'. This means that the measure should meet the standards of accessibility and foreseeability: it must be accessible to the persons concerned, and sufficiently precise to allow them to reasonably foresee its consequences.[183] In this respect, the ECtHR held in *Kruslin v France* that

> tapping and other forms of interception of telephone conversations represent a serious interference with private life and must accordingly be based on a 'law' that is particularly precise. It is essential to have clear, detailed rules on the subject, especially as the technology available for use is continually becoming more sophisticated.[184]

In *Malone v United Kingdom* the Court stressed that

> [the] law must be sufficiently clear in its terms to give citizens an adequate indication as to the circumstances in which and the conditions on which public authorities are empowered to resort to ... secret and potentially dangerous interference with the right to respect for private life and correspondence.[185]

The AG in his Opinion discussed the 'provided for by law' requirement in detail and held that where the limitation on fundamental rights stems from the legislation of the European Union itself, as in the case of the Directive, the legislature has a responsibility to set out in detail the guarantees necessary to regulate the limitation on fundamental rights.[186] In this regard, he found that the Data Retention Directive was as a whole incompatible with the 'provided for by law' requirement, because it did not include the guarantees needed to regulate access to the data and their use.[187] Unlike the AG, the Court did not discuss the 'provided for by law' requirement at all, probably assuming that this was satisfied by the Directive.[188]

C. Objective of General Interest Recognised by the Union

Both the AG and the CJEU agreed that the Data Retention Directive 'genuinely satisfied an objective of general interest'.[189] In this regard, the Court recalled its

---

[183] *Sunday Times v United Kingdom* (1979) Series A no 30, para 49.

[184] *Kruslin v France* (1990) Series A no 176-A, para 33.

[185] *Malone v United Kingdom* (1984) Series A no 82, para 66.

[186] Opinion of AG Cruz Villalón, n 99 above, para 117.

[187] ibid, para 131. See also Privacy International, 'Memorandum of laws concerning the legality of data retention with regard to the rights guaranteed by the European Convention on Human Rights', 10 October 2003, 8–9.

[188] Bignami has argued that the democratic character of the Data Retention Directive was enhanced by the fact that it was adopted under the first pillar. F Bignami, 'Privacy and Law Enforcement in the European Union: The Data Retention Directive' (2007) 8 *Chicago Journal of International Law* 233, 249.

[189] *Digital Rights Ireland*, n 119 above, para 44.

established case law, according to which both the fight against international terrorism in order to maintain international peace and security[190] and the fight against serious crime in order to ensure public security[191] constitute objectives of general interest recognised by the EU. The CJEU also noted that Article 6 EUCFR lays down the right of any person not only to liberty, but also to security.

D. Proportionality

The CJEU recalled that the principle of proportionality entails two tests: it requires that EU measures are appropriate for attaining the legitimate objectives pursued by the legislation, but that they do not exceed the limits of what is necessary in order to achieve those objectives. It should be noted that the ECtHR has interpreted in a similar way the 'necessary in a democratic society' requirement under Article 8(2) ECHR. According to the Strasbourg Court, this requirement is satisfied when the interference 'corresponds to a pressing social need' and is 'proportionate to the legitimate aim pursued'.[192] Nevertheless, the ECtHR accepts that national authorities enjoy a certain margin of appreciation, depending on a variety of factors, such as the importance of the legitimate aim or the seriousness of the interference involved.[193] The CJEU, however, held in *Digital Rights Ireland*, citing *S and Marper*[194] by analogy, that the EU legislature's discretion may be limited where interferences with fundamental rights are at issue, depending on a number of factors, including, in particular, the area concerned, the nature of the right at issue guaranteed by the Charter, the nature and seriousness of the interference and the object pursued by the interference.[195] It concluded, therefore, that the EU legislature's discretion in the case of the Data Retention Directive was reduced 'in view of the important role played by the protection of personal data in the light of the fundamental right to respect for private life and the extent and seriousness of the interference with that right caused by the Directive'.[196] Consequently, the judicial review of that discretion had to be strict in that case.[197]

The CJEU found data retention was appropriate for fighting serious crime because, having regard to the growing importance of means of electronic communication, data which must be retained pursuant to the Data Retention Directive

---

[190] Cases C-402/05 P and C-415/05 P *Kadi and Al Barakaat International Foundation v Council and Commission* EU:C:2008:461, para 363, and Cases C-539/10 P and C-550/10 P *Al-Aqsa v Council* EU:C:2012:711, para 130. See M Tzanou, 'Case-note on Joined Cases C-402/05 P & C-415/05 P *Yassin Abdullah Kadi & Al Barakaat International Foundation v Council of the European Union & Commission of the European Communities*' (2009) *German Law Journal*, 121.

[191] Case C-145/09 *Tsakouridis* EU:C:2010:708, paras 46 and 47.

[192] *Leander v Sweden* App no 9248/81 (1987), para 58.

[193] ibid.

[194] *S and Marper v United Kingdom* ECHR 2008-V [GC], § 102.

[195] *Digital Rights Ireland*, n 119 above, para 47.

[196] ibid, para 48.

[197] ibid.

allow the national authorities which are competent for criminal prosecutions to have 'additional opportunities' to shed light on serious crime and, in this respect, they are therefore a 'valuable tool' for criminal investigations.[198] The Court, however, did not examine at all the effectiveness of metadata retention in fighting serious crime, on the basis of empirical evidence. In this regard, the Commission in its Evaluation Report of the Directive noted that 'Member States generally reported data retention to be at least valuable, and in some cases indispensable, for preventing and combating crime, including the protection of victims and the acquittal of the innocent in criminal proceedings'[199] and provided some examples from Member States where retained communications' data were useful for constructing evidence trails, starting criminal investigations and prosecuting crimes. This cannot be considered as sufficient and robust empirical evidence proving the effectiveness of blanket metadata retention[200] and it is regrettable that the CJEU missed the opportunity to engage with this issue given that after the invalidation of the Directive many Member States have considered maintaining or re-introducing data retention measures in their national law.

Despite being deemed appropriate to attain its objective, the Directive failed the necessity test for three main reasons. The first concerned its comprehensive, all-encompassing scope that covered in a generalised manner all persons, all means of electronic communication and all types of metadata without any differentiation, limitation or exception being made for individuals with no link whatsoever to serious crime or for special types of communication that are subject to professional secrecy.[201] In this regard, the Article 29 Working Party had proposed the so-called 'data preservation' or 'quick-freeze procedure',[202] as an alternative to blanket data retention. Under this procedure, operators served with a court order should be obliged to retain data relating only to specific individuals suspected of criminal activity.[203] This alternative was discarded at the EU level because data

---

[198] ibid, para 49.

[199] Evaluation report on the Data Retention Directive, n 20 above, p 23.

[200] In his Opinion on the Commission's Evaluation Report, the EDPS noted: 'the quantitative and qualitative information provided by the Member States is not sufficient to confirm the necessity of data retention as it is developed in the Data Retention Directive.' See EDPS, Opinion on the Evaluation Report from the Commission to the Council and the European Parliament on the Data Retention Directive (Directive 2006/24/EC), 31 May 2011, para 44.

[201] See Art 29 WP, Opinion 3/2006 on the Directive 2006/XX/EC of the European Parliament and of the Council on the retention of data processed in connection with the provision of public electronic communication services and amending Directive 2002/58/EC, as adopted by the Council on 21 February 2006, 2.

[202] See Opinion of the European Data Protection Supervisor on the proposal for a Directive of the European Parliament and of the Council on the retention of data processed in connection with the provision of public electronic communication services and amending Directive 2002/58/EC (COM(2005) 438 final) (2005/C 298/01) OJ C 298/1 of 29.11.2005, 20; Art 29 WP, Opinion 4/2005 on the proposal for a Directive of the European Parliament and of the Council on the retention of data processed in connection with the provision of public electronic communication services and amending Directive 2002/58/EC (COM(2005)438 Final of 21.09.2005), 6.

[203] Evaluation report on the Data Retention Directive, n 20 above, p 5.

preservation did not guarantee the ability to establish evidence trails prior to the preservation order, did not allow investigations where a target was unknown, and did not allow for evidence to be gathered on movements of victims of or witnesses to a crime.[204] Secondly, the Directive was not deemed to comply with the necessity requirement because it did not determine the limits of the access of the competent national authorities to the data and their subsequent use by imposing substantive and procedural conditions relating to this. This pronouncement of the Court shows that the two types of processing—data retention by the electronic communications providers, and data access and use by the competent public authorities—are inextricably intertwined and, as many national court decisions highlighted, cannot be artificially separated by making the one subject of EU law and the other subject of national law. Finally, the data retention period was not deemed proportionate because it was not based on objective criteria and made no distinction between the different categories of data retained on the basis of their possible usefulness.

Insofar as the proportionality of the interference with the fundamental right to data protection was concerned, the Court referred once again to the data security principle. In particular, it stated that EU legislation must lay down clear and precise rules governing the scope and application of the measure in question and imposing minimum safeguards so that the persons whose data have been retained have sufficient guarantees to effectively protect their personal data against the risk of abuse and against any unlawful access and use of that data.[205] The need for such safeguards is all the greater where personal data are subjected to automatic processing and where there is a significant risk of unlawful access to those data.[206] In this respect, the Court found that the relevant safeguards provided in the Directive were not 'sufficient'[207] because this did not lay down rules relating to (i) the vast quantity of data whose retention was required, (ii) the sensitive nature of that data, and (iii) the risk of unlawful access to that data, rules which would serve, in particular, to govern the protection and security of the data in question in a clear and strict manner in order to ensure their full integrity and confidentiality.[208] Moreover, according to the Court, the Directive did not ensure that a particularly high level of protection and security was applied by the providers by means of technical and organisational measures, but permitted those providers to have regard to economic considerations when determining the level of security which they applied, as regards the costs of implementing security measures.[209] In addition, the Directive did not ensure the irreversible destruction of the data at the end of the data retention period and it did not require the data to be retained within the

---

[204] ibid.
[205] *Digital Rights Ireland*, n 119 above, para 54.
[206] ibid, para 55.
[207] ibid, para 66.
[208] ibid.
[209] ibid, para 67.

European Union, where these were subject to control by an independent authority as required by Article 8(3) EUCFR.[210] These pronouncements are significant because they demonstrate that the Court discussed three different data protection principles in its proportionality assessment regarding the right to data protection: data security, data minimisation and the control by an independent supervisory authority. The CJEU could have referred to these principles when examining the interference posed by data retention on the right to data protection instead of assessing this on the basis of the mere fact that the Directive entailed processing of personal data. Nevertheless, the Court should be praised for reaching its apogee regarding the proportionality analysis of the fundamental right to data protection.

That said, the Court failed to mention that the use of communications data for fighting terrorism interferes with the purpose limitation principle, which mandates that personal information should be collected for specified, explicit and legitimate purposes and not further processed in a way incompatible with those purposes. Fighting serious crime is a purpose incompatible with their retention, initially foreseen solely for reasons directly related to the communication itself, such as billing purposes. The retention of metadata for criminal law enforcement introduces an exception to the purpose limitation principle, as individuals that use telecommunications services and networks and provide their data to the relevant providers for contractual purposes are not capable of foreseeing that this data combined and aggregated can reveal an accurate picture of their lives. This lack of foreseeability and transparency of the further processing was hardly remedied by the fact that the Directive provided the basis for the retention of the data itself. Most EU citizens that use communications services and networks were probably not aware of the Data Retention Directive or its various national transposition laws in their respective Member States. But, even if they were, the further use of their communications' data for law enforcement purposes could have had a chilling effect on their behaviour and the exercise of other fundamental freedoms, such as freedom of speech or freedom of association. Processing for purposes that are incompatible with their initial collection, such as those introduced by the Data Retention Directive, goes against the right to informational self-determination. It is submitted that this affects the principle of purpose limitation as such and should, therefore, be considered under the permissible limitations to the right to data protection, and not under the requirement of 'provided for by the law', as the AG did in his Opinion. In light of the increasing cooperation between private and public actors for fighting terrorism and serious crime, it is crucial that courts address the purpose limitation principle and decide whether this still has a meaning in the modern era of surveillance.

---

[210] ibid, para 68.

V. METADATA RETENTION AFTER THE INVALIDATION OF THE DATA RETENTION DIRECTIVE

A. The Imminent Consequences of the *Digital Rights Ireland* Judgment

The CJEU did not limit the temporal effect of its judgment and, therefore, the declaration of invalidity of the Data Retention Directive took effect *ab initio*, namely from the date on which the Directive entered into force.[211] This means that a number of important consequences arose from the judgment in *Digital Rights Ireland*. First, at the EU level, infringement proceedings initiated against Member States for non-implementation of the Data Retention Directive had to be duly terminated. In this regard, the Commission announced that the fine that Sweden had paid for failing to implement the Directive had to be paid back.[212] Furthermore, the proceedings brought against Germany ordering it to pay a penalty for failure to implement the Data Retention Directive were withdrawn and the case was closed.[213] Second, the CJEU's judgment is legally binding for the Irish Court and the Austrian Verfassungsgerichtshof that made preliminary references to the Court.[214] Indeed, the Verfassungsgerichtshof rendered its decision on 27 June 2014 declaring the national data retention law unconstitutional.[215] The Irish High Court is also expected to deliver its decision regarding the Irish data retention law.[216] Third, the CJEU's judgment in *Digital Rights Ireland* was decisive for challenges of domestic data retention laws before national courts. The Slovak Constitutional Court suspended the domestic data retention law until this was amended and brought into conformity with the CJEU judgment.[217] On 8 July 2014, the Romanian Constitutional Court declared the national law unconstitutional.[218] On 11 July 2014, the Slovenian Constitutional Court repealed mandatory data

---

[211] See press release no 54/14, 'The Court of Justice declares the Directive to be invalid', 8 April 2014, http://curia.europa.eu/jcms/upload/docs/application/pdf/2014-04/cp140054en.pdf, fn 2.

[212] Summary of the meeting of the European Parliament Committee on Civil Liberties, Justice and Home Affairs, held in Brussels on 10 April 2014, document 8940/14, 11 April 2014, http://register.consilium.europa.eu/doc/srv?l=EN&f=ST%208940%202014%20INIT, 4.

[213] Case C-329/12 *Commission v Germany*.

[214] Art 91(1) of the Rules of Procedure of the Court of Justice.

[215] Verfassungsgerichtshof, decision no G 47/2012-49, G 59/2012-38, G 62/2012-46, G 70/2012-40, G 71/2012-36, 27 June 2014 available in German at www.vfgh.gv.at/cms/vfgh-site/attachments/5/9/4/CH0007/CMS1363700023224/vds_schriftliche_entscheidung.pdf, press release in English at www.vfgh.gv.at/cms/vfgh-site/attachments/1/5/8/CH0006/CMS1409900579500/press_releasedataretention.pdf and extract in English at www.vfgh.gv.at/cms/vfgh-site/attachments/5/9/4/CH0007/CMS1363700023224/vdseng28082014.pdf.

[216] See Open Rights Group, Data retention in the EU following the CJEU ruling, updated April 2015, www.openrightsgroup.org/assets/files/legal/Data_Retention_status_table_updated_April_2015_uploaded_finalwithadditions.pdf.

[217] See Press Information by European Information Society Institute, available in Slovak at www.eisionline.org/index.php/sk/projekty%E2%80%90m/ochrana%E2%80%90sukromia/75%E2%80%90ussr%E2%80%90pozastavil%E2%80%90sledovanie.

[218] Romanian Constitutional Court decision of 8 July 2014, press release in Romanian, www.ccr.ro/noutati/COMUNICAT-DE-PRES-99.

retention and ordered Internet service providers to delete stored metadata.[219] The Polish Constitutional Court ruled on 30 July 2014 that access to data must be subjected to independent control and more safeguards; and, if the national law was not changed appropriately in 18 months, all provisions on data retention will become invalid.[220] On 12 March 2015, the Bulgarian Constitutional Court declared the national data retention regulation invalid.[221] On 11 June 2015, the Belgian Constitutional Court annulled the Belgian data retention law on the basis that it interfered disproportionately with the right to privacy.[222] Data retention was also questioned in criminal cases before different national courts where the retained data were used as evidence.[223]

Following the CJEU's judgment in *Digital Rights Ireland*, an important question arose regarding the fate of national rules implementing the Data Retention Directive in different Member States. The European Parliament's legal service took the view that invalidation of the Directive with retroactive effect 'in principle did not affect national legislation'.[224] The position that 'national rules remain valid and applicable'[225] after the invalidation of the Directive is problematic. In fact, in a memo on frequently asked questions published about the Directive on the date the CJEU's judgment was delivered, the Commission answered the question 'what happens to national legislation following the decision by the Court?' as follows:

> National legislation needs to be amended only with regard to aspects that become contrary to EU law after a judgment by the European Court of Justice. Furthermore, a finding of invalidity of the Directive does not cancel the ability for Member States under the e-Privacy Directive (2002/58/EC) to oblige retention of data.[226]

This means that while national legislation transposing the Directive is not automatically void, this should, nevertheless, take into account the safeguards introduced by the CJEU and—if necessary—it should be repealed to do so.[227] Nevertheless, that was a matter of national law and indeed certain Member States decided not to

---

[219] Slovenian Constitutional Court decision of 3 July 2014, press release in English at http://odloc-itve-old.us-rs.si/usrs/us-odl.nsf/o/4AFCECAACABDD309C1257D4E002AB008.

[220] See FRA Annual report 2014, 'Information society, privacy and data protection', http://fra.europa.eu/sites/default/files/fra_uploads/information_society_chapter_fra-annual-report-2014_en.pdf, 115.

[221] Bulgarian Constitutional Court Decision No 2 of 12 March 2015 on constitutional case No 8/2014 available in Bulgarian, http://constcourt.bg/contentframe/contentid/4467.

[222] Belgian Constitutional Court Decision 84/20015 of 11 June 2015, available in French at https://nurpa.be/files/20150611_ruling-const-cour-dataretention-belgium_fr.pdf, press release in English available at https://nurpa.be/actualites/2015/06/const-court-repeals-data-retention-belgium.

[223] See Fundamental Rights Agency (FRA) Report 2016, Ch 5: 'Information society, privacy and data protection', http://fra.europa.eu/sites/default/files/fra_uploads/fra-2016-frr-chapter-5-data-protection_en.pdf, 124.

[224] Summary of the meeting of the European Parliament Committee on Civil Liberties, Justice and Home Affairs, held in Brussels on 10 April 2014, document 8940/14, 11 April 2014, p 5.

[225] Tracol, n 120 above, p 744.

[226] Memo, 'Frequently Asked Questions: The Data Retention Directive', 8 April 2014, http://europa.eu/rapid/press-release_MEMO-14-269_en.htm.

[227] J Kühling and S Heitzer, 'Returning through the national back door? The future of data retention after the ECJ judgment on Directive 2006/24 in the UK and elsewhere' (2015) *European Law Review* 263, 267.

change anything, or considered that their data retention schemes were compatible with the CJEU's judgment.[228] Others, however, sought to review and re-evaluate their national data retention laws in the light of judgment and decided to partially amend these or introduce new data retention laws altogether.[229] Given that the Commission is not planning to introduce a new data retention regime at the EU legal order any time soon,[230] it should be examined whether the national data retention laws fall within the purview of the EU Charter of Fundamental Rights.

B. National Data Retention Measures and EU Fundamental Rights

There are several questions surrounding national data retention measures after the invalidation of the Data Retention Directive. Can they be adopted, does EU law apply to them and if so, what safeguards do they need to guarantee in order to comply with the CJEU's judgment in *Digital Rights Ireland*? All these issues are raised in two pending cases before the CJEU, *Tele2 Sverige v Post- och telestyrelsen* (C-203/15) and *Secretary of State for the Home Department v Tom Watson, Peter Brice, Geoffrey Lewis* (C-698/15), which were joined together.[231] The first case arose in the proceedings between Tele2 Sverige, a Swedish telecommunications company and the Swedish Post and Telecommunications Authority (PTS). In particular, on 9 April 2014, one day after the CJEU handed down its decision in *Digital Rights Ireland*, Tele2 Sverige informed the PTS of its decision to cease retaining data under the relevant provisions of the Swedish law (the LEK) and to delete the data which had been retained until then. The PTS ordered Tele2 Sverige to resume the retention of data after it had received complaints from the *Rikspolisstyrelsen* (the National Police Board, Sweden, 'the RPS'). Tele2 Sverige challenged the PTS's decision before the Administrative Court of Sweden, and upon dismissal brought a further appeal before that Court, which decided to stay the proceedings and make a preliminary reference to the CJEU. The second case concerned the Data Retention and Investigatory Powers Act 2014 ('the DRIPA'), which was adopted in the UK after the invalidation of Data Retention Directive. DRIPA was challenged before the High Court of Justice (England and Wales), Queen's Bench Division (Administrative Court), which concluded on 17 July 2015 that the regime in question was inconsistent with EU law. The Home Secretary appealed against that

---

[228] See FRA Report, n 223 above, p 126.

[229] ibid, p 115; N Vainio and S Miettinen, 'Telecommunications data retention after *Digital Rights Ireland*: legislative and judicial reactions in the Member States' (2015) 23 *International Journal of Law and Information Technology* 290.

[230] See EU executive plans no new data retention law www.reuters.com/article/us-eu-data-telecommunications-idUSKBN0M82CO20150312; Speech of Commissioner Avramopoulos at the LIBE Committee in the European Parliament, 3 December 2014 http://europa.eu/rapid/press-release_SPEECH-14-2351_en.htm.

[231] Joined Cases C-203/15 and C-698/15 *Tele2 Sverige v Post- och telestyrelsen* and *Secretary of State for the Home Department v Tom Watson, Peter Brice, Geoffrey Lewis*, pending.

judgment before the Court of Appeal (England and Wales) (Civil Division), which decided to stay the proceedings and refer a number of preliminary questions to the CJEU.

The questions referred by the two national courts concerned essentially two issues: whether, in the light of *Digital Rights Ireland*, Member States were precluded from imposing on service providers a general obligation to retain data; and if not, whether all the safeguards laid down by the Court in paragraphs 60 to 68 of *Digital Rights Ireland* in connection with access to the data, the period of retention and the protection and security of the data had to be included in the national data retention framework.

C. The Opinion of the Advocate General

At the time of writing, the CJEU had not pronounced on these questions, but it is worth taking a look at AG Saugmandsgaard Øe's Opinion, delivered on 19 July 2016.[232] The AG commenced his analysis by considering whether the Member States were entitled to avail themselves of the possibility offered by Article 15(1) of the ePrivacy Directive in order to impose a general data retention obligation. He found that the wording of Article 15(1) of the ePrivacy Directive confirmed that retention obligations imposed by the Member States fell within the scope of the Directive.[233] In fact, a general data retention obligation was to be considered as 'a measure implementing Article 15(1) of Directive 2002/58'.[234] Subsequently, the AG stated that the provisions of the Charter are applicable to national measures implementing EU law, in accordance with Article 51(1) EUCFR.[235]

AG Saugmandsgaard Øe went on to consider the compatibility of such laws with the requirements laid down in Article 15(1) of the ePrivacy Directive and Articles 7, 8 and 52(1) EUCFR. Citing the relevant pronouncements from *Digital Rights Ireland*, he found that a general data retention obligation poses a 'serious' interference to the fundamental rights to privacy and data protection and to 'several rights' enshrined in the ePrivacy Directive.[236] He then turned to examine whether such interference was justified on the basis of both Article 15(1) of the ePrivacy Directive and Article 52(1) EUCFR, read in the light of *Digital Rights Ireland*.[237]

Regarding the requirement of necessity of the measure, the AG dismissed the UK's argument that the criteria established in *Digital Rights Ireland* were irrelevant

---

[232] Opinion of Advocate General Saugmandsgaard Øe in Joined Cases C-203/15 and C-698/15 *Tele2 Sverige v Post- och telestyrelsen* and *Secretary of State for the Home Department v Tom Watson, Peter Brice, Geoffrey Lewis*, delivered on 19 July 2016.

[233] ibid, para 90.

[234] ibid, para 91.

[235] ibid, para 122.

[236] ibid, paras 127–28.

[237] ibid, para 130.

to the case at issue because that case concerned not a national regime but a regime established by the EU legislature. According to the AG, 'it is not possible to interpret the provisions of the Charter differently depending on whether the regime under consideration was established at EU level or at national level.' However, the AG left it to the national courts to consider whether it would be possible to limit the substantive scope of a retention obligation while at the same time preserving the effectiveness of such a measure in the fight against serious crime.[238] In this respect, the AG held that all the safeguards included in paragraphs 60 to 68 of *Digital Rights Ireland* were to be regarded as mandatory for national retention regimes. The AG also considered the proportionality *stricto sensu* of national data retention regimes and took the view that a national regime which includes all of the safeguards set out in *Digital Rights Ireland* 'may nevertheless be considered disproportionate, within a democratic society, as a result of a lack of proportion between the serious risks engendered by such an obligation, in a democratic society, and the advantages it offers in the fight against serious crime.'[239] He opined, however, that it was a matter for the national courts to decide.[240]

The Opinion of AG Saugmandsgaard Øe in *Tele2 Sverige* provides a detailed answer to all the questions regarding national data retention that arose after the invalidation of the Data Retention Directive in *Digital Rights Ireland*. In fact, the AG's analysis goes further than *Digital Rights Ireland*. Unlike the CJEU, which concluded its discussion in this case with the absence of the requirement of necessity, the AG provided a reflection on the consequences of metadata retention in a democratic society under the scope of proportionality *stricto sensu*. The final assessment, however, is left to national courts, and this opens up the possibility for divergent interpretations in different Member States. National data retention regimes, even if they contain all the safeguards laid down by the CJEU in *Digital Rights Ireland*, might be deemed disproportionate *stricto sensu* before certain national courts, while accepted by others. The CJEU's judgment on the matter is, therefore, very important. For the moment, however, it seems that the Opinion of the AG has struck another blow against mass electronic surveillance.

---

238 ibid, para 211.
239 ibid, para 262.
240 ibid, para 261.

4

Travel Data Surveillance

I. PNR

A. Defining Passenger Name Record (PNR)

ACCORDING TO THE European Commission, a 'Passenger Name Record' (PNR) is a computerised 'record of each passenger's travel requirements which contains all information necessary to enable reservations to be processed and controlled by the booking and participating airlines.'[1] PNR data sets may contain 'as many as 60 data fields',[2] including name, address, e-mail, contact telephone numbers, passport information, date of reservation, date of travel, travel itinerary, all forms of payment information, billing address, frequent flyer information, travel agency and travel agent, travel status of passenger (such as confirmations and check-in status), ticketing field information (including ticket number, one-way tickets and Automated Ticket Fare Quote), date of issuance, seat number, seat information, general remarks, no-show history, baggage information, go show information, OSI (Other Service-related Information), and SSI/SSR (Special Service Information/Special Service Requests). PNR data can further contain information on individuals who are not travelling by air,[3] such as, for instance, the details (e-mail address, telephone number) for contacting a person (eg a friend or a family member).[4] PNR data may also reveal religious or ethnic information (for example from the meal preferences of the passenger),[5]

---

[1] Commission Decision 2004/535/EC of 14 May 2004 on the adequate protection of personal data contained in the Passenger Name Record of air passengers transferred to the United States' Bureau of Customs and Border Protection (notified under document number C(2004) 1914), para 4. 'Booking airline' denotes the airline with which the passenger made his original reservations or with which additional reservations were made after commencement of the journey. 'Participating airline' is any airline on which the booking airline has requested space, on one or more of its flights, to be held for a passenger.

[2] House of Lords European Union Committee, 'The EU/US Passenger Name Record (PNR) Agreement', 21st Report of Session 2006–07, para 12.

[3] R Rasmussen, 'Is International Travel Per Se Suspicion of Terrorism? The Dispute Between the United States and European Union over Passenger Name Record Data Transfers' (2009) 26 *Wisconsin International Law Journal* 551, 553.

[4] Art 29 WP, Opinion 6/2002 on Transmission of Passenger Manifest Information and other data from airlines to the United States.

[5] ibid.

affiliation to a particular group,[6] as well as medical data (for example medical assistance required by the passenger, or any disabilities or health problems that are made known to the airline).[7] Few airlines hold PNR data in their own databases; those are normally stored centrally in the databases of the 'Computerized Reservation Systems' (CRSs), of which there are currently three operating worldwide: Amadeus, Sabre, and Travelport. PNR data are never deleted from the CRSs; once created, they are archived and retained indefinitely.[8]

PNR data is normally distinguished from APIS (Advanced Passenger Information System) data, which include information, such as names, gender, date of birth, nationality, type of travel document, country of issue, and expiry date.[9] The basic difference is that APIS data comprise normally the biographical information included in the machine-readable part of a passport,[10] and is therefore considered more accurate than PNR data, which is 'unverified information provided by passengers for enabling reservations and carrying out the check-in process.'[11] APIS data is most commonly used for identification purposes in border controls,[12] while PNR data is intended to detect criminal or terrorist activity.[13]

B. Why is Airline Passenger Surveillance Needed? Uses of PNR data

Michael Chertoff, US Secretary of Homeland Security, noted in an article in the *Washington Post*, in 2006: 'If we learned anything from Sept. 11, 2001, it is that we need to be better at connecting the dots of terrorist-related information.'[14] In fact, it is remarkworthy that nine of the 19 hijackers of 11 September 2001 were identified as threat risks by the Airline Passenger Screening Programme operating at that time in the US,[15] but were nevertheless allowed to board the planes.[16]

---

[6] ibid.

[7] ibid.

[8] E Hasbrouck, 'What's in a Passenger Name Record?', https://hasbrouck.org/articles/PNR.html. According to Hasbrouck, of the four CRSs that used to operate worldwide, two (Worldspan and Galileo) merged in 2007 to form Travelport, but continue to operate two distinct technology platforms under different brand names. Of the three that currently operate, only Amadeus is based in Europe.

[9] Council Directive 2004/82/EC of 29 April 2004 on the obligation of carriers to communicate passenger data, [2004] OJ L261/24.

[10] House of Lords European Union Committee, n 2 above, para 11.

[11] Commission Communication on the global approach to transfers of Passenger Name Record (PNR) data to third countries, COM(2010) 492 final, 3.

[12] According to the Commission, 'API data are ... primarily used as an identity management tool.' Ibid, p 4.

[13] European Parliament recommendation to the Council on the negotiations for an agreement with the United States of America on the use of passenger name records (PNR) data to prevent and combat terrorism and transnational crime, including organised crime (2006/2193(INI)), P6_TA(2006)0354.

[14] M Chertoff, 'A Tool We Need to Stop the Next Airliner Plot', *Washington Post*, 29 August 2006.

[15] CAPPS I. See below.

[16] House Select Committee on Homeland Security: Subcommittee on Econ Sec, Infrastructure Prot & Cybersecurity Hearing on Air Passenger Pre-Screening, 109th Cong (29 June 2005) (statement of James Dempsey, Exec Dir Ctr For Democracy & Tech). See also S Dummer, 'COMMENT: Secure Flight and

'Connecting the dots',[17] therefore, is crucial to identifying terrorists and preventing future terrorist attacks.[18] The aviation counter-terrorism and safety measures employed until recently have been criticised as inefficient, because they focused on objects instead of people.[19] Following 9/11, law enforcement authorities are not merely expected to act proactively;[20] they are expected to focus on people.[21] The question is no longer about screening the baggage of passengers, it is about screening the passengers themselves.

The pre-screening of passengers is carried out through the help of PNR data. It is normally argued that unlike API data that is mainly used as an identity verification tool, PNR data is useful as a criminal intelligence tool.[22] As the US Department of Homeland Security (DHS) explains, 'PNR information is a critical tool used … in such screening of travellers to identify individuals of interest who are planning to travel to the United States.'[23] But, what is the exact role of PNR data in the detection of 'individuals of interest'? In its 2010 Communication on the global approach to transfers of PNR data to third countries, the European Commission identified three different uses of PNR data: first, 'reactive' use in investigations and prosecutions. PNR data is utilised to unravel networks after a crime has been committed.[24] Second, 'real-time' use, where PNR data is used in order to prevent a crime, observe or arrest persons before a crime has been committed or because a crime has been or is being committed. In such cases PNR data is necessary for running against predetermined fact-based risk indicators in order to identify previously 'unknown' suspects and for running against various databases of persons and objects sought.[25] Third, 'proactive' use for trend analysis and creation of fact-based travel and general behaviour patterns, which can then be used in real time.[26] The uses of PNR data are, therefore, classified chronologically: past-present-future. In this way, however, especially the present and future uses seem to be intertwined in an unduly circular relationship: PNR data are used to create patterns (future) which will be subsequently used to

---

Dataveillance, A New Type of Civil Liberties Erosion: Stripping Your Rights When You Don't Even Know It' (2006) 75 *Mississippi Law Journal* 583, 584.

[17] See KA Taipale, 'Data Mining and Domestic Security: Connecting the Dots to Make Sense of Data' (2003) 5 *Columbia Science & Technology Law Review* 1.

[18] M Ozcan and F Yilmaz, 'Pendulum Swings in Between Civil Rights and Security: EU Policies Against Terrorism in the Light of the PNR Case', (2008) *Ysak Yearbook of International Policy & Law* 51, 54.

[19] T Ravich, 'Is Airline Passenger Profiling Necessary?' (2007) 62 *University of Miami Law Review* 1, 2.

[20] Taipale, n 17 above, p 4.

[21] Ravich, n 19 above.

[22] Commission Communication, n 11 above, p 4.

[23] US Department of Homeland Security, Privacy Office, 'A Report concerning Passenger Name Record Information derived from flights between the US and the European Union', 18 December 2008, www.dhs.gov/xlibrary/assets/privacy/privacy_pnr_report_20081218.pdf, 4.

[24] Commission Communication, n 11 above, p 5.

[25] ibid.

[26] ibid.

identify 'unknown' suspects (present), which in their turn may generate further patterns (future), etc.

Regarding the specific uses of PNR data, the Commission notes:

> The uses of PNR are mainly the following: (i) risk assessment of passengers and identification of 'unknown' persons …, (ii) earlier availability than API data, and provision of an advantage to law enforcement authorities in allowing more time for its processing, analysis and any follow-up action, (iii) identification to which persons specific addresses, credit cards etc. that are connected to criminal offences belong, and (iv) matching of PNR against other PNR for the identification of associates of suspects, for example by finding who travels together.[27]

C. 'Born in the USA': A Brief History of Airline Passenger Screening

The screening of airline passengers was not an invention of the post-9/11 era. In the USA, passenger profiling was taking place in the 1960s in order to deal with the increased number of airline hijackings in that period.[28] More particularly, the US Federal Aviation Administration ('FAA') had established 'approximately twenty-five characteristics empirically linked with hijackers historically'.[29] The scheme, however, was abandoned in 1972, as it was found ineffective.[30] In 1996, after an airline tragedy,[31] President Clinton announced the creation of the 'White House Commission on Aviation Safety and Security' which was mandated 'to look at the changing security threat'[32] in the field of aviation, and 'develop and recommend to the President a strategy designed to improve aviation safety and security, both domestically and internationally.'[33] The White House Commission on Aviation Safety and Security, also known as Gore Commission, in its final report made a number of recommendations in order to make flights safer.[34] It noted that:

> Profiling can leverage an investment in technology and trained people. Based on information that is already in computer databases, passengers could be separated into a very

---

[27] ibid, p 5.

[28] Ravich, n 19 above, p 9.

[29] ibid.

[30] ibid, p 10.

[31] On 17 July 1996, 12 minutes after take-off, TWA flight 800 from New York to Rome, with a stopover in Paris, exploded and crashed into the Atlantic Ocean, killing all 230 persons on board. Initially, it was believed that a terrorist attack was the cause of the accident; afterwards, however, it was found that the cause might have been an explosion of flammable fuel/air vapours in a fuel tank. See National Transportation Safety Board, Aircraft Accident Report 'In-flight breakup over the Atlantic Ocean Trans World Airlines Flight 800 Boeing 747–131, 17 July 1996', www.ntsb.gov/doclib/reports/2000/AAR0003.pdf.

[32] White House Commission on Aviation Safety and Security, Final Report to President Clinton, 1997, www.fas.org/irp/threat/212fin~1.html, 3.

[33] Executive Order No 13015, 61 Fed Reg 43, 937 (22 August 1996). See also Ravich, n 19 above, pp 10–11.

[34] White House Commission on Aviation Safety and Security, n 32 above. See also R Hahn, 'The Economics of Airline Safety and Security: An Analysis of the White House Commission's Recommendations' (1997) 20 *Harvard Journal of Law & Public Policy* 791.

large majority who present little or no risk, and a small minority who merit additional attention.[35]

The Commission, therefore, recommended three steps:

First, FBI, CIA, and ATF should evaluate and expand the research into known terrorists, hijackers, and bombers needed to develop the best possible profiling system. They should keep in mind that such a profile would be most useful to the airlines if it could be matched against automated passenger information which the airlines maintain.

Second, the FBI and CIA should develop a system that would allow important intelligence information on known or suspected terrorists to be used in passenger profiling without compromising the integrity of the intelligence or its sources...

Third, the Commission will establish an advisory board on civil liberties questions that arise from the development and use of profiling systems.[36]

The Report seemed to be mandating two things: first, the creation of profiles for potential hijackers and terrorists through the use of intelligence information; second, the matching of those profiles with PNR data in order to get to the 'real' people.

The plan did not take long to be implemented. The first 'Computer Assisted Passenger Screening' (CAPS) programme was developed by Northwest Airlines in 1997 with a grant from the FAA.[37] CAPS was then turned by the FAA into the 'Computer Assisted Passenger Pre-screening System' ('CAPPS'), and offered to all major airlines with hopes that it would eventually be adopted on a voluntary basis.[38] FAA rules required that 'selectees', namely those who were regarded as a risk to the aircraft, were subjected to a secondary screening only of their checked baggage;[39] additional screening of the person or the carry-on baggage was not required.[40] CAPPS utilised approximately 40 pieces of passenger data to identify passengers fitting predetermined profiles.[41] The criteria used by CAPPS in order to profile individuals remain unknown.[42] According to the 'Gore Commission' report, 'no profile should contain or be based on material of a constitutionally suspect nature—e.g., race, religion, national origin of U.S. citizens.' Therefore, the elements of the profiling system were required to be developed in such a way that

---

[35] White House Commission on Aviation Safety and Security, n 32 above, para 3.19.

[36] ibid.

[37] Ravich, n 19 above, p 11; Dummer, n 16 above, p 587.

[38] M AuBuchon, 'Comment: Choosing How Safe Is Enough: Increased Antiterrorist Federal Activity and Its Effect on the General Public and the Airport/airline Industry' (1999) 64 *Journal of Air Law & Communications* 891, 904.

[39] United States National Commission for Terrorist Attacks, 'The Aviation Security System and the 9/11 Attacks', Staff Statement No 3, 6.

[40] ibid. For this reason, the 9/11 suicide bombers that were identified by CAPPS were allowed to board their flight.

[41] Dummer, n 16 above, p 588.

[42] See C Chandrasekhar, 'Flying While Brown: Federal Civil Rights Remedies to Post-9/11 Airline Racial Profiling of South Asians' (2003) 10 *Asian Law Journal* 215, 221. AuBuchon, n 38 above, p 904.

ensures that 'selection is not impermissibly based on national origin, racial, ethnic, religious or gender characteristics'.[43] Despite this, CAPPS was criticised for lacking transparency[44] and targeting passengers of a certain racial group as 'increased threats',[45] and was ultimately abandoned.[46]

Following the 9/11 terrorist attacks, Congress passed in November 2001 the Aviation and Transportation Security Act (ATSA),[47] which was intended to change 'both the way in which passengers are screened and the entities responsible for conducting the screening.'[48] ATSA also created the Transport Security Administration (TSA) within the Department of Transportation.[49] The TSA was mandated to carry out 'security screening operations for passenger air transportation and intrastate air transportation.'[50] It assumed responsibility for civil aviation security from the Federal Aviation Administration, and for passenger and baggage screening from the air carriers.[51] TSA was charged to develop the second generation of the 'Computer-Assisted Passenger Pre-screening System' ('CAPPS II'),[52] in order to 'confirm the identities of passengers and identify foreign terrorists or persons with terrorist connections before they board a US aircraft'.[53] The system operated as follows: during the reservation process, the passenger was required to provide four pieces of information: full name, home address, home phone number, and date of birth. This information was sent electronically to CAPPS II. Before the flight, CAPPS II would request an identity authentication from commercial data provider(s), meaning that the PNR data obtained during the reservation process would be verified by information held in the databases of one or more of the commercial data providers.[54] After obtaining the passenger's authentication scores, CAPPS II would conduct risk assessments using government databases, including classified and intelligence data, to generate a risk score categorising the passenger as an acceptable risk, an unknown risk, or an unacceptable risk.[55] When the passenger checked in for a flight at the airport, his risk category would be transmitted

---

[43] White House Commission on Aviation Safety and Security, n 32 above, para 3.19.
[44] J Rhee, 'Comment, Rational and Constitutional Approaches To Airline Safety In The Face Of Terrorist Threats' (2000) 49 *Depaul Law Review* 847, 865; Chandrasekhar, n 42 above, p 222.
[45] Chandrasekhar, n 42 above, p 217.
[46] ibid, p 222.
[47] Aviation and Transportation Security Act of 2001, Pub L No 107-71 § 36, 115 Stat 597, 637 (2001).
[48] United States General Accounting Office, Report to Congressional Committees, 'Aviation Security Computer-Assisted Passenger Pre-screening System faces significant Implementation Challenges', GAO Report, February 2004, www.gao.gov/new.items/d04385.pdf, 6.
[49] The Homeland Security Act of 2002, Pub L No 107-296, § 403, 116 Stat 2135, 2178, transferred TSA from the Department of Transportation to the Department of Homeland Security (DHS).
[50] Aviation and Transportation Security Act, para 101. See also Rasmussen, n 3 above, p 570.
[51] United States General Accounting Office Report, n 48 above, p 6.
[52] Notice to amend a system of records, 68 Fed Reg 2101, 15 January 2003.
[53] See LA Kite, 'Red Flagging Civil Liberties and Due Process Rights of Airline Passengers: Will a Redesigned CAPPS II System Meet the Constitutional Challenge' (2004) 61 *Washington & Lee Law Review* 1385, 1396.
[54] United States General Accounting Office Report, n 48 above, p 6.
[55] ibid, 7.

from CAPPS II to the check-in counter. Passengers of an acceptable or unknown risk would receive a boarding pass encoded with their risk level so that checkpoint screeners would know the level of scrutiny required. Passengers whose risk assessment was determined to be unacceptable would not be issued boarding passes, and appropriate law enforcement agencies would be notified.[56] Following CAPPS' fate, CAPPS II was revoked by TSA in August 2004, due to increased civil liberties concerns.[57]

'Secure Flight' was the successor of CAPPS II, specifically developed to address the problems of its 'controversial predecessor'.[58] It was created under the Intelligence Reform and Terrorism Prevention Act (IRTPA) of 2004, through which the Congress mandated TSA to 'commence testing of an advanced passenger pre-screening system that will allow the Department of Homeland Security to assume the performance of comparing passenger information ... to the automatic selectee and no fly lists.'[59] The differences between Secure Flight and CAPPS were not so obvious. According to the Government Accountability Office Report on Secure Flight, the system 'among other changes, [would] only pre-screen passengers flying domestically within the United States, rather than passengers flying into and out of the United States'.[60] Also, the CAPPS rules would not be implemented as part of Secure Flight, but rather the rules would continue to be applied by commercial air carriers.[61] Secure Flight operated on the Transportation Vetting Platform (TVP), the underlying infrastructure (hardware and software) to support the Secure Flight application, including security, communications, and data management. The Secure Flight application aimed to perform the functions associated with 'receiving, vetting, and returning requests related to the determination of whether passengers are on government watch lists.'[62] Under Secure Flight, when a passenger made a reservation, the system accepting it, such as the air carrier's reservation office or a travel agent, would enter the passenger's PNR data, which would then be stored in the air carrier's reservation system.[63] The PNR data required by Secure Flight included information such as names, phone numbers, number of bags, seat number, and form of payment.[64] Approximately 72 hours prior to the flight, portions of the passenger data contained in the PNR would be sent

[56] United States Government Accountability Office, Testimony before the Committee on Commerce, Science, and Transportation, US Senate, Aviation Security, 'Significant Management Challenges May Adversely Affect Implementation of the Transportation Security Administration's Secure Flight Program', GAO Report, 9 February 2006, www.gao.gov/new.items/d06374t.pdf, 7.

[57] United States General Accounting Office Report, n 48 above, p 42. See also, Ravich, n 19 above, pp 17–19; Kite, n 53 above, p 1401; E Baker, 'Flying While Arab—Racial Profiling and Air Travel Security' (2002) 67 *Journal of Air Law & Commerce* 1375.

[58] Ravich, n 19 above, p 20.

[59] Intelligence Reform and Terrorism Prevention Act of 2004, Pub L No 108-458, § 102, 118 Stat 3638, 3715.

[60] United States Government Accountability Office Testimony, n 56 above, p 9.

[61] ibid.

[62] ibid.

[63] ibid.

[64] ibid.

to Secure Flight through a network connection provided by DHS's CBP.[65] TSA processed the PNR data through the Secure Flight application running on the TVP.[66] During this process, Secure Flight was to determine 'if the passenger data match the data extracted daily from TSC's Terrorist Screening Database (TSDB)— the information consolidated by TSC from terrorist watch lists to provide government screeners with a unified set of terrorist-related information.'[67] TSA also screened the information against its own watch list composed of individuals who did not have a nexus to terrorism but who may have posed a threat to aviation security.[68] When the passenger checked in for the flight at the airport, he received a level of screening based on his designated category. A cleared passenger was to be provided a boarding pass and allowed to proceed to the screening checkpoint in the normal manner. A selectee passenger was to receive additional security scrutiny at the screening checkpoint. A no-fly passenger would not be issued a boarding pass, and law enforcement authorities would be notified.[69]

Although Secure Flight appears to have removed certain elements criticised in CAPPS II, such as some 'computer-based risk assessment algorithms mined from vast commercial databases, in its verification process',[70] the system has been characterised as 'a stripped-down version of the old CAPPS II … with a more consumer-friendly name.'[71] In its 2006 Report on Secure Flight, the United States Government Accountability Office (GAO) concluded that 'TSA has not followed a disciplined life cycle approach in developing Secure Flight, in accordance with best practices for large-scale information technology programs.'[72] The programme was eventually abandoned in 2006,[73] and the development of subsequent programmes going under the names 'Registered Traveller',[74] and 'Trusted Traveller'[75] were announced.[76] In August 2009, the TSA announced that it would begin implementing the second phase of the Secure Flight programme in late 2009[77] and that

---

[65] ibid, 10.
[66] ibid.
[67] ibid.
[68] ibid.
[69] ibid, 13.
[70] Dummer, n 16 above, p 590.
[71] B Scannell, 'TSA Cannot Be Trusted' *USA Today*, 27 September 2004.
[72] United States Government Accountability Office Testimony, n 56 above, p 13.
[73] Electronic Privacy Information Centre, 'Spotlight on Surveillance: Secure Flight Should Remain Grounded Until Security and Privacy Problems Are Resolved', https://epic.org/privacy/airtravel/secureflight.html.
[74] Registered Traveller, www.tsa.gov/approach/rt/index.shtm. See also ACLU, 'Why the "Registered Traveler" Program Will Not Make Airline Passengers Any Safer', www.aclu.org/other/why-registered-traveler-program-will-not-make-airline-passengers-any-safer?redirect=why-registered-traveler-program-will-not-make-airline-passengers-any-safer.
[75] Bruce Schneier, 'An Easy Path for Terrorists', *Boston Globe*, 24 August 2004.
[76] Rasmussen, n 3 above, p 571.
[77] Press Release, TSA, 'TSA's Secure Flight Program Enters Next Public Phase', www.tsa.gov/press/releases/2009/0812.shtm. See also Y Kleiner, 'Racial Profiling in the Name of National Security: Protecting Minority Travelers' Civil Liberties in the Age of Terrorism' (2010) 30 *British Columbia Third World Law Journal* 103, 134.

it expected 'all international carriers with direct flights to the U.S. to begin using Secure Flight by the end of 2010'.[78]

II. THE EU–US PASSENGER NAME RECORD (PNR) AGREEMENTS: A CHRONOLOGY

A. The First EU–US PNR Agreement

i. EU Airlines between a Rock and a Hard Place

The EU–US Passenger Name Record (PNR) saga began two months after the tragic events of 11 September 2001.[79] It is a story fraught with a myriad of complex issues: counter-terrorism, air security, human rights, 'different cultures of privacy',[80] EU law internal cross-pillar controversies and international aviation law.[81] It is also fraught with conflicts: security versus privacy,[82] US anti-terrorist legislation versus EU data protection law, EU versus US legal privacy regime, European Parliament versus Council and Commission, 'commercial processing' of data versus 'law enforcement processing', data protection versus data mining.

The first dilemma was faced by European airline companies that had to choose between violating EU data protection legislation or paying heavy fines and losing landing rights in the US.[83] More specifically, the Aviation and Transportation Security Act (ATSA), adopted on 19 November 2001, required airlines flying into US territory to transfer to the Commissioner of Customs data relating to passengers and cabin crew (Passenger Manifest Information).[84] The airlines were also obliged to provide Customs with PNR information upon request.[85] The purpose was to identify individuals 'who may pose a threat to aviation safety or national security'.[86] The Department of Homeland Security (DHS) also passed legislation

---

[78] Press Release, 'Secretary Napolitano Announces Major Aviation Security Milestone, DHS performs 100 percent watchlist matching for domestic flights', 7 *June 2010*, www.tsa.gov/press/releases/2010/0607.shtm.

[79] For a general analysis of the EU–US counter-terrorism cooperation see W Rees, *Transatlantic Counter-Terrorism Cooperation: The New Imperative* (London, Routledge, 2006); E Fahey and D Curtin, *Transatlantic Community of Law: Legal Perspectives on the Relationship between the EU and US Legal Orders* (Cambridge, Cambridge University Press, 2014).

[80] See J Whitman, 'Two Western Cultures of Privacy: Dignity Versus Liberty' (2003) 113 *Yale Law Journal* 1151.

[81] P Mendes De Leon, 'The Fight Against Terrorism Through Aviation: Data Protection Versus Data Production' (2006) XXXI *Air & Space Law* 320, 328.

[82] M Roos, 'Definition of the Problem: The Impossibility of Compliance with Both European Union and United States Law' (2005) 14 *Transnational Law & Contemporary Problems* 1137, 1138.

[83] ibid, 1137.

[84] 49 USC § 44909 (Passenger Manifests Law). See Art 29 WP Opinion 6/2002, n 4 above, p 2.

[85] ibid, § 44909(3). According to § 44909(5), information 'may be shared with other Federal agencies for the purpose of protecting national security'. See Roos, n 82 above, p 1139.

[86] ATSA, 49 USC § 114 (h) (4).

requiring airlines to make available to US Customs PNR information relating to a passenger's identity and travel plans when that passenger is flying to or from the US.[87] The information was to be transmitted no later than 15 minutes after the departure of the aircraft.[88] The data transmitted was stored in the central-ised Interagency Border Inspection System ('IBIS') database, accessible by more than 20 different agencies, including the FBI, Interpol, Drug Enforcement Agency, Alcohol Tobacco and Firearms, the Internal Revenue Service, the Coast Guard, the Federal Aviation Administration, the Secret Service, and the Animal and Plant Health Inspection Service.[89] Failure to forward the information required, or for-warding incorrect or incomplete information, was punishable with loss of landing rights and the payment of a fine of up to $6,000 per passenger whose data had not been appropriately transmitted.[90]

There are number of risks associated with transborder data transfers,[91] which have prompted governments around the world to regulate them in order to pro-tect the fundamental rights to data protection and privacy of individuals and to ensure their own 'informational sovereignty'.[92] Under EU data protection law, transborder data flows are allowed to third countries only on condition that these ensure in principle an 'adequate' level of protection of personal data.[93] The Data Protection Directive applied to the data processed by the air carriers, as PNR information is data related to an identified person, and therefore 'personal data';[94] and its collection, storage, and transfer to the US authorities constitutes 'processing',[95] which is 'commercial' and does not fall within the exceptions of Article 3(2). Furthermore, European airlines were considered 'controllers' of personal data[96] under the Data Protection Directive. Thus, they could be subject to fines from EU national Data Protection Authorities (DPAs) for not comply-ing with their obligations under the Directive,[97] given that there was no general adequacy finding of personal data protection for the USA.

---

[87] Passenger Name Record (PNR) Regulation, 19 CFR § 122.49(a) and 122.49b(2).

[88] ibid. 19 CFR § 122.49a(b)(2)(i).

[89] US Government Accountability Office, 'Terrorist Watch List Screening Efforts to Help Reduce Adverse Effects on the Public', September 2006, www.gao.gov/new.items/d061031.pdf.

[90] E Guild and E Brouwer, 'The political life of data: the ECJ decision on the PNR Agreement between the EU and the US', CEPS Policy Brief No 109, July 2006; Art 29 WP Opinion 6/2002, n 4 above, p 4.

[91] C Kuner, *Transborder Data Flows and Data Privacy Law* (Oxford, Oxford University Press, 2013) 103–06.

[92] See Report of the Commission on Transnational Corporations of the UN Economic and Social Council of 6 July 1981. See also A Gotlieb, C Dalfen and K Katz, 'The Transborder Transfer of Informa-tion by Communications and Computer Systems: Issues and Approaches to Guiding Principles', (1974) 68 *American Journal of International Law* 227; W Fishman, 'Introduction to Transborder Data Flows', (1980) 16 *Stanford Journal of International Law* 3.

[93] Data Protection Directive, Art 25. See also GDPR, Art 45(1).

[94] Data Protection Directive, Art 2(a).

[95] ibid, Art 2(b).

[96] ibid, Art 2(d).

[97] On an initial assessment of the data protection problems of the transfer of PNR see Art 29 WP Opinion 6/2002, n 4 above, pp 8–9.

European airline companies were, thus, caught 'between a rock and a hard place' (if they followed Community law, they were liable to US sanctions; if they gave in to the US authorities' demands, they fell foul of EU data protection requirements),[98] and the European Commission had to intervene to find a solution to this conundrum.[99] In June 2002, the Commission informed the US authorities that the PNR data transfers to US law enforcement authorities for counter-terrorism purposes could conflict with Community and Member States' legislation on data protection, and with some provisions of the Regulation on Computerised Reservation Systems (CRSs).[100] The US authorities agreed to postpone the entry into force of the new requirements only until 5 March 2003.[101] The Commission and the US administration entered into negotiations to reach a compromise, and on 18 February 2003 they issued a joint statement, recalling their shared interest in combating terrorism and setting out initial data protection undertakings agreed by US Customs in order to pursue talks with a view to allowing the Commission to make a decision of adequacy of the US privacy regime in accordance with Article 25(6) of the Data Protection Directive.[102] The main objective of the Commission's negotiations was to allow the transfer of PNR data to the US authorities, while reaching a compromise regarding EU data protection requirements. Indeed, as a commentator cynically noted, 'the discussions essentially sought to enhance US data protection standards and reduce those of the EC.'[103]

Meanwhile, the European Parliament and the Article 29 Data Protection Working Party actively joined the debate on the side of fundamental rights. In two Resolutions, the European Parliament highlighted that that there was 'an imperative and urgent need to give passengers, airlines and reservation systems clear indications as soon as possible on which measures are to be taken in response to the demands made by the US authorities',[104] and criticised the Commission for its February 2003 joint declaration with the US on the ground that it lacked 'any legal basis and could be interpreted as an indirect invitation to the national authorities to disregard Community law'.[105] Nevertheless, recognising the need for

---

[98] European Parliament Resolution on transfer of personal data by airlines in the case of transatlantic flights, 13 March 2003, P5_TA(2003)0097.

[99] E De Busser, *Data Protection in EU and US criminal cooperation: A substantive law approach to the EU internal and transatlantic cooperation in criminal matters between judicial and law enforcement authorities* (Antwerpen, Maklu Publishers, 2009).

[100] Council Regulation (EEC) No 2299/89 of 24 July 1989 on a code of conduct for computerised reservation systems [1989] OJ L220/1, as amended by Council Regulation (EC) No 323/1999 of 8 February 1999 [1999] OJ L40/1.

[101] It should be mentioned that since then (and before the entry into force of the first PNR Agreement on 28 May 2004), European airlines were providing PNR data to the US authorities.

[102] European Commission/US Customs Talks on PNR transmission, Brussels, 17/18 February Joint Statement, http://ec.europa.eu/transport/air_portal/security/doc/prn_joint_declaration_en.pdf.

[103] I Ntouvas, 'Air Passenger Data Transfer to the USA: The Decision of the ECJ and Latest Developments' (2007) 16 *International Journal of Law and Information Technology* 73, 79.

[104] European Parliament Resolution, n 98 above.

[105] ibid, para 3.

negotiations in order to ensure a genuine cooperation with the US authorities,[106] it called for an Agreement where: 1) there is no discrimination against non-US passengers and no retention of data beyond the length of a passenger's stay on US territory; 2) passengers are provided with full and accurate information before purchasing their ticket and give their informed consent regarding the transfer of such data to the USA; and 3) passengers have access to a swift and efficient appeals procedure, should any problem arise.[107] Similar concerns were also raised by the Article 29 Working Party in a series of Opinions it issued when the EU–US PNR conflict broke out.[108]

ii. Appeasing the Conflict: The 2004 PNR Agreement

Amidst the concerns voiced by the Parliament and the Working Party, the Commission announced,[109] on 16 December 2004, 'the successful conclusion of negotiations',[110] which reflected a 'balanced, integrated, multi-strand approach'.[111] The draft decision on adequacy, alongside with the draft CBP Undertakings attached to it, was put before the Parliament on 1 March 2004. In its Resolution of 31 March 2004, the European Parliament heavily criticised the draft decision on adequacy.[112] Having noted its regret at 'the fact that, throughout 2003, the Commission did not heed the repeated requests from Parliament and the data-supervision authorities',[113] it stated that the draft decision went 'beyond the executive powers conferred on the Commission'.[114] In fact, according to the Parliament the draft decision was

> not (and could not be) a legal basis capable of enabling, within the European Union, the purpose for which the data were collected in the PNR to be changed and enabling them to be transferred by the airlines, in whole or in part, to third parties; its effect, however, may well be a lowering of the data-protection standards established by means of Directive 95/46/EC within the EU or the creation of new standards in agreement with third countries.[115]

---

[106] ibid.

[107] ibid.

[108] See Article 29 WP Opinion 6/2002, n 4 above; European Data Protection Authorities, Opinion on the transfer of Passengers' data to the United States, 17.6.2003; Article 29 WP, Opinion 2/2004 on the adequate protection of personal data contained in the PNR of air passengers to be transferred to the US' Bureau of Customs and Border Protection (US CBP).

[109] See Address of Frits Bolkestein to European Parliament Committees on Citizens' Freedoms and Rights, Justice and Home Affairs and Legal Affairs and the Internal Market, 'EU/US talks on transfers of airline passengers' personal data' SPEECH/03/613 of 16 December 2003.

[110] ibid. Ntouvas, n 103 above, p 80.

[111] ibid.

[112] European Parliament Resolution on the draft Commission decision noting the adequate level of protection provided for personal data contained in the Passenger Name Records (PNRs) transferred to the US Bureau of Customs and Border Protection (2004/2011(INI)), P5_TA(2004)0245.

[113] ibid.

[114] ibid.

[115] ibid.

The European Parliament also expressed its doubts regarding the binding nature of the US Undertakings and the use of the 'pull' system for the transmission of the data,[116] and concluded by calling upon the Commission to withdraw its draft decision on adequacy.[117]

Notwithstanding this, on 14 May 2004 the Commission adopted a decision, on the basis of Article 25(6) of the Data Protection Directive, confirming the adequate protection of personal data contained in the Passenger Name Record of air passengers transferred to the United States' Bureau of Customs and Border Protection.[118] Following the Commission's decision on the adequacy of the protection of personal data in the US, on 17 May 2004 the Council adopted a decision authorising the conclusion of an agreement between the EC and the US on the transfer of PNR data by air carriers to the US DHS, Bureau of Customs and Border Protection.[119] The legal basis for the Council's decision was Article 95 EC (now Article 114 TFEU) in conjunction with the first sentence of the first subparagraph of Article 300(2) EC. On 28 May 2004, an Agreement permitting the transfer of PNR data to the United States was signed in Washington DC.[120] The Agreement entered into force the same day.[121]

iii. The Commission's Adequacy Decision and the CBP Undertakings

It should be stated from the outset that the Commission's adequacy decision is based on the assumption (proved wrong later by the CJEU) that the transfer of PNR data by European air carriers to the US authorities constitutes commercial processing, therefore it is a matter falling within Community law (former First Pillar), and the Data Protection Directive applies.[122] That being said, let us take a closer look at the 'adequacy requirement' and the decision itself. Simply put, the adequacy requirement means that personal data cannot travel to third countries that do not offer an 'adequate' level of protection.[123] According to the Data Protection Directive, the adequacy of the level of protection afforded by a third country is assessed

---

[116]   ibid.

[117]   ibid.

[118]   Commission Decision 2004/535/EC of 14 May 2004 on the adequate protection of personal data contained in the Passenger Name Record of air passengers transferred to the United States Bureau of Customs and Border Protection, [2004] OJ L235/11.

[119]   Council Decision 2004/496/EC of 17 May 2004 on the conclusion of an Agreement between the European Community and the United States of America on the processing and transfer of PNR data by Air Carriers to the United States Department of Homeland Security, Bureau of Customs and Border Protection, [2004] OJ L183/83, and corrigendum at [2005] OJ L255/168.

[120]   Agreement between the European Community and the United States of America on the processing and transfer of PNR data by Air Carriers to the United States Department of Homeland Security, Bureau of Customs and Border Protection.

[121]   ibid, para 7.

[122]   V Papakonstantinou and P de Hert, 'The PNR Agreement and Transatlantic Anti-Terrorism Co-operation: No Firm Human Rights Framework on Either Side of the Atlantic' (2009) 46 *Common Market Law Review* 885, 901.

[123]   Data Protection Directive, Art 25(1). See also GDPR, Art 45(1).

in the light of all the circumstances surrounding a data transfer operation or a set of data transfer operations; particular consideration shall be given to the nature of the data, the purpose and duration of the proposed processing operation or operations, the country of origin and country of final destination, the rules of law, both general and sectoral, in force in the third country in question and the professional rules and security measures which are complied within that country.[124]

The adequacy requirement has been characterised as 'notorious regulatory gunboat diplomacy'[125] that has prompted many countries to change their data protection rules—or indeed introduce new ones—in order to be able to receive data transfers from the EU.[126] The adequacy test and its interpretation by the CJEU will be discussed in detail below in the context of the *Schrems*[127] judgment, but for the moment the analysis will focus on the Commission's PNR adequacy decision. Adequacy seemed to be easily satisfied in the Commission's decision.[128] Indeed, the assessment of the data protection principles affected by the transfer of PNR data was not undertaken on particularly stringent standards of protection. Air passengers' data could be processed for several broad purposes;[129] as many as 34 PNR data categories were to be transferred to the US; and data retention periods were particularly long.[130]

Nevertheless, the Commission considered its adequacy finding as not permanent and rebuttable.[131] In particular, competent authorities in Member States could suspend data flows to CBP where a competent US authority had determined that CBP was in breach of the applicable standards of protection; or where there was a substantial likelihood that the standards of protection agreed with CBP were being infringed; there were reasonable grounds for believing that CBP was not taking adequate and timely steps to settle the case at issue; the continuing transfer would have created an imminent risk of grave harm to data subjects, and the competent authorities in the Member State have made reasonable efforts in the circumstances to provide CBP with notice and an opportunity to respond.[132] Furthermore, if the basic principles necessary for an adequate level of protection were no longer being complied with, the Commission had the right to repeal or

---

[124]   Data Protection Directive, Art 25(2). See also GDPR, Art 45(2).

[125]   Papakonstantinou and de Hert, n 122 above, p 899; P de Hert and B de Schutter, 'International Transfers of Data in the Field of JHA: The Lessons of Europol, PNR and Swift' in B Martenczuk and S Van Thiel (eds), *Justice, Liberty, Security: New Challenges for EU External Relations* (Brussels, VUBRESS, Brussels University Press, 2008) 303, 315–16. See also E Fahey, 'On the Use of Law in Transatlantic Relations: Legal Dialogues between the EU and US' (2014) 20(3) *European Law Journal* 368.

[126]   See M Birnhack, 'The EU data protection directive: an engine of a global regime' (2008) 24 *Computer Law & Security Report* 508.

[127]   Case C-362/14, *Maximillian Schrems v Data Protection Commissioner* (CJEU (GC), 6 October 2015).

[128]   Commission decision on adequacy, Recital 14.

[129]   ibid, Recital 15.

[130]   ibid, Recital 16.

[131]   ibid, Art 5.

[132]   ibid, Art 3(1).

suspend its adequacy decision.[133] The Commission's adequacy finding applied for a period of three years and six months, after which the PNR Agreement should be renegotiated.[134]

The Council's decision itself was laconic. In only two Articles the Council solemnly announced that the Community approved the conclusion of the Agreement for the transfer of PNR data to the US authorities.[135] Similarly, the EU–US Agreement for the transfer of PNR data contained a mere seven Articles.[136]

Annexed to the Commission's decision were the 48 CBP Undertakings that regulated the details of the DHS processing.[137] The legal nature of the Undertakings was not clear. In the Commission's own words the Undertakings had 'varying degrees of legal effect'[138] because they were incorporated in a variety of different legal documents: statutes, regulations, directives or other policy instruments in the United States.[139] Nevertheless, because the Undertakings were to be published in full in the Federal Register under the authority of the DHS, the Commission considered that they represented 'a serious and well considered political commitment on the part of the DHS.'[140] This was problematic for a number of reasons. First of all, political commitments do not have the binding nature and the enforceability of legal obligations. Indeed, as the Working Party correctly observed, the US undertakings were not legally binding on the US side.[141] This is confirmed by taking a look at Undertaking 47: 'these Undertakings do not create or confer any right or benefit on any person or party, private or public.' Moreover, individuals lacked legal certainty as how to challenge the measures since they were enshrined in legal texts of different nature. The Commission's assertion, therefore, that non-compliance 'could be challenged through legal, administrative and political channels'[142] seemed rather difficult to take place in practice. The European Parliament[143] and the Article 29 Working Party[144] echoed similar concerns about the Undertakings on the draft adequacy decision.

On the substance, the Undertakings include the commitments assumed by the CBP for the use of the PNR data. CBP required access to 34 categories of data,[145] even if it believed that only in rare cases an individual PNR will include a full set of the identified data.[146] The PNR data were used for three purposes: preventing

---

[133] ibid, Art 4(3).
[134] ibid, Art 7.
[135] Council's decision on the conclusion of the Agreement, Art 1.
[136] EU–US PNR, Art 3.
[137] See I Tukdi, 'Transatlantic Turbulence: The Passenger Name Record Conflict' (2008) 45 *Houston Law Review* 587, 601.
[138] Commission decision on adequacy, Recital 13.
[139] ibid.
[140] ibid.
[141] Art 29 WP, Opinion 2/2004, n 108 above, p 5.
[142] Commission decision on adequacy, Recital 13.
[143] European Parliament Resolution, n 112 above.
[144] Art 29 WP, Opinion 2/2004, n 108 above, p 5.
[145] The data elements were listed in Attachment A of the CBP Undertakings.
[146] Undertaking 4.

and combating 1) terrorism and related crimes, 2) other serious crimes, including organised crime, that are transnational in nature, and 3) flight from warrants or custody for these crimes.[147] CBP assured that it would not use 'sensitive' data,[148] and an automated system which filtered and deleted such codes was implemented.[149] With regard to the method of accessing the PNR data, CBP 'pulled' passenger information from air carrier reservation systems 72 hours prior to the departure of the flight with the possibility to re-check them a further three times.[150] PNR data were accessed by authorised CBP users for a period of three years and six months, unless they were manually consulted. In this case, they could be kept for another eight years in a deleted record file.[151] CBP could provide, at its discretion, PNR data to other government authorities, including foreign government authorities, with counter-terrorism or law-enforcement functions, on a case-by-case basis, for purposes of preventing and combating criminal offences.[152] The data could also be disclosed in any criminal judicial proceedings or as otherwise required by law.[153] CBP assured that it would provide information to the travelling public regarding the transfer of its PNR data to the US authorities and its use[154] and would rectify the data at the request of the data subject.[155] Finally, the CBP and the Commission agreed on a joint review of the implementation of the Undertakings.[156]

iv. The CJEU PNR *Decision and 'the Decline and Fall'*[157] *of the 2004 Agreement*

While the dilemma faced by the European airline companies regarding their compliance to US counter-terrorism policies or EU data protection legislation seemed to be resolved after the 2004 PNR Agreement, another controversy emerged. This time the conflict was an internal European one: the European Parliament sought the annulment before the CJEU of both the Commission's adequacy decision and the Council's decision approving the signing of the Agreement.[158] As astutely noted, 'the Parliament's quarrel was in fact not so much with the legality of ... the Decision as with the substance of the data protection undertakings, which

---

[147] Undertaking 3.
[148] Undertaking 9.
[149] Undertaking 10.
[150] Undertaking 14.
[151] Undertaking 15.
[152] Undertaking 29.
[153] Undertaking 35.
[154] Undertakings 36 and 37.
[155] Undertakings 39, 40.
[156] Undertaking 43. See Commission Staff Working Paper, Joint Review of the Implementation by the US Bureau of Customs and Border Protection of the Undertakings set out in Commission Decision 2004/535/EC of 14 May 2004, Washington, 20–21 September 2005 (COM (2005) final, 12 December 2005.
[157] House of Lords European Union Committee, n 2 above, para 21.
[158] Joined Cases C-317/04 and C-318/04 *European Parliament v Council and Commission (PNR)* [2006] ECR I-4721.

the Parliament regarded as inadequate. The proposal to link a challenge to the legality of the Decision with its main complaint on the substance proved fatal to its case.'[159]

On 27 July 2004, the Parliament filed an action of annulment of the Commission's adequacy decision (Case C-318/04), based on four pleas:

1) the adoption of the Commission's decision was *ultra vires* because the provisions laid down in the Data Protection Directive were not complied with;
2) the adequacy decision breached the fundamental principles of the Data Protection Directive;
3) it infringed fundamental rights, and in particular the right to privacy; and
4) it breached the principle of proportionality.[160]

In its action against the Council's decision on the conclusion of the Agreement (Case C-317/04), the Parliament advanced six pleas for annulment:

1) incorrect choice of Article 95 EC as legal basis;
2) infringement of the second subparagraph of Article 300(3) EC;
3) infringement of the right to protection of personal data;
4) breach of the principle of proportionality;
5) lack of a sufficient statement of reasons for the decision at issue; and
6) breach of the principle of cooperation in good faith laid down in Article 10 EC.[161]

a. The Opinion of the Advocate General

In his Opinion, Advocate General (AG) Léger argued that the Commission's adequacy decision was excluded *ratione materiae* from the scope of the Data Protection Directive, because the use by CBP and the making available to the latter of air passenger data from air carriers' reservation systems constitute data processing operations which concern public security and relate to state activities in areas of criminal law.[162] This is supported by the wording of the adequacy decision, which provides that PNR data will be used strictly for purposes of preventing and combating terrorism and serious transnational crimes.[163] The AG admitted that the collection and recording of air passenger data by airlines had, in general, a 'commercial purpose' in so far as it was connected with the operation of the flight by the air carrier, but the processing which was regulated in the adequacy decision was different in nature, because it concerned the safeguarding of public

---

[159] House of Lords European Union Committee, n 2 above, para 52.

[160] Joined Cases C-317/04 and C-318/04 *(PNR)*, n 158 above, para 50.

[161] ibid, para 62.

[162] Opinion of AG Léger in Joined Cases C-317/04 and C-318/04, delivered on 22 November 2005, para 97.

[163] ibid, para 99.

security and covered 'a stage subsequent to the initial collection of the data.'[164] Consequently, according to the AG, the fact that personal data had been collected in the course of a business activity could not justify the application of the Data Protection Directive.[165]

Along the same lines, the AG rejected Article 95 EC as the appropriate legal basis for the adoption of the Council's decision on the conclusion of the PNR Agreement.[166] Even if it was to be accepted that the EU–US PNR Agreement had as its purpose to remove 'any distortion of competition between the Member States' airlines and between the latter and the airlines of third countries'[167] this purpose was '*incidental* in character to the two main objectives of combating terrorism and other serious crimes and protecting passengers' personal data.'[168] According to the 'centre of gravity' theory applied by the Court, if a Community measure pursues more than one purpose and if one is identifiable as the main or predominant purpose, whereas the other is merely incidental, the measure must be founded on a single legal basis, namely the one required by the main or predominant purpose or component.[169] The AG, considered therefore, that since the principal aim and content of the agreement were not about the functioning of the internal market, Article 95 EC was not the correct legal basis for its adoption.[170]

Advocate General *Léger* also dealt with the Parliament's plea alleging an infringement of fundamental rights, in particular privacy and data protection. The way he viewed the function of the two rights will be discussed in detail below. On the substance of his analysis, the AG followed the usual formula employed by the ECtHR when assessing limitations to the right to privacy. In particular, after having established an interference with the right to privacy, he went on to examine whether this was disproportionate, by seeing whether the requirements 'in accordance with the law', 'legitimate aim', and 'necessary in a democratic society' were complied with. The AG was satisfied that the 'in accordance with the law' condition, and in particular the accessibility and foreseeability requirement, was complied with, because the airlines covered by the PNR regime were informed of the obligations imposed on them under the agreement, and airline passengers were informed of their rights, in particular as regards access to and rectification of data.[171] Furthermore, the interference pursued the legitimate aim of combating terrorism.[172] As regards his analysis on the necessity requirement, the AG opined that in the light of the nature and importance of the objective of combating terrorism, the Court should recognise that the Council and the Commission had a

---

[164] ibid, para 102.
[165] ibid, para 103.
[166] ibid, para 140.
[167] ibid, para 144.
[168] ibid, para 147.
[169] ibid, para 154.
[170] ibid, para 155.
[171] ibid, para 219.
[172] ibid, para 222.

wide margin of appreciation in negotiating with the US authorities the content of the PNR regime. Therefore, the review of the necessity of the interference should 'be limited to determining whether there was any manifest error of assessment on the part of those two institutions. By carrying out a restricted review of that kind, the Court would thus avoid the pitfall of substituting its own assessment for that of the Community political authorities as to the nature of the most appropriate and expedient means of combating terrorism and other serious crimes.'[173] In this regard, the AG found that the list of 34 PNR data was not excessive, as 'the need to profile potential terrorists may require access to a large number of pieces of data;'[174] and the retention period of PNR data was not manifestly excessive bearing in mind that investigations conducted following terrorist attacks or other serious crimes sometimes last several years.[175] Therefore, he concluded that 'the Council and the Commission did not exceed the limits placed on their margin of appreciation when adopting the PNR regime.'[176]

b. The Judgment of the Court

The CJEU delivered its judgment in the PNR case on 30 May 2006. In a rather laconic reasoning, the Court agreed with the Advocate General that the Commission's adequacy decision was not adopted on the correct legal basis,[177] because the transfer of PNR data to the CBP did not constitute processing necessary for a supply of services, but processing necessary for safeguarding public security and law-enforcement purposes.[178] Therefore, it did not fall within the scope of the Data Protection Directive pursuant to the provision of Article 3(2).[179] The CJEU reached the same conclusion concerning the Council's decision. Article 95 EC could not justify Community competence to conclude the Agreement,[180] because this related to 'the same transfer of data as the decision on adequacy and therefore to data processing operations which … are excluded from the scope of the Directive.'[181] As a result, the CJEU annulled both the Commission's adequacy decision[182] and the Council's decision on the conclusion of the Agreement.[183] It was very careful, however, regarding the implications of its judgment.[184]

---

[173] ibid, para 231.
[174] ibid, para 238.
[175] ibid, para 242.
[176] ibid, para 254.
[177] Joined Cases C-317/04 and C-318/04 (*PNR*), n 158 above, para 60.
[178] ibid, para 57.
[179] ibid, para 59.
[180] ibid, para 67.
[181] ibid, para 69.
[182] ibid, para 61.
[183] ibid, para 70.
[184] J Rijpma and G Gilmore, 'Joined Cases C-317/04 and C-318/04, *European Parliament v. Council and Commission*, Judgment of the Grand Chamber of 30 May 2006, [2006] ECR I-4721' (2007) 44 *Common Market Law Review* 1081, 1087.

It preserved the effect of the adequacy decision for 90 days, until 30 September 2006, in order to allow the political institutions to negotiate a new arrangement.

The judgment of the Court of Justice brought forward new problems and controversies.[185] The European Parliament welcomed the annulment of the Council and the Commission decisions,[186] but regretted that the Court did not respond to its concerns about the legal structure of the agreement and the congruency of its content with the data protection principles.[187] Indeed, the decision of the Court was characterised as a 'Pyrrhic victory'[188] for the European Parliament. The annulment of the Community instruments as a basis for the PNR data transfer meant that the Agreement had to be renegotiated within the framework of the (former) third pillar, with all the consequences therein, among which was the limited role of the European Parliament itself.[189] For the European Data Protection Supervisor, therefore, the judgment created 'a loophole in the protection of European citizens whereby their data are used for law enforcement purposes.'[190] Along the same lines, for the Article 29 Working Party, the Court's ruling showed 'once more the difficulties arising from the artificial division between the pillars and the need for a consistent cross pillar data protection framework.'[191]

The Court seemed to have got it wrong everywhere. On the pillars issue, the PNR case was considered an example of the difficulty of allocating an international agreement to the correct legal base (and pillar), and of the consequences of getting it wrong.[192] On the distinction between 'commercial' and 'law enforcement' processing, despite the efforts of the Court to distinguish the two, the judgment failed ultimately to place the two Community measures under their corresponding processing regime.[193] The EC had nothing to do with the law enforcement

---

[185] See M Mendez, 'Passenger Name Record Agreement—European Court of Justice' (2007) 3 *European Constitutional Law Review* 127; Guild and Brouwer, n 90 above, p 3; M Botta and M Viola de Azevedo Cunha, 'La Protezione dei dati personali nelle relazioni tra UE e USA, Le Negoziazioni sul trasferimento dei PNR' (2010) XXVI *Il Diritto dell' Informazione e dell'Informatica* 315, 326.

[186] European Parliament, Committee on Civil Liberties, Justice and Home Affairs, 'Report with a proposal for a European Parliament Recommendation to the Council on the Negotiations for an Agreement with the United States of America on the use of Passenger Name Records (PNR) data to prevent and combat terrorism and transnational crime, including organised crime', 19 July 2006, (2006/2193(INI)) 4.

[187] ibid.

[188] Rijpma and Gilmore, n 184 above, p 1081.

[189] C Patton, 'No Man's Land: The EU-U.S. Passenger Name Record Agreement and What It Means for the European Union's Pillar Structure' (2008) 40 *George Washington International Law Review* 527, 539–40.

[190] European Data Protection Supervisor, Press Release, 'PNR: EDPS First Reaction to the Court of Justice Judgment' (2006).

[191] Art 29 WP, Opinion 5/2006 on the ruling by the European Court of Justice of 30 May 2006 in Joined Cases C-317/04 and C-318/04 on the transmission of Passenger Name Records to the United States, 3.

[192] M Cremona, 'EU External Action in the JHA Domain: A legal perspective' EUI Working Papers LAW 2008/24, 17.

[193] See De Hert and de Schutter, n 125 above, p 330.

processing of the PNR data. That was a demand by the US; the data would be used for counter-terrorism and law enforcement purposes only there. The EU data protection regime governed the initial processing of the data by the air carriers for commercial purposes.[194] As regards the EU's external relations, the judgment illustrated the extent to which EU internal inter-institutional and cross pillar conflicts[195] can affect its 'capacity to conduct meaningful relations with third countries'.[196] Finally, on the balance between fundamental rights and counter-terrorism, the Court got the worst of both worlds—even if, in fact it did not pronounce on the issue at all. On the one hand, the question of the potential fundamental rights infringements of the EU–US PNR Agreement was not discussed by the Court, despite being the Parliament's main plea. Furthermore, the fundamental rights ramifications of the judgment were severe: a new agreement had to be negotiated under a framework with significantly reduced fundamental rights' protection compared to the Community one. On the other hand, complaints voiced on the other side of the Atlantic alleged that by invalidating the decisions of the Commission and the Council, the CJEU had 'essentially sacrificed the security of both the United States and the European Union'.[197] According to this argument, PNR data was an 'important tool in combating crime and terrorism' and its lack could lead to a 'less secure environment' for both the US and the EU.[198]

B. The Second (Interim) EU–US PNR Agreement

Following the CJEU's decision, the Council and the Commission notified the US government on 3 July 2006 that the PNR Agreement had to be terminated with effect from 30 September 2006.[199] On 27 June 2006, the EU entered a second round of negotiations with the US administration to conclude a new PNR Agreement under the (former) third pillar. The actors conducting the negotiations on the EU's side were different this time. Instead of the Commission authorised

---

[194] See E Harris, 'Tradeoffs in Personal Data Privacy: A Swedish Church Lady, Austrian Public Radio Employees and Transatlantic Air Carriers Show That Europe Does Not Have the Answers' (2007) 22 *American University International Law Review* 745, 791–92.

[195] See B de Witte, 'Too Much Constitutional Law in the European Union's Foreign Relations?' in M Cremona and B de Witte (eds), *EU Foreign Relations Law: Constitutional Fundamentals* (Oxford, Hart Publishing, 2008) 3, 11.

[196] Rijpma and Gilmore, n 184 above, p 1096; V Serrano, 'Comment: The European Court of Justice's Decision to Annul the Agreement Between the United States and European Community Regarding the Transfer of Personal Name Record Data, Its Effects, and Recommendations for a New Solution' (2007) 13 *ILSA Journal of International & Comparative Law* 453, 468.

[197] Harris, n 194 above, p 793.

[198] ibid, p 794.

[199] Council Notice concerning the denunciation of the Agreement between the European Community and the United States of America on the processing and transfer of PNR data by air carriers to the United States Department of Homeland Security, Bureau of Customs and Border Protection, [2006] OJ C219/1.

by the Council—as was the case in the 2004 PNR Agreement—this time it was the Presidency assisted by the Commission, according to Article 24(1) TEU. On 6 October 2006 the negotiations were completed and on 16 October 2006, the Council authorised the Presidency to sign the Agreement.[200] The Agreement was signed on behalf of the US at Washington DC on 19 October 2006 and applied provisionally from the same date.[201] The Agreement, unless otherwise terminated, would remain into force until 31 July 2007.[202]

The 2006 Interim Agreement comprised of seven points and did not seem to add anything to its 2004 predecessor, apart from Point 1 which read as follows:

> In reliance upon DHS's continued implementation of the aforementioned Undertakings *as interpreted in the light of subsequent events*, the European Union shall ensure that air carriers operating passenger flights in foreign air transportation to or from the United States of America process PNR data contained in their reservation systems as required by DHS.[203]

The phrase 'as interpreted in the light of subsequent events' referred to the letter sent by Stewart Baker, Assistant Secretary for Policy at the DHS, to the Presidency and the Commission (the 'Baker letter')[204] concerning the US administration's 'understandings with regard to the interpretation of a number of provisions'[205] of the 2004 PNR Undertakings, since 'things have changed in Washington in the last couple of years'.[206] The Baker letter in essence introduced a number of unilateral changes to the 2004 Undertakings[207] rendering the US's commitments under the Interim Agreement 'markedly different from those under the 2004 Agreement.'[208]

Under the new US understanding of the Undertakings, PNR data would be shared with further government authorities, besides the DHS, in order to fight terrorism.[209] For PNR data 'pulled' from the airlines, the US authorities reserved

---

[200] Council Decision 2006/729/CFSP/JHA of 16 October 2006 on the signing, on behalf of the European Union, of an Agreement between the European Union and the United States of America on the processing and transfer of passenger name record (PNR) data by air carriers to the United States Department of Homeland Security, [2006] OJ L298/27.

[201] See Point 7 of the Agreement between the European Union and the United States of America on the processing and transfer of passenger name record (PNR) data by air carriers to the United States Department of Homeland Security, [2006] OJ L298/29 and Art 3 of Council Decision 2006/729/CFSP/JHA.

[202] ibid.

[203] Emphasis added.

[204] Letter to the Council Presidency and the Commission from the Department of Homeland Security (DHS) of the United States of America, concerning the interpretation of certain provisions of the undertakings issued by DHS on 11 May 2004 in connection with the transfer by air carriers of passenger name record (PNR) data, [2006] OJ C259/1.

[205] ibid.

[206] See Jonathan Faul testimony in House of Lords European Union Committee, n 2 above, para 60.

[207] See E Guild, 'Inquiry into the EU-US Passenger Name Record Agreement', CEPS, Policy Brief No 125, March 2007.

[208] House of Lords European Union Committee, n 2 above, para 60.

[209] Letter to the Council Presidency and the Commission, n 204 above. See also the Preamble of the Interim Agreement.

the right to obtain them more than 72 hours prior to the departure of a flight.[210] Moreover, PNR data could be used for further purposes than fighting terrorism and international crime in order to protect the 'vital interests' of the data subject or of other persons. According to the Baker letter, 'vital interests' encompassed circumstances in which the lives of the data subject or of others could be at stake and included access to information necessary to ensure that those who might have been exposed to a dangerous communicable disease could be readily identified, located, and informed without delay.[211] The reference to the retention periods of PNR data in the Baker letter was confusing. The letter started by pointing out that 'several important uses for PNR data help to identify potential terrorists; even data that is more than 3.5 years old can be crucial in identifying links among terrorism suspects.'[212] It then went on to explain that Undertaking 15 of the 2004 Agreement might have required the destruction of data, but nevertheless questions of whether and when to destroy PNR data collected in accordance with the Undertakings would be addressed by the United States and the European Union as part of future discussions.[213] This suggested that CBP had no intention of deleting the PNR data after the 3.5-year period, even when collected under the (previous) 2004 Agreement.[214]

C. The Third EU–US PNR Agreement

i. The 2007 PNR Agreement

With the Interim PNR Agreement deemed to expire on 31 July 2007, the EU had to start a new round of negotiations with the United States for a new agreement. On 22 February 2007, the Council authorised the Presidency, assisted by the Commission, to open negotiations for a long-term PNR agreement. The Parliament, having noted that 'a future agreement must have more democratic legitimacy, with the full involvement of the European Parliament and/or ratification by national parliaments',[215] called for an assessment of the effectiveness of the previous agreements before the adoption of a new one[216] and asked that the principles of purpose limitation[217] and proportionality,[218] as well as the rights to information, access and rectification of the data subjects, be respected.[219] In an attempt to exercise

---

[210] ibid.
[211] ibid.
[212] ibid.
[213] ibid.
[214] See House of Lords European Union Committee, n 2 above, paras 67, 69, 71–72.
[215] European Parliament resolution on SWIFT, the PNR agreement and the transatlantic dialogue on these issues P6_TA(2007)0039.
[216] ibid.
[217] ibid.
[218] ibid.
[219] ibid.

some political pressure, the US Secretary of Homeland Security Michael Chertoff addressed, on 14 May 2007, the LIBE Committee of the European Parliament, stating that PNR data transfer is 'a tool which at minimal cost of civil liberty has the tremendous potential to save lives.'[220]

On 28 June 2007 the draft agreement between the EU and the US was sent to the European Parliament LIBE Committee. In its July 2007 Resolution, the Parliament having expressed its disappointment on 'the lack of democratic oversight of any kind'[221] concerning the new Agreement, which was 'negotiated and agreed without any involvement of the European Parliament and leaving insufficient opportunity for national parliaments to exercise any influence over the negotiating mandate',[222] concluded that the draft agreement was 'substantively flawed in terms of legal certainty, data protection and legal redress for EU citizens, in particular as a result of open and vague definitions and multiple possibilities for exceptions.'[223]

Despite the Parliament's objections, the Agreement was signed on 23 July 2007.[224] Following the general pattern of the previous PNR Agreements, the text of the 2007 Agreement was not consolidated in a unique document. As Commissioner Franco Frattini explained, the agreement was divided into three parts: first, an agreement signed by both parties; second, a letter which the United States sent to the EU in which it set out assurances on the way in which it would handle European PNR data in the future; third, a letter from the EU to the United States acknowledging the receipt of assurances and confirming that on that basis it considered the level of protection afforded by the US Department of Homeland Security to be adequate for European PNR data.[225] This form, while not new in the PNR context (letter of Undertakings in the first PNR, Baker letter in the Interim PNR Agreement), raised again concerns, especially as regards the legal nature of the DHS letter and its relationship with the Agreement.[226]

As regards its substance, the 2007 Agreement[227] appeared unbalanced; while obligations were imposed on the EU side, the US authorities provided mere

---

[220] US Homeland Security Secretary Michael Chertoff's Address before the Civil Liberties Committee of the European Parliament, Brussels 14 May 2007.

[221] European Parliament resolution of 12 July 2007 on the PNR agreement with the United States of America P6_TA-PROV(2007)0347.

[222] ibid.

[223] ibid.

[224] Council Decision 2007/551/CFSP/JHA of 23 July 2007 on the signing, on behalf of the European Union, of an Agreement between the European Union and the United States of America on the processing and transfer of Passenger Name Record (PNR) data by air carriers to the United States Department of Homeland Security (DHS) (2007 PNR Agreement), [2007] OJ L204/16.

[225] European Parliament Debates, Monday, 9 July 2007, Strasbourg, www.europarl.europa.eu/sides/getDoc.do?pubRef=-//EP//TEXT+CRE+20070709+ITEM-018+DOC+XML+V0//EN&language=EN.

[226] European Parliament resolution, n 221 above.

[227] Agreement between the European Union and the United States of America on the processing and transfer of Passenger Name Record (PNR) data by air carriers to the United States Department of Homeland Security (DHS) (2007 PNR Agreement) [2007] OJ L204/18.

'assurances'[228] on the use of the data.[229] The DHS letter, intended to explain how the US Department of Homeland Security handled the collection, use and storage of PNR data,[230] appeared to be the most important part of the Agreement. Concerning the purposes for the collection of PNR data, the Baker letter had already broadened these beyond the prevention and combating of terrorism and other serious crimes, to the protection of the vital interests of the data subject or other persons. The DHS letter confirmed this[231] and added that PNR data could be further used where necessary in any criminal judicial proceedings, or as otherwise required by law.[232] The DHS letter also clarified that PNR data could be exchanged with government authorities in third countries 'in support of counterterrorism, transnational crime and public security related cases (including threats, flights, individuals and routes of concern) they are examining or investigating.'[233] Consequently, the EU could 'not interfere with relationships between the United States and third countries for the exchange of passenger information on data protection grounds.'[234] The categories of PNR data collected were reduced from 34 in the 2004 Agreement to 19. This reduction, however, was characterised by the European Parliament as 'cosmetic', since it essentially merged the 34 categories into 19 data fields.[235] Article 29 Working Party's examination suggested even an extension of the data transmitted to the DHS.[236] Furthermore, the DHS letter assured that sensitive data collected would be filtered and promptly deleted, unless there was an exceptional case 'where the life of a data subject or of others could be imperilled or seriously impaired'.[237] In this case, sensitive data could be accessed and used by DHS officials, and deleted 'within 30 days once the purpose for which it has been accessed is accomplished and its retention is not required by law'.[238] The overall retention period of the data prescribed in the 2007 Agreement was 15 years: seven years in an active analytical database[239] and eight years in a dormant, non-operational status.[240] According to the DHS letter, this retention period

---

[228] See European Parliament resolution, n 221 above and Papakonstantinou and de Hert, n 122 above, pp 909–10.

[229] See for instance 2007 EU–US PNR Agreement, Art 1.

[230] DHS letter.

[231] ibid, Art I.

[232] ibid. This change of the scope of the Agreement was criticised by the Art 29 Working Party. See Art 29 WP, Opinion 5/2007 on the Follow-up Agreement between the European Union and the United States of America on the processing and transfer of Passenger Name Record (PNR) data by air carriers to the United States Department of Homeland Security concluded in July 2007.

[233] ibid, Art II. For criticism see European Parliament resolution, n 221 above.

[234] Art 6 of the Agreement.

[235] ibid.

[236] See Art 29 WP, Opinion 5/2007, n 232 above.

[237] DHS letter, Art III.

[238] ibid.

[239] The length of the retention period was strongly criticised by the European Parliament. See European Parliament resolution of 12 July 2007 on the PNR agreement with the United States of America, n 227 above.

[240] ibid. DHS letter, Art VII. The DHS letter was not very clear, however, on the deletion of the PNR data after the 15-year period.

also applied to the PNR data collected on the basis of the 2004 and 2006 Agreements, raising questions as to whether the data collected under the two previous agreements were ever deleted in the respective periods required by those Agreements. Concerning the never resolved issue of the use of a 'push' system for the transfer of the data,[241] the DHS letter noted that 13 airlines had implemented it, and the responsibility rested with the remaining air carriers to migrate their systems and comply with DHS' technical requirements. For the airlines that did not implement such a system, the 'pull' system remained in effect.[242] Insofar as the data subjects' rights were concerned, the DHS letter extended administrative Privacy Act protections to 'PNR data stored in the ATS regardless of the nationality or country of residence of the data subject, including data that relates to European citizens.'[243] Individuals also had the right to access the data held on them in accordance with the US Privacy Act and the US Freedom of Information Act (FOIA).[244]

The EU's reply to the DHS letter formed part of the 2007 Agreement, but did not add any substantial point itself.[245] It merely noted that 'the assurances explained in [the DHS] letter allow the European Union to deem … that DHS ensures an adequate level of data protection.'[246] The same verbal economy applied to the agreement, which contained only nine Articles. The most ambiguous provision of the Agreement was Article 5, which read as follows:

> By this Agreement, DHS expects that it is not being asked to undertake data protection measures in its PNR system that are more stringent than those applied by European authorities for their domestic PNR systems. DHS does not ask European authorities to adopt data protection measures in their PNR systems that are more stringent than those applied by the U.S. for its PNR system. If its expectation is not met, DHS reserves the right to suspend relevant provisions of the DHS letter while conducting consultations with the EU with a view to reaching a prompt and satisfactory resolution.

The language of this provision cannot go unnoticed: it represented a unilateral statement by the US authorities warning the EU on its future positions regarding PNR negotiations.[247]

From a fundamental rights point of view, the 2007 PNR Agreement did 'not stand a chance'.[248] It 'markedly weakened' the safeguards provided by its predecessors, which were already considered 'weak' themselves, and contained 'too many emergency exceptions' and shortcomings.[249]

---

[241] See European Parliament resolution, n 221 above; Art 29 WP, Opinion 5/2007, n 232 above.
[242] DHS letter, Art VIII.
[243] ibid, Art IV.
[244] ibid.
[245] The value of the EU's reply letter to DHS has been questioned. See Papakonstantinou and de Hert, n 122 above, p 910.
[246] EU letter to US.
[247] See Art 29 WP, Opinion 5/2007, n 232 above.
[248] Papakonstantinou and de Hert, n 122 above, p 913.
[249] Art 29 WP, Opinion 5/2007, n 232 above.

*ii. The Implementation of the 2007 PNR Agreement: An Insight into
the DHS Privacy Office Report*

On 18 December 2008, the DHS Privacy Office published its Report concerning Passenger Name Record Information derived from flights between the US and the EU.[250] The purpose of the report was to determine whether DHS and, in particular, the US Customs and Border Protection (CBP) were operating 'in compliance with the Automated Targeting System (ATS) System of Records Notice (SORN) published on August 6, 2007 in the Federal Register and the 2007 Letter of Agreement between the United States and the Council of the European Union dated July 26, 2007 (2007 Letter).'[251] ATS SORN was adopted by the DHS in order to implement the provisions of the 2007 PNR Agreement.[252]

A closer examination of the ATS SORN reveals several inconsistencies with the 'assurances' laid down in the DHS letter. For instance, on the issue of the sharing of PNR data, the DHS letter provided that 'DHS shares EU PNR data only for the purposes named in Article I.'[253] However, ATS SORN stated that 'in addition to those disclosures generally permitted under 5 U.S.C. 552a (b) of the Privacy Act, all or a portion of the records or information contained in this system may be disclosed outside DHS as a *routine use* pursuant to 5 U.S.C. 552a (b)(3).'[254] This meant that PNR data was shared with a variety of authorities outside DHS, including federal, state, local, tribal, or foreign governmental agencies or multilateral governmental organisations; federal and foreign government intelligence or counterterrorism agencies; and organisations or individuals in either the public or private sector, for purposes ranging from fighting terrorism or potential threats to national or international security to assisting enforcement of applicable civil or criminal laws, protecting the life, property, or other vital interests of a data subject and preventing exposure to or transmission of a communicable or quarantinable disease or combatting other significant public health threats.[255] The disclosure of PNR data to other US authorities for routine (and not case-by-case, use, as was envisaged in the previous Agreements), was not mentioned anywhere in the DHS letter. According to Report, the DHS Privacy Office found that in addition to the types of terrorism related, flights from warrants related, and transnational crimes related disclosures, PNR data was 'regularly shared by the National Targeting Centre (NTC-P) with the Centre for Disease Control (CDC) to properly coordinate appropriate responses to health concerns associated with international air transportation.'[256]

---

[250] US Department of Homeland Security, Privacy Office, n 23 above.

[251] ibid, p 4.

[252] ibid. See also M Yano, 'Come Fly the (Unfriendly) Skies: Negotiating Passenger Name Record Agreements Between the United States and European Union' (2010) 5 *I/S Journal of Law and Policy* 479, 501.

[253] DHS letter, Art II.

[254] See US Department of Homeland Security, Privacy Office, n 23 above, p 15. Emphasis added.

[255] ibid.

[256] See Routine Uses A, B, C and D USC § 552a (b)(1), (b)(3), b(8) and (e)(10).

Concerning the extension by the DHS letter of the rights of access and redress of individuals that was much 'triumphed over by the European side',[257] the Privacy Office reviewed seven requests for PNR data and three other requests related to searches for all information held by CBP. According to the Report, 'the requests for PNR took more than one year to process and were inconsistent in what information was redacted.'[258] A similar conclusion was also reached in the February 2010 joint review of the 2007 Agreement.[259] Finally, ATS SORN confirmed the concerns raised in the EU about the retention periods of the collected PNR data[260] by clearly stating that data were not be deleted even after the 15-year retention period if it is related to a specific case or investigation.[261]

D. The Fourth EU–US PNR Agreement

i. *The 2012 EU–US PNR Agreement*

Following the entry into force of the Lisbon Treaty in December 2009, the Council sent the 2007 EU–US PNR Agreement to the European Parliament requesting its consent for the conclusion pursuant to Article 218 TFEU. The Parliament adopted a Resolution[262] on 5 May 2010 in which it decided to postpone its vote on the requested consent and requested the negotiation of a new EU–US PNR Agreement[263] that would comply with certain fundamental rights requirements in accordance with the EUCFR, which had become by then binding EU primary law. After negotiations between the EU and the US, a new PNR Agreement was initialled by the Commission in November 2011[264] and adopted by the Council 13 December 2011. Both the EDPS[265] and the Working Party[266] voiced their

---

[257] Papakonstantinou and de Hert, n 122 above, p 912.

[258] US Department of Homeland Security, Privacy Office, n 23 above, p 26. Exercising a right to access to PNR data was also found to be almost impossible, given the complexity of the procedure.

[259] Report on the Joint Review of the implementation of the Agreement between the European Union and the United States of America on the processing and transfer of Passenger Name Record (PNR) data by air carriers to the United States Department of Homeland Security (DHS) 8–9 February 2010, 7 April 2010, 11.

[260] See above.

[261] US Department of Homeland Security, Privacy Office, n 23 above, p 30.

[262] European Parliament resolution of 5 May 2010 on the launch of negotiations for Passenger Name Record (PNR) agreements with the United States, Australia and Canada, P7_TA(2010)0144.

[263] ibid.

[264] Proposal for a Council Decision on the conclusion of the Agreement between the United States of America and the European Union on the use and transfer of Passenger Name Records to the United States Department of Homeland Security, COM(2011) 807 final.

[265] Opinion of the European Data Protection Supervisor on the Proposal for a Council Decision on the conclusion of the Agreement between the United States of America and the European Union on the use and transfer of Passenger Name Records to the United States Department of Homeland Security, 9 December 2011.

[266] Art 29 Working Party Letter to the LIBE Committee of the European Parliament, 6 January 2012, Ref Ares(2012)15841-06/01/2012. See also European Commission Legal Service, Note for the Attention

concerns regarding the draft Agreement, which they considered that it incorporated only 'modest improvements'[267] compared to its predecessors. In her Report to the LIBE Committee,[268] rapporteur Sophie In't Veld MEP recommended the European Parliament should withhold its consent to the conclusion of the Agreement, on the basis that this did not fulfil 'to a satisfactory level' the criteria laid down in the EP's Resolution of 5 May 2010.[269] Nevertheless, the Agreement was approved by the LIBE Committee with 31 votes in favour, 23 against and one abstention[270] and finally adopted by the European Parliament on 19 April 2012. The new Agreement[271] entered into force on 1 July 2012, replacing the previous one from 2007 and due to expire in seven years.[272]

In terms of form, the 2012 EU–US PNR Agreement resembles more an international agreement than all its predecessors. All its provisions are included in the text of the Agreement itself without any Undertakings or side letters. In terms of substance, however, little has changed. Article 4 of the Agreement determines the use of PNR data for the purposes of preventing, detecting, investigating and prosecuting 'terrorist offences and related crime',[273] and 'other crimes that are punishable by a sentence of imprisonment of three years or more and that are transnational in nature'.[274] 'Terrorist offences and related crime' are defined with reference to European standards, but the definition of 'other transnational crimes punishable by a sentence of imprisonment of three years or more' lacks clarity. There are different crimes that are punishable by imprisonment of more than three years in the US and in the various EU Member States, and even minor offences could fall within this definition.[275] This concern is exacerbated by the wide-ranging definition of 'transnational crimes', which includes crimes 'committed in one country and the offender is in or intends to travel to another country'.[276] Paragraphs (2), (3) and (4) of Article 4 open up further the scope of PNR data to uses that go beyond terrorism and transnational crime. Article 4(2) provides that

---

of Mr Stefano Manservisi Director General, DG HOME, Subject: Draft Agreement on the Use of Passenger Name Records (PNR) between the EU and the United States, SJ1 (2011) 603245, 18 May 2011.

[267] ibid, p 1.
[268] Draft Recommendation on the draft Council decision on the conclusion of the Agreement between the United States of America and the European Union on the use and transfer of Passenger Name Records (PNR) to the United States Department of Homeland Security (17433/2011—C7-... –2011/0382(NLE)) of 30.1.2012.
[269] ibid.
[270] See Press Release, 'Civil Liberties Committee green light for air passenger data deal with the US', www.europarl.europa.eu/pdfs/news/expert/infopress/20120326IPR41838/20120326IPR41838_en.pdf.
[271] Agreement between the United States of America and the European Union on the use and transfer of passenger name records to the United States Department of Homeland Security, [2012] OJ L215/5.
[272] ibid, Art 26(1).
[273] ibid, Art 4(1)(a).
[274] ibid, Art 4 (1) (b).
[275] See EDPS Opinion, n 265 above, p 4.
[276] 2012 EU–US PNR Agreement, Art 2(1)(b)(v).

PNR data can be used 'on a case-by-case basis' where necessary in view of a serious threat and for the protection of vital interests of any individual or if ordered by a court. Article 4(3) states that PNR data be used for border control purposes 'to identify persons who would be subject to closer questioning or examination upon arrival to or departure from the United States or who may require further examination.' This suggests that PNR data is used for border control purposes[277]— as the Commission indeed notes in the FAQ on the 2012 Agreement.[278] Finally, Article 4(4) allows for the use of PNR data for 'domestic law enforcement, judicial powers, or proceedings, where other violations of law or indications thereof are detected in the course of the use and processing of PNR.'

Regarding the PNR data transferred to the US, the Agreement contains 19 data categories—identical to the 2007 Agreement—which were deemed disproportionate by the EDPS and the WP.[279] Carriers are required to transfer PNR data to DHS initially at 96 hours before the scheduled flight departure and additionally either in real time or for a fixed number of routine and scheduled transfers.[280] The Agreement provides that all air carriers should be required to acquire the technical ability to use the 'push' method not later than 24 months following its entry into force,[281] thus, raising doubts whether the 'push' system was ever fully implemented in the previous EU–US PNR Agreements.[282] Sensitive data are not deleted under the 2012 Agreement, but filtered and masked out and can be accessed and processed in exceptional circumstances where the life of an individual could be imperilled or seriously impaired.[283] The data retention period continues to be 15 years, this time under a different arrangement: DHS retains PNR data in an active database for five years; after the initial six months of this period, data are depersonalised and masked and transferred to a dormant database for another 10 years.[284] It is not clear from the 2012 Agreement whether PNR data would be deleted after the 15-year retention period. In fact, Article 8(4) provides that, following this period, data 'must be rendered fully anonymised'. This is puzzling given, as the WP noted, 'the difficulty of truly anonymising data and the lack of further explaining why the (anonymised) data is still needed.'[285] While the Agreement requires the DHS to provide information to the travelling public regarding its use and processing of PNR data through publications in the Federal Register, on its website, notices that may be incorporated by the carriers into contracts of carriage, statutorily required

---

[277] Art 29 WP Letter to LIBE Committee, n 266 above, p 2.
[278] European Commission Memo, 'Frequently asked questions: The EU–US agreement on the transfer of Passenger Name Record (PNR) data', 27 November 2013, http://europa.eu/rapid/press-release_MEMO-13-1054_en.htm.
[279] EDPS Opinion, n 265 above.
[280] 2012 EU–US PNR Agreement, Art 15(3).
[281] ibid, Art 15(4).
[282] Art 29 WP Letter to LIBE Committee, n 266 above, p 4.
[283] 2012 EU–US PNR Agreement, Art 6.
[284] ibid, Art 8.
[285] Art 29 WP Letter to LIBE Committee, n 266 above, p 3.

reporting to Congress and other appropriate measures,[286] there have been no significant improvements regarding the individual's access and redress rights. The Agreement stipulates that individuals have a right to request their PNR data from DHS[287]—but not the right to know if these have been processed—to correct and rectify such data,[288] and to seek 'effective administrative and judicial redress in accordance with US law'.[289] This entails the right to 'administratively challenge DHS decisions related to the use and processing of PNR'[290] and 'petition for judicial review in US federal court of any final agency action by DHS.'[291] Nevertheless, Article 21 explicitly states that the Agreement does 'not create or confer, under US law, any right or benefit on any person or entity, private or public.' Finally, the 2012 Agreement provides for a joint review of its implementation.[292]

On the basis of these provisions, Article 19 stipulates that DHS is deemed to provide, within the meaning of relevant EU data protection law, an adequate level of protection for PNR data processing and use and carriers which have provided PNR data to DHS in compliance with the Agreement are deemed to have complied with applicable EU legal requirements.

Besides its specific shortcomings analysed above, the Agreement does not address the general concern raised by the EP in its 2010 Resolution regarding the necessity and proportionality of bulk transfers of PNR data in general. There is no empirical evidence on the effectiveness of the use of PNR data to fight terrorism and transnational organised crime and no Privacy Impact Assessment as requested by the European Parliament. There are also doubts that the Agreement complies with EU fundamental rights after the CJEU's judgments in *Digital Rights Ireland*[293] and *Schrems*.

Besides the EU–US Agreement, the EU has also signed bilateral PNR agreements with Canada and Australia.[294] The latest EU–Canada PNR agreement was signed on 25 June 2014[295] and the Council has requested the Parliament's approval for the conclusion of the Agreement. On 25 November 2014, the Parliament asked

---

[286] 2012 EU–US PNR Agreement, Art 10.

[287] ibid, Art 11.

[288] ibid, Art 12.

[289] ibid, Art 13.

[290] ibid, Art 13 (2).

[291] ibid, Art 13 (3).

[292] ibid, Art 23.

[293] Joined Cases C-293/12 and C-594/12 *Digital Rights Ireland Ltd v Minister for Communications, Marine and Natural Resources* [2014] ECR I-238.

[294] Agreement between the European Union and Australia on the processing and transfer of Passenger Name Record (PNR) data by air carriers to the Australian Customs and Border Protection Service, [2012] OJ L186/4.

[295] Proposal for a Council Decision on the conclusion of the Agreement between Canada and the European Union on the transfer and processing of Passenger Name Record Data (COM(2013) 528 final).

the Court to provide an Opinion on a number of questions concerning the compatibility of this agreement with primary EU law and the appropriate legal basis for the Council decision on its conclusion.[296] The Court's Opinion is still pending at the time of writing, but Advocate General Mengozzi in his Opinion delivered on 8 September 2016,[297] formulated a number of recommendations regarding the draft agreement and found that certain of its provisions were incompatible with Articles 7 and 8 EUCFR.[298] His pronouncements to the extent that they are relevant to the present discussion are examined below.

III. THE US PRIVACY REGIME

It has been argued on both sides of the Atlantic that 'the drama that played out between the United States and the European Union over PNR-data transfers is a prominent example of the clash between conflicting philosophies on privacy protection.'[299] Indeed, American scholars have criticised the strict pro-privacy stance adopted by the EU in the PNR negotiations as detrimental to the efforts of preventing terrorism.[300] Before turning to the substantive analysis of travel data surveillance, it is worth taking a look at the US privacy regime, at the attempts to create a transatlantic data protection framework, and at the EU's own travel data surveillance PNR programme.

A. The Constitutional Protection of Privacy

Legal scholar Gregory Shaffer noted with regard to the US privacy regime: 'data privacy regulation in the United States is fragmented, *ad hoc*, and narrowly targeted to cover specific sectors and concerns. It is decentralised and uncoordinated, involving standard setting and enforcement by a wide variety of actors, including federal and state legislatures, agencies and courts, industry associations, individual companies, and market forces.'[301] US privacy law can be found in a number of

---

[296] Opinion 1/15 Request for an opinion submitted by the European Parliament, pending.

[297] Opinion of AG Mengozzi in Opinion 1/15, delivered on 8 September 2016.

[298] ibid, para 328(3).

[299] Rasmussen, n 3 above, p 588. See also F Mendez and M Mendez, 'Comparing Privacy Regimes: Federal Theory and the Politics of Privacy Regulation in the European Union and the United States' (2009) 40 *Publius: The Journal of Federalism* 617; A Shoenberger, 'Privacy Wars: EU Versus US: Scattered Skirmishes, Storm Clouds Ahead' (2007) 17 *Indiana International & Comparative Law Review* 375; P Swire, 'The Second Wave of Global Privacy Protection: Symposium Introduction' (2013) 74 (6) *Ohio State Law Journal* 841.

[300] J Rosen, 'Continental Divide: Americans See Privacy as a Protection of Liberty, Europeans as a Protection of Dignity. Will One Conception Trump the Other—or Are Both Destined to Perish?' (2004) *Legal Affairs*, https://legalaffairs.org/issues/September-October-2004/review_rosen_sepoct04.msp.

[301] G Shaffer, 'Globalization and Social Protection: The Impact of EU and International Rules in the Ratcheting up of U.S. Data Privacy Standards' (2000) 25 *Yale Journal of International Law* 1, 22.

different sources: the US Constitution, Supreme Court case law, federal legislation, state legislation and the theory of torts.[302] The first two that are most pertinent to the present discussion are analysed below.

The Constitutional protection of privacy is mainly based on the First Amendment (protection of free speech and freedom of assembly), the Fourth Amendment (protection from unreasonable searches and seizures), and the Fifth Amendment (privilege against self-incrimination).[303] As the Supreme Court has stated, 'the overriding function of the Fourth Amendment is to protect personal privacy and dignity against unwarranted intrusion by the State.'[304] In particular, the Fourth Amendment provides:

> The right of the people to be secure in their persons, houses, papers, and effects, against unreasonable searches and seizures, shall not be violated, and no Warrants shall issue, but upon probable cause, supported by Oath or affirmation, and particularly describing the place to be searched, and the persons or things to be seized.[305]

The Fourth Amendment contains two clauses: the first, the substantive one, protects against certain government activities; the second, the procedural one, regulates government power through the process of obtaining a warrant.[306] A warrant can be obtained when there is a 'probable cause' for conducting a search or seizure.[307] In *Olmstead v United States*,[308] the Supreme Court held that wiretaps attached to telephone wires on the public streets did not constitute a Fourth Amendment search, because '[t]here was no entry of the houses or offices of the defendants'. In *Katz v United States*,[309] the Court stated that the Fourth Amendment 'protects people, not places' and established that the protection of the Fourth Amendment against government intrusion applies, when an individual has a 'reasonable expectation of privacy'.[310] Justice Harlan in his concurring opinion in

---

[302] Papakonstantinou and de Hert, n 122, p 892.

[303] S Brenner, 'Constitutional Rights and New Technologies in the United States' in R Leenes, BJ Koops and P De Hert (eds), *Constitutional Rights and new technologies: A comparative Study* (The Hague, TMC Asser Press, Distributed by Cambridge University Press, 2008) 225, 230.

[304] *Schmerber v California*, 384 US 757 (1966). It should be noted, however, that the Fourth Amendment has not been interpreted to afford a 'comprehensive right to personal data protection'. See F Bignami, 'The US legal system on data protection in the field of law enforcement. Safeguards, rights and remedies for EU citizens', Study for the LIBE Committee, PE 519.215, Brussels, European Union, 2015, 8.

[305] US Constitution, IV Amendment.

[306] D Solove, 'Digital Dossiers and the Dissipation of Fourth Amendment Privacy' (2002) 75 *Southern California Law Review* 1083, 1118.

[307] D Solove and P Schwartz, *Information Privacy Law* (New York, Wolters Kluwer Law & Business, 2009) 237. In *Riley v California* 134 S Ct 2473 (2014), the Supreme Court held that law officers must obtain a warrant to search data on a mobile phone seized from an individual at the time of arrest.

[308] *Olmstead v United States* 277 US 438 (1928).

[309] See C Slobogin, *Privacy at Risk: The New Government Surveillance and the Fourth Amendment* (Chicago, University of Chicago Press, 2007) 13.

[310] *Katz v United States*, 389 US 347 (1967).

Katz articulated the twofold requirement, known as the 'reasonable expectation of privacy test'[311] that triggers the application of the Fourth Amendment:

> first, that a person have exhibited an actual (subjective) expectation of privacy and, second, that the expectation be one that society is prepared to recognise as 'reasonable'.[312]

This means, according to Justice Harlan, that 'conversations in the open would not be protected against being overheard, for the expectation of privacy under the circumstances would be unreasonable.'[313] A similar statement was made by the majority opinion, which held that 'what a person knowingly exposes to the public, even in his own home or office, is not a subject of Fourth Amendment protection.'[314] On this basis, the Court has found that US citizens lack a reasonable expectation of privacy in open fields,[315] anything they say to a friend,[316] their bank records,[317] and their garbage.[318] More recently, the Court held in *United States v Jones*[319] that the use of Global Positioning System (GPS) monitoring technology combined with a physical intrusion upon private property constitutes a search, and therefore requires a warrant.[320]

In *Smith v Maryland*,[321] the Court applied the *Katz* reasoning on phone records. The police, without a warrant, asked the telephone company to install a pen register[322] to record the numbers dialled from the defendant's home.[323] The Court found that there was no reasonable expectation of privacy regarding the numbers someone dials on his phone. The Court reasoned:

> First, we doubt that people in general entertain any actual expectation of privacy in the numbers they dial. All users realise that they must 'convey' phone numbers to the telephone company, since it is through telephone company switching equipment that their calls are completed. All subscribers realise, moreover, that the phone company has facilities for making permanent records of the numbers they dial, for they see a list of their long-distance (toll) calls on their monthly bills. In fact, pen registers and similar devices are routinely used by telephone companies 'for the purposes of checking billing

---

[311] C Slobogin and J Schumacher, 'Reasonable Expectations of Privacy and Autonomy in Fourth Amendment Cases: An Empirical Look at Understandings Recognized and Permitted by Society' (1993) 42 *Duke Law Journal* 727, 731.

[312] *Katz*, n 310 above, Justice John Harlan concurring.

[313] ibid.

[314] ibid.

[315] *Oliver v United States* 466 US 170 (1984).

[316] *United States v White* [1971] 401 US 745.

[317] *United States v Miller* [1976] 425 US 435, 437.

[318] *California v Greenwood* [1988] 486 US 3.

[319] *United States v Jones*, 132 S Ct 948–49 (2012).

[320] E Raviv, 'Homing In: Technology's Place in Fourth Amendment Jurisprudence' (2015) 28 (2) *Harvard Journal of Law & Technology* 593, 596; F Cate and B Cate, 'The Supreme Court and information privacy' (2012) 2 (4) *International Data Privacy Law* 255.

[321] *Smith v Maryland* US 735 (1979).

[322] A pen register is a device that records outgoing telephone calls.

[323] Solove, n 306 above, p 1134; O Kerr, 'The Fourth Amendment and New Technologies: Constitutional Myths and the Case for Caution', (2004) 102 *Michigan Law Review* 801.

operations, detecting fraud and preventing violations of law.' … Telephone users, in sum, typically know that they must convey numerical information to the phone company; that the company has facilities for recording this information; and that the phone company does in fact record this information for a variety of legitimate business purposes. Although subjective expectations cannot be scientifically gauged, it is too much to believe that telephone subscribers, under these circumstances, harbour any general expectation that the numbers they dial will remain secret.[324]

Smith v Maryland established, therefore, a general rule, also known as the 'third party doctrine', according to which, 'if information is in the hands of third parties, then an individual can have no reasonable expectation of privacy in that information, which means that the Fourth Amendment does not apply.'[325] As Christopher Slobogin noted, this decision suggests that 'transaction surveillance'[326] is immune from the restrictions of the Fourth Amendment.[327]

The third party doctrine has been praised as ensuring 'technological neutrality in Fourth Amendment rules', by preventing criminals from conducting their crimes privately and subsequently hiding the public aspects of those crimes.[328] However, there have also been criticisms of the third party doctrine,[329] alleging that it was articulated before data storage in the modern information era and gives the government too much power in areas where individuals can reasonable expect privacy, such as bank records, phone records, and other third-party records.[330] In her concurrence in *United States v Jones,* Justice Sotomayor voiced concerns regarding 'technological advances that have made possible nontresspassory surveillance techniques', such as GPS monitoring which can generate 'a precise, comprehensive record of a person's public movements that reflects a wealth of detail about her familial, political, professional, religious, and sexual associations.'[331] In this respect, Justice Sotomayor called for a reconsideration 'of the premise that an individual has no reasonable expectation of privacy in information voluntarily disclosed to third parties.' According to Justice Sotomayor,

This approach is ill suited to the digital age, in which people reveal a great deal of information about themselves to third parties in the course of carrying out mundane tasks. People disclose the phone numbers that they dial or text to their cellular providers; the URLs that they visit and the e-mail addresses with which they correspond to their Internet service providers; and the books, groceries, and medications they purchase to

---

[324] *Smith v Maryland*, n 321 above.

[325] See Solove, n 306 above, p 1135.

[326] Slobogin explains that 'transaction surveillance involves accessing *recorded* information about communications, activities, and other transactions'. See Slobogin, n 309 above, p 3.

[327] ibid, p 16.

[328] O Kerr, 'The Case for the Third-Party Doctrine', (2009) 107 *Michigan Law Review* 561, 561.

[329] D Bedley, 'A Look at the Proposed Electronic Communications Privacy Act Amendments Act of 2011: Where is Smart Grid Technology, and How Does Inevitable Discovery Apply?' (2012) 36 *Nova Law Review* 521, 538.

[330] A Bagley, 'Don't Be Evil: The Fourth Amendment in the Age of Google, National Security, and Digital Papers and Effects' (2011) 21 *Albany Law Journal of Science and Technology* 153, 174.

[331] *United States v Jones*, n 319 above, Sotomayor J concurring.

online retailers. Perhaps, … some people may find the 'tradeoff' of privacy for conveni-ence 'worthwhile', or come to accept this 'diminution of privacy' as 'inevitable', and per-haps not. I for one doubt that people would accept without complaint the warrantless disclosure to the Government of a list of every Web site they had visited in the last week, or month, or year. But whatever the societal expectations, they can attain constitutionally protected status only if our Fourth Amendment jurisprudence ceases to treat secrecy as a prerequisite for privacy. I would not assume that all information voluntarily disclosed to some member of the public for a limited purpose is, for that reason alone, disentitled to Fourth Amendment protection.[332]

Leaving aside the obvious similarities of *Smith v Maryland* with the EU Data Retention Directive discussed in Chapter 3 above, the third party doctrine estab-lished in that case and in *United States v Miller*[333] discussed above, is also perti-nent to PNR data. Applying the *Smith v Maryland* reasoning, PNR data cannot be covered by the Fourth Amendment protection, since travellers cannot enjoy any reasonable expectation of privacy of data they, themselves, granted to the airline companies in order to effectuate their ticket reservation.[334] At the EU level, the reasonable expectation of privacy as interpreted through the lens of the third party doctrine goes against the heart of the purpose limitation principle, as will be seen below. Finally, it is worth noting that the Fourth Amendment does not protect persons overseas, such as EU citizens.[335]

B. Federal Privacy Laws

At federal level, statutes are 'narrowly tailored to specific privacy problems'[336] and have often being adopted as a reaction to specific problems or 'public scandals'.[337] The most significant and 'the only federal omnibus'[338] piece of privacy legislation is the Privacy Act of 1974.[339] The Privacy Act embodies fair information principles in a statutory framework governing the means by which federal agencies collect, maintain, use, and disseminate personally identifiable information. The Privacy Act applies to information that is maintained in a 'system of records'. A system of records is a group of any records under the control of an agency from which infor-mation is retrieved by the name of the individual or by some identifying num-ber, symbol, or other identifying particular assigned to the individual. While the

---

[332] ibid.
[333] *United States v Miller* 425 US 435 (1976).
[334] To what extent PNR is covered under the European notion of privacy will be discussed below.
[335] In *United States v Verdugo-Urquidez* 494 US 1092 (1990), the Supreme Court held that the Fourth Amendment does not apply to a physical search of a premise overseas where the person invok-ing the right is a foreign citizen or resident.
[336] Solove, n 306 above, p 1440.
[337] Shaffer, n 301 above, p 25 and references therein.
[338] ibid.
[339] Pub L No 93-579, 88 Stat 1896 (2000) (codified at 5 USC § 552a).

Privacy Act applies to government records, it is ambiguous as to whether it applies to 'commercial data brokers who supply information to the government'.[340] As noted by an American scholar, 'it is not clear whether a database which originates in the private sector, and is then used by the government, is subject to the Act.'[341] This could be problematic in the case of the PNR data that originate in air carrier databases. The Privacy Act applies only to US citizens and lawful permanent residents (hereinafter 'US persons').[342]

As already mentioned above, an important limitation to the Privacy Act is the so-called 'routine use' exception, according to which, information may be disclosed for any 'routine use' if disclosure is 'compatible' with the purpose for which the agency collected the information.[343] PNR data, as seen above, are disclosed by the DHS for 'routine use'. Moreover, there are several 'general' and 'specific' exemptions to the Privacy Act regarding law enforcement agencies. 'General exemptions' may be established for any system of records maintained by an agency which 'performs as its principal functions any activity pertaining to the enforcement of criminal laws' if the agency publishes a rule claiming the exemption.[344] 'Specific exemptions' may be applied to a system of records involving classified national defence or foreign policy material compiled for law enforcement purposes; such content may also be exempted from the Privacy Act safeguards[345] if the agency publishes a rule to that effect.[346] The Privacy Act is also further limited, as its primary enforcement mechanism is a civil action in federal court, generally for damages[347] excluding damages for 'mental or emotional distress'.[348]

Another important piece of federal legislation is the Freedom of Information Act (FOIA), adopted in 1966.[349] FOIA permits any person (regardless of nationality or country of residence) to access a US federal agency's records, except to the extent such records (or a portion thereof) are protected from disclosure by an

---

[340] C Hoofnagle, 'Big Brother's Little Helpers: How ChoicePoint and Other Commercial Data Brokers Collect, Process, and Package Your Data for Law Enforcement' (2004) 29 *North Carolina Journal of International Law & Commercial Regulation* 595, 622.

[341] A Ramasastry, 'Lost in Translation—Data Mining, National Security and the Adverse Inference Problem' (2006) 22 *Santa Clara Computer & High Technology Law Journal* 757, 793.

[342] 5 USC § 552a(a)(2). See EPIC, 'The Privacy Act 1974' (2015), https://epic.org/privacy/1974act/. On the Judicial Redress Act of 2015 that extends judicial actions to non-US persons, see below. See also B Petkova, 'The Safeguards of Privacy Federalism' (2016) 20 (2) *Lewis & Clark Law Review* 595.

[343] D Solove, 'A Brief History of Information Privacy Law' in *Proskauer on Privacy*, GWU Law School Public Law Research Paper No. 215 (2006) 1, 26; P Schwartz, 'Privacy and Participation: Personal Information and Public Sector Regulation in the United States' (1995) 80 *Iowa Law Review* 553, 585; D Solove, 'The Origins and Growth of Information Privacy Law' (2003) 748 *PLI/PAT* 29.

[344] 5 USC § 552a(j).

[345] These safeguards include the proportionality duty related to relevance and necessity and individual access. See Bignami, n 304 above, p 12.

[346] 5 USC § 552a(k).

[347] F Bignami, 'European Versus American Liberty: A Comparative Privacy Analysis of Antiterrorism Data Mining' (2007) 48 *Boston College Law Review* 609, 633.

[348] *FAA v Cooper*, 132 S Ct 1441, 1456 (2012).

[349] 5 USC § 552(a)(3)(A).

applicable exemption under the FOIA. According to the 2012 EU–US PNR Agreement, individuals are entitled to petition for judicial review in accordance with applicable law and relevant provisions of the FOIA.[350]

C. The Need for a Comprehensive Framework?

i. *The EU–US High Level Contact Group on Information Sharing and Privacy and Personal Data Protection*

The seriously limited US privacy regime discussed above, creates problems to unimpeded transatlantic data flows. As the PNR experience proved, negotiations are difficult, with data protection differences being at the heart of the conflict.[351] A possible solution could, therefore, be an international agreement setting down certain data protection guarantees that would govern data exchanges between the two parties, in order to raise restrictions on data flows.

On 6 November 2006, the EU–US Justice and Home Affairs Ministerial Troika decided to establish an informal high-level advisory group[352] to start discussions on privacy and personal data protection in the context of the exchange of information for law enforcement purposes. On 28 May 2008, the Presidency of the Council of the European Union announced to the Committee of Permanent Representatives (COREPER), that the EU–US High-Level Contact Group (hereafter HLCG) on information-sharing and privacy and personal data protection had finalised its report.

The report, which was made public on 26 June 2008,[353] aimed to identify a set of core principles on privacy and personal data protection, acceptable as 'minimum standards' when processing personal data for law enforcement purposes.[354] These should be included preferably in an international agreement binding both the EU and the US,[355] instead of non-binding instruments or politically declarations.[356] Both sides recognised that a binding instrument would provide the greatest level

---

[350] 2012 EU–US PNR Agreement, Art 13(3). Under the same provision, individuals can petition judicial review also in accordance with the Computer Fraud and Abuse Act and the Electronic Communications Privacy Act (ECPA). On the ECPA, see C Doyle, *Privacy: An Overview of the Electronic Communications Privacy Act* (Congressional Research Service, 2012) 7-5700.

[351] Besides PNR, a number of other EU–US Agreements refer to the exchange of personal data. For instance, the Extradition and Mutual Legal Assistance Agreement (2003); the Agreements governing personal data exchange between the United States and Europol (2002) and Eurojust (2006); the TFTP Agreement (discussed below).

[352] The group was composed of senior officials from the Commission, the Council Presidency (supported by the Council Secretariat) and the US Departments of Justice, Homeland Security and State.

[353] Council of the European Union, Reports by the High Level Contact Group (HLCG) on information sharing and privacy and personal data protection, 9831/08 JAI 275 DATAPROTECT 31 USA 26.

[354] ibid, p 3.

[355] ibid, p 8.

[356] ibid, p 9.

of legal security and certainty and 'the advantage of establishing the fundamentals of effective privacy and personal data protection for use in any future agreements relating to the exchange of specific law enforcement information that might arise between the EU and the US.'[357]

The HLCG, indeed, agreed on a number of principles. These were: 1) purpose specification and purpose limitation; 2) integrity and data quality; 3) necessity and proportionality; 4) information security; 5) sensitive data; 6) accountability; 7) independent and effective oversight; 8) individual access and rectification; 9) transparency and notice; 10) redress; 11) automated individual decisions; and 12) restrictions on onward transfers to third countries.[358]

Nevertheless, there were a number of outstanding issues: the question of redress;[359] consistency regarding private entities' obligations during data transfers;[360] the equivalent and reciprocal application of privacy and personal data protection law;[361] the impact of the agreement on relations with third countries; specific agreements regulating information exchanges and privacy and personal data protection;[362] and issues related to the institutional framework of the EU and US. The main problem, however, was that the two sides seemed to have different understandings of 'law enforcement purposes',[363] which was central for the agreement. For the EU, 'law enforcement purposes' meant use of the personal data 'for the prevention, detection, investigation or prosecution of any criminal offence.' For the US, 'law enforcement purposes' was a somewhat broader notion that comprised 'the prevention, detection, suppression, investigation, or prosecution of any criminal offence or violation of law related to border enforcement, public security, and national security, as well as for non-criminal judicial or administrative proceedings related directly to such offences or violations.'[364] Nonetheless, the HLCG did not seem to find these differences important. For the HLCG, these two different ways of describing 'law enforcement purposes' reflected 'respective domestic legislation and history but may in practice coincide to a large extent'.[365] The initiative was welcomed by the EDPS, who expressed, nevertheless, a number of concerns.[366]

---

[357] ibid, p 8.

[358] ibid, p 4.

[359] On 2 October 2009, the HLCG agreed on a text with regard to the redress principle. See Addendum to the Final Report by EU–US High-Level Contact Group on information-sharing and privacy and personal data protection, Report and Agreed Text from the High-Level Contact Group as of 28 October 2009 and Reports by the High-Level Contact Group (HLCG) on information-sharing and privacy and personal data protection, Brussels, 23 November 2009, 15851/09, JAI 822 DATAPROTECT 74 USA 102.

[360] ibid.

[361] ibid.

[362] ibid.

[363] Council of the European Union, Reports by the HLCG, n 353 above, p 3.

[364] ibid, 4.

[365] ibid.

[366] European Data Protection Supervisor, Opinion on the Final Report by the EU–US High-Level Contact Group on Information-Sharing and Privacy and personal data protection, 11 November 2008.

ii. The EU–US Umbrella Agreement

a. A Chronology

In May 2010, the European Commission, taking up the work done by the HLCG, asked the Council to authorise the opening of negotiations with the United States for an agreement, based on Article 16 TFEU, when personal data are transferred and processed for the purpose of preventing, investigating, detecting or prosecuting criminal offences, including terrorism, in the framework of police and judicial cooperation in criminal matters.[367] The Commission noted that the aims of the EU–US agreement should be fourfold. First, the agreement should ensure a high level of protection of the fundamental rights and freedoms of individuals, in particular the right to protection of personal data, in line with the requirements of the EUCFR.[368] Second, it should provide a clear and coherent legally binding framework of personal data protection standards. Such a framework should remove the uncertainties and bridge the gaps in protection created in the past because of significant differences between EU and US data protection laws and practices. The agreement itself should therefore, according to the Commission, provide enforceable data protection standards and establish mechanisms for implementing them effectively.[369] Third, the agreement should provide a high level of protection for personal data transferred to and subsequently processed in the US for law enforcement purposes.[370] Finally, the agreement would not do away with the requirement for a specific legal basis for transfers of personal data between the EU and the US, with specific data protection provisions tailored to the particular category of personal data in question.[371]

On 3 December 2010, the Council adopted a decision authorising the Commission to open negotiations on an agreement between the EU and the US on the protection of personal data when transferred and processed for the purpose of preventing, investigating, detecting or prosecuting criminal offences, including terrorism, in the framework of police cooperation and judicial cooperation in criminal matters (the 'Umbrella Agreement'). In March 2011, the Commission opened negotiations with the US[372] and on 8 September 2015 the text of the

---

[367] European Commission, Proposition de Recommandation du Conseil Autorisant l'ouverture de Negociations en vue d'un Accord entre l'Union Europeene et les Etats-Unis d'Amerique sur la protection des donnees personnelles lors de leur transfert et de leur traitement a des fins de prevention, d' investigation, de detection ou de poursuite d'actes criminels y compris le terrorism, dans le cadre de la Cooperation Policiaire et Judiciaire en matiere penale COM(2010) 252/2.

[368] ibid.

[369] ibid.

[370] ibid.

[371] ibid.

[372] Press Release, EU–US Negotiations on an agreement to protect personal information exchanged in the context of fighting crime and terrorism, http://europa.eu/rapid/pressReleasesAction. do?reference=MEMO/11/203.

Agreement was initialled.[373] However, the signing of the Umbrella Agreement was made conditional on the passage of the Judicial Redress Act by the US Congress. The bill was approved by Congress on 10 February 2016 and was signed into law by President Obama on 24 February 2016.[374]

b. The Judicial Redress Act of 2015

According to the European Commission, the Judicial Redress Act of 2015 provides 'for the first time, equal treatment of EU citizens with US citizens' by extending to EU citizens 'three core judicial redress avenues' under the 1974 US Privacy Act, previously reserved to US citizens and permanent residents. Thus, EU citizens are able to 'avail themselves of rights of general application' for any transatlantic data transfers in the criminal law enforcement sector.[375]

A closer look at the Judicial Redress Act, however, reveals that the Commission's celebration of the equal treatment of EU citizens with US citizens is somewhat misplaced. First, the scope of judicial redress actions for non-US persons as compared to US persons is limited under the Act. In particular, US persons are granted four causes of action under the Privacy Act on the basis of the following criteria: i) an agency's failure to amend a US person's record upon his request; ii) an agency's refusal to comply with a US person's request for access to his records; iii) an agency's failure to maintain their records with the accuracy, relevance, timeliness and completeness necessary for a fair adjudication of rights or benefits whereby the agency subsequently makes an adverse decision; and iv) an agency's failure to comply with any other provision of the Privacy Act or any relevant promulgated regulations. The Judicial Redress Act extends these causes of action to non-US citizens only with respect to disclosures 'intentionally or wilfully' made in violation of section 552a(b), which prohibits disclosure of personal information without consent unless the disclosure is subject to the enumerated exceptions. This means that under the Judicial Redress Act, non-US persons are unable to pursue damages for adverse determinations based on inaccurate or otherwise unlawful personal data[376] or for failure of the agency to comply with any other provision of the Privacy Act.[377] Moreover, the Privacy Act applies to all agencies of the US Government, including all executive departments, military

---

[373] Statement by EU Commissioner Věra Jourová on the finalisation of the EU–US negotiations on the data protection 'Umbrella Agreement', http://europa.eu/rapid/press-release_STATEMENT-15-5610_en.htm.

[374] HR 1428: Judicial Redress Act of 2015. See also Statement by Commissioner Věra Jourová on the signature of the Judicial Redress Act by President Obama, http://europa.eu/rapid/press-release_STATEMENT-16-401_en.htm.

[375] Communication from the Commission to the European Parliament and the Council, 'Transatlantic Data Flows: Restoring Trust through Strong Safeguards', COM(2016) 117 final, 29.2.2016, 12–13.

[376] Bignami, n 304 above, p 13.

[377] EPIC Statement on Judicial Redress Act of 2015, S 1600, 12 January 2006, https://epic.org/foia/eu-us-data-transfer/EPIC-Ltr-S1600.pdf, 3.

departments, government corporations, government-controlled corporations, independent regulatory agencies, or other establishments in the executive branch. In contrast, the Judicial Redress Act stipulates that non-US citizens have redress rights for improper disclosure of personal information only against 'designated federal agencies'. Federal agencies are 'designated' by the Attorney General—with the concurrence of any agency head beyond the Department of Justice—who enjoys complete discretion as to the agencies they would designate. As a consequence, non-US citizens do not enjoy redress rights against federal agencies that have not been designated, even if those in fact maintain records of these persons.[378]

In addition, the Judicial Redress Act grants redress rights to citizens of the so-called 'covered countries' designated by the US Government. The designation of the countries in order to become 'covered' by the Act is, however, conditional on the following criteria: (a) the country or regional economic organisation has an agreement with the United States on privacy protections for information shared for the purpose of preventing, investigating, detecting, or prosecuting criminal offences: (b) the country or regional economic organisation permits the transfer of personal data for commercial purposes between it and the United States; and (c) the policies regarding the transfer of personal data for commercial purposes and related actions of the country or regional organisation, do not materially impede the national security interests of the United States.[379] This means that redress mechanisms under the Privacy Act are extended to non-US nationals only if their respective countries or regional organisations actually transfer personal data for commercial purposes to the US and their data protection laws do not impede the security interests of the US.[380] As eloquently observed by EPIC in their Statement regarding the Judicial Redress Act, 'this provision turns privacy protections on their head, requiring data transfer before privacy protections are established.'[381] Furthermore, according to the Judicial Redress Act, the Attorney General may with the concurrence of the Secretary of State, the Secretary of the Treasury and the Secretary of Homeland Security revoke the designation of a foreign country or regional organisation without any provision made as to what would happen to the non-US persons' data held in the US in these cases.[382] Finally, the Judicial Redress Act clarifies that no provision of this can be construed to 'waive any applicable privilege or require the disclosure of classified information'. Thus overall, it is unclear why the Commission celebrated the enactment of this Act as a victory of judicial redress rights for EU citizens' personal data breaches in the US.

---

[378] ibid.

[379] s 2(d)(1) Judicial Redress Act 2015.

[380] As the Electronic Privacy Information Centre (EPIC) noted, '[t]he Act fails to extend Privacy Act protections to non-US citizens, and as adopted, coerces EU countries to transfer data to the US, even without adequate protection, or be denied legal rights.' See www.epic.org/alert/epic_alert_23.03.html.

[381] EPIC Statement on Judicial Redress Act of 2015, n 377 above, p 5.

[382] ibid.

c. The Umbrella Agreement

Following the enactment of the Judicial Redress Act, on 29 April 2016 the Commission put forward a proposal for a Council decision on the signing of the EU–US Umbrella Agreement.[383] The legal basis for this proposal is Article 16 TFEU, in conjunction with Article 218(5) TFEU. The proposed Agreement includes five categories of provisions: i) horizontal provisions (Articles 1–5) determining the purpose, scope and effect of the Agreement; ii) data protection principles and safeguards (Articles 6–15); iii) data subject rights (Articles 16–20); iv) aspects relating to oversight (Articles 21–23); and v) the final provisions.

Article 1 stipulates that the purpose of the agreement is twofold: on the one hand, ensuring a high level of protection of personal information and, on the other hand, enhancing cooperation between the US and the EU and its Member States in relation to the prevention, investigation, detection or prosecution of criminal offences, including terrorism. To attain these objectives, the Agreement 'establishes the framework for the protection of personal information' when transferred between the US and the EU or its Member States.[384] The Umbrella Agreement does not constitute a general legal basis for transfers of personal information to the US. A specific legal basis is always required for such transfers.[385]

The Agreement applies to two types of transfers of personal data: those transferred between the competent law enforcement authorities of the EU and the US, and those transferred in accordance with an agreement concluded between the US and the EU for law enforcement purposes. According to the Commission, this includes transfers on the basis of domestic laws; EU–US agreements, such as the EU–US Mutual Legal Assistance Treaty; Member States–US agreements, such as Mutual Legal Assistance Treaties, Agreements on Enhancing Cooperation in Preventing and Combating Serious Crime, Terrorist Screening Information Agreements or Arrangements; and specific agreements providing for the transfer of personal data by private entities for law enforcement purposes, such as the EU–US PNR Agreement and the Terrorist Finance Tracking Programme (TFTP) Agreement.[386] The relationship between these specific agreements and the Umbrella Agreement, however, remains unclear in case of potential conflicts

---

[383] Commission Proposal for a Council Decision on the signing, on behalf of the European Union, of an Agreement between the United States of America and the European Union on the protection of personal information relating to the prevention, investigation, detection, and prosecution of criminal offences, COM(2016) 238 final, 29.4.2016.

[384] Umbrella Agreement, Art 1(2).

[385] ibid, Art 1(3). The legal basis for such transfers will generally be EU–US data transfer agreements, such as the PNR Agreement, the EU–US Mutual Legal Assistance (MLAT) Agreement that covers transfers of data from law enforcement agencies (LEAs) in the EU (such as Europol) to LEAs in the US and bilateral MLAT Agreements between EU Member States and the US. See D Korff, Note on the EU–US Umbrella Data Protection Agreement, Fundamental Rights European Experts Group (FREE), 14 October 2015, www.statewatch.org/news/2015/oct/eu-usa-umbrella-freegroup-Korff-Note.pdf, 4.

[386] Commission Proposal on the signing of the Umbrella Agreement, n 383, p 6.

arising from their provisions.[387] Furthermore, the Umbrella Agreement explicitly excludes its application to transfers of personal data or other forms of cooperation between US and Member States' authorities 'responsible for safeguarding national security'.[388] While the Agreement includes a broad definition of law enforcement 'competent authorities'[389] to which it applies, it does not define 'authorities responsible for safeguarding national security'. Nevertheless, this provision seems to exclude the activities of intelligence agencies from the purview of the Umbrella Agreement.

Article 4 of the proposed Agreement enshrines a general clause of non-discrimination regarding its implementation. However, this provision has been criticised because it guarantees the respect of the principle of non-discrimination only with regard to US nationals and EU citizens, but excludes from its personal scope non-EU citizens that nevertheless have their personal data transferred to the US.[390] Similarly, Article 19 on judicial redress only applies to 'citizens' of the Parties. Thus, the Agreement does not be comply with Articles 7, 8 and 47 EUCFR that all grant rights to 'everyone' in the EU, irrespective of their nationality.[391]

There are a number of substantive data protection principles and safeguards enshrined in the Umbrella Agreement. These include provisions on purpose limitation (Article 6(1)), necessity and proportionality (Article 6(5)), information security (Article 9), data retention (Article 12), sensitive data (Article 13), accountability (Article 14) and automated decisions (Article 15). Nonetheless, several of these provisions lack clarity or include significant limitations, omissions or exceptions that result in watering down the relevant basic EU data protection principles.

The purpose limitation provision of the Agreement limits the transfer of personal information to 'specific purposes authorised by the legal basis for the transfer'[392] and prohibits further processing incompatible with the purposes for which it was transferred.[393] The same Article provides that personal data must be processed '*in a manner* that is directly relevant to and not excessive or overbroad in relation to the purposes of such processing.'[394] This formulation of 'processing the data in a manner relevant to the purposes of the processing', besides being tautological, is also different to the relevant EU data protection provisions that stipulate

---

[387] D Korff, Note on the EU–US Umbrella Data Protection Agreement, Fundamental Rights European Experts Group (FREE) Annex, 5.

[388] Umbrella Agreement, Art 3(2).

[389] ibid, Art 2(5).

[390] Giovanni Buttarelli, 'EU–US "Umbrella Agreement"', Presentation of EDPS Preliminary Opinion 1/2016 before Civil Liberties, Justice and Home Affairs Committee (LIBE) of the European Parliament, 15 February 2016, https://secure.edps.europa.eu/EDPSWEB/webdav/site/mySite/shared/Documents/EDPS/Publications/Speeches/2016/16-02-15_Umbrella_Agreement_LIBE_EN.pdf, 3.

[391] ibid.

[392] Umbrella Agreement, Art 6(1).

[393] ibid, Art 6(2).

[394] Emphasis added.

that the data themselves must be relevant and not excessive to the purposes of the processing. Such formulation is suspiciously unclear because it seems to allow the transfer of excessive and irrelevant data as soon as these are processed in a relevant manner.[395]

The Umbrella Agreement permits the onward transfer of personal data to states not bound by this if the competent authority originally sending such data has given its consent after taking into account 'all the relevant factors'.[396] Notwithstanding that the competent authority that originally sent the personal information is not a DPA but a law enforcement authority, this provision is further problematic, for two reasons. First, it is unclear whether it allows for the transfer of data in bulk.[397] Second, it stipulates that the level of data protection in a third state or body 'shall not be the basis for denying consent for, or imposing conditions on … transfers'.[398] This goes directly against the requirement of 'adequate' protection of personal data for their transfer to third countries under EU law and suggests that constraints could be imposed on NDPAs if they try to ban such transfers. Such a provision is not compatible with the CJEU's judgment in *Schrems*, where it was held that NDPAs must be able to examine, with complete independence, whether transfers of data to third countries comply with fundamental rights and the requirements of the Data Protection Directive.[399]

Article 8 obliges the Parties to take 'reasonable steps' to ensure that 'personal information is maintained with such accuracy, relevance, timeliness and completeness as is necessary and appropriate for lawful processing of the information', including where the transferring Competent Authority becomes aware of 'significant doubts' as to the relevance, timeliness, completeness or accuracy of such personal information. In these cases, 'where feasible' it must advise the receiving Competent Authority. Again the protections enshrined in this provision are watered down from the ones of EU law: only 'reasonable steps' are required where it is 'feasible'.

Similarly, the Agreement guarantees information security,[400] but incidents involving accidental loss or destruction or unauthorised access to the personal data would be dealt with only where there is a 'significant risk of damage' to individuals.[401] Furthermore, the notification of information security incidents to the transferring Competent Authority (and not NDPAs) may be 'delayed' or

---

[395] See also Korff, n 387 above, p 12.

[396] Umbrella Agreement, Art 7(1).

[397] ibid, Art 7(3). See also EDPS, Opinion 1/2016, Preliminary Opinion on the agreement between the United States of America and the European Union on the protection of personal information relating to the prevention, investigation, detection and prosecution of criminal offences, 12 February 2016, 12.

[398] Umbrella Agreement, Art 7(4).

[399] *Schrems*, n 127 above, para 57.

[400] Umbrella Agreement, Art 9.

[401] ibid, Art 10(1).

'omitted' when such notification 'may endanger national security'.[402] Notification of data security incidents can be withheld from the individual when this 'may endanger' a) public or national security; b) official inquiries, investigations or proceedings; c) the prevention, detection, investigation, or prosecution of criminal offences; and d) rights and freedoms of others, in particular the protection of victims and witnesses.[403] Given that the Umbrella Agreement refers to data transfers for the above law enforcement purposes, this provision seems to suggest that data security breaches will not be notified to the individual concerned in the majority of cases.

Regarding the data retention period, the Agreement mandates the Parties 'to ensure that personal information is not retained for longer than is necessary and appropriate.'[404] For bulk transfers of data, it is stipulated that the relevant agreements governing these, such as the EU–US PNR Agreement should 'include a specific and mutually agreed upon provision on retention periods.'[405] The principles of necessity and proportionality should have been mentioned here[406] and the Umbrella Agreement should also stipulate expressly the obligation to delete the data after the relevant retention periods have expired, something that is unclear whether it has taken place under the EU–US PNR Agreements.

The proposed Umbrella Agreement allows the processing of sensitive data[407] 'under appropriate safeguards in accordance with the law.'[408] Notwithstanding that it not clear in accordance with which law the data will be processed, this falls short to EU data protection legislation that prohibits in principle the processing of sensitive data unless certain limited exceptions apply. Moreover, the EDPS has raised concerns regarding the 'possibility of having bulk transfers of sensitive data' under Article 13(2), requesting that bulk transfers of sensitive data be excluded from the scope of the Agreement.[409]

The data subject rights contained in the Agreement include a right to access (Article 16), rectification (Article 17), administrative (Article 18) and judicial redress (Article 19) and a right to be informed (Article 20). However, there are significant limitations to these rights. First, they are all made conditional to 'the applicable legal framework of the State in which relief is sought',[410] namely US law with its significant restrictions of data subject's rights—even after the adoption of the Judicial Redress Act. Secondly, certain data subjects' rights are constrained considerably with respect to their equivalents under EU primary or secondary law. For instance, the right to access is made subject to 'reasonable restrictions provided

---

[402] ibid, Art 10(2)(b).
[403] ibid, Art 10(3).
[404] ibid, Art 12(1).
[405] ibid, Art 12(2).
[406] EDPS Opinion 1/2016, n 397 above, p 13.
[407] See Korff, n 387 above, p 23.
[408] Umbrella Agreement, Art 13(1).
[409] EDPS Opinion 1/2016, n 397 above, p 13.
[410] Umbrella Agreement, Arts 16(1), 17(1), 18(1) and 19(2).

under domestic law' for broad purposes,[411] such as to 'protect law enforcement sensitive information',[412] to 'avoid obstructing official or legal inquiries, investigations or proceedings'[413] and to 'protect interests provided for in legislation regarding freedom of information and public access to documents.'[414] The last limitation seems to refer to the further exceptions of the FOIA,[415] but nevertheless it appears overall extremely difficult—if not impossible—for the data subject to exercise any access rights on the basis of these limitations. As observed by the EDPS, 'it is difficult to conceive of a situation in which personal data transferred for the purposes of the [Umbrella] Agreement will not be considered "law enforcement sensitive information" by the competent authority, in the absence of specific criteria to determine what "law enforcement sensitive information" means.'[416]

The right to administrative redress is granted to individuals under the Umbrella Agreement in two cases: where they believe that their request for access or rectification of inaccurate information or improper processing has been 'improperly denied'.[417] Individuals are entitled to authorise 'an oversight authority or other representative', such as their NDPA, to seek administrative redress on their behalf.[418] However, it is worth noting that the right to administrative redress is obtained from a Competent Authority and not from an independent authority, such as the NDPA.[419]

The right to judicial redress is expressly limited to citizens of the Parties to the Agreement and can be exercised, after administrative redress is exhausted, only in the following three instances: a) when a Competent Authority has denied access to records containing the individual's personal information; b) when a Competent Authority has declined to amend the records containing his personal information; and c) for unlawful disclosure of such information that has been 'wilfully or intentionally made'.[420] This excludes any possibility for data subjects to pursue legal remedies on other grounds, such as for instance to obtain erasure of their data[421] and it is overall doubtful whether it complies with the CJEU's pronouncement in *Schrems* concerning the essence of Article 47 EUCFR.[422]

The Agreement provides that the individual will be given notice as to his personal information 'through publication of general notices or through actual notice' with regard to the purposes of processing, purposes for which the information

---

[411]   ibid, Art 16(2).
[412]   ibid, Art 16(2)(c).
[413]   ibid, Art 16(2)(d)
[414]   ibid, Art 16(2)(f).
[415]   Korff, n 387 above, pp 32–33.
[416]   EDPS Opinion 1/2016, n 397 above, p 13.
[417]   Umbrella Agreement, Art 18(1).
[418]   ibid, Art 18 (2).
[419]   EDPS Opinion 1/2016, n 397 above, p 15.
[420]   Umbrella Agreement, Art 19(1).
[421]   EDPS Opinion 1/2016, n 397 above, p 15.
[422]   See *Schrems*, n 127 above, para 95.

may be shared with other authorities, laws or rules under which such process-ing takes place, third parties to whom such information is disclosed, and access, correction or rectification, and redress available.[423] While the recognition of the right to information in the Umbrella Agreement is certainly welcome, this is made subject to 'the law applicable to the authority providing notice' and 'the reasonable restrictions under domestic law' applying to the right to access.[424]

The oversight of the application of the Agreement is carried out by public authorities that are granted the power to review, investigate and intervene,[425] to accept and act upon complaints made by individuals[426] and to refer violations of law related to the Agreement for prosecution or disciplinary action.[427] On the EU side, the authorities responsible for oversight are the European and national DPAs.[428] On the US side, oversight is to be provided 'cumulatively through more than one authority, which may include, *inter alia*, inspectors general, chief pri-vacy officers, government accountability offices, privacy and civil liberties over-sight boards, and other applicable executive and legislative privacy or civil liberties review bodies.'[429] This provision lacks clarity as to which authority in the US individuals can raise their complaints with. In addition, it is dubious whether it complies with Article 8(3) EUCFR that requires that respect for the rules on data protection has to be supervised by an independent authority, in the light of its interpretation by the CJEU, according to which an authority must be able to make decisions independently from any direct or indirect external influence.[430]

Article 5 stipulates that any processing carried out by the Parties with respect to matters falling within the scope of the Umbrella Agreement 'shall be deemed to comply with their respective data protection legislation restricting or condition-ing international transfers of personal information, and no further authorisation under such legislation shall be required.'[431] This establishes, therefore, a *quasi*-adequacy finding,[432] although the Agreement expressly states that it 'supplements, as appropriate, but does not replace, provisions regarding the protection of personal information' in international agreements between the EU and the US or the US and the Member States.[433] Finally, the implementation of the Umbrella Agreement is made subject to periodic joint reviews by the Parties[434] and a suspension of the Agreement is allowed 'in the event of a material breach' of its provisions.[435]

---

[423] Umbrella Agreement, Art 20(1).
[424] ibid, Art 20(2).
[425] ibid, Art 21(1)(a).
[426] ibid, Art 21(1)(b).
[427] ibid, Art 21(1)(c).
[428] ibid, Art 21(2).
[429] ibid, Art 21(3).
[430] Case C-288/12 *Commission v Hungary* (CJEU (GC), 8 April 2014), para 47; *Schrems*, n 127 above, para 40. See also EDPS Opinion 1/2016, n 397 above, p 16.
[431] Umbrella Agreement, Art 5(3).
[432] See EDPS Opinion 1/2016, n 397 above, pp 7–8.
[433] Umbrella Agreement, Art 5(1).
[434] ibid, Art 23.
[435] ibid, Art 26.

IV. THE EU PNR

A. The Proposal for an EU PNR Framework Decision

An American author predicted in 2002 that

> since EU and US political interests are largely aligned … against terrorism, it is possible that the European Union will move closer to the United States as a result of the [September 11] attacks, rather than the United States moving away from the European Union. To the extent that Europeans feel vulnerable as a result of terrorism, they may shift their emphasis away from data privacy and toward protective anti-terrorist surveillance programs.[436]

PNR is a prominent example of this. The European Council in the Stockholm Programme invited the Commission to present a proposal on the establishment of an EU PNR system.[437] Following this, on 6 November 2007, the Commission introduced its proposal for a Council Framework decision on the use of PNR data for law enforcement purposes under the then third pillar.[438] The draft Framework decision had as its purpose 'the making available by air carriers of PNR data of passengers of international flights to the competent authorities of the Member States, for the purpose of preventing and combating terrorist offences and organised crime, as well as the collection and retention of those data by these authorities and the exchange of those data between them.'[439] For this reason, the Framework decision required each Member State to designate a competent authority ('Passenger Information Unit'—PIU), which would be responsible for collecting the PNR data of international flights arriving or departing from its territory.[440] The PIU would further be responsible for analysing the PNR data and for carrying out a risk assessment of the passengers, in order to: identify persons who are or may be involved in a terrorist or organised crime offence; create and update risk indicators for the assessment of such persons; provide intelligence on travel patterns and other trends relating to terrorist offences and organised crime; and use the risk assessment in criminal investigations and prosecutions of terrorist offences and organised crime.[441]

The PNR data to be transmitted according to the proposed Framework decision were almost identical to the categories listed in the then EU–US Agreement

---

[436] S Salbu, 'The European Union Data Privacy Directive and International Relations' (2002) 35 *Vanderbilt Journal of Transnational Law* 655, 694.

[437] European Council, 'The Stockholm Programme—An Open and Secure Europe Serving and Protecting Citizens', [2010] OJ C115/1, 19.

[438] Proposal for a Council Framework Decision on the use of Passenger Name Record (PNR) for law enforcement purposes COM(2007) 654 final.

[439] ibid, Art 1.

[440] ibid, Art 3.

[441] ibid, Art 3(5).

in place.[442] The draft Framework decision asked for (exactly) 19 data fields as the 2007 EU–US PNR Agreement.[443] Air carriers would be required to make available the data to the relevant PIU twice: 24 hours before the scheduled flight departure, and immediately after flight closure.[444] The PNR data would be retained for a period of 13 years in total: for five years in a PIU database, and subsequently for another eight years, during which access would be limited in exceptional circumstances.[445] Concerning the data protection principles applicable to the EU PNR system, the draft Framework decision could not be briefer. Two Articles referred to data protection, one of which was dedicated to data security.[446] The other prohibited any enforcement action to be taken by the PIUs or the Member States based only on the automated processing of PNR data or by reason of a person's race or ethnic origin, religious or philosophical belief, political opinion or sexual orientation.[447] The proposed PNR Framework decision stated that relevant EU applicable data protection applicable legislation would be the Framework decision on the Protection of Personal Data Processed in the Framework of Police and Judicial Co-operation in Criminal Matters (not yet adopted, back then).[448]

The proposal on the Framework decision establishing an EU PNR regime was received with fierce criticisms by the Article 29 Working Party, the EDPS, the Fundamental Rights Agency (FRA), and the European Parliament. In particular, the Article 29 Working Party in its joint opinion with the Working Party on Police and Justice characterised the proposal as 'a further milestone towards a European surveillance society in the name of fighting terrorism and organised crime.'[449]

Indeed, the reaction of the above institutions and bodies was even more severe than the criticisms they voiced for the EU–US PNR Agreements. Both the Working Party and the EDPS demanded that an EU PNR system must be 'demonstrably necessary'.[450] The necessity of the EU–US PNR Agreements was also questioned, but given the position of the European airlines and the pressure exercised by the US authorities for the prompt conclusion of an agreement, the Working Party, the EDPS, and the Parliament had been focusing more on the substantial assessment of the relevant provisions interfering with the right to data protection. Having to deal with an EU measure this time, their position

---

[442] House of Lords European Union Committee, 'The Passenger Name Record (PNR) Framework Decision' 15th Report of Session 2007–08, para 22. See also M Tzanou, 'The War Against Terror and Transatlantic Information Sharing: Spillovers of Privacy or Spillovers of Security?' (2015) 31 (80) *Utrecht Journal of International and European Law* 87.

[443] See Annex of the PNR proposal for a Council Framework Decision.

[444] PNR proposal for a Council Framework Decision, Art 5.

[445] ibid, Art 9.

[446] ibid, Art 11 (Protection of personal data) and Art 12 (Data security).

[447] ibid, Art 11(3).

[448] ibid, Art 11(1).

[449] Art 29 WP, WP on Police and Justice, Joint Opinion on the Proposal for a Council Framework Decision on the Use of Passenger Name Record (PNR) for Law Enforcement Purposes, Presented by the Commission on 6 November 2007.

[450] ibid, p 5.

became clearly stricter: the Commission had to prove beyond doubt the added value of an EU PNR system.[451]

Another criticism raised against the proposal by all four institutions concerned the profiling aspirations of the EU PNR regime. As the EDPS noted eloquently, unlike the API data that are supposed to help identifying individuals, PNR data 'would contribute to carrying out risk assessments of persons, obtaining intelligence and making associations between known and unknown people.'[452] The purpose of a PNR system covers not only the apprehension of *known* persons, but also the identification of persons that may be of interest for law enforcement reasons.[453] A substantial part of FRA's Opinion concerning the draft PNR Framework decision is dedicated to a human rights' assessment of the 'profiling purposes' of the proposal, mainly on the basis of the prohibition of discrimination found in Article 21 EUCFR.[454] The European Parliament also raised similar concerns in its Resolution.[455]

Finally, there were numerous problems identified in the proposal: the excessive categories of data to be retained,[456] the disproportionate retention periods,[457] the uncertainty on the individuals' rights,[458] the questions on the applicable legal framework,[459] and the role of PIUs and intermediaries.[460]

B. The EU PNR Directive

Upon the entry into force of the Lisbon Treaty on 1 December 2009, the Commission's proposal of 6 November 2007 for a Framework decision on PNR, which had not been adopted by the Council by that date, became obsolete. On 2 February 2011, the Commission introduced a new proposal on the establishment of an EU PNR system—this time for a Directive.[461] The proposal was based

---

[451] ibid, p 6.

[452] Opinion of the European Data Protection Supervisor on the draft Proposal for a Council Framework Decision on the use of Passenger Name Record (PNR) data for law enforcement purposes [2008] OJ C110/1, para 6.

[453] ibid, para 15.

[454] Fundamental Rights Agency, Opinion on the Proposal for a Council Framework Decision on the Use of Passenger Name Record (PNR) Data for Law Enforcement Purposes (2008), http://fra.europa. eu/fraWebsite/attachments/FRA_opinion_PNR_en.pdf, 7.

[455] European Parliament resolution of 20 November 2008 on the proposal for a Council framework decision on the use of Passenger Name Record (PNR) for law enforcement purposes P6_TA(2008)0561.

[456] ibid. Art 29 WP, WP on Police and Justice, n 449 above.

[457] ibid.

[458] ibid.

[459] Opinion of the European Data Protection Supervisor, n 452 above, para 39.

[460] ibid, para 68.

[461] Proposal for a Directive of the European Parliament and of the Council on the use of Passenger Name Record data for the prevention, detection, investigation and prosecution of terrorist offences and serious crime COM(2011) 32 final.

once again on the need for harmonisation of the Member States' relevant provisions. This time, however, the Commission seemed slightly more convincing. According to the Explanatory Memorandum, the UK already had its PNR system, while France, Denmark, Belgium, Sweden and the Netherlands had either enacted relevant legislation or were testing using PNR data. According to the Commission, other Member States were also considering setting up PNR systems that might diverge in several respects. The Commission, therefore, foresaw the creation of up to 27 considerably diverging PNR systems that 'would result in uneven levels of protection of personal data across the EU, security gaps, increased costs and legal uncertainty for air carriers and passengers alike.'[462] The Commission explained that it carried out an Impact Assessment for the development of an EU PNR system, which concluded that a legislative proposal applicable to travel by air with decentralised PNR data collection for the purpose of preventing, detecting, investigating and prosecuting terrorist offences and other serious crime was the best policy option.[463]

Following the criticisms raised against the proposed PNR Framework decision, the Commission has taken great pains to prove that a PNR system at the EU level has indeed an added value. The Commission's justification is long and in many aspects irrelevant, as it cites an extensive amount of information and statistical data on criminal offences in general in the Member States; on the economic cost of crimes in industrialised economies; on the annual cocaine-related deaths in the EU; on the number of opioid users in Europe; and, on the total Member States' expenditure relating to illicit drugs.[464] Concerning the value of a PNR system, it notes, first, that the absence of harmonised provisions on the collection and processing of PNR data at EU level, explains why detailed statistics on the extent to which such data are useful to combat terrorism and crime are not available.[465] It then goes on to provide information on the experiences of the use of PNR data by other countries. A great part of the analysis is no more than anecdotal.[466] According to the Commission, statistical data prove that with respect to drugs, 'the majority of seizures are made due to the use of PNR data in real-time and pro-actively.'[467] The Commission's analysis on the necessity of an EU PNR system

---

[462] ibid, p 4.

[463] ibid.

[464] ibid, p 2.

[465] ibid, 6.

[466] See E Brouwer, *Ignoring Dissent and Legality—The EU's proposal to share the personal information of all passengers* (Brussels, CEPS, 2011) 2–3.

[467] According to the Commission, Belgium reported that 95 per cent of all drugs seizures in 2009 were exclusively or predominantly due to the processing of PNR data. Sweden reported that 65–75 per cent of all drugs seizures in 2009 were exclusively or predominantly due to the processing of PNR data. The United Kingdom reported that during a period of six months in 2010, 212 kilos of cocaine and 20 kilos of heroin were seized exclusively or predominantly due to the processing of PNR data.

has been clearly more elaborated than the one provided in the draft Framework decision, but nevertheless still lacking strong empirical evidence.[468]

On 29 April 2013 the LIBE Committee voiced concerns regarding the effectiveness of an EU PNR system and its compatibility with the fundamental right to data protection and the principle of proportionality, and voted against the proposal.[469] The debate was stalled temporarily, but not completely abandoned. The terrorist attacks in Paris on 7 January 2015 and in Copenhagen on 14–15 February 2015, as well as the attacks in Paris on 13 November 2015 and in Brussels on 22 March 2016, pushed toward a rapid adoption of the EU PNR Directive. In its Special Meeting of 30 August 2014, the European Council emphasised that an EU PNR was necessary in order to detect and disrupt suspicious travel and investigate and prosecute foreign fighters, and called the Council and the EP to finalise work on the proposal before the end of 2014.[470] An agreement was reached between the Parliament and the Council in December 2015 and endorsed by the LIBE Committee.[471] The text of the EU PNR Directive was approved by the Parliament on 14 April 2016[472] and adopted by the Council.[473] Member States have two years to transpose the provisions of the Directive into national law.[474]

The PNR Directive is based on Articles 82(1)(d) and 87(2)(a) TFEU, and regulates the transfer by air carriers of PNR data of passengers of extra-[475] and intra-EU flights,[476] as well as the processing of such data, including its collection, use and retention by the Member States and its exchange between them.[477] The PNR data collected may be processed for the purposes of preventing, detecting, investigating, and prosecuting 'terrorist offences' and 'serious crimes'.[478]

---

[468] Opinion of the European Data Protection Supervisor on the Proposal for a Directive of the European Parliament and of the Council on the use of Passenger Name Record data for the prevention, detection, investigation and prosecution of terrorist offences and serious crime, Brussels, 25 May 2011, para 10; Art 29 WP, Opinion 10/2011 on the proposal for a Directive of the European Parliament and of the Council on the use of Passenger Name Record data for the prevention, detection, investigation and prosecution of terrorist offences and serious crime.

[469] M Marx, 'The EP Committee Rejects the Proposal for an European Passenger Name Record System (PNR)' (European Area of Freedom Security & Justice, 1 May 2013) http://free-group.eu/2013/05/01/the-ep-committee-rejects-the-proposal-for-an-european-passanger-name-record-system-pnr/#_ftn5.

[470] Conclusions of the Special Meeting of the European Council of 30 August 2014, EUCO 163/14 CO EUR 11 CONCL 4, para 18.

[471] Press release, 'EU Passenger Name Record (PNR): Civil Liberties Committee backs EP/Council deal', www.europarl.europa.eu/news/en/news-room/20151207IPR06435/EU-Passenger-Name-Record-(PNR)-Civil-Liberties-Committee-backs-EPCouncil-deal.

[472] 'EU Passenger Name Record (PNR) directive: An overview', www.europarl.europa.eu/news/en/news-room/20150123BKG12902/EU-Passenger-Name-Record-(PNR)-directive-an-overview.

[473] Directive (EU) 2016/681 of the European Parliament and of the Council of 27 April 2016 on the use of passenger name record (PNR) data for the prevention, detection, investigation and prosecution of terrorist offences and serious crime, [2016] OJ L119/132.

[474] PNR Directive, Art 18.

[475] ibid, Art 1(1)(a).

[476] ibid, Art 2.

[477] ibid, Art 1(1)(b).

[478] ibid, Art 1(2).

Terrorist offences entail the offences provided for in Framework Decision 2002/475/JHA[479] and a list of 'serious crimes', punishable for a maximum period of at least three years, is found in Annex II of the Directive.[480] Member States are required to establish or designate an authority to act as their PIU.[481] PIUs are responsible for both collecting PNR data from air carriers, processing and transferring those data to the competent national law enforcement authorities and for exchanging PNR data and the result of their processing with the PIUs of other Member States and with Europol.[482] Similarly to the 2012 EU–US PNR, the Directive stipulates that 19 categories of PNR data must be transmitted.

PNR data are processed by PIUs for three purposes: first, in order to carry out an assessment of passengers prior to their scheduled arrival or departure to identify persons who require further examination; secondly, to respond to a request from the competent authorities to provide and process PNR data in specific cases; and thirdly, to analyse PNR data for the purpose of updating or creating new criteria to be used in the passenger assessments in order to identify persons who may be involved in a terrorist offence or serious crime.[483] When carrying out the passenger assessment, PIUs are allowed to compare the PNR data against law enforcement databases and databases on persons or objects sought or under alert and process these data against 'pre-determined criteria'.[484] The Directive stipulates that the assessment of passengers must be carried out in a non-discriminatory manner and the pre-determined criteria must be targeted, proportionate and specific and not based on a person's race or ethnic origin, political opinions, religion or philosophical beliefs, trade union membership, health, sexual life or sexual orientation.[485]

The result of the processing of PNR data by a PIU should be transmitted to the PIUs of the other Member States.[486] Europol is also entitled to request PNR data or the result of their processing from the PIUs in order to perform its tasks.[487] PNR data may also be transferred by Member States to third countries in certain circumstances on a case-by-case basis.[488]

Air carriers are obliged to transmit the PNR data 24 to 48 hours before the scheduled flight departure time and immediately after flight closure.[489] The Directive requires Member States to ensure that air carriers transmit PNR data using the 'push method'.[490] The data are retained in a database at the PIU for a

---

[479] Council Framework Decision 2002/475/JHA on combatting terrorism, [2002] OJ L164/3.
[480] PNR Directive, Art 3(9).
[481] ibid, Art 4(1).
[482] ibid, Art 4(2).
[483] ibid, Art 6(2).
[484] ibid, Art 6(3).
[485] ibid, Art 6(4).
[486] ibid, Art 9.
[487] ibid, Art 10.
[488] ibid, Art 11.
[489] ibid, Art 8(3).
[490] ibid, Art 8(1).

period of five years:[491] initially for six months after the transfer, and for the rest of the retention period the PNR data must be depersonalised through masking out data elements, such as names, addresses, contact, payment and frequent flyer information, which could serve to identify directly the relevant passengers.[492] Upon expiry of the initial period of six months, the full PNR data can be disclosed only where necessary in specific cases after obtaining the approval by a judicial authority or another national authority competent to verify whether the conditions for disclosure are met.[493] The Directive expressly stipulates that PNR data must be permanently deleted after the five year period has passed.[494]

The PNR Directive enshrines a number of data protection safeguards. Each PIU is required to appoint an independent data protection officer responsible for monitoring the processing of PNR data and implementing relevant safeguards.[495] The data protection officer must have access to all data processed by the PIU and if he considers that unlawful processing of data has taken place, he may refer the matter to the national supervisory authority.[496] Data subjects have the right to contact the data protection officer at PIU, as a single point of contact, on all issues relating to the processing of their PNR data.[497] The Directive prohibits national competent authorities from taking decisions on the basis of a person's race or ethnic origin, political opinions, religion or philosophical beliefs, trade union membership, health, sexual life or sexual orientation.[498] Decisions that produce an adverse legal effect on a person or significantly affect a person cannot be made only by reason of automated processing of PNR data.[499]

Article 13 entitled 'Protection of personal data' provides that every passenger must have the 'same right to protection of their personal data, rights of access, rectification, erasure and restriction and rights to compensation and judicial redress' as those adopted under national law in implementation of Articles 17, 18, 19 and 20 of the Framework Decision on the Protection of Personal Data Processed in the Framework of Police and Judicial Co-operation in Criminal Matters.[500] Articles 21 and 22 of the Data Protection Framework Decision concerning confidentiality of processing and data security also apply to the processing of PNR data.[501] The Directive prohibits the processing of PNR data revealing sensitive information and obliges the PIUs to delete immediately such information.[502] PIUs must keep records of the collection, consultation, disclosure and erasure of the data and

---

[491] ibid, Art 12(1).
[492] ibid, Art 12(2).
[493] ibid, Art 12(3).
[494] ibid, Art 12(4).
[495] ibid, Art 5(1).
[496] ibid, Art 6(7).
[497] ibid, Art 5(3).
[498] ibid, Art 7(6).
[499] ibid.
[500] ibid, Art 13(1).
[501] ibid, Art 13(2).
[502] ibid, Art 13(4).

must make these available, upon request, to the national supervisory authority.[503] The national supervisory authority established under Article 25 of Framework Decision 2008/977/JHA is responsible for monitoring the application of the EU PNR Directive.[504] The supervisory authority can investigate complaints lodged by data subjects and verify the lawfulness of the data processing, conduct investigations, inspection and audits.[505]

V. AIR PASSENGER SURVEILLANCE AND THE RIGHTS TO
PRIVACY AND DATA PROTECTION

A. The Rights to Privacy and Data Protection and the Standard of Judicial Review: The Case of PNR

Fundamental rights concerns have been at the heart of the PNR conflict. Air passenger screening has been alleged to interfere with the right to privacy, the right to data protection, the prohibition of discrimination[506] and the right to travel freely.[507] The problem with PNR data is that these do not allow 'very precise conclusions concerning the private life of passengers to be drawn',[508] but they relate to 'normal border control procedures'[509] and, therefore, cannot be seen as 'a genuine surveillance mechanism'.[510] The Opinion of Advocate General Léger in the *Parliament v Commission and Council (PNR)* case followed this approach. When examining the 2004 EU–US PNR, the AG found it difficult to explain why PNR data, which includes data on names, contact details, baggage information, etc, interferes with the private life of individuals. To the extent that sensitive data is included, such as health or dietary requirements revealing religious beliefs for instance, this could be accepted. But, what about the great bulk of the PNR data? On the other side of the Atlantic, such questions were similarly perplexing. As US Homeland Security Secretary Chertoff noted in his address to the European Parliament concerning PNR: 'It's basic information. It's nothing that's particularly confidential by its very nature.'[511] In essence, under US constitutional law, PNR data cannot be expected to enjoy a 'reasonable expectation of privacy'.[512] Privacy protection in Europe certainly differs significantly from the US notion of 'reasonable expectation', but the problem with PNR data still remains. If we exclude the

---

[503] ibid, Art 13(6).
[504] ibid, Art 15(1).
[505] ibid, Art 15(3).
[506] See below.
[507] Kite, n 53 above, p 1410; Dummer, n 16 above, p 599.
[508] Opinion of AG Mengozzi, n 297 above, para 148.
[509] ibid, para 152.
[510] ibid.
[511] US Homeland Security Secretary Michael Chertoff, n 220 above.
[512] See analysis above.

category of sensitive data for the moment, we are faced with the difficulty of how to explain conceptually the harm caused by PNR to the right to private life. If this cannot be seen, then the collection of PNR data presents no interference, or even if it does, its proportionality cannot be assessed on the correct basis. This was the fallacy committed by the Advocate General in *Parliament v Commission and Council (PNR)*. Having to assess PNR on the basis of Article 8 ECHR, the AG had to engage in a discussion on why PNR affected the right to privacy. An interference in the private life of the passengers was indeed confirmed,[513] but even so, the Advocate General noted some difficulties:

> … the interference in the private life of airline passengers appears to me to be established *even though certain PNR data elements, considered in isolation, could be regarded as not individually infringing the privacy of the passengers concerned.*[514]

However, it was more difficult to explain why such interference could be considered as disproportionate. This is evident in his reasoning, but also in his conclusions. Concerning his reasoning, the Advocate General had to make a distinction based on the nature of the data, because

> the review of proportionality by the European Court of Human Rights varies according to parameters such as the nature of the right and activities at issue, the aim of the interference and the possible presence of a common denominator in the States' legal systems.[515]

Therefore, according to the AG:

> As regards the nature of the right and activities at issue, where the right is one which *intimately affects the individual's private sphere*, such as the right to confidentiality of health-related personal data, the European Court of Human Rights seems to take the view that the State's margin of appreciation is more limited and that its own judicial review must be stricter.[516]

Following the Advocate General's reasoning, PNR data did not seem to 'intimately affect the individual's private sphere', and consequently the margin of appreciation left to the executive would be wider and the judicial review more lenient. It is regrettable, however, that by using the right to privacy to make his assessment, AG Léger decided that the level of judicial review should be decreased in the name of the fight against terrorism. This approach is understandable since at the time, the Charter was not legally binding. In his recent Opinion on the draft EU–Canada PNR Agreement, AG Mengozzi rightly called for a 'strict review' of compliance

---

[513] Opinion of Advocate General Léger in Joined Cases C-317/04 and C-318/04, n 162 above, para 211.

[514] ibid, para 212 (emphasis added). AG Mengozzi also opined that the interference constituted by the draft EU–Canada PNR Agreement is 'less extensive than that provided for in Directive 2006/24 and is also less intrusive into the daily life of everyone.' Opinion of AG Mengozzi, n 297 above, para 240.

[515] Opinion of AG Léger, n 162 above, para 228.

[516] ibid, para 229 (emphasis added).

with the principle of proportionality and fundamental rights in the case of PNR[517] on the basis of 'the important role which the protection of personal data plays in the light of the fundamental right to respect for private life' and because of 'the extent and seriousness of the interference with that right, which may include the large number of persons whose fundamental rights are liable to be infringed where personal data is transferred to a third country.'[518]

B. The Added Normative Value of the Fundamental Right to Data Protection in the Case of PNR

The right to privacy is relevant in the PNR case in particular as far as sensitive data relating to the personal or family life of the person are at issue. PNR data that reveal confidential information about potential health problems of the individual, or his credit card details, or the contact details of his family or friends, or his religious beliefs based on the meal he ordered during the flight within the scope of the right to privacy under Article 7 EUCFR. Such data come also within the scope of the right to data protection that provides for enhanced protection in these cases.

It is difficult to justify, however, why the rest of the PNR data can be protected by the right to privacy, as AG Léger's analysis demonstrated. A further argument that could be made is that the right to privacy applies insofar as PNR data is confidential commercial information of the air carriers on the basis of the contractual rights and obligations arising from the legally binding agreement concluded between the air carrier and the customer/passenger. This, however, means that the application of the fundamental right to privacy is made subject to private law obligations assumed in the process of a contract concluded between two private parties. Certainly, the air carrier is bound by the obligation not to reveal the information communicated to it for the execution of the contract, but this is a mere contractual private law obligation that cannot be given equal standing with the public law purpose of combating terrorism and serious crime. The question has been brought before US Federal Courts, which, not surprisingly, held that, 'without a specific showing of damages, passengers have no cause of action against airlines that disclose or transfer PNR data to third parties.'[519] More particularly, in *Re Northwest Airlines Privacy Litigation*, passengers claimed that the transfer by Northwest of PNR data to the National Aeronautical and Space Administration to assist in a study of airline security violated the airline's privacy policy.[520] The US Court dismissed the claim, stating that 'general statements of policy are not

---

[517] See Opinion of AG Mengozzi, n 297 above, paras 199–204.
[518] ibid, para 201.
[519] For a more detailed analysis see Rasmussen, n 3 above, p 567.
[520] *Re Northwest Airlines Privacy Litigation*, No Civ 04-126 (PAM/JSM), 2004 WL 1278459, 1 (D Minn 6 June 2004).

contractual'.[521] This demonstrates that an argument based on passengers' privacy arising from the contractual obligations assumed by the air carriers has limited value in the use of PNR data for law enforcement purposes.

Such problems do not arise with regard to the right to data protection. All the categories of data contained in the PNR constitute information relating to an identified person and, therefore, personal data, regardless of whether they are connected to the intimate private sphere of the person or not. An assessment therefore of the PNR case on the basis of the specific data protection principles enshrined in the fundamental right to data protection would not encounter the difficulties found in the Advocate General's analysis, carried out on the basis of the right to privacy. But the fundamental right to data protection is not only useful for a finding of interference in the PNR case. Such an interference was found by AG Léger, albeit with some difficulties, with regard to the right to privacy as well. The most important contribution of the fundamental right to data protection lies in the assessment of whether the interference posed by PNR is disproportionate or not. Data protection provides for specific principles, on the basis of which such an assessment can be undertaken: among others, purpose limitation, proportionality concerning the amount of data processed and the periods of their retention, consent of the data subject, individual due-process rights, enhanced protection of sensitive data, and independent supervision.

It is submitted, therefore, that data protection is the correct fundamental rights basis to assess PNR data transfers for two reasons: first, because all PNR data, despite their level of intimacy, are personal data, and consequently their processing may interfere with the right to data protection if it does not comply with the requirements of Article 8 EUCFR. This approach avoids making fundamental rights protection subject to private law obligations. Second, the specific data protection principles are the right forum to discuss whether such interference is disproportionate, instead of the general privacy right that cannot catch all the problems posed by the PNR transfer.

VI. A SUBSTANTIVE ASSESSMENT OF PNR UNDER THE FUNDAMENTAL RIGHT TO DATA PROTECTION

According to Article 52(1) EUCFR, a) any limitation of a right of the Charter should: b) be provided for by law; c) meet objectives of general interest recognised by the Union or the need to protect the rights and freedoms of others; d) be necessary; e) be subject to the principle of proportionality; and f) respect the essence of the right. The analysis below employs this formula with regard to the fundamental right to data protection.

---

[521] ibid.

A. Limitation of the Right to Data Protection

In order to assess whether a limitation of the right to data protection exists, it must be examined, at the outset, if this right is applicable at all to the transmission of PNR data by air carriers to the United States Department of Homeland Security and the processing of these data by the latter. The fundamental right to data protection indeed applies in the present case because all the fields of data contained in the Passenger Name Record are 'personal data' to the extent that they are related to an identified person; and the collection and transmission of the data to DHS by the air carriers, as well as the operations undertaken on the data by the latter constitute 'processing' of personal data.

A clarification is further needed at this point for the sake of accuracy of the analysis. In the case of PNR data transfer, we are dealing with two phases of processing of the same data: at the first phase, the airlines collect the data for the purpose of issuing the ticket; at the second phase, the DHS receives the data from the airlines—through the 'push' method even though the 'pull' method might still be applied—stores and processes them for law enforcement purposes. Both the airline companies and DHS are 'controllers' of personal data, since they determine the purposes and means of the processing of the data. Indeed, we have two different controllers processing the same data and two distinct processing operations. The method of transfer of the data ('push' or 'pull') does not seem to make any significant difference to this assessment, DHS is in both cases a controller.[522]

The separation of these two different types of processing is not an easy task. The CJEU dealt with this issue in its 2006 *PNR* judgment, where it attempted to separate the two types of processing in order to decide in which pillar they fell. The conclusion it reached based on the separation of processing was criticised for many reasons, as seen above. Such a strict separation, as the one followed by the Court for its legal basis analysis, is obsolete in the post-Lisbon era, and it will not be adopted here for a further important reason: apart from the obligation on air carriers to transmit the PNR data to DHS, the rest of the 2012 EU–US PNR Agreement (and its predecessors) deal with the processing of the data by the DHS. This will, therefore, be the centre of the present analysis.

Having assessed that the fundamental right to data protection is applicable in the PNR case, it needs to be established whether this right has been limited by the 2012 EU–US PNR Agreement. The conditions for the transmission of PNR data to DHS and their processing thereof poses limitations to the following data protection principles: the purpose limitation principle, the data minimisation principle, the proportionality principle concerning the period of the retention of the data, and the non-discrimination principle. It also interferes with the due

---

[522] Contra Ntouvas, n 103 above, p 88.

process and individual participation rights of the data subject[523] and the requirement for an independent supervision under Article 8(3) EUCFR. Finally, it raises questions with regard to sensitive data to the extent they are also transmitted, and the consent of the data subject. In particular, Article 8(2) EUCFR requires that data must be processed 'on the basis of the consent of the data subject.' Consent, however, has limited value in the PNR case. The data subject has given his consent for the processing of his data from the airline company in order to purchase a ticket, but no consent has been given for the transfer of the data to intelligence and law enforcement authorities and data subjects cannot object to giving their PNR data if they wish to travel.[524] Indeed, there is no issue of consent, but rather a 'take it or leave it' deal. As one airline CEO astutely put it: 'You want to travel on the airline system? You give up your privacy. You don't want to give up your privacy? Don't fly.'[525]

It is worth noting that AG Mengozzi found that the EU–Canada draft PNR Agreement interferes with both privacy and data protection. According to the AG, PNR data 'taken as a whole, touches on the area of the privacy, indeed intimacy, of persons and indisputably relates to one or more "identified or identifiable individual or individuals".'[526] While the AG did not provide any further explanation as to why PNR data affect the intimacy of individuals, he concluded that the systematic transfer of such a volume of data to the Canadian public authorities, the access and the use of such data, its retention for a period of five years by those public authorities and in certain cases its subsequent transfer to other public authorities and third countries 'fall within the scope of the fundamental right to respect for private and family life guaranteed by Article 7 of the Charter and to the "closely connected" but nonetheless distinct right to protection of personal data guaranteed by Article 8(1) of the Charter and constitute an interference with those fundamental rights.'[527] This assessment is not affected by the fact that most persons will not suffer any inconvenience as a result of that interference[528] and the fact that most information transferred does not concern sensitive data.[529] In my view, the AG should have based his analysis solely on the fundamental right to data protection since all the reasons he identified explaining the interference posed by PNR essentially relate to this right. The AG's approach seems to suggest that the 'close connectivity' of data protection to privacy still prevents it

---

[523]   E Fahey, 'Law and Governance as Checks and Balances in Transatlantic Security: Rights, Redress, and Remedies in EU–US Passenger Name Records and the Terrorist Finance Tracking Program' (2013) *Yearbook of European Law* 1.

[524]   Opinion of AG Mengozzi, n 297 above, para 184.

[525]   R Crandall, 'Security for the Future: Let's Get Our Airlines Flying', 2001 Airline Security and Economic Symposium (2002) 67 *Journal of Air Law & Commerce* 9, 19.

[526]   Opinion of AG Mengozzi, n 297 above, para 170.

[527]   ibid.

[528]   ibid, 172. See to that effect *Digital Rights Ireland*, n 293 above, para 33; *Schrems*, n 127 above, para 87.

[529]   ibid, 173.

from operating on its own without privacy on its side. It also implies an implicit hierarchy of the value of the two rights: privacy is more important than data protection, therefore, this is needed, even though it is touched only tangentially by the measure at issue in order to establish the 'seriousness' of the interference.[530] However, there is no reason why an interference cannot be considered as 'serious' when only the right to data protection is at stake. Given that the fundamental right to data protection has been fully recognised as an autonomous right in the case law of the CJEU, the approach that considers this right void of any value of its own should be rejected.

B. Provided for by Law

Following the established case law of the European Court of Human Rights, any interference with a fundamental right should be provided by law that is foreseeable and accessible. Previous EU–US PNR Agreements had difficulties satisfying these conditions, because the US assurances or undertakings regarding their processing of the data were found in different instruments with a dubious legally binding nature. The 2012 EU–US PNR, however, appears to provide a legal basis for the transfer of PNR data to the US and therefore complies with the 'provided by law' requirement.

C. Objectives of General Interest Recognised by the Union

Under Article 4 of the 2012 PNR Agreement, PNR is collected and used by the US for the following purposes: i) preventing and combating terrorism and related crimes, or ii) other serious crimes that are punishable by a sentence of imprisonment of three years and are transnational, iii) for the protection of vital interests of any individual or if ordered by a court, and iv) to identify persons who would be subject to closer questioning or examination upon arrival to or departure from the United States or who may require further examination.

Preventing and combating terrorism and other serious transnational crimes is an objective of general interest recognised by the Union. The same could be argued for the protection of the vital interests of the individuals, although it is not clear how such an objective can be achieved by collecting and processing PNR data. It is difficult to see, however, how US border management purposes can be considered as meeting objectives of general interest recognised by the EU.

---

[530] Opinion of AG Mengozzi, n 297 above, para 201.

D. Necessity

The necessity of the PNR system is one of the most disputed issues. According to AG Mengozzi, this requires an assessment of whether a 'fair balance' has been struck between the objective of combating terrorism and serious transnational crime and the objective of protecting personal data and respecting the private life of the persons concerned.[531] Such a fair balance must be reflected in the agreement, which must establish clear and precise rules governing the scope and the application of a measure interfering with Articles 7 and 8 EUCFR and impose a 'minimum' of requirements, so that the persons concerned have sufficient guarantees that their data will be afforded effective protection against the risks of abuse and also against any unlawful access to and any unlawful use of that data.[532] It should also be investigated if there are other less intrusive measures that can achieve in an effective manner the purpose of fighting terrorism.[533]

Regarding the effectiveness of PNR, Secretary of Homeland Security Chertoff provided, in a letter of 14 May 2007 to the European Parliament, eight examples that 'illustrate the necessity of analysing and sharing PNR data'.[534] Among them only one refers to terrorism, and in a rather indirect way.[535] Some of the rest have mere anecdotal value and are not based on robust empirical evidence.[536] The processing of API data could be considered as a less restrictive measure to PNR, however, it is generally accepted that such data 'does not reveal information about the booking methods, payment methods used and travel habits, the cross-checking of which can be useful for the purposes of combating terrorism and other serious transnational criminal activities.'[537]

E. Proportionality

As seen above, PNR interferes with a number of data protection principles. First, it affects the purpose limitation principle. The use of PNR data for law enforcement purposes is a purpose incompatible with the commercial purpose of their initial collection by the airline companies, namely to effectuate the purchase of a plane ticket. Such use constitutes a 'purpose deviation'[538] that, coupled with the

---

[531]   ibid, para 207.
[532]   ibid, para 208.
[533]   ibid.
[534]   Chertoff, n 220 above.
[535]   ibid.
[536]   ibid.
[537]   Opinion of AG Mengozzi, n 297 above, para 214.
[538]   E de Busser, 'EU Data Protection in Transatlantic Cooperation in Criminal Matters: Will the EU Be Serving Its Citizens an American Meal?' (2010) 6 *Utrecht Law Review* 86, 95.

quantities of data processed and the extensive retention periods, turn the 'function creep' into a 'function rush' problem.[539] Moreover, the processing, collation, and comparison of these data against unknown patterns make the 'powerlessness' and 'vulnerability'[540] of the data subjects even greater, especially taking into account that they lack any meaningful form of participation in this form of processing.

Law enforcement authorities' access to commercial data is a central problem identified in different cases of information processing.[541] Where does this leave the purpose limitation data protection principle? It can be assumed that this has no bite and data, already available to the private sector for commercials reasons, will be used for law enforcement purposes as well, as long as such use respects the 'essence' of the fundamental right to data protection. This approach reduces the content of the purpose limitation principle to a mere declaration that data are to be used for certain purposes, which can be easily complied with in most cases. Such a reading of this principle is adopted for instance in the EU–US Umbrella Agreement, which provides in Article 6(1) entitled 'Purpose and Use Limitations': 'The transfer of personal information shall be for specific purposes authorised by the legal basis for the transfer …'. Besides being tautological, this provision suggests that the meaning of purpose and use limitation is that personal data can be processed for certain determined purposes, even if these are completely different from the ones for which the data were initially collected. This interpretation of the purpose limitation principle is confirmed in Article 16 of the 2012 EU–US PNR Agreement, that allows for the domestic sharing of the PNR between the DHS and other US government authorities for purposes consistent with the purposes of their transfer.

AG Mengozzi did not refer in his Opinion on the draft EU–Canada PNR to this issue, but found that this agreement was incompatible with Articles 7 and 8 EUCFR to the extent that it allows 'the possibilities of processing PNR data to be extended beyond what is strictly necessary, independently of the stated purposes of the agreement envisaged'.[542] Similar concerns are also raised with regard to the 2012 EU–US PNR, which permits the processing of PNR data on a case-by-case basis where necessary in view of a serious threat and for the protection of vital interests of any individual or if ordered by a court[543] and in order to identify persons who would be subject to closer questioning or examination upon arrival to or departure from the US.[544]

---

[539] BJ Koops, 'Law, Technology, and Shifting Power Relations' (2010) 25 *Berkeley Technical Law Journal* 973, 989.

[540] D Solove, 'Privacy and Power: Computer Databases and Metaphors for Information Privacy' (2001) 53 *Stanford Law Review* 1393, 1423.

[541] See F Cate, J Dempsey and I Rubinstein, 'Systematic government access to private-sector data' (2012) 2(4) *International Data Privacy Law* 195; S Pell, 'Systematic government access to private-sector data in the United States' (2012) 2(4) *International Data Privacy Law* 245.

[542] Opinion of AG Mengozzi, n 297 above, paras 236–37.

[543] EU–US PNR, Art 4(2).

[544] ibid, Art 4(3).

Another fair information principle interfered with in the PNR case is the data minimisation principle. This requires that personal data must be adequate, relevant and not excessive in relation to the purposes for which they were collected and further processed. The 2012 PNR Agreement and the EU PNR Directive require the transmission of 19 data categories. There are certain data fields in the Passenger Name Record that raise questions as to why they are required. For instance, the 2012 Agreement requires the transmission of general remarks, including OSI (Other Service-related Information), SSI (Special Service Information), and SSR (Special Service Requests).[545] These data categories could reveal information concerning racial and ethnic origin (for instance on the meal ordered) or the health data of the passengers (for instance if a wheelchair was requested). The Agreement provides that the DHS employs automated systems to filter and mask out sensitive data from PNR data and does not further process or use such information, unless required in exceptional circumstances 'where the life of an individual could be imperilled or seriously impaired'.[546] It is not clear why sensitive data are collected in the first place, since they are masked out and not further processed. It should also be recalled that the right to privacy applies as well insofar as this type of information is concerned, because it may affect the private and family life of the individual. Furthermore, the relevant data protection principle prohibits the processing of sensitive information, because it can lead to discrimination. For these reasons, it is difficult to see how the proportionality principle has been complied with in connection to the data minimisation principle. A similar conclusion was reached by AG Mengozzi, who highlighted the 'risk of stigmatising a large number of individuals' entailed in the processing of sensitive personal data[547] and found that this was incompatible with Articles 7 and 8 EUCFR.[548]

A further data protection principle stipulates that data should be kept no longer than is necessary for the purposes for which they were collected or further processed. The retention of PNR data for an overall period of 15 years raises questions regarding its proportionality. Firstly, the EU–US PNR Agreement does not state the objective reasons justifying that this retention period is necessary in order to attain the purposes of fighting terrorism and transnational crime.[549] As seen above, the Commission has identified three uses of PNR data: the reactive, the real-time, and the proactive. Reactive and real-time use cannot justify a retention period of 15 years. This means that such a long retention period is required for the proactive use of PNR data, namely drawing terrorist patterns and profiles. Nevertheless, even for this reason, a retention period of 15 years appears unjustified. In his Opinion on the EU–Canada PNR draft Agreement that stipulates five

---

[545] Annex item 17.
[546] 2012 EU–US PNR, Art 6(1) and (3).
[547] Opinion of AG Mengozzi, n 297 above, para 222.
[548] ibid, paras 221 and 225.
[549] See *Digital Rights Ireland*, n 293 above, para 64; ibid, para 280.

years of data retention, AG Mengozzi wonders whether information, such as frequent flyer, check-in status, ticketing or ticket price and code sharing, has 'genuine added value' that justifies its retention for such a long period.[550] Furthermore, as Article 29 WP has pointed out, the distinction between 'active/analytic' and 'dormant' status does not make a difference from a data protection point of view, taking into account that the data remain available and can still be accessed and processed during the dormant period.[551] In any case, the fact that the data are depersonalised and masked out after the initial six months does not make their overall retention period proportionate.

The requirement of control of an independent supervisory authority, according to Article 8(3) EUCFR is not addressed in the 2012 EU–US PNR Agreement. The DHS that is made responsible for supervising the data protection safeguards regarding the transfer of PNR data to the US and to ensure the rights of access, rectification and erasure is hardly an independent supervisory authority. This makes compliance of the Agreement with the data protection principle of independent supervision very problematic.

F. Respect the 'Essence' of the Fundamental Right to Data Protection

In his Opinion, AG Mengozzi considered that the draft EU–Canada PNR Agreement did not compromise the essence of the right to privacy since the nature of the PNR data 'does not permit any precise conclusions to be drawn as regards the essence of the private life of the persons concerned', the data processed is limited to the pattern of air travel between the EU and Canada and the Agreement contains a series of guarantees.[552] As regards the essence of the fundamental right to protection of personal data, the AG also concluded that this was not affected because the said agreement requires Canada to 'ensure compliance verification and the protection, security, confidentiality and integrity of the data', and 'to implement regulatory, procedural or technical measures to protect PNR data against accidental, unlawful or unauthorised access, processing or loss', and provides for effective and dissuasive corrective measures which might include sanctions for data security breaches.[553] This pronouncement reduces again the essence of the fundamental right to data protection to minimum data security safeguards and protection from data security breaches and disregards the data protection principles expressly mentioned in Article 8(2) and (3). It should be recognised that it is indeed difficult to carry out an 'essence' analysis with regard to the right to data protection taking into account the elusiveness of its content, but data protection and its essence should not be equated to data security.

---

[550] ibid.
[551] Art 29 WP, Opinion 5/2007, n 232 above.
[552] Opinion of AG Mengozzi, n 297 above, para 186.
[553] ibid, para 187.

The blanket collection of the PNR data of every passenger, irrespective of whether he is considered to be under suspicion, its retention for long periods and its processing in order to develop terrorist profiles, without granting adequate procedural rights to the individuals concerned to challenge it, affects cumulatively the essence of several different fair information principles and, might, therefore, be considered to touch upon the essence of the fundamental right to data protection.

VII. DATA-MINING PNR DATA

A. The Question of Effectiveness

The analysis above focused mainly on the interferences to the right to data protection posed by the collection and retention of PNR data by law enforcement authorities in order to fight terrorism. However, the use of PNR data is another issue that has not been dealt with yet. As mentioned above, PNR data can be used reactively, in real time or proactively. The two last uses are particularly interesting: PNR data are necessary to create patterns (proactive use) which will then be employed to identify 'unknown' suspects (real-time use).[554] This practice, referred to as data mining, allegedly constitutes the added value for the processing of PNR data by law enforcement authorities. What exactly is data mining? Numerous definitions have been offered.[555] The CATO Report on data mining and counterterrorism defines it as 'the process of searching data for previously unknown patterns and using those patterns to predict future outcomes.'[556]

A 2007 Report for Congress[557] explains:

[d]ata mining involves the use of sophisticated data analysis tools to discover previously unknown, valid patterns and relationships in large data sets. These tools can include statistical models, mathematical algorithms, and machine learning methods (algorithms that improve their performance automatically through experience, such as neural networks or decision trees). Consequently, data mining consists of more than collecting and managing data, it also includes analysis and prediction.[558]

---

[554] ibid.

[555] J Dempsey and L Flint, 'Commercial Data and National Security' (2004) 72 *The George Washington Law Review* 1459, 1464. See also J Thai, 'Is Data Mining Ever a Search Under Justice Stevens's Fourth Amendment?' (2006) 74 *Fordham Law Review* 1731, 1736; I Witten and E Frank, *Data mining* (San Francisco, Morgan Kaufmann, 2000); F Birrer, 'Data mining to combat terrorism and the roots of privacy concerns' (2005) 7 *Ethics and Information Technology* 211.

[556] J Jonas and J Harper, 'Effective Counterterrorism and the limited role of predictive data mining' (2006) *CATO Report* 1.

[557] J Seifert, *Data mining and Homeland Security: An Overview, Library of Congress* (Washington DC, Congressional Research Service, 2007).

[558] ibid, p 1.

Data mining has been used extensively as a marketing strategy to increase sales.[559] This is because, as the Congressional Report explains, it has a clear added value compared to simpler analytical tools that use, for instance, a verification-based approach.[560] Furthermore, data mining in direct marketing works effectively because the sample used is very broad: millions of consumer-behaviour patterns are analysed in order to draw up the profile of each customer[561] to be subsequently targeted by individualised offers or advertisements. Even if the data mining identifies a wrong pattern, the harm made is minimal: the marketer might lose some money for the imperfectly aimed mail, and the customer a moment of his time.[562]

The issue is not the same, however, when it comes to counter-terrorism data mining. It has been argued that in this context, data mining is not only ineffective; it is also disproportionate with regard to its effects. Starting from its potential benefits, experts explain that data mining cannot be effective for counter-terrorism, because it lacks a necessary pre-requisite: terrorist patterns.[563] As explained by a scholar:

> With a relatively small number of attempts every year and only one or two major terrorist incidents every few years -each one distinct in terms of planning and execution- there are no meaningful patterns that show what behaviour indicates planning or preparation for terrorism. Unlike consumers' shopping habits and financial fraud, terrorism does not occur with enough frequency to enable the creation of valid predictive models.[564]

Data mining, therefore, is not an effective mean to predict terrorism, because it lacks 'well-constructed algorithms based on extensive historical patterns'.[565] This deficit cannot be remedied by collecting the data of virtually every person, as in the case of PNR. Having every air passenger's data does not mean that a terrorist attack would be prevented. Unlike direct marketing, where consumers' profiles are based on 'millions of previous instances of the same particular behaviour',[566] terrorist profiles cannot be predicted so accurately, since incidents of terrorist attacks—fortunately—are very few.[567] But even if it is assumed that an accurate terrorist profile can be drawn based on information about known terrorists, it does not necessarily mean that the system is capable of identifying suspects whose behaviour 'significantly deviates from the original model'.[568] The limited

---

[559] Jonas and Harper, n 556 above, p 6. See also United States General Accounting Office, Report to the ranking minority member, Subcommittee on Financial Management, The Budget, and International Security, Committee on governmental affairs, US Senate, 'Data Mining—Federal Efforts cover a wide range of uses', May 2004, 2.
[560] Seifert, n 557 above, p 2.
[561] Jonas and Harper, n 556 above, p 7.
[562] ibid.
[563] ibid.
[564] ibid, p 8.
[565] ibid.
[566] Seifert, n 557 above, p 3.
[567] Ramasastry, n 341 above, p 773.
[568] Seifert, n 557 above, p 3.

frequency and individuality of terrorist acts within the EU and the US necessarily has made counter-terrorism data mining efforts 'backwards focused'.[569] For instance, Cate observes that since the 9/11 terrorists used box cutters to take over the aircraft, the US government banned box cutters and everything that resembled them, such as nail clippers, nail files, pocket knives, etc. When, subsequently, a terrorist attack was attempted by using detonating explosives hidden in a terrorist's shoes, the TSA officials began screening shoes; when British officials uncovered a plot to blow up aircraft with liquid explosives, restrictions on liquids carried on planes were introduced.[570]

Commentators often distinguish between subject-based and pattern-based analysis of data.[571] Subject-based data analysis aims to 'trace links from known individuals or things to others'.[572] Pattern-based analysis is more probabilistic: it aims to develop patterns that will be used to unveil previously unknown suspects.[573] The main use of PNR data and their alleged added value is found exactly in the pattern-based analysis that can be performed on this set of data.[574] For a subject-based analysis, which is based on suspicion and not on uncertain patterns, the use of API data would have been enough.

However, data mining is very limited: it can merely reveal patterns; it cannot explain the significance of these patterns or identify a casual relationship.[575] It can only provide information about the '*what*' and not about the '*why*'.[576] Checking, for instance, whether a passenger purchased a one-way ticket or a ticket within a short time before the departure of the flight, because such behaviour was followed by the 9/11 terrorists, is not enough to reveal future terrorists. People might purchase one-way tickets within a short time before the departure for various reasons that have nothing to do with terrorism (for instance, because of the nature of their profession, their personal circumstances or because they merely found a good offer, etc).[577]

Moreover, whatever the technological capabilities of the data-mining system, its effectiveness depends also on other factors, especially, where 'commercial data' are used as in the case of PNR. In this context, a first problem has to do with the accuracy and the completeness of the data.[578] The Congressional Report emphasises that data quality is a 'multifaceted issue that represents one of the biggest

---

[569] F Cate, 'Government Data Mining: The Need for a Legal Framework' (2008) 43 *Harvard Civil Rights—Civil Liberties Law Review* 435, 474.

[570] ibid.

[571] Dempsey and Flint, n 555 above, p 1466; Jonas and Harper, n 556 above, p 6.

[572] ibid.

[573] ibid. Unlike subject-based analysis, pattern-based analysis is characterised more by prediction than by the traditional notion of suspicion.

[574] See above.

[575] Ramasastry, n 341 above, p 770; D Steinbock, 'Data Matching, Data Mining, and Due Process' (2005) 40 *Georgia Law Review* 82; Seifert, n 557 above, p 3.

[576] Dempsey and Flint, n 555 above, p 1470.

[577] Ramasastry, n 341 above, p 770.

[578] Seifert, n 557 above, p 21.

challenges for data mining'.[579] In this context, 'the presence of duplicate records, the lack of data standards, the timeliness of updates, and human error can significantly impact the effectiveness of the more complex data mining techniques, which are sensitive to subtle differences that may exist in the data.'[580] Moreover, PNR data have an additional problem that adds to their limited data quality: they are subjective. PNR are completed at the time of reservation of an airline ticket by customers themselves, who can provide inaccurate or false data, or even use fraudulent identification documents. In such instances, not only are the patterns drawn inaccurate; wrong people might be identified as potential terrorists.[581]

Finally, as experts point out, the statistical likelihood of false identifications (either false positives or false negatives) in data mining make it prohibitive.[582] In particular, even if it is assumed that a terrorist data-mining system works very accurately with a 99 per cent accuracy rate—which is very difficult, taking into account the problems identified above—still the 1 per cent of false negatives is unduly large with regard to the millions of travellers that fly from Europe to the US or between European destinations every year.[583]

B. Fundamental Rights Affected

Unlike marketing data mining, which is normally efficient and has minimal negative effects, counter-terrorism data mining does not merely have limited effectiveness, it also has serious consequences on fundamental rights. Three rights mainly are affected: the right to privacy (Article 7 EUCFR),[584] the right to data protection (Article 8 EUCFR), and the prohibition of discrimination (Article 21 EUCFR).[585]

Starting with the right to privacy, it has been argued that

the greatest impact of data mining on individual privacy is that individuals will change their behaviour as a result of their awareness that the government may, without probable cause or other specific authorisation, obtain access to myriad distributed stores of information about them.[586]

---

[579] ibid.
[580] ibid.
[581] Cate, n 569 above, p 472.
[582] ibid, p 479.
[583] See also Opinion of AG Mengozzi, n 297 above, para 255.
[584] Technology and Privacy Advisory Committee, US Department of Defence, 'Safeguarding Privacy in the fight against terrorism', TAPAC Report, March 2004, 48.
[585] The EU Fundamental Rights Agency Opinion concerning the establishment of an EU PNR system focused exactly on these three rights. See Fundamental Rights Agency, n 454 above, p 1.
[586] Cate, n 569 above, p 477. See also M Tzanou, 'The EU as an Emerging "Surveillance Society": The Function Creep Case Study and Challenges to Privacy and Data Protection' (2010) 4 *Vienna Online Journal of International Constitutional Law* 407; House of Lords, Select Committee on the Constitution, Surveillance: Citizens and the State, 2nd Report of Session 2008–09.

More specific and concrete interferences are found with regard to the right to data protection. Besides the problems posed on the purpose limitation principle analysed above, data mining also raises questions regarding the due process rights of the data subject. As Steinbock notes,

> [t]he most striking aspect of virtually all antiterrorist … data mining decisions is the total absence of even the most rudimentary procedures for notice, hearing, or other opportunities for meaningful participation.[587]

Setting aside the consequences that data mining might have on those individuals identified as potential terrorists because they fit the profiles (no-fly lists, terrorist investigations, arrest, greater scrutiny, inclusion in watch-lists,[588] humiliation)[589] that call for enhanced due process rights, terrorist profiles raise more general due process issues. Profiling is generally defined as the 'systematic association of sets of physical, behavioural or psychological characteristics with particular offences and their use as a basis for making law-enforcement decisions.'[590] How are terrorist profiles drawn up? What characteristics make a terrorist? How can someone disagree with such a profile? Profiles are secret, because otherwise terrorists would try to evade them.[591] How is it possible to control them, then, in order to verify that they are not abusive or discriminative? If they cannot be made known to the general public, why cannot they be controlled by the judiciary? For instance, a pattern-based analysis could be reviewed by a court.[592] This raises further questions: What should be the standard of review? When can terrorist data-mining be allowed and when not?

Advocate General Mengozzi raised similar concerns in his examination of the draft EU–Canada PNR Agreement. He noted that the main added value of the processing of the PNR data lies in 'the comparison of the data received with scenarios or predetermined risk assessment criteria or databases which, with the assistance of automated processing, makes it possible to identify "targets" who can subsequently be subjected to more thorough checks.'[593] However, none of the terms of the PNR agreements or systems currently in place make any specific reference to either such databases or those scenarios or assessment criteria, which

---

[587] Steinbock, n 575 above, p 82.

[588] Dempsey and Flint, n 555 above, p 1471.

[589] M Scheinin, Report of the Special Rapporteur on the promotion and protection of Human Rights and Fundamental Freedoms while Countering Terrorism, A/HRC/4/26, 29 January 2007, para 56.

[590] ibid, para 33. See also D Moeckli, 'Terrorist Profiling and the Importance of a Proactive Approach to Human Rights Protection' (2006), https://a1papers.ssrn.com/sol3/papers.cfm?abstract_id=952163; T Ojanen, 'Terrorist Profiling: Human Rights Concerns' (2010) 3 *Critical Studies on Terrorism* 295; MD Kielsgard, 'A human rights approach to counter-terrorism' (2006) 36(2) *California Western International Law Journal* 249.

[591] D Solove, 'Data Mining and the Security-Liberty Debate' (2008) 74 *University of Chicago Law Review* 343, 359.

[592] Dempsey and Flint, n 555 above, p 1501.

[593] Opinion of AG Mengozzi, n 297 above, para 252.

therefore continue to be determined and used at the entire discretion of public authorities.[594]

The issue of terrorist profiles was brought up in the seminal *Rasterfahndung* decision of the German Constitutional Court.[595] The case concerned the notorious *Rasterfahndung* ('dragnet investigation') implemented by police and intelligence agencies in Germany after the 9/11 terrorists attacks for the purpose of identifying Muslim terrorist sleepers.[596] The programme was initiated after it became known that some of the terrorists who had participated in the 9/11 attacks had been residing in Germany and had studied at German universities.[597] The criteria used for the screening were: male, aged 18 to 40, student or former student, of Islamic religious affiliation, coming from a country with predominantly Islamic population.[598] These criteria would then be combined with further information in order to lead to the discovery of 'terrorist sleepers'. In October 2001, the programme was approved by the Amtsgericht Düsseldorf (Düsseldorf Local Court) at the request of the police department of Düsseldorf pursuant to § 31 of the *Polizeigesetz des Landes Nordrhein-Westfalen* (Police law of North Rhine-Westphalia state).[599] In accordance with the programme, universities, colleges, health and social insurance agencies, registry offices, the central registry of immigrants, employers and other institutions were asked to provide data,[600] which were held at the *Bundeskriminalamt* (Federal Criminal Police Office), in a file called '*Schläfer*' ('Sleeper').[601] It is estimated that within the first four months alone of the programme the data of more than 30,000 male students had been collected in Hamburg.[602] Overall, around 8 million personal data of up to 300,000 persons were gathered,[603] and approximately 32,000 people were identified as potential terrorist sleepers.[604] It is worth noting that *Rasterfahndung*, despite its massive scale, did not lead to the opening of a single criminal case for terrorist-related offences.

The programme was challenged by a Moroccan student who had been screened. After his appeals were rejected in the lower courts, the student filed a complaint before the Federal Constitutional Court. The Constitutional Court concluded that

---

[594] ibid, para 253.

[595] BVerfGE 115, 320, 1 BvR 518/02, 4 April 2006.

[596] ibid, para 9.

[597] V Zöller, 'Liberty Dies by Inches: German Counter-Terrorism Measures and Human Rights' (2004) 5 *German Law Journal* 469, 487.

[598] 1 BvR 518/02, n 595 above, para 8. See also G Kett-Straub, 'Data Screening of Muslim Sleepers Unconstitutional' (2006) 7 *German Law Journal* 967, 970; M Kaufmann, *Ethnic Profiling and Counter-terrorism: Examples of European Practice and Possible Repercussions* (Münster, LIT Verlag, 2010).

[599] F Müller and T Richter, 'Report on the Bundesverfassungsgericht's (Federal Constitutional Court) Jurisprudence in 2005/2006' (2008) 9 *German Law Journal* 161, 179–80.

[600] ibid.

[601] ibid.

[602] 'Kleine Anfrage der PDS zur Rasterfahndung', 18 Feb 2002 *Bundestagsdrucksache* 14/8257. See also Zöller, n 597 above, p 487.

[603] 1 BvR 518/02, n 595 above, para 28.

[604] ibid.

the *Rasterfahndung* programme constituted a serious infringement of the fundamental right to informational self-determination.[605] According to the Court, all the information collected in the course of the programme was personal data regarding the religious affiliation, the nationality, the family status, and the field of study of the individuals concerned. This information was combined with other data sets in order to produce new information with 'very intense personality relevance' (*besonders starke Persönlichkeitsrelevanz*).[606] 'Personality profiles' (*Persönlichkeitsbilder*) could be, thus, created[607] and people were made subject to screening methods that had a 'stigmatising effect' (*stigmatisierende Wirkung*) and increased the risk of discrimination.[608] The Court stated that a dragnet investigation targeting Muslim people could augment the stereotypes and stigmatise a whole group in the public perception.[609] The Court also criticised the secrecy covering the programme,[610] which implicated people who had no information about it[611] and people who had never aroused any suspicion.[612] Finally, the Court held that since the infringement of fundamental rights was serious, a 'concrete threat' was needed before such an investigation could be carried out.[613]

The *Rasterfahndung* case is illuminating for the present discussion as well. The Constitutional Court found that the drawing up of terrorist profiles, such as those used by the programme interfered disproportionately with the right to informational self-determination. Similar concerns apply to the PNR case. The drawing up of predictive terrorist profiles interferes with the right to data protection, as understood by the German Constitutional Court through the concept of 'informational self-determination', because it goes against individual autonomy and makes the asymmetry of power between data subject and data controller—the secret services, law enforcement authorities—even greater. Furthermore, the criteria used in the *Rasterfahndung* programme were clearly discriminatory and could lead to the stigmatisation of a certain group of the population. While the criteria used for building up terrorist profiles in the case of PNR data are not known, a similar danger might exist.

Terrorist data mining might also interfere with Article 21 EUCFR, which prohibits discrimination based on any ground such as sex, race, colour, ethnic or social origin, genetic features, language, religion or belief, political or any other opinion, membership of a national minority, property, birth, disability, age or sexual orientation. The FRA in its Opinion concerning the establishment of an EU PNR system

---

[605] ibid, para 37.
[606] ibid, para 101.
[607] ibid, para 106.
[608] ibid, para 108.
[609] ibid.
[610] ibid, para 110.
[611] ibid.
[612] ibid.
[613] ibid, para 125.

was categorical on this point: '[a]ny mass profiling using stereotypical assumptions based on racial or religious criteria should be conceived as unjustifiable.'[614]

Terrorist data mining and profiling are, thus, not only ineffective, but also have serious implications on human rights. As the FRA correctly observed, 'they affect thousands of innocent people, without producing concrete results.'[615] There is currently no concrete information on how PNR data are being data-mined and terrorist profiles are drawn, but there is an increased risk that such a practice seriously interferes with the fundamental right to informational self-determination and the prohibition of discrimination. In this respect, AG Mengozzi proposed that the draft EU–Canada PNR should expressly state that 'neither the scenarios or the predetermined assessment criteria nor the databases used can be based on an individual's racial or ethnic origin, his political opinions, his religion or philosophical beliefs, his membership of a trade union, his health or his sexual orientation;[616] where 'the comparison of PNR data with the predetermined criteria and scenarios leads to a positive result, that result must be examined by non-automated means';[617] and the relevant criteria, scenarios and databases used for profiling should be the subject of control by an independent authority.[618] Such safeguards should be adopted also in the context of all the other EU PNR bilateral agreements as well as the EU's own PNR system.

[614] Fundamental Rights Agency, n 454 above, para 39. On ethnic profiling in general see also EU Network of Independent Experts on Fundamental Rights, 'Ethnic Profiling', CFR-CDF Opinion 4/2006, December 2006; O De Schutter and J Ringelheim, 'Ethnic Profiling: A Rising Challenge for European Human Rights Law' (2008) 71 *Modern Law Review* 358; Fundamental Rights Agency, 'Towards more effective policing understanding and preventing discriminatory ethnic profiling: A Guide', October 2010, http://fra.europa.eu/sites/default/files/fra_uploads/1133-Guide-ethnic-profiling_EN.pdf; Open Society, 'Justice Initiative, Ethnic Profiling in the European Union: Pervasive, Ineffective, and discriminatory', www.opensocietyfoundations.org/sites/default/files/profiling_20090526.pdf; D Moeckli, 'Discriminatory Profiles: Law Enforcement After 9/11 and 7/7' (2005) 5 *European Human Rights Law Review* 517; D Moeckli, *Human Rights and Non-Discrimination in the 'War on Terror'* (Oxford, Oxford University Press, 2008).
[615] Fundamental Rights Agency, n 454 above, para 38.
[616] Opinion of AG Mengozzi, n 297 above, para 258.
[617] ibid, para 259.
[618] ibid, para 260.

5

Financial Data Surveillance

I. THE SWIFT AFFAIR

A. The Secret Operations

O N 23 SEPTEMBER 2001, two weeks after the 11 September attacks, the US President issued Executive Order 13224.[1] The Order, which was characterised by President Bush as 'draconian',[2] declared a national emergency on the basis that the 9/11 terrorist attacks constituted 'an unusual and extraordinary threat to the national security, foreign policy, and economy of the United States'.[3] The Order also imposed financial sanctions to 'foreign persons that support or otherwise associate with foreign terrorists'[4] and asked the Secretary of the Treasury to

> make all relevant efforts to cooperate and coordinate with other countries, including through technical assistance, as well as bilateral and multilateral agreements and arrangements, to achieve the objectives of th[e] order, including … the sharing of intelligence about funding activities in support of terrorism.[5]

Furthermore, section 314(a) of the USA Patriot Act urged law enforcement authorities

> to share with financial institutions information regarding individuals, entities and organisations engaged in or reasonably suspected … of engaging in terrorist acts or money laundering activities.[6]

Based on the International Emergency Economic Powers Act of 1977 (IEEPA) and the Executive Order 13224, as implemented through the Global Terrorism

---

[1] Executive Order 13224, 'Blocking Property and Prohibiting Transactions With Persons Who Commit, Threaten to Commit, or Support Terrorism', 66 Fed Reg 49,079, 23 September 2001.

[2] See L Donohue, 'Anti-terrorist Finance in the United Kingdom and United States' (2006) 27 *Michigan Journal of International Law* 303, 377.

[3] Executive Order 13224, n 1 above.

[4] ibid, s. 1.

[5] ibid, s 6. See also s 7.

[6] Uniting and Strengthening America by Providing Appropriate Tools Required to Intercept and Obstruct Terrorism Act of 2001, Pub L No 107-56, 115 Stat 272, 307. See D Shetterly, 'Starving the Terrorists of Funding: How the United States Treasury Is Fighting the War on Terror' (2006) 18 *Regent University Law Review* 327, 340; Donohue, n 2 above, p 374.

Sanctions Regulations, the United States Department of the Treasury (UST) established the Terrorist Finance Tracking Programme (TFTP). Under the Programme, UST was authorised to require any person to furnish financial transaction data in connection with a terrorism investigation.[7] The purpose was to identify, track, and pursue terrorists and their networks by unravelling their money flows.[8] According to the US Treasury Department,

> terrorists depend on a regular cash flow to pay operatives, arrange for travel, train new members, forge documents, pay bribes, acquire weapons, and stage attacks. In order to send money through the banking system, they often provide information that yields the kinds of concrete leads that can advance a terrorism investigation. This is why counterterrorism officials place a high premium on financial intelligence, including that derived from programs such as the TFTP, which has proved to be of inestimable value in combating global terrorism.[9]

James Gurule, then Under Secretary for Enforcement of the US Department of Treasury, stated at the hearing before the Committee on Finance of the US Senate that the objective was 'to follow the money trail, and dismantle entire financial networks and channels from moving money to finance terror.'[10]

Private law entities of the financial sector were enlisted by UST in this effort.[11] In particular, the US Treasury Department, seeking information on suspected international terrorist networks under the TFTP, started issuing administrative subpoenas to the US operations centre of the Society for Worldwide Interbank Financial Telecommunication (SWIFT).[12] SWIFT is a cooperative limited liability company governed by Belgian law[13] that operates a worldwide messaging system used to transmit financial transaction information. SWIFT supplies its customers, who are banks or other financial institutions, with automated, standardised messaging services and interface software aimed at transmitting financial messages between financial institutions worldwide.

According to the company's own data, SWIFT is used for the exchange of financial messages by more than 9,700 banking organisations, securities institutions and corporate customers in 209 countries.[14] SWIFT was seen by the US administration as 'the mother lode, the Rosetta stone of financial data',[15] since it represents 80 per cent

---

[7] US Department of the Treasury, 'Terrorist Financing Tracking Program: Fact Sheet', 23.06.2006 available at www.treasury.gov/press-center/press-releases/Pages/js4340.aspx.

[8] ibid.

[9] Processing of EU originating Personal Data by United States Treasury Department for Counter Terrorism Purposes—'SWIFT'(2007/C166/09)—Terrorist Finance Tracking Program—Representations of the United States Department of the Treasury, [2007] OJ C166/18.

[10] Financial War on Terrorism: New Money Trails Present Fresh Challenges: Hearing Before the Committee on Finance, US Senate, 107th Cong 5, 2002.

[11] Shetterly, n 6 above, p 339.

[12] US Department of the Treasury, n 7 above.

[13] Its registered office is in La Hulpe.

[14] See www.swift.com/info?lang=en.

[15] See J Santolli, 'Note: The Terrorist Finance Tracking Program: Illuminating the Shortcomings of the European Union's Antiquated Data Privacy Directive' (2008) 40 *The George Washington International Law Review* 553, 561. According to media information, the idea to target SWIFT with

of the market for international bank transfers globally[16] and its database contains billions of financial messages. When the US Department of Treasury started targeting SWIFT with administrative subpoenas under the TFTP, the company had two operation centres located in SWIFT branches, one in Europe[17] and one in the United States.[18] All messages processed by SWIFT were stored and mirrored at both operation centres for 124 days, as a 'back-up recovery tool' for customers in case of disputes between financial institutions or data loss. After this period the data was deleted.

Administrative subpoenas are orders 'from a government official to a third party, instructing the recipient to produce certain information'.[19] The advantage of administrative subpoenas is that they can be issued as quickly as the development of an investigation requires, because they are issued directly by an agency official. The administrative subpoenas addressed to SWIFT by UST were very broad in nature. They demanded information on transactions which related or might relate to terrorism, related to x number of countries and jurisdictions, on y date, or from … to … dates ranging from one to several weeks.[20] The geographical scope of the subpoenas was also very wide covering messages of inter-bank transactions within the US, to or from the US, as well as messages with no territorial connection to the US, such as messages exchanged within the EU.[21]

As the Belgian Privacy Commission explained, SWIFT messages 'can be compared with an "envelop" and a "letter"'.[22]

> The 'envelop' … contains non-identifying data of the sender, i.e. standardized data of the institution that issues the message, such as its BIC-code, data for the identification of the recipient institutions, and the date and time of the message. The 'letter' contains the actual message, i.e. information on the amount of the transaction, the currency, the value, the date, the beneficiary's name, the beneficiary's financial institution, the customer requesting the financial transaction and the customer's financial institution requesting the transaction.[23]

administrative subpoenas for counter-terrorism purposes came from a conversation between a senior official of the US administration and a Wall Street broker, who pointed out to the former that there are billions of international financial transactions included in SWIFT's database.

[16] Deutsche Welle, 'US Accesses European Bank Data under Controversial SWIFT Agreement', August 2010, www.dw.com/en/us-accesses-european-bank-data-under-controversial-swift-agreement/a-5855750.

[17] In Zoeterwonde in the Netherlands.

[18] In Culpepper in Virginia.

[19] Hearing before the United States Senate Judiciary Committee, Subcommittee on Terrorism, Technology and Homeland Security: 'Tools to Fight Terrorism: Subpoena Authority and Pretrial Detention of Terrorists', Testimony of Rachel Brand, Principal Deputy Assistant Attorney General, Office of Legal Policy, US Department of Justice 22 June 2004, http://kyl.senate.gov/legis_center/subdocs/062204_brand.pdf. See *United States v Allis-Chalmers Corp* 498 F Supp 1027, 1028–30 (ED Wis 1980), 29.

[20] See Belgian Privacy Commission, Opinion No 37/2006 of 27 September 2006 on the Transfer of Personal Data by the CSLR SWIFT by virtue of UST (OFAC) Subpoenas.

[21] ibid.

[22] ibid.

[23] Belgian Privacy Commission, Decision of 9 December 2008, Control and Recommendation Procedure initiated with respect to the Company SWIFT SCRL, 33.

These data, however, which constitute personal data, were encrypted, and SWIFT did not have access to them. This meant that SWIFT could not search its database for specific data requested by the Treasury Department, such as for instance make a search on the basis of the name of a particular person.[24] Furthermore, SWIFT stored copies of financial messages in its archiving system only for a period of 124 days; this storage period was considered too short by the UST for its investigations. For these reasons, a new arrangement had to be negotiated between SWIFT and the Department of Treasury.[25] Pursuant to this, the messages relating to suspicious periods should be isolated, copied and protected from destruction in order to be usefully exploited by the US authorities.[26] According to the agreement reached, SWIFT had to deliver from its US operation centre the data required under the subpoena to a so-called 'black box' owned by the US and retained at UST facilities; the US Treasury Department would perform, subsequently, its searches on the data transferred to the 'black box'.[27] SWIFT never challenged the administrative subpoenas before the courts because it was in general satisfied with the guarantees given by UST regarding the searches performed,[28] and considered that there was a risk that American judges would have obliged it to communicate all data without any restrictions.[29] Ironically, the TFTP was carried out secretly for six years and SWIFT had already been targeted and complied with 64 subpoenas by UST before the EU finally realised, due to media disclosures.

B. Disclosure and European reactions

On 23 June 2006 a series of articles in the *New York Times*,[30] the *Wall Street Journal*,[31] the *Los Angeles Times*,[32] and the *Washington Post*[33] revealed the secret TFTP scheme that had been in place since 2001, under which the US Department of Treasury in collaboration with the Central Intelligence Agency (CIA) had

---

[24] See W Hummer, 'Die SWIFT-Affaire US-Terrorismusbekämpfung Versus Datenschutz' (2011) 49 *Archiv des Völkerrechts* 203, 211; G González Fuster, P De Hert and S Gutwirth, 'SWIFT and the Vulnerability of Transatlantic Data Transfers' (2008) 22 (1) *International Review of Law, Computers & Technology* 194.

[25] Belgian Privacy Commission, Decision of 9 December 2008, n 23 above, p 12.

[26] ibid.

[27] See Art 29 WP, Opinion 10/2006 on the Processing of Personal Data by the Society for Worldwide Interbank Financial Telecommunication (SWIFT), 8–9.

[28] See Belgian Privacy Commission, Decision of 9 December 2008, n 23 above, p 13; Belgian Privacy Commission, Opinion No 37/2006, n 20 above.

[29] ibid.

[30] E Lichtblau and J Risen, 'Bank Data Is Sifted by U.S. in Secret to Block Terror', *The New York Times*, 23 June 2006.

[31] G Simpson, 'Treasury Tracks Financial Data In Secret Program', *The Wall Street Journal*, 23 June 2006.

[32] J Meyer and G Miller, 'US Secretly Tracks Global Bank Data', *Los Angeles Times*, 23 June 2006.

[33] B Gellman et al, 'Bank Records Secretly Tapped', *The Washington Post*, 23 June 2006.

collected and analysed for counter-terrorism purposes huge amounts of data from SWIFT's database.[34]

The revelation caused a wave of criticisms[35] in the EU. In a Resolution of 6 July 2006, the European Parliament having noted that 'the information stored by SWIFT to which the US authorities have had access concerns hundred of thousands of EU citizens, as European banks use the SWIFT messaging system for the worldwide transfer of funds between banks, and ... SWIFT generates millions of transfers and banking transactions on a daily basis,[36] stressed that it strongly disapproved of 'any secret operations on EU territory that affect the privacy of EU citizens'[37] and that it was deeply concerned that such operations were taking place without the citizens of Europe and their parliamentary representation having being informed.[38] In this respect, it asked the Commission, the Council and the European Central Bank (ECB) to 'explain fully the extent to which they were aware of the secret agreement between SWIFT and the US government',[39] and urged 'the USA and its intelligence and security services to act in a spirit of good cooperation and notify their allies of any security operations they intend to carry out on EU territory.'[40] Concerning the TFTP, the Parliament noted that access to data managed by SWIFT could reveal information on the economic activities of the individuals and the countries concerned with the danger of resulting to 'large-scale forms of economic and industrial espionage.'[41]

Along the same lines, the Belgian Data Protection Authority found that SWIFT had made a 'secret, systematic and large scale violation of the basic European principles of data protection, which went on for years',[42] and as data controller it had failed to comply with its obligations, in particular, the duty to provide information to the data subjects, and to notify the Data Protection Authority of the processing.[43]

In its Opinion of 22 November 2006, the Article 29 Working Party confirmed the finding of the Belgian Privacy Commission that SWIFT was a controller of

---

[34] SWIFT responded the same day by issuing a statement on compliance policy, www.swift.com/about_swift/legal/compliance/statements_on_compliance/swift_statement_on_compliance_policy/index.page.

[35] C Shea, 'A Need for Swift Change: The Struggle Between the European Union's Desire for Privacy in International Financial Transactions and the United States' Need for Security from Terrorists as Evidenced by the Swift Scandal' (2008) 8 *Journal of High Technology Law* 143, 155; SE Exten, 'Major Developments in Financial Privacy Law 2006: The SWIFT Database Incident, and Updates to the Gramm-Leach-Bliley and Fair Credit Reporting Acts' (2008) 3 *ISJLP* 649, 656; J Shrader, 'Secrets Hurt: How SWIFT Shook Up Congress, the European Union, and the US Banking Industry' (2007) 11 *North Carolina Banking Institute* 397.

[36] European Parliament resolution on the interception of bank transfer data from the SWIFT system by the US secret services (P6_TA-PROV(2006)0317).

[37] ibid.
[38] ibid.
[39] ibid.
[40] ibid.
[41] ibid.
[42] Belgian Privacy Commission, Opinion No 37/2006, n 20 above.
[43] ibid.

personal data under EU data protection law.[44] The Working Party criticised SWIFT for failing to notify the transfer of financial data to UST to its customers and to the data protection supervisory authorities.[45] It commented that by deciding to mirror all data processing activities in an operating centre in the US, SWIFT had placed itself in a situation where it was subject to subpoenas under US law.[46] The Working Party observed that the further purpose for which SWIFT's data were used—ie for terrorist investigations—was 'completely different from the original purpose and its treatment of the personal data involved, and may have direct consequences for the individuals whose personal data are being processed.'[47] The Working Party found that the principles of purpose limitation and compatibility, proportionality and necessity of the personal data processed were not respected.[48] Regarding the TFTP, the Working Party held that

> the hidden, systematic, massive and long-term transfer of personal data by SWIFT to the UST in a confidential, non-transparent and systematic manner for years without effective legal grounds and without the possibility of independent control by public data protection supervisory authorities constitutes a violation of fundamental European principles as regards data protection and is not in accordance with Belgian and European law.[49]

In this respect, the Working Party called upon SWIFT to immediately take measures in order to remedy the illegal state of affairs, and to return to a situation where international money transfers were 'in full compliance with national and European law',[50] or otherwise it could be made subject to sanctions imposed by the competent authorities.

The EDPS also entered the discussion but from a slight different perspective: he was asked by the European Parliament to pronounce on the role of the ECB in the SWIFT case and on 1 February 2007, he issued his opinion on the matter.[51] The EDPS explained that SWIFT was subject to cooperative oversight by the Central Banks of the Group of Ten countries (G-10 Group),[52] among which was the ECB.[53] In 2002, the G-10 Group was informed by SWIFT about the data transfers to US authorities. However, considering that this issue fell outside the scope of its oversight role, and that it was bound by rules of professional secrecy, the ECB

---

[44] Art 29 WP, Opinion 10/2006, n 27 above, p 11.

[45] ibid, p 20.

[46] ibid, p 15.

[47] ibid.

[48] ibid.

[49] ibid, p 26.

[50] ibid, p 27.

[51] European Data Protection Supervisor, Opinion on the role of the European Central Bank in the *SWIFT* case, 1 February 2007.

[52] The G-10 Group is composed of the National Bank of Belgium, Bank of Canada, Deutsche Bundesbank, European Central Bank, Banque de France, Banca d' Italia, Bank of Japan, De Nederlandsche Bank, Sveriges Riksbank, Swiss National Bank, Bank of England and the Federal Reserve System (USA), represented by the Federal Reserve Bank of New York and the Board of Governors of the Federal Reserve System.

[53] The major instrument for the oversight of SWIFT is 'moral suasion', and overseers can formulate recommendations to SWIFT.

'did not address the consequences of the transfers to US authorities for personal data protection, and neither informed relevant authorities nor used its powers of moral suasion to urge SWIFT to do so.'[54] The EDPS recognised that the participation of ECB in the cooperative oversight on SWIFT as such did not confer to it the responsibilities of a 'controller', but nevertheless, found 'the secrecy that surrounded the data transfers carried out by SWIFT for more than 4 years' regrettable, and called for a clarification of both the oversight on SWIFT and the rules on confidentiality.[55]

C. A Temporary Solution

Following the revelation of the TFTP by media reports, the US authorities sought to obtain the continuation of the scheme by sending a set of unilateral statements to the EU.[56] In particular, on 28 June 2007, UST sent a letter to the EU Council[57] and the Commission containing eight pages of unilateral representations ('the Representations') which described the controls and safeguards governing the handling, use and dissemination of data under the Treasury Department's Terrorist Financing Tracking Programme.[58] Having noted that the TFTP 'represents exactly what citizens expect and hope their governments are doing to protect them from terrorist threats',[59] the UST went on to explain why the programme was 'grounded in law, carefully targeted, powerful and successful, and bounded by privacy safeguards'.[60] The US Treasury Department asserted that:

> From its inception, the TFTP has been designed and implemented to meet applicable US legal requirements, to contribute meaningfully to combating global terrorism, and to respect and protect the potential commercial sensitivity of and privacy interests in the SWIFT data held in the United States... The programme contains multiple, overlapping layers of governmental and independent controls to ensure that the data, which are limited in nature, are searched only for counterterrorism purposes and that all data are maintained in a secure environment and properly handled.[61]

According to the UST, the assertion that the data processed did not contain sensitive information appeared enough to justify that no infringement of the Data Protection Directive took place in the SWIFT case.[62] For the rest, the Treasury

---

[54] European Data Protection Supervisor, n 51 above, para 29.
[55] ibid, p 11.
[56] Hummer, n 24 above, p 204.
[57] Letter from United States Department of the Treasury regarding SWIFT/Terrorist Finance Tracking Programme (2007/C 166/08), [2007] OJ C166/17.
[58] Processing of EU originating Personal Data by United States Treasury Department for Counter Terrorism Purposes—'SWIFT' (2007/C 166/09) Terrorist Finance Tracking Program—Representations of the United States Department of the Treasury, [2007] OJ C166/18.
[59] ibid.
[60] ibid.
[61] ibid.
[62] ibid.

Department guaranteed that the data security principle was safeguarded under the TFTP because SWIFT data were 'maintained in a secure physical environment, stored separately from any other data, and the computer systems have high-level intrusion controls and other protections to limit access to the data...'.[63] Furthermore, the Representations assured that the TFTP did not involve data mining or any other type of algorithmic or automated profiling or computer-filtering[64] and that information derived from the SWIFT data was shared 'under strict controls' with other US agencies in the intelligence and law enforcement communities to be used exclusively for counter-terrorism purposes.[65] Concerning the rights of redress of the data subject, the US Representations were quite ambiguous. The Treasury Department contended that such rights were not available because responding to a privacy-related inquiry from a natural person as to whether information about that individual was included in the database 'would require, in almost all instances, accessing data that would never be accessed in the normal operation of the TFTP'.[66] According to the UST, such access would be inconsistent with the TFTP requirement that every search have a pre-existing nexus to terrorism.[67] Moreover, because there was no alteration, manipulation, deletion or addition of the data within the searchable database, there existed no basis to 'rectify' any information.[68] This meant essentially that individuals did not have any rights of access to their data held under the TFTP because access to the system was restricted only to counter-terrorism purposes. Uncertainties also existed regarding the period of retention of the SWIFT data as the Representations provided that this was 'a function of numerous, well-established factors, including investigative requirements, applicable statutes of limitation, and regulatory limits for claims or prosecution.'[69] Nevertheless, the Representations stated that non-extracted data received from SWIFT would be deleted by the Treasury Department not later than five years after receipt.[70] Finally, the UST invited the EU to appoint in consultation with the Treasury Department 'an eminent European person' to confirm that the programme was implemented in accordance with the unilateral representations for the purpose of verifying the protection of EU-originating personal data and to monitor that processes for deletion of non-extracted data had been carried out.

The EU replied to UST by sending a letter signed by the Commission and the Council welcoming the unilateral Representations and the opportunity that was given to the European Union to 'have its views and concerns duly reflected in the Representations'.[71] It also informed the Treasury Department that it would

---

[63] ibid.
[64] ibid.
[65] ibid.
[66] ibid.
[67] ibid.
[68] ibid.
[69] ibid.
[70] ibid.
[71] Reply from European Union to United States Treasury Department—SWIFT/Terrorist Finance Tracking Programme (2007/C 166/10), [2007] OJ C166/26.

begin the process of identifying appropriate candidates for the position of the 'eminent European'.[72] Indeed, on 7 March 2008 the Commission announced the designation of Judge Jean-Louis Bruguière as the SWIFT/TFTP 'eminent European person'.[73] Judge Bruguière produced two Reports on TFTP in December 2008[74] and January 2010[75] where he found that the programme was respecting, in general, the safeguards included in the Representations.

Meanwhile on 20 July 2007, SWIFT obtained registration for the Safe Harbour programme of the US Department of Commerce.[76] The EU welcomed this development as it meant that SWIFT would be in compliance with its respective legal responsibilities under EU data protection law.[77]

D. SWIFT's New Architecture and the Need for a New Arrangement

Both the Belgian Privacy Commission and the Article 29 Working Party found that SWIFT was in breach of its obligations under Belgian data protection law and the Data Protection Directive. In particular, the Working Party criticised SWIFT for mirroring its data in an operating centre in the US, and thus, placing itself under the jurisdiction of the US authorities.[78] In order to address these criticisms, SWIFT announced on 4 October 2007 that it would restructure its messaging architecture.[79] The new architecture, which would become operational from January 2010, would store the EU originating financial data solely in Europe,[80] thus excluding them from being targeted with subpoenas from the UST under the TFTP. Peter Hustinx, the European Data Protection Supervisor noted with satisfaction that this change in the SWIFT architecture

> was encouraged and welcomed by the European data protection authorities, as it was designed to bring all data originating in Europe within the jurisdiction and control of

---

[72] ibid.

[73] Commission press release announcing the designation of Judge Jean-Louis Bruguière as the SWIFT/TFTP 'eminent European person' IP/08/400, 7 March 2008, http://europa.eu/rapid/press ReleasesAction.do?reference=IP/08/400&format=HTML&aged=0&language=en&guiLanguage=en.

[74] Summary of the First Annual Report on the Processing of EU Originating Personal Data by the United States Treasury Department For Counter Terrorism Purposes, Terrorist Finance Tracking Programme, Judge Jean-Louis Bruguière, www.statewatch.org/news/2011/apr/eu-usa-tftp-swift-1st-report-2008-judge-bruguiere.pdf.

[75] Second Report on the Processing of EU-Originating Personal Data by the US Treasury Department for Counter-terrorism purposes, TFTP, Judge Jean-Louis Bruguière, www.statewatch.org/news/2010/aug/eu-usa-swift-2nd-bruguiere-report.pdf.

[76] Press release, 'SWIFT completes transparency improvements and obtains registration for Safe Harbor', www.swift.com/about_swift/legal/compliance/statements_on_compliance/swift_completes_transparency_improvements_and_files_for_safe_harbor/index.page.

[77] Reply from European Union to United States Treasury Department SWIFT/Terrorist Finance Tracking Programme, n 71 above.

[78] Belgian Privacy Commission, Opinion No 37/2006, n 20 above; Art 29 WP, Opinion 10/2006, n 27 above.

[79] Press release, 'SWIFT Board approves messaging re-architecture', www.swift.com/about_swift/legal/compliance/statements_on_compliance/swift_board_approves_messaging_re_architecture/index.page.

[80] SWIFT's new operations centre is in Diessenhofen, Switzerland.

European authorities and thus ensure that the European standards for the protection of fundamental rights, including the protection of personal data, would fully apply.[81]

Ironically, however, SWIFT's decision on restructuring created problems not only for the US authorities, since transfers of SWIFT data to UST under administrative subpoenas could no longer take place, but it affected the EU side as well, that had compelled SWIFT to negotiate a new framework for the transfer of financial data. A new agreement for the transfer of such data was required for two reasons: first, the EU was subject to political pressures by the US administration that was pointing out that 'an important security gap'[82] might arise if European financial transactions were not available to UST for terrorism investigations under the TFTP, and wanted to demonstrate that it actively cooperated with its transatlantic partner for such a vital purpose as counter-terrorism.[83] Second, the EU did not have its own TFTP system and the relevant information coming from the US processing of the financial data to EU governments would otherwise be lost.[84]

On 27 July 2009, the Council authorised the Presidency, assisted by the Commission, to begin negotiations with UST for the conclusion of a short-term Agreement allowing the transfer of EU originating SWIFT data to the US.[85] The Agreement would fall under the (former) third pillar and in particular Articles 24 and 38 TEU.[86] The timing was not without relevance: it was the end of July 2009 and the Lisbon Treaty was due to enter into force on 1 December 2009. The Interim Agreement's fate seemed, therefore, closely linked to the new constitutional developments at the EU level.[87] In this respect, the negotiating directives provided that in the event of the entry into force of the Lisbon Treaty, the 'Agreement shall provide that the Contracting parties resume negotiations for a new Agreement under the conditions of the appropriate legal framework.'[88]

The negotiations of the Interim TFTP Agreement were surrounded by secrecy. Both the negotiating mandate of the Commission and the comments of the EDPS were characterised as EU-restricted and were not published. The European Parliament was only briefed on the main lines of the EDPS opinion in a Joint Meeting

[81]   P Hustinx, European Data Protection Supervisor, Speaking points to Joint Meeting of LIBE and ECON Committees on EU-US interim agreement following the entry into force of the new SWIFT architecture, European Parliament, Brussels, 3 September 2009.

[82]   Council of the European Union, Press Release, 'EU-US Agreement on the Transfer of Financial Messaging Data for purposes of the Terrorist Finance Tracking Programme', Brussels, 9 February 2010 6265/10 (Presse 23).

[83]   M Cremona, 'Justice and Home Affairs in a Globalised World: Ambitions and Reality in the Tale of the EU–US SWIFT Agreement', Austrian Academy of Sciences, Institute for European Integration Research, Working Paper No 04/2011, March 2011, 13.

[84]   ibid.

[85]   Council of the European Union, 'Negotiating directives for negotiations between the European Union and the United States of America for an international agreement to make available to the United States Treasury Department financial payment messaging data to prevent and combat terrorism and terrorist financing.'

[86]   ibid.

[87]   Cremona, n 83 above, p 14.

[88]   Council of the European Union, n 85 above.

of the LIBE and ECON Committees on the EU–US interim TFTP Agreement, held in Brussels on 3 September 2009.[89] In a Resolution of 17 September 2009, the European Parliament noted the fact that a number of negotiating documents, including the draft Agreement, were classified as 'EU-restricted' and asked the Commission and the Presidency to ensure that the European Parliament and all national parliaments were given 'full access to the negotiation documents and directives.'[90] It pointed out that a framework for the exchange of data with the US, the EU–US agreement on legal assistance, was already in place and provided for a sounder legal basis for the transfer of SWIFT data than the proposed interim agreement.[91] In this respect, the Parliament asked the Council and the Commission to explain the necessity of an interim TFTP agreement.[92] Finally, it set out a number of data protection safeguards that the Agreement must ensure 'as a very minimum.'[93]

On 30 November 2009, one day before the entry into force of the Lisbon Treaty, the Council authorised the Presidency to sign an Agreement between the EU and the USA on the processing and transfer of Financial Messaging Data from the European Union to the United States for purposes of the Terrorist Finance Tracking Programme.[94] The Agreement would apply provisionally as from 1 February 2010 and expire the latest on 31 October 2010.[95]

E. The Interim TFTP Agreement and its 'Historic' Rejection

The Interim TFTP Agreement had a twofold purpose: on the one hand, to make available to the US Treasury Department financial payment messaging and related data stored in the territory of the European Union by providers of international financial payment messaging services, for the purpose of fighting terrorism; and, on the other hand, to make available to law enforcement, public security, or counter

---

[89] Hustinx, n 81 above.

[90] European Parliament resolution of 17 September 2009 on the envisaged international agreement to make available to the United States Treasury Department financial payment messaging data to prevent and combat terrorism and terrorist financing, P7_TA(2009)0016. MEP Sophie In' t Veld also made a request under Regulation 1049/2001 in July 2009 to access the Opinion of the Council's Legal Service regarding the Commission's recommendation to the Council to authorise the opening of the TFTP negotiations. The Council denied the request and In' t Veld challenged this before the Court. See Case T- 529/09 *In' t Veld v Council* [2012] and the appeal judgment Case C-350/12P *Council v In' t Veld*, Judgment of the Court (First Chamber) of 3 July 2014.

[91] European Parliament resolution of 17 September 2009, n 90 above.

[92] ibid.

[93] ibid.

[94] Council Decision 2010/16/CFSP/JHA of 30 November 2009 on the signing, on behalf of the European Union, of the Agreement between the European Union and the United States of America on the processing and transfer of Financial Messaging Data from the European Union to the United States for purposes of the Terrorist Finance Tracking Programme, [2010] OJ L8/9.

[95] Agreement between the European Union and the United States of America on the processing and transfer of Financial Messaging Data from the European Union to the United States for purposes of the Terrorist Finance Tracking Programme, [2010] OJ L8/11.

terrorism authorities of Member States, Europol or Eurojust relevant information obtained through the TFTP for the same counter-terrorism purposes.[96]
The Agreement did not mention SWIFT expressly. Instead, it provided that the
data would be made available to the US authorities by 'providers of international
financial payment messaging services' designated by the Parties (the 'Designated
Providers').[97]

The procedure envisaged for the transfer of the data to the US was described
in Article 4 of the Agreement. First, the US Treasury Department had to issue a
request based on an ongoing terrorist investigation concerning a specific conduct
that had been committed or 'where there was, based on pre-existing information
or evidence, a reason to believe that it could be committed.'[98] The request had to be
transmitted by the US Department of Justice to the central authority of the Member State either in which the designated financial provider was based or where it
stored the requested data.[99] A copy of the request would also be simultaneously
transmitted to the central authority of the other Member State and to the national
Members of Eurojust of those Member States.[100] On receipt of the request, the
central authority of the requested Member State had to verify that it accorded with
the TFTP Agreement and the applicable requirements of the bilateral mutual legal
assistance agreement. After such verification, the request would be transmitted to
the competent authority for its execution under the law of the requested Member
State.[101] The request was to be executed as a matter of urgency and the data would
be transferred between the designated authorities of the requested Member State
and of the United States.[102] If the provider was not able to identify and produce
the specific data that would respond to the request because of technical reasons, all
potentially relevant data should have been transmitted in bulk to the competent
authority of the requested Member State.[103]

The procedure for transfer of financial data was unclear. What was meant by
'central authority of the Member State', which was 'the other Member State', what
was 'the competent authority for execution' and which were 'the designated authorities'? The Interim Agreement did not provide any definition of these notions, and
the whole transfer procedure was, thus, fraught with uncertainties. This was not
remedied by the safeguards applicable to the processing of provided data,[104] which
in essence repeated the assurances found in the Unilateral Representations.

Insofar as the retention periods were concerned, the Interim Agreement
stipulated that non-extracted data was to be deleted five years from receipt, while
information extracted from Provided Data was made subject to 'the retention

[96] TFTP Agreement, Art 1.
[97] ibid, Art 3.
[98] ibid, Art 4(1). See also Art 4(2).
[99] ibid, Art 4(3).
[100] ibid, Art 4(4).
[101] ibid, Art 4(5).
[102] ibid.
[103] ibid, Art 4(6).
[104] ibid, Art 5.

period applicable to the particular government authority according to its particular regulations and record retention schedules.'[105] Concerning the rights of redress, these were limited to a 'confirmation' obtained from the relevant data protection authority on whether any processing of the individual's personal data had taken place in breach of the Agreement.[106] In this regard, any person who considered his personal data to have been processed in breach of the Agreement was entitled to seek 'effective administrative and judicial redress in accordance with the laws of the European Union, its Member States, and the United States, respectively.'[107]

The Interim TFTP Agreement was unduly complex and very weak from the point of view of fundamental rights, but that was not its only problem. With the entry into force of the Lisbon Treaty on 1 December 2009, one day after its signature, the procedure of Article 218 TFEU for the conclusion of international agreements came into application, according to which the European Parliament's consent was required for the formal conclusion of the TFTP Agreement. For this reason, on 17 September 2009, the Commission introduced a proposal for a Council Decision on the conclusion of the TFTP Agreement with the US.[108] On the basis of Article 218(6)(a) TFEU, the Commission recommended to the Council, to adopt a decision concluding the Agreement, after obtaining the consent of the European Parliament.[109] The new legal bases for the decision would be Articles 82(1)(d) (judicial cooperation in criminal matters) and 87(2)(a) TFEU (police cooperation).[110]

On 5 February 2010, the LIBE Committee of the Parliament recommended that the Parliament withhold its consent to the conclusion of the TFTP Agreement.[111] The Rapporteur, Jeanine Hennis-Plasschaert made several very critical remarks concerning the SWIFT case in the Recommendation:

> [W]hat might have kicked off as an urgent temporary measure (in reply to 9/11) became *de facto* permanent without specific approval or authorisation by EU authorities or a real transatlantic evaluation of its impact and forward looking transatlantic negotiations covering at the same time security, judicial cooperation and data protection impact.[112]

Concerning the Interim TFTP Agreement, the Recommendation noted, first, that this violated the basic principles of data protection law, i.e. the principles of necessity and proportionality, because SWIFT was not in a position technically to

---

[105] ibid, Art 5(2)(m).

[106] ibid, Art 11.

[107] ibid, Art 11(3).

[108] Proposal for a Council Decision on the conclusion of the Agreement between the European Union and the United States of America on the processing and transfer of Financial Messaging Data from the European Union to the United States for purposes of the Terrorist Finance Tracking Programme, COM(2009/0703 final)—NLE 2009/0190/.

[109] ibid.

[110] ibid.

[111] LIBE Committee Recommendation on the proposal for a Council decision on the conclusion of the Agreement between the European Union and the United States of America on the processing and transfer of Financial Messaging Data from the European Union to the United States for purposes of the Terrorist Finance Tracking Programme (05305/1/2010REV—C7-0004/2010—2009/0190(NLE)).

[112] ibid, p 7.

provide specific data related to an individual. It could only, therefore, provide data in bulk, and, hence, it was not possible to refer to so-called limited requests.[113] The LIBE Recommendation also identified a number of other problems in the Interim Agreement: the transfer requests were not subject to judicial authorisation; the conditions for sharing TFTP data with third countries were not clearly defined; the public control and oversight of the authorities' access to SWIFT data was not regulated; the Agreement provided no indication of the data retention periods; the rights of access, rectification, compensation and redress were not defined adequately; and it was impossible to claim true reciprocity.[114]

These, however, were not the sole reasons for recommending the rejection of the Interim TFTP Agreement. Inter-institutional relations were at stake, not least because the Lisbon Treaty gave new powers to the Parliament and the Agreement was adopted one day before its entry into force. The LIBE Recommendation did not fail to mention this:

> By requesting Parliament's consent for the conclusion of the FMDA in conditions in which it was impossible for practical reasons for Parliament to react before the provisional application came into operation, the Council has in effect set Parliament a deadline *in breach of the spirit of Article 218(6)(a) TFEU*, and *undermined in part the legal effect and the practical impact of Parliament's decision in the consent procedure*, in particular as regards its provisional application.[115]

The LIBE Report also stressed that the Parliament should have been informed 'fully and immediately at all stages of the procedure',[116] something that did not happen in the negotiations of the Interim TFTP that were in general covered by secrecy.

On 9 February 2010, two days before the vote of the Parliament on the conclusion of the Interim TFTP Agreement, 'in an unusual move',[117] the Council issued a Press Release, responding essentially to the allegations raised by the LIBE Committee.[118] It explained that it was impossible to wait for the entry into force of the Lisbon Treaty before starting the negotiations for the TFTP Agreement, which in any case would have a transitional nature and would be applicable for a short term, having a maximum duration of nine months.[119] The Council also stated diplomatically that it was 'looking forward' to the new situation created by the Lisbon Treaty that would allow the Parliament to 'fully exercise its role' in order that the longer-term TFTP Agreement would meet its concerns regarding the protection of

---

[113] ibid, p 8.
[114] ibid.
[115] ibid. Emphasis added.
[116] ibid, p 10.
[117] Cremona, n 83 above, p 16.
[118] Council of the European Union, Press Release, n 82 above.
[119] ibid.

personal data, while ensuring that it continued to provide EU Member States with significant lead information to investigate and disrupt terrorism.[120]

Despite the Council's mobilisation, the Parliament voted on 11 February 2010 against the Agreement—with 378 against, 196 in favour and 31 abstentions— requesting the Commission to immediately submit recommendations to the Council with a view to a long-term TFTP Agreement with the US that would comply with the new legal framework established by Lisbon Treaty and the EUCFR.[121]

This historic rejection of an almost concluded international agreement with the US was, according to commentators, largely due to the Council's handling of the TFTP Agreement.[122] It presented it to the Parliament as a *fait accompli*,[123] assuming that the latter 'would reluctantly, and probably with much verbal protesting, nevertheless agree. The strategy failed and as a result the legislative initiative failed too. Instead of an imperfect agreement there was no agreement.'[124]

F. Renegotiating a TFTP Agreement

After the rejection of the Interim TFTP Agreement by the European Parliament, the Commission and the Council had to open a new round of negotiations with the US for a second TFTP Agreement, this time paying due respect to the role of the European Parliament. On 24 March 2010, the Commission asked the Council to authorise the opening of negotiations for a long-term TFTP agreement.[125] According to the Commission's Recommendation, the legal bases for the new Agreement would be Articles 82, 87 and 216 TFEU.[126] The Commission stressed that the long- term agreement would address the concerns set out in the European Parliament's Resolution of 17 September 2009, particularly with regard to the protection of personal data.[127] For this reason, the Commission proposed that a judicial public authority should be designated in the EU with the responsibility

---

[120] ibid.

[121] European Parliament legislative resolution of 11 February 2010 on the proposal for a Council decision on the conclusion of the Agreement between the European Union and the United States of America on the processing and transfer of Financial Messaging Data from the European Union to the United States for purposes of the Terrorist Finance Tracking Programme (05305/1/2010 REV 1—C7-0004/2010—2009/0190(NLE)) P7_TA(2010)0029.

[122] Cremona, n 83 above, p 17; J Monar, 'Editorial Comment: The Rejection of the EU–US TFTP Interim Agreement by the European Parliament: A Historic Vote and Its Implications' (2010) 15 *European Foreign Affairs Review* 143, 146.

[123] ibid.

[124] Cremona, n 83 above, p 17.

[125] Recommendation from the Commission to the Council to authorise the opening of negotiations for an agreement between the EU and the USA to make available to the US Treasury Department financial payment messaging data to prevent and combat terrorism and terrorist financing, Brussels, 24.3.2010, SEC (2010) 315 final.

[126] ibid, p 2.

[127] ibid, p 3.

to receive requests from UST.[128] The authority would verify whether the request met the requirements of the Agreement in order for the transfer to take place. On 22 April 2010, the Council adopted the Negotiating Directives and on 11 May it authorised the Commission to open negotiations with the US.

On 5 May 2010, the Parliament adopted a Resolution concerning the opening of negotiations for a second TFTP Agreement.[129] The Parliament welcomed 'the new spirit of cooperation demonstrated by the Commission and the Council and their willingness to engage with Parliament, taking into account their Treaty obligation to keep Parliament immediately and fully informed at all stages of the procedure', and urged the two institutions to explore ways of establishing a transparent and legally sound procedure for the authorisation of the transfer and extraction of relevant data as well as for the conduct and supervision of data exchanges in full compliance with the principles of necessity and proportionality and full respect for fundamental rights requirements under EU law.[130] Along the lines of the Commission's Recommendation on the negotiating Directives, the Parliament requested that a judicial public authority should be designated in the EU with the responsibility to receive requests from the United States Treasury Department.[131]

On 15 June 2010, the Commission introduced a Proposal for a Council Decision on the conclusion of a TFTP Agreement with the US. On 28 June, the Council adopted a decision on the signing of the TFTP Agreement, subject to its conclusion at a later stage.[132] On 5 July, the LIBE Committee recommended the Parliament to give its consent to the conclusion of the Agreement.[133] The Rapporteur, Alexander Alvaro, explained that compared to the Interim Agreement, rejected by Parliament, the second TFTP represented 'an improvement' that had been achieved due to 'Parliament's consistent demands for solutions to key issues.'[134] Following the Recommendation of the LIBE Committee, and the political pressure exercised by the US on the European Parliament that had become now an

---

[128] ibid, p 5.

[129] European Parliament resolution of 5 May 2010 on the Recommendation from the Commission to the Council to authorise the opening of negotiations for an agreement between the European Union and the United States of America to make available to the United States Treasury Department financial messaging data to prevent and combat terrorism and terrorist financing P7_TA-PROV(2010)0143.

[130] ibid.

[131] ibid.

[132] Council Decision of 28 June 2010 on the signing, on behalf of the Union, of the Agreement between the European Union and the United States of America on the processing and transfer of financial messaging data from the European Union to the United States for the purposes of the Terrorist Finance Tracking Programme (2010/411/EU), [2010] OJ L195/1.

[133] LIBE Committee Recommendation on the draft Council decision on the conclusion of the Agreement between the European Union and the United States of America on the processing and transfer of Financial Messaging Data from the European Union to the United States for the purposes of the Terrorist Finance Tracking Programme (11222/1/2010/REV 1 and COR 1—C7-0158/2010—2010/0178(NLE)) A7-0224/2010, Rapporteur: Alexander Alvaro.

[134] ibid.

important actor in the negotiations,[135] on 8 July, the Parliament voted in favour of the Agreement.[136] The Parliament's change of approach was due to the improvements introduced in the Agreement and to the fact that this time the Parliament had been kept informed and involved in the negotiations, and had to act as an institution with 'real joint legislative power' rather than an institution 'with only the power of expressing its opinion'.[137] Having received the consent of the Parliament, the Council adopted on 13 July a decision on the conclusion of the TFTP Agreement between the EU and the US.[138] The Agreement entered into force on 1 August 2010.

G. The Long-Term TFTP Agreement: An Improvement?

The second TFTP Agreement[139] was received with enthusiasm and considered an improvement compared to its predecessor that was rejected in the beginning of 2010. In fact, the Parliament gave its consent for the conclusion of the long-term TFTP Agreement, as the LIBE Committee had identified in its report eight major improvements in comparison to the Interim TFTP: access to and extraction of data on US soil by US agencies would be monitored and when required, blocked by a European official; the procedure regarding judicial redress for European citizens was regulated in greater detail; the right to rectification, erasure, or blocking was more comprehensive; the regulation on transparency of the US TFTP was more detailed; the procedure regarding onward data transfers to third countries was regulated more precisely; the scope for fighting terrorism was defined and clarified; Europol was entrusted with the task of verifying whether the US request

---

[135] Several MEPs were invited to Washington DC and Vice-President Joe Biden addressed the European Parliament on 6 May 2010. See A Ripoll Servent and A MacKenzie, 'The European Parliament as a Norm Taker? EU-US Relations after the SWIFT Agreement' (2012) 17 *European Foreign Affairs Review* 71; M de Goede, 'The SWIFT affair and the global politics of European security' (2012) 50 (2) *Journal of Common Market Studies* 214.

[136] European Parliament legislative resolution of 8 July 2010 on the draft Council decision on the conclusion of the Agreement between the European Union and the United States of America on the processing and transfer of Financial Messaging Data from the European Union to the United States for the purposes of the Terrorist Finance Tracking Programme (11222/1/2010/REV 1 and COR 1—C7-0158/2010—2010/0178(NLE)) P7_TA(2010)0279.

[137] M Cremona, 'Risk in Three Dimensions: The EU–US Agreement on the Processing and Transfer of Financial Messaging Data' in H Micklitz and T Tridimas (eds), *Risk and EU Law* (Cheltenham, Edward Elgar, 2015) 69, 85.

[138] Council Decision of 13 July 2010 on the conclusion of the Agreement between the European Union and the United States of America on the processing and transfer of Financial Messaging Data from the European Union to the United States for the purposes of the Terrorist Finance Tracking Programme (2010/412/EU), [2010] OJ L195/3.

[139] Agreement between the European Union and the United States of America on the processing and transfer of Financial Messaging Data from the European Union to the United States for the purposes of the Terrorist Finance Tracking Programme, [2010] OJ L195/5.

for financial data met the requirements of the Agreement as well as whether it was tailored as narrowly as possible before the data provider was authorised to transfer the data; the US Treasury Department was obliged to delete financial data transmitted that was not requested; and SEPA (Single Euro Payments Area) data were excluded from the transfers.[140]

A closer look at the Agreement is required in order to assess whether it can be considered an improvement. The purpose of the long-term TFTP Agreement is identical with the Interim one: on the one hand, the transfer of financial payment data to UST for counter-terrorism objectives; on the other hand, the making available of information obtained through the TFTP to law enforcement, public security, or counter-terrorism authorities of Member States, Europol and Eurojust.[141] It has been argued that the scope of defining terrorism has been clarified,[142] as the notion of terrorism found in Article 2 of the second TFTP Agreement builds on the definition of terrorism[143] found in the Council Framework Decision 2002/475/JHA.[144] The alleged improvement is, however, minimal since the Interim Agreement contains the same definition with small differences. Similarly to its predecessor, the long-term TFTP Agreement stipulates that 'providers of international financial payment messaging services' are to be jointly designated by the Parties ('Designated Providers') in order to provide the relevant data to UST.[145] Unlike the Interim Agreement, however, this time in the Annex of the Agreement we find the name of the 'designated provider', SWIFT.

Certainly, the second TFTP excludes the transfer of data relating to SEPA[146] and lays down more clearly the requirements under which a request by UST should be made: a) identify as clearly as possible the data, including the specific categories of data requested, that are necessary for the purpose of the prevention, investigation, detection, or prosecution of terrorism or terrorist financing; b) clearly substantiate the necessity of the data; and c) be tailored as narrowly as possible in order to minimise the amount of data requested.[147] However, the solution found on the judicial authority entrusted with the task to receive requests is rather disappointing. It is Europol that was given the role to verify that UST requests comply with the Agreement in order for the transfer to take place.[148] The problem is that Europol is not a judicial authority and it has interests on its own on the financial

---

[140] LIBE Committee Recommendation, n 133 above, pp 7–8.

[141] TFTP II Agreement, Art 1.

[142] European Data Protection Supervisor, Opinion on the Proposal for a Council Decision on the conclusion of the Agreement between the European Union and the United States of America on the processing and transfer of financial messaging data from the European Union to the United States for purposes of the Terrorist Finance Tracking Programme (TFTP II), 22 June 2010.

[143] TFTP II Agreement, Art 2.

[144] Council Framework Decision of 13 June 2002 on combating terrorism (2002/475/JHA), [2002] OJ L164/3.

[145] TFTP II Agreement, Art 3.

[146] ibid, Art 4(2)(d).

[147] ibid, Art 4(2).

[148] ibid, Art 4(3), (4) and (5).

data. Furthermore, the Agreement stipulates that data transmitted while not requested will be deleted 'promptly and permanently' by UST[149] and that all non-extracted data should be deleted no later than five years from receipt.[150] However, the retention period of extracted data, which may only be retained 'for no longer than necessary for specific investigations or prosecutions for which they are used', is equally unclear as its equivalent in the Interim TFTP.[151]

Moreover, while the Interim Agreement spoke only of sharing 'terrorist leads' obtained through the TFTP with law enforcement, public security, or counter terrorism authorities in the United States, EU, or third states; the second TFTP Agreement contains a whole new Article on onward transfers of information 'extracted from the provided data.'[152] In the case that such information involves a citizen or a resident of a Member State, the Agreement provides that sharing should be subject to the prior consent of competent authorities of the concerned Member State, unless it is essential for the prevention of an immediate and serious threat to public security.[153]

Concerning the individual rights of the data subject, the long-term TFTP Agreement did not introduce any significant improvements. A right of access is granted to individuals through their data protection authorities in the EU to verify whether any processing of their data has taken place in breach of the Agreement.[154] The person must send a relevant request to the relevant national data protection authority, which will transmit it to the Privacy Officer of UST, who shall make all necessary verifications pursuant to the request.[155] Such a procedure, however, as the Article 29 Working Party has pointed out limits the national data protection authorities to the role of a 'postbox' for assessments made by UST 'instead of being able to obtain themselves all relevant information, to independently assess such information and to assess full data protection compliance.'[156] Individuals have the right to seek rectification, erasure, or blocking of their data processed by UST, following a procedure similar to the one regarding the right to access.[157] Insofar as redress rights are concerned, there seems to be an improvement with regard to the Interim Agreement, as the second TFTP states that 'all persons, regardless of nationality or country of residence, shall have available under US law a process for seeking judicial redress from an adverse administrative action.'[158] However, there

---

149   ibid, Art 6(2).
150   ibid, Art 6(4).
151   ibid, Art 6(7).
152   ibid, Art 7.
153   ibid, Art 7(d).
154   ibid, Art 15.
155   ibid, Art 15(3).
156   Article 29 Working Party & Working Party on Police and Justice, Press Release, 'EU–US TFTP Agreement not in line with privacy legislation: European Data Protection Authorities not satisfied with safeguards in EU-US financial transactions agreement', Brussels, 28 June 2010.
157   TFTP II Agreement, Art 16.
158   ibid, Art 18(2).

are questions about the enforceability of this provision since the Agreement states at the same time that it does not create or confer any right or benefit on any person or entity, private or public.[159] Finally, the new transparency provisions that were much welcomed by the European Parliament refer only to the posting of detailed information concerning the TFTP on the Department of Treasury's website.[160]

Besides the provision on joint review[161] that existed in the Interim TFTP Agreement, the current Agreement provides also for the monitoring of the TFTP by independent overseers, who will have the authority to review 'in real time and retrospectively all searches made of the provided data, and the authority to query such searches and … to request additional justification of the terrorism nexus.'[162] Independent overseers also have the authority to block any or all searches that do not respect the data protection safeguards set out in the Agreement.[163]

Overall, the long-term TFTP is longer and more detailed than its predecessor, but remains silent concerning the issue of most concern to the Parliament, the EDPS[164] and the Article 29 Working Party: bulk transfers of data. Since SWIFT's system does not allow for targeted searches, it is questionable whether the principles of proportionality and purpose limitation are respected under the second TFTP. Also, the indispensability of a Terrorist Financing Tracking Programme is still not proved. In a Communication on the Joint Report conducted by the Commission and the UST regarding the value of TFTP provided data issued in November 2013, the Commission concluded that TFTP data, including information retained for multiple years, 'have been delivering very important value for the counter terrorism efforts in the United States, Europe, and elsewhere.'[165]

H. The Role of Europol under the TFTP: A Fox Guarding the Henhouse?

Despite not being a judicial authority, Europol has been assigned the task of verifying the US requests and giving the green light for the transmission of the data by SWIFT. In particular, as discussed above, Europol examines whether: a) the UST request identifies the data as clearly as possible, including the specific categories of

---

[159] ibid, Art 20(1).
[160] ibid, Art 14.
[161] ibid, Art 13.
[162] ibid, Art 12(1).
[163] ibid.
[164] European Data Protection Supervisor, Opinion on the Proposal for a Council Decision, n 142 above.
[165] Joint Report from the Commission and the US Treasury Department regarding the value of TFTP Provided Data pursuant to Article 6(6) of the Agreement between the European Union and the United States of America on the processing and transfer of Financial Messaging Data from the European Union to the United States for the purposes of the Terrorist Finance Tracking Program, Brussels, 27.11.2013, COM(2013) 843 final, 2.

data requested, that are necessary for the purpose of the prevention, investigation, detection, or prosecution of terrorism or terrorist financing; b) the necessity of the data is clearly substantiated; c) the request is tailored as narrowly as possible in order to minimise the amount of data requested, taking due account of past and current terrorism risk analyses focused on message types and geography as well as perceived terrorism threats and vulnerabilities, geographic, threat, and vulnerability analyses; and d) the request does not seek any data relating to the Single Euro Payments Area (SEPA).[166]

Europol has two further interests under the Agreement concerning the TFTP data. On the one hand, it can receive spontaneously by UST information obtained through the TFTP that may contribute to the investigation, prevention, detection, or prosecution by the EU of terrorism or its financing.[167] On the other hand, it can request searches of the TFTP data if it determines that there is reason to believe that a person or entity has a nexus to terrorism.[168] It is, therefore, difficult to see how Europol's verification task on the necessity and proportionality of the US requests can be reconciled with its own interests on the financial data.

Specific questions on Europol's level of scrutiny were raised by the Europol Joint Supervisor Body (JSB) in its inspection concerning Europol's implementation of the TFTP Agreement. In particular, pursuant to Article 34(1) of the Europol Council Decision,[169] the JSB has the task of reviewing the activities of Europol in order to ensure that the rights of the individual are not violated by the storage, processing and utilisation of data by Europol. In its inspection of 11 November 2010, the findings of which were classified as 'EU-Secret',[170] the JSB stated that due to the abstract nature and terms of the UST requests—broad types of data, also involving EU Member States' data—proper verification of whether the requests were in line with the conditions of Article 4(2) of the TFTP Agreement was—on the basis of the available documentation—'impossible.'[171] A problem highlighted by the JSB was the provision of information orally to certain Europol staff by the

---

[166] TFTP II Agreement, Art 4.

[167] ibid, Art 9.

[168] ibid, Art 10.

[169] Council Decision 2009/371/JHA of 6 April 2009 establishing the European Police Office (Europol), [2009] OJ L121/37. Art 34(1) provides that an independent Joint Supervisory Body has the task to review, the activities of Europol in order to ensure that the rights of the individuals are not violated by the storage, processing and use of the data held by Europol. The Joint Supervisory Body can also monitor the permissibility of the transmission of data originating from Europol. The Joint Supervisory Body is composed of a maximum of two members or representatives of each of the independent national supervisory bodies, having the necessary abilities and appointed for five years by each Member State.

[170] Report on the Inspection of Europol's Implementation of the TFTP Agreement, Conducted in November 2010 by the Europol Joint Supervisory Body, JSB Europol inspection report 11–07, Brussels, 1 March 2011.

[171] ibid.

US Treasury Department with the stipulation that 'no written notes' were to be made.[172] In this respect, the JSB noted in its Report:

> where requests lack the necessary written information to allow proper verification of compliance with Article 4(2) of the TFTP Agreement, it is impossible to check whether this deficiency is rectified by the orally provided information. The significant involvement of oral information renders proper internal and external audit, by Europol's Data Protection Office and the JSB respectively, impossible.[173]

The three reports on the joint review of the implementation of the TFTP Agreement[174] appear more satisfied with the procedures in place and Europol's role.

On 8 April 2011, Europol issued an Information Note to the European Parliament explaining its activities in relation to the TFTP Agreement.[175] The Agreement does not mention anything on bulk transfers of data, but Europol's explanations were illuminating on this point. According to Europol,

> Article 4 regulates the transfer of *bulk data* from the Designated Provider (based on standardised data categories) to the US Department of the Treasury, as clearly understood during the negotiation of the Agreement. Strictly within the context of Article 4 the provisions aim at transferring information on a bulk and generic level according to the criteria established (limited in geographical scope, time period, and list of data categories). Identifying a nexus to terrorism in specific cases is a requirement under other provisions in the Agreement and forms no part of the request as submitted by the US Department of the Treasury to the Designated Provider under Article 4 ... Europol does not see or manage the provided data, which is transmitted directly from the Designated Provider to the US Department of the Treasury.[176]

Furthermore, replying essentially to the allegations raised by JSB that most information related to a UST request is transmitted to certain Europol officials orally, Europol described in its Note the set of documents that it receives from the Treasury Department on the basis of a request under Article 4.[177] As Europol

---

[172] ibid.

[173] ibid.

[174] Commission Staff Working Paper, Report on the joint review of the implementation of the Agreement between the European Union and the United States of America on the processing and transfer of Financial Messaging data from the European Union to the United States for the purposes of the Terrorist Finance Tracking Programme 17–18 February 2011, Brussels, 30.03.2011, SEC(2011) 438 final; Commission Staff Working Document, Report on the second joint review of the implementation of the Agreement between the European Union and the United States of America on the processing and transfer of Financial Messaging data from the European Union to the United States for the purposes of the Terrorist Finance Tracking Program, October 2012, Brussels, 14.12.2012, SWD(2012) 454 final; Staff Working Document, Joint Review Report of the implementation of the Agreement between the European Union and the United States of America on the processing and transfer of Financial Messaging Data from the European Union to the United States for the purposes of the Terrorist Finance Tracking Programme, Brussels, 11.8.2014, COM(2014) 513 final.

[175] Europol Activities in Relation to the TFTP Agreement, Information Note to the European Parliament 1 August 2010–1 April 2011, The Hague, 8 April 2011, File no 2566-566.

[176] ibid, p 4.

[177] See Europol's Information Notice to the European Parliament.

explained, the request for financial messaging data usually covers a period of four weeks.[178] Europol had received eight requests prior to April 2011 and verified all of them, asking for additional information in five out of them.[179] Normally, Europol is required to complete its verification task in 48 hours from the receipt of the request, but as stated in its Information Note to the Parliament in six cases it had failed to meet this deadline, taking 16 days to complete its work in one case.[180]

I. A European Terrorist Finance Tracking System

Since SWIFT does not have the technical capability to transfer individualised data and Europol does not perform a strict scrutiny of the US requests, European financial messaging data are available in bulk to the US Treasury Department for its searches. In order to address the problem of the lack of an effective minimisation of financial data, it has been proposed that the EU establish a 'legal and technical framework for the extraction of data on EU territory'[181] with the overall aim to ensure that the processing of such data would take place in accordance with the EU Charter of Fundamental Rights and secondary data protection legislation.

Following the PNR precedent and the more general trend to internalise highly controversial counter-terrorism policies in the EU, on 13 July 2011, the Commission tabled a proposal for the development of an EU Terrorist Financing Tracking System (TFTS).[182] The difference with the EU PNR is that this time, an EU system was considered necessary both by the Council[183] and the Parliament,[184] not only to fight terrorism, but also to achieve an effective minimisation of data at the EU level. The EU–US TFTP Agreement also provides that the Commission will carry out a study into the possible introduction of 'an equivalent system allowing for a more targeted transfer of data.'[185] The paradox is that the EU TFTS was presented, therefore, as a path towards the proportionality of the EU–US TFTP Agreement. Hence, ironically, it was not merely a measure internalising external security needs—as in the PNR case—but also a measure rationalising these security needs.

---

[178] ibid.

[179] ibid, p 8.

[180] ibid.

[181] Council Decision on the conclusion of the Agreement between the European Union and the United States of America on the processing and transfer of Financial Messaging Data from the European Union to the United States for the purposes of the Terrorist Finance Tracking Program, n 138 above, Art 2.

[182] Communication from the Commission to the European Parliament and the Council, 'A European terrorist finance tracking system: available options', Brussels, 13.7.2011, COM(2011) 429 final.

[183] See Council Decision on the conclusion of the Agreement between the European Union and the United States of America on the processing and transfer of Financial Messaging Data from the European Union to the United States for the purposes of the Terrorist Finance Tracking Program, n 138 above.

[184] See European Parliament resolution of 5 May 2010, n 129 above.

[185] TFTP II Agreement, Art 11.

In its proposal, the Commission laid down the two purposes of the EU TFTS: the system would provide an effective contribution to the fight against terrorism and its financing within the EU; and, it would contribute to limiting the amount of personal data transferred to third countries.[186] The US influence was evident on the EU TFTS.[187] The TFTS could be seen as going even further than the TFTP in a number of aspects. First, the Commission was wondering whether access to financial messaging data would be useful not only to combat terrorism but also other forms of serious crime, in particular organised crime and money laundering.[188] Second, the Commission was considering, whether, besides SWIFT, which is clearly the most important world-wide provider of financial messaging services, other providers that operate on the market should be requested to transmit their data.[189] A third question that arose with regard to the EU TFTS was whether it should be limited to requesting international transactions of financial data or whether the option of including financial messaging services exchanged between Member States could be considered.[190] Finally, the Commission was reflecting whether, besides the particular type of financial messaging data that is currently requested, other different types of financial messaging data used in the international banking system might be useful for the purposes of the TFTS.[191]

The Commission set out in its Communication three options for an EU TFTS, depending on whether a centralised EU solution or a decentralised model were to be adopted.[192] The first option envisaged the creation of an EU central TFTS unit, with most of the tasks and functions being implemented at the EU level.[193] The second option involved the establishment of an EU central TFTS unit, whose tasks would comprise issuing requests for 'raw data' to the Designated Providers, verifying these requests and running searches. Under this option, the EU TFTS unit would not be allowed to analyse the search results and compare them with other available information or intelligence—its role would be limited to preparing and distributing search results in a presentable manner.[194] The third and more decentralised option comprised the establishment of an upgraded Financial Intelligence Unit (FIU) Platform, made up of all the FIUs of the Member States. The EU level authority would issue requests for 'raw data' to the Designated Providers, by compiling the needs specified by the national FIUs into a single request, which would also be verified and authorised at central level. However, the national FIUs

---

[186] Communication from the Commission to the European Parliament and the Council, 'A European terrorist finance tracking system: available options', n 182 above, p 2.
[187] ibid, p 4.
[188] ibid, p 7.
[189] ibid.
[190] ibid, p 8.
[191] ibid.
[192] ibid.
[193] ibid, p 9.
[194] ibid, p 10.

would be responsible for running searches and managing search results on behalf of their Member States.[195]

In a Communication issued in November 2013, the Commission concluded that at this stage the case to present a proposal for an EU TFTS was not clearly demonstrated,[196] given that the added benefits of such a system do not outweigh the significant cost to private companies and the damage to privacy and data protection rights that it would entail.[197]

II. THE TERRORIST FINANCE TRACKING PROGRAMME AND THE RIGHTS TO PRIVACY AND DATA PROTECTION

TFTP interferes with both the fundamental rights to privacy and data protection.[198] The messages transmitted through the SWIFT platform contain personal data, which are found in the so-called 'content' of the message. As explained by the Belgian Privacy Commission, the 'content' of the financial message includes the name and the account number of the payee; the name and the bank details of the beneficiary; the amount transferred and the currency; and in some cases, an unstructured (free format) text.[199] This information constitutes 'personal data' to the extent that it relates to an identified person. The fact that SWIFT does not have the technical capacity to make individual searches in its databases is not important in the context of the present analysis. The data are transmitted in bulk to UST, which performs searches on certain entities or individuals. Both the transmission of the data to UST and the searches performed on this constitute 'processing' of personal data. The right to data protection is, thus, applicable in the case of TFTP, which interferes with a number of data protection principles. As in the case of PNR, the main problem posed to the right to the fundamental right to data protection is once again the deviation of the purpose limitation principle. Data initially collected for a commercial purpose (for the performance of the money transfer) are being used for a totally unrelated objective (to combat terrorism). The data protection principle of proportionality is also interfered with: due to SWIFT's technical organisation the information has to be transmitted in bulk and there is no minimisation of the personal data. Furthermore, retention periods are uncertain as they depend on whether the data have been 'extracted' or not and in any case are unduly long. In addition, the supervision of the TFTP is minimal, since Europol is not a judicial authority and has its own interests on the data. The due process rights of the data subject are also almost non-existent. Indeed, data subjects in most cases have no knowledge that their financial information can be

---

[195] ibid, p 11.
[196] Communication from the Commission to the European Parliament and the Council, n 182 above, p 14.
[197] ibid, p 12.
[198] See for instance Art 29 WP, Opinion 10/2006, n 27 above; Cremona, n 83 above.
[199] Belgian Privacy Commission, Opinion No 37/2006, n 20 above, p 4.

used to identify terrorist networks and, consequently, it is very difficult for them to exercise their judicial and administrative rights. This absence of knowledge of the US government's access to SWIFT's information makes even deeper the asymmetry of power between the data subject and the data controller.

TFTP also interferes with the right to privacy. Similarly to the PNR data, TFTP data might reveal information about racial or ethnic origin (on the basis of the personal details of the payee and the currency used for the transfer), or religious beliefs or trade-union membership (if the beneficiary is a church or a foundation).[200] But, contrary to what was concluded with regard to PNR, the right to privacy in the present context does not only cover sensitive data. The transfer of financial data constitutes a form of communication before the payee and the beneficiary. This communication, albeit limited to financial information, enjoys confidentiality. Data obtained from TFTP can reveal a person's financial movements, his potential network of business associates, family and friends to whom he transfers money, or even his donations to charitable organisations and NGOs. This, in addition to being confidential information of the payee, also involves necessarily the beneficiary, who is a passive subject of the intercommunication relationship.[201] In this way, charities organisations or other entities and individuals are made subject of suspicion before law enforcement authorities.[202]

US constitutional law, with its 'third party doctrine',[203] does not offer much help in the TFTP case.[204] *United States v Miller*,[205] mentioned in Chapter 1, bears many similarities with the TFTP issue. In that case, federal law enforcement officials issued subpoenas to two banks to produce a customer's financial records. The Supreme Court rejected the customer's complaint that the subpoenas violated his Fourth Amendment rights, on the basis that he had already voluntarily conveyed that information to a third party, ie his bank, and therefore he lacked any reasonable expectation of privacy.[206] This rationale also applies to the TFTP. Customers provide personal data to their banks, which use the SWIFT platform in order to effect a money transfer.[207] Consequently, customers do not enjoy any Fourth Amendment protection because they have already voluntarily revealed the data to third parties.

Federal legislation does not seem to be of much help either. Two years after the Supreme Court's decision in *United States v Miller*, and in order to remedy the

---

[200] See Donohue, n 2 above, p 379.

[201] See the Romanian court's pronouncements with regard to the Data Retention Directive in Ch 3.

[202] Donohue, n 2 above, p 379.

[203] For a detailed analysis see D Solove, 'A Taxonomy of Privacy' (2006) 154 *University of Pennsylvania Law Review* 477, 528.

[204] See Ch 4.

[205] *United States v Miller* 425 US 435, 437 (1976).

[206] ibid.

[207] It should be noted that customers transferring money are often not aware that their bank uses the SWIFT platform.

situation, Congress passed the Right to Financial Privacy Act (RFPA)[208] that makes the access of government authorities to financial information subject to certain conditions.[209] Among them, government authorities are required to obtain a warrant or an administrative subpoena before accessing financial records. According to RFPA, the subpoena should provide 'a reason to believe that the records sought are relevant to a legitimate law enforcement inquiry'.[210] In this case, a copy of the subpoena must be given to the customer, along with the opportunity to file a motion before the US courts.[211] However, the notification obligation does not apply when the disclosure of financial records is required by a government authority 'authorised to conduct investigations of, or intelligence or counterintelligence analyses related to, international terrorism for the purpose of conducting such investigations or analyses.'[212] RFPA was also amended by the Patriot Act to permit the disclosure of financial information to any intelligence in any investigation related to international terrorism.[213]

III. A SUBSTANTIVE FUNDAMENTAL RIGHTS' ASSESSMENT OF TFTP

The interference of TFTP with the rights to privacy and data protection can be justified if it complies with the requirements laid down in Article 52(1) EUCFR. In particular, a) it should be provided for by law; b) meet objectives of general interest recognised by the Union or the need to protect the rights and freedoms of others; c) be necessary; d) be proportionate; and e) respect the essence of the right.

A. Provided by Law

The transfer of financial messaging data from SWIFT to the US Department of Treasury is provided for by law since the TFTP Agreement entered into force on 1 August 2010. The Terrorist Finance Tracking Programme, however, had been operating in secret since 2001. It was disclosed by media reports in 2006, but was not terminated. A kind of 'soft law' solution was opted for through the unilateral

---

[208] Right to Financial Privacy Act, 12 U.S.C. § 3401 *et seq.* (1978). For an analysis see G Trubow and D Hudson, 'The Right to Financial Privacy Act of 1978: New Protection from Federal Intrusion' (1979) 12 *J Marshall J Prac & Proc* 487.

[209] Access is permitted when 1) the customer has authorised the disclosure; 2) the financial records are disclosed in response to an administrative subpoena or summons; 3) the financial records are disclosed in response to a search warrant; 4) the financial records are disclosed in response to a judicial subpoena; or 5) the financial records are disclosed in response to a formal written request.

[210] Right to Financial Privacy Act § 3404.

[211] Ibid.

[212] Ibid, § 3413. See also Santolli, n 15 above, p 575.

[213] US Patriot Act, Section 358.

Representations sent to the EU by UST. It is settled case law of the ECtHR that secret state schemes, whatever their purpose, cannot be tolerated in a democratic entity operating under the rule of law.[214] The Court stated in *Klass* that the Contracting States do not

> enjoy an unlimited discretion to subject persons within their jurisdiction to secret surveillance. The Court, being aware of the danger such a law poses of undermining or even destroying democracy on the ground of defending it, affirms that the Contracting States may not, in the name of the struggle against espionage and terrorism, adopt whatever measures they deem appropriate.[215]

The TFTP was operating without satisfying the requirement of 'provided for by law' under Article 52(1) EUCFR and the 'in accordance with the law' condition under Article 8(2) ECHR on the basis of Article 52(3) EUCFR as understood by the Strasbourg Court for nine years—and under total secrecy for five of those years. Besides the repercussions that this might have had on the EU–US relations, huge amounts of financial data had been transferred to the US authorities without any foreseeable and accessible legal basis.

B. Objectives of General Interest Recognised by the Union

According to the EU–US TFTP Agreement, the 'exclusive' purpose of the transfer of financial messaging data is the 'prevention, investigation, detection, or prosecution of terrorism or terrorist financing'.[216] This constitutes an objective of general interest recognised by the Union.

C. Necessary

The assessment of the necessity of the TFTP, as in the PNR case, has to be based on the US authorities' assertions on the necessity of the SWIFT data in the fight against terrorism. Concerning the Programme's effectiveness the US officials have been very positive:

> The TFTP has proven to be a powerful investigative tool that has contributed significantly to protecting US citizens and other persons around the world and to safeguarding America's and other countries' national security. The programme has been instrumental in identifying and capturing terrorists and their financiers, and it has generated many

---

[214] See among others *Rotaru v Romania* ECHR 2000-V, para 52; *S and Marper v United Kingdom* [2008] ECHR 1581, para 95; and *Malone v United Kingdom* (1984) Series A no 82, para 66.
[215] *Klass and Others v Germany* (1978) Series A no 28, paras 48-49.
[216] See TFTP II Agreement, Art 1.

leads that have been disseminated to counterterrorism experts in intelligence and law enforcement agencies around the world.[217]

Besides general statements, however, concrete information on the effectiveness of TFTP is missing. SWIFT data do not capture the various alternative systems of money remittance allegedly used by terrorist networks.[218] For instance, *hawala* (which is used as a synonym of 'trust' in Arabic) is a fast and cost-effective method for the worldwide remittance of money or value, particularly for persons who may be outside the reach of the traditional financial sector.[219] *Hawala* relies upon personal connections to transfer money across international borders[220] and has allegedly been used by terrorists.

But even if it is accepted that the TFTP is actually effective in fighting terrorism and has generated many leads, as the US authorities claim, the question of the availability of less extensive alternatives should be examined in order to assess its necessity. As the European Parliament has pointed out, there are indeed other alternative routes for the exchange of information with the US. Besides the various bilateral agreements between the Member States and the US, the EU–US Agreement on Mutual Legal Assistance[221] allows the exchange of bank information for wider purposes than counter-terrorism and without being limited to the data contained in a specific provider's databases, such as the SWIFT company. In particular, Article 4 of the EU–US Agreement on Mutual Legal Assistance provides:

> Upon request of the requesting State, the requested State shall, in accordance with the terms of this Article, promptly ascertain if the banks located in its territory possess information on whether an identified natural or legal person suspected of or charged with a criminal offence is the holder of a bank account or accounts. The requested State shall promptly communicate the results of its enquiries to the requesting State.[222]

The same action may also be taken for the purpose of identifying information in the possession of non-bank financial institutions; or financial transactions unrelated to accounts.[223] According to the Agreement, such assistance cannot be refused on grounds of bank secrecy.[224]

The alternative ways of exchanging financial information are not limited to the EU (or Member States') agreements with the US. At the international level, there exists a framework of financial information exchange based primarily on initiatives against money-laundering, such as for instance, the 40 Recommendations for

---

[217] See UST Representations and the Preamble of the TFTP Agreement.

[218] Hearing before the Committee on Finance US Senate, n 10 above, p 35; Donohue, n 2 above, p 365.

[219] ibid.

[220] Donohue, n 2 above, p 366.

[221] Agreement on Mutual Legal Assistance between the European Union and the United States of America, [2003] OJ L181/34.

[222] Agreement on Mutual Legal Assistance, Art 4(1).

[223] ibid, Art 4(1)(b).

[224] ibid, Art 4(5).

fighting money laundering and promoting good financial governance issued by the Financial Action Task Force (FATF),[225] and the Egmont Group.[226]

D. Proportionate

Due to SWIFT's technical capacities, data must be transferred in bulk to the US Treasury Department. This includes vast amounts of financial communications of people totally unrelated to terrorism. This is particularly worrying, despite the assurances of the Treasury Department that the data are exclusively searched for counter-terrorism purposes.[227] Furthermore, it is unclear why non-extracted data, namely data not used for counter-terrorism investigations, must only be deleted five years after the receipt. Insofar as the extracted data are concerned, an indeterminate retention time depending on the usefulness of the information for investigations without any meaningful supervision from independent data protection authorities or courts raises questions regarding its proportionality. Furthermore, even if it is accepted that TFTP, unlike PNR, does not involve any data mining or profiling, as Article 5(3) of the Agreement stipulates, the interference is disproportionate with regard to the purpose limitation, the adequacy, and the proportionality fair information principles.

Moreover, the data subjects lack any kind of meaningful participation to the processing of their personal data within the TFTP context. Before the media disclosure of the SWIFT case in 2006, EU citizens did not even have the basic right to know that their data might have been transferred to the US for law enforcement purposes. The current TFTP Agreement only guarantees the provision of information to the data subjects, by posting on the website of UST information concerning the TFTP.[228] The other data subject rights are mere proclamations. The right to access is turned to a right to obtain confirmation by the US authorities, through a request by the national data protection authority, that

---

[225] The FATF is an inter-governmental body founded in 1989, whose purpose is the development and promotion of national and international policies to combat money laundering and terrorist financing. In 1990, FATF adopted 40 Recommendations that 'provide a complete set of counter-measures against money laundering covering the criminal justice system and law enforcement, the financial system and its regulation, and international co-operation.' On 31 October 2001, the FATF issued the nine Special Recommendations on terrorist financing. See www.fatf-gafi.org/pages/0,2987,en_32250379_32235720_1_1_1_1_1,00.html.

[226] The Egmont Group is a group of Financial Intelligence Units (FIUs) established in 1995, whose aim is to improve cooperation in the fight against money laundering and the financing of terrorism and to foster the implementation of domestic programmes in this field. The FIU is a 'central, national agency responsible for receiving, (and as permitted, requesting) analyzing and disseminating to the competent authorities, disclosures of financial information: (i) concerning suspected proceeds of crime and potential financing of terrorism, or (ii) required by national legislation or regulation, in order to combat money-laundering or terrorism financing.' See Interpretative Note concerning the Egmont definition of a Financial Intelligence Unit.

[227] See TFTP II Agreement, Art 5(2).

[228] ibid, Art 14.

no processing has taken place in breach of the Agreement. The same applies to the right of rectification, while the enforceability of the right to redress is very uncertain since the Agreement does not create or confer any right or benefit on any person or entity.[229]

Finally, an integral part of the right to data protection, as this is laid down in Article 8(3) EUCFR, is control of compliance with the data protection principles by independent authorities.[230] Such a control is not guaranteed by the TFTP Agreement that grants Europol a minimal verification role, and turns essentially the national data protection authorities to mere 'post-boxes of assessments made by the US authorities'.[231]

E. Respect the Essence of the Right

It should be recalled that the CJEU found in *Schrems*[232] that legislation permitting generalised access to the content of electronic communications compromises the essence of the fundamental right to privacy established in Article 7 EUCFR,[233] and legislation not providing for legal remedies to individuals to access and obtain rectification or erasure of their data affects the essence of the fundamental right to effective judicial protection enshrined in Article 47 EUCFR.[234] The bulk transfer of SWIFT financial messaging data to UST, without the possibility of minimisation or effective supervision as to whether they are related to counter-terrorism purposes, and no enforceable data subject rights, touches the essence of the rights to privacy and data protection.

---

[229] ibid, Art 20(1).
[230] See Art 8(3) EUCFR.
[231] See above.
[232] Case C-362/13 *Maximillian Schrems v Data Protection Commissioner*, 6 October 2015, (CJEU (Grand Chamber), 6 October 2015).
[233] ibid, para 94.
[234] ibid, para 95.

6

Internet Data Surveillance

I. COMMUNICATIONS SURVEILLANCE IN THE US

A. The Snowden Revelations

O N 6 JUNE 2013, two articles published in the *Guardian*[1] and the *Washington Post*[2] revealed that the US was operating a secret mass electronic surveillance programme granting it access to Internet data, such as email, chat, videos, photos, file transfers and social networking details held by leading US Internet companies, including Microsoft, Yahoo, Google, Facebook, PalTalk, AOL, Skype, Youtube and Apple. In particular, it was reported that the programme, code-named PRISM, 'facilitates extensive, in-depth surveillance on live communications and stored information' to 'the content of communications and not just the metadata'.[3] With this programme, the National Security Agency (NSA) and the Federal Bureau of Investigation (FBI) 'are tapping directly into the central servers'[4] of 'the world's largest internet brands' and 'obtain both stored communications as well as perform real-time collection on targeted users'[5] that 'enable analysts to track foreign targets.'[6] The UK Government Communications Headquarters (GCHQ) 'also has been secretly gathering intelligence from the same internet companies through an operation set up by the NSA' which allows it 'to circumvent the formal legal process required in Britain to seek personal material such as emails, photos and videos from an internet company based outside of the country.'[7] On 9 June 2013, it was revealed that the whistle-blower behind the

---

[1] G Greenwald and E MacAskill, 'NSA Prism program taps in to user data of Apple, Google and others', *The Guardian*, 7 June 2013, www.theguardian.com/world/2013/jun/06/us-tech-giants-nsa-data.

[2] B Gellman and L Poitras, 'U.S., British intelligence mining data from nine U.S. Internet companies in broad secret program', *Washington Post*, 7 June 2013, www.washingtonpost.com/investigations/us-intelligence-mining-data-from-nine-us-internet-companies-in-broad-secret-program/2013/06/06/3a0c0da8-cebf-11e2-8845-d970ccb04497_story.html.

[3] Greenwald and MacAskill, n 1 above.

[4] Gellman and Poitras, n 2 above.

[5] Greenwald and MacAskill, n 1 above.

[6] Gellman and Poitras, n 2 above.

[7] ibid.

NSA revelations was Edward Snowden, a former technical assistant for the Central Intelligence Agency (CIA) and the NSA.[8]

The media revelations raised serious concerns about the fundamental rights implications of the US surveillance programmes and sparked outrage on the other side of the Atlantic.[9] Before turning to the European reactions and the EU fundamental rights issues, it is worth taking a closer look at the US surveillance programme.

B. A Brief History of US Communications Surveillance

In the aftermath of the 9/11 terrorist attacks, on 4 October 2001, President George Bush issued a classified presidential authorisation ordering the NSA to collect in bulk metadata and content information of international telephone and Internet communications for foreign intelligence purposes.[10] The authorisations permitting the acquisition of bulk content and metadata were renewed,[11] with some modifications, approximately until 2007.[12] The programme allowing for the collection of international communications' data under these presidential authorisations became known as the Terrorist Surveillance Programme (TSP).[13] The general public became aware of the TSP only in December 2005, when the *New York Times* published an article revealing that the Bush administration had been authorising the NSA to monitor 'the international telephone calls and international

---

[8] G Greenwald, E McAskill and L Poitras, 'Edward Snowden: the whistleblower behind the NSA surveillance revelations', *The Guardian*, 9 June 2013, www.theguardian.com/world/2013/jun/09/edward-snowden-nsa-whistleblower-surveillance.

[9] See D Wright and R Kreissl, 'European responses to the Snowden revelations: A discussion paper', December 2013, Increasing Resilience in Surveillance Societies (IRISS), http://irissproject.eu/wp-content/uploads/2013/12/IRISS_European-responses-to-the-Snowden-revelations_18-Dec-2013_Final.pdf.

[10] Authorization for Specified Electronic Surveillance Activities During a Limited Period to Detect and Prevent Acts of Terrorism Within the United States, Oct. 4, 2001, cited in Office Of The Inspector Gen, Nat'l Sec Agency Cent Sec Serv, Working Draft ST-09-0002, 1, 7–8, 11, 15 (2009). See 'DNI Announces the Declassification of the Existence of Collection Activities Authorized by President George W. Bush Shortly After the Attacks of September 11, 2001' (21 December 2013), http://icontherecord.tumblr.com/post/70683717031/dni-announces-the-declassification-of-the.

[11] A Report prepared by the Office of Inspectors General of several defence and intelligence agencies noted that the programme 'became less a temporary response to the September 11 terrorist attacks and more a permanent surveillance tool.' See Unclassified Report on the President's Surveillance Program, Prepared by the Office of Inspectors General of the Department of Defence, Department of Justice, Central Intelligence Agency, National Security Agency and the Office of the Director of National Intelligence, 2009, 31.

[12] Privacy and Civil Liberties Oversight Board (PCLOB), Report on the Surveillance Program Operated Pursuant to Section 702 of the Foreign Intelligence Surveillance Act, 2 July 2014, www.pclob.gov/Library/702-Report-2.pdf, 16.

[13] On a discussion of the legal bases on which the US Administration based the programme, see L Donohue, 'Section 702 and the Collection of International Telephone and Internet Content' (2015) 38 *Harvard Journal of Law & Public Policy* 117, 126.

e-mail messages of hundreds, perhaps thousands, of people' inside and outside the United States.[14]

In the light of public concerns, the US administration sent a letter to congressional leaders explaining that the programme was required because the Foreign Intelligence Surveillance Act (FISA) 'lacked the flexibility needed to identify potential threats.' The TSP was subsequently transferred under the FISA and the Government sought authorisation under this to continue carrying out the content collection undertaken under the TSP.[15] In January 2007, the Foreign Intelligence Surveillance Court (FISC) granted the US Government authorisation to conduct communications' surveillance under the condition that the targeted email addresses and telephone numbers were reasonably believed to be used by persons located outside the United States. The FISC's authorisation, known as the 'Foreign Telephone and Email Order', replaced the TSP. When the US Government applied to further renew the Foreign Telephone and Email Order, a different FISC judge imposed some restrictions and required some changes in the collection programme[16] that created an 'intelligence gap', according to the Government.[17] At the same time and separate from the Foreign Telephone and Email Order, the US Government was obtaining individual orders from FISC under FISA to require private US companies to grant access to communications of individuals located overseas who were suspected of engaging in terrorism and who used United States-based communication service providers.[18]

In order to deal with the 'perceived inefficiencies of obtaining FISC approval to target persons located outside the US',[19] the US Congress passed the Protect America Act (PAA) of 2007,[20] which covered the collection of communications previously undertaken under the Foreign Telephone and Email Orders and the TSP. Under PAA, the Attorney General and the Director of National Intelligence issued authorisations for up to one year to acquire communications directed at persons reasonably believed to be outside the United States.[21] The Attorney General was required to submit targeting procedures to the FISC and to certify that the communications to be intercepted were not purely domestic in nature.[22] Upon

---

[14] J Risen and E Lichtblau, 'Bush Lets U.S. Spy on Callers Without Courts', *New York Times*, 16 December 2005, www.nytimes.com/2005/12/16/politics/bush-lets-us-spy-on-callers-without-courts.html.

[15] PCLOB Report, n 12 above, p 17.

[16] ibid, p 17.

[17] E Lichtblau, J Risen, and M Mazzetti, 'Reported Drop in Surveillance Spurred a Law', *New York Times*, 11 August 2007, www.nytimes.com/2007/08/11/washington/11nsa.html.

[18] PCLOB Report, n 12 above, p 18.

[19] ibid.

[20] Protect America Act of 2007, Pub L No 110-55, § 2, 121 Stat 552 (2007).

[21] ibid. Access to the communications was granted under five conditions: 1) reasonable procedures had to be in place in order to determine that the acquisition concerned persons reasonably believed to be located outside the United States; 2) the acquisition did not involve solely domestic communications; 3) it involved obtaining the communications data from or with the assistance of a communications service provider who had access to communications; 4) a significant purpose of the acquisition was to obtain foreign intelligence information; and 5) minimisation procedures under FISA would be used. See also Donohue, n 13 above, 136.

[22] ibid.

certification, the FISC had to grant the order. Service providers were granted immunity under the PAA for providing information to the Government. The PAA was a temporary measure that expired in February 2008.

It was replaced by the FISA Amendments Act (FAA) of 2008.[23] The FAA introduced section 702 of FISA as the new legal basis for the collection of the communications of non-US persons abroad, as well as sections 703 and 704 that target US persons outside of the United States for electronic surveillance and other types of acquisitions. The FAA was renewed in December 2012[24] and is due to expire in December 2017. The Snowden revelations referred to the surveillance programme under section 702, and this is examined below.

C. Section 702, PRISM and Upstream Surveillance

According to the PCLOB, section 702 of FISA is a 'complex law'.[25] It permits the Attorney General (AG) and the Director of National Intelligence (DNI) to jointly authorise, for a period of up to one year, the targeting of non-US persons[26] who are reasonably believed to be located outside the United States, 'with the compelled assistance of an electronic communication service provider'[27] in order to acquire foreign intelligence information.[28] Foreign intelligence information concerning non-US persons is defined in FISA as information that relates to the ability of the United States to protect against an actual or potential attack by a foreign power; sabotage, international terrorism, the proliferation of weapons of mass destruction by a foreign power; or clandestine intelligence activities by a foreign power.[29] Foreign intelligence information also refers to information that relates to the national defence or security of the United States or the conduct of the foreign affairs of the United States, insofar as that information concerns a foreign power (such as international terrorist groups or foreign governments) or foreign territory.[30]

The AG's and DNI's section 702 annual certifications, as well as targeting and minimisation procedures, are subject to review by the FISC. The certifications must be accompanied by affidavits of national security officials that demonstrate to the FISC that only persons outside the US are targeted, and that domestic communications are excluded.[31] However, the FISC's role is 'limited'[32] to reviewing

---

[23] FISA Amendments Act of 2008, Pub L No 110-261, 122 Stat 2436 (2008).
[24] FISA Amendments Act Reauthorization Act of 2012, Pub L No 112-238, 126 Stat 1631 (2012).
[25] PCLOB Report, n 12 above, p 20.
[26] According to PCLOB, 'a foreign government or international terrorist group could qualify as a "person," but an entire foreign country cannot be a "person" targeted under Section 702.' Ibid, p 21.
[27] 50 USC § 1881a(g)(2)(A)(vi).
[28] ibid.
[29] 50 USC § 1801(e)(1).
[30] 50 USC § 1801(e)(2).
[31] 50 USC § 1881a(g)(2)(C).
[32] Donohue, n 13 above, p 140.

the certification and the targeting and minimisation procedures.[33] As soon as it establishes that those are present, it must issue an order approving the certification and the use of the data acquired.[34] Furthermore, under section 702 the AG's and the DNI's annual certifications authorising the targeting of non-US abroad do not need to identify the particular individuals to be targeted and specify these to the FISC.[35] Instead, the certifications identify 'categories of foreign intelligence information' and there is no requirement that the AG and the DNI show probable cause to believe that a 'Section 702 target is a foreign power or agent of a foreign power, as is required under traditional FISA.'[36]

Once the FISC has authorised the acquisition, the AG and the DNI send 'written directives to electronic communication service providers compelling their assistance in the acquisition.'[37] The definition of electronic communication service providers under FISA is broad and includes telephone, Internet service, and other communications providers. Providers are allowed to challenge the legality of a section 702 directive before the FISC,[38] and the Government may file a petition before the same court to compel a provider to comply with a directive.[39] Non-US persons are targeted through the 'tasking' of 'selectors'. A selector is 'a specific communications facility that is assessed to be used by the target', such as the target's email address or telephone number.[40] As soon as a selector has been tasked, it is sent to an electronic communications service provider requiring it to collect the communications. The PCLOB observed in its report that 'although targeting decisions must be individualized, this does not mean that a substantial number of persons are not targeted under the Section 702 program. The government estimates that 89,138 persons were targeted under Section 702 during 2013.'[41] Under the procedures for targeting, the NSA is required to make two determinations: it must determine the assessed location and the non-US person status of the potential target (referred to as 'the foreignness determination') and whether the target 'possesses and/or is likely to communicate or receive foreign intelligence information' (referred to as the 'foreign intelligence purpose determination').[42]

Two types of data acquisition occur under section 702: PRISM and 'upstream' collection. Under PRISM, the FBI sends selectors—such as an email address or a telephone number—to US-based electronic communications service providers that have been served a directive compelling them to transfer to the Government the communications sent 'to' or 'from' that selector.[43] The raw data acquired via

---

[33] PCLOB Report, n 12 above, p 27.
[34] 50 USC § 1881(i)(3)(A).
[35] 50 USC § 1881a(a). See also PCLOB Report, n 12 above, p 24.
[36] ibid, p 25.
[37] 50 USC § 1881a(h). Ibid, p 32.
[38] 50 USC § 1881a(h)(4).
[39] 50 USC § 1881a(h)(5).
[40] PCLOB Report, n 12 above, p 32.
[41] ibid, p 33.
[42] ibid, p 42.
[43] ibid, p 34.

PRISM collection can be used by the NSA, the CIA and the FBI. The 'upstream' collection involves the acquisition of communications 'as they transit the "internet backbone" facilities.'[44] As the PCLOB explains, 'the collection ... does not occur at the local telephone company or email provider with whom the targeted person interacts ..., but instead occurs "upstream" in the flow of communications between communication service providers.'[45] Unlike PRISM that only collects communications 'to' and 'from' the tasked selector, under upstream collection, the NSA acquires Internet communications 'to' and 'from' as well as 'about' the selector.[46] According to PCLOB, 'an "about" communication is one in which the tasked selector is referenced within the acquired Internet transactions, but the target is not necessarily a participant in the communication.'[47] 'About' communications can even involve the 'Internet activity of the targeted person.'[48] The PCLOB report states that since 2011, the NSA has acquired approximately 26.5 million Internet transactions a year as a result of upstream collection.[49] The raw data acquired via upstream collection are sent only to the NSA.[50]

II. TRANSATLANTIC DATA TRANSFERS AND EU FUNDAMENTAL RIGHTS

A. The European Reaction to the Snowden Revelations

The Snowden revelations caused numerous concerns in Europe as regards the protection of fundamental rights and provoked the reaction of European institutions. The European Council noted that a lack of trust between the EU and the USA 'could prejudice the necessary cooperation in the field of intelligence gathering.'[51] In a Communication to the Parliament and the Council entitled 'Rebuilding Trust in EU–US Data Flows', the Commission stated that trust in the transatlantic partnership had been negatively affected and needed to be restored.[52] According to the

---

[44] Statement of Rajesh De, General Counsel, NSA at the Privacy and Civil Liberties Oversight Board: Public Hearing Regarding the Surveillance Program Operated Pursuant to Section 702 of the Foreign Intelligence Surveillance Act 26, 19 March 2014.

[45] PCLOB Report, n 12 above, p 35.

[46] See Donohue, n 13 above, pp 160–61.

[47] PCLOB Report, n 12 above, p 37.

[48] ibid, p 38.

[49] ibid, p 37. According to the PCLOB, 'an Internet transaction refers to any set of data that travels across the Internet together such that it may be understood by a device on the Internet. An Internet transaction could consist of a single discrete communication, such as an email that is sent from one server to another.' Sometimes, however, however, 'a single Internet transaction might contain multiple discrete communications (MCTs) ... If a single discrete communication within an MCT is to, from, or about a Section 702-tasked selector, and at least one end of the transaction is foreign, the NSA will acquire the entire MCT.'

[50] ibid, p 35.

[51] See 'EU-US spying row stokes concern over anti-terror campaign', *EU Business*, 26 October 2013, www.eubusiness.com/news-eu/us-intelligence.r38.

[52] Communication from the Commission to the European Parliament and the Council, 'Rebuilding Trust in EU–US Data Flows', 27.11.2013 COM(2013) 846 final, 2.

Commission, 'large-scale US intelligence collection programmes, such as PRISM affect the fundamental rights of Europeans and, specifically, their right to privacy and to the protection of personal data.'[53] Having noted that 'mass surveillance of private communication, be it of citizens, enterprises or political leaders, is unacceptable',[54] the Commission put forward five steps to be taken 'to restore trust in data transfers for the benefit of the digital economy, security both in the EU and in the US, and the broader transatlantic relationship.'[55] It called for a timely adoption of the EU data protection reform package; for the strengthening of data protection safeguards in law enforcement cooperation, mainly through the adoption of the 'Umbrella' Agreement; for the promotion of privacy standards internationally; for a review and reform of US national security activities to address European concerns; and proposed 'making Safe Harbour safer'.[56]

In its Resolution of 12 March 2014,[57] the European Parliament stated that the fight against terrorism can 'never be a justification for untargeted, secret, or even illegal mass surveillance programmes' and took the view that such programmes are 'incompatible with the principles of necessity and proportionality in a democratic society.'[58] It condemned 'the vast and systemic blanket collection of the personal data of innocent people, often including intimate personal information', emphasising that privacy is 'the foundation stone of a free and democratic society.'[59] Furthermore, it pointed out that mass surveillance has potentially severe effects on other fundamental rights, such as freedom of the press, freedom of assembly and of association and it entails 'a significant potential for abusive use of the information gathered' and possible 'illegal actions by intelligence services'. In this respect, it called the US authorities and the EU Member States to prohibit blanket mass surveillance activities, and asked for the suspension of Safe Harbour as 'the legal instrument used for the transfer of EU personal data to the US', since it failed to provide adequate protection for EU citizens.[60]

B.   The Snowden Revelations and Safe Harbour

Transatlantic trade is of critical importance for the economies of both the EU and the US.[61] A crucial aspect of this relation, which makes possible the realisation

---

[53] ibid, p 3.
[54] ibid.
[55] ibid, pp 5–10.
[56] ibid, p 6.
[57] European Parliament resolution of 12 March 2014 on the US NSA surveillance programme, surveillance bodies in various Member States and their impact on EU citizens' fundamental rights and on transatlantic cooperation in Justice and Home Affairs (2013/2188(INI)), P7_TA(2014)0230.
[58] ibid.
[59] ibid.
[60] ibid.
[61] Communication from the Commission, n 52 above, p 2.

of transatlantic commercial transactions, is the transatlantic flow of personal data.[62] Under the EU data protection legal framework, personal data can cross the EU's external borders only if an 'adequate' level of protection is ensured in the country of destination.[63] As mentioned above, the EU regulation of transborder data flows has been broadly based on a centralised model according to which the Commission, decide whether a third country ensures adequate protection. In terms of the criteria used to assess the adequacy of protection, Directive 95/46/EC on the protection of individuals with regard to the processing of personal data and on the free movement of such data (the 'Data Protection Directive') stipulates that all the circumstances surrounding a data transfer, and more particularly the nature of the data, the purpose of the proposed processing operation and the rules of law in force in the third country in question, should be taken into consideration.[64] According to the Working Document adopted by the Article 29 Working Party on the protection of individuals with regard to the processing of personal data, an adequacy analysis essentially focuses on two basic elements: the content of the rules applicable and the means for ensuring their effective application.[65]

The Commission has recognised a number of countries or jurisdictions as providing adequate protection.[66] However, there has been no general adequacy finding for the US, given that it lacks comprehensive data protection legislation.[67] In order to allow for international trade, transatlantic data flows between the EU and the US were made possible through the Safe Harbour scheme.[68] Safe Harbour was based on a system of voluntary self-certification and self-assessment of US-based companies that they abide by certain data protection principles, the 'Safe Harbour principles'[69] implemented in accordance with the guidance provided by the frequently asked questions (the 'FAQs') issued by the US Department of Commerce on 21 July 2000.[70] Under the scheme, US companies were required to self-register

---

[62] See I Tourkochoriti, 'The Transatlantic Flow of Data and the National Security Exception in the European Data Privacy Regulation: In Search for Legal Protection Against Surveillance' (2014) 36 (2) *University of Pennsylvania Journal of International Law* 459.

[63] Directive 95/46/EC [1995] OJ L281/31 (Data Protection Directive), Art 25(1).

[64] ibid, Art 25(2).

[65] Article 29 Working Party, 'Transfers of Personal Data to Third Countries: Applying Articles 25 and 26 of the EU Data Protection Directive', 24 July 1998, 5.

[66] Switzerland, Canada, Andorra, Argentina, Guernsey, Isle of Man, Faroe Islands, Israel, Jersey, New Zealand and Uruguay.

[67] See V Papakonstantinou and P de Hert, 'The PNR Agreement and Transatlantic Anti-Terrorism Co-Operation: No Firm Human Rights Framework on Either Side of the Atlantic' (2009) 46 *Common Market Law Review* 885, 892; G Greenleaf, 'The influence of European data privacy standards outside Europe: implications for globalization of Convention 108' (2012) 2 (2) *International Data Privacy Law* 68, 70.

[68] See Commission Decision 2000/520/EC of 26 July 2000 pursuant to Directive 95/46/EC of the European Parliament and of the Council on the adequacy of the protection provided by the safe harbour privacy principles and related frequently asked questions issued by the US Department of Commerce (notified under document number C(2000) 2441).

[69] Commission Decision 2000/520/EC, Annex I.

[70] ibid, Annex II. Safe Harbour included the following principles: notice, choice, onward transfer, security, data integrity, access and enforcement.

their compliance with the Safe Harbour principles with the US Department of Commerce, while the US Federal Trading Commission (FTC) was responsible for enforcing the agreement.[71] On the basis of this, the Commission issued Decision 2000/520/EC (hereafter 'the Safe Harbour Decision') recognising the adequacy of protection provided by the Safe Harbour principles.[72] The Safe Harbour decision served as the legal basis for transfers of personal data from the EU to US-based companies which have adhered to the Safe Harbour privacy principles. Safe Harbour proved to be an important tool of transatlantic commercial relations,[73] with approximately 3,246 companies signing up to the scheme.

In a Report issued in November 2013, the Commission identified several problematic aspects regarding the functioning of the Safe Harbour. First, it found that there was a variance as to the degree of compliance by US self-certified companies with the transparency obligations.[74] Secondly, false claims of Safe Harbour adherence were made by US companies which had never been participants of the Safe Harbour, and by companies which had once joined the scheme but then failed to resubmit their self-certification to the Department of Commerce.[75] Thirdly, many companies had not correctly incorporated the Safe Harbour Privacy Principles and there was no full evaluation of the actual practice in the self-certified companies.[76] Fourthly, the Commission found that there were many weaknesses in the enforcement of the scheme and its oversight by US public authorities.[77]

The Snowden revelations in 2013 raised additional concerns about the systematic access of US law enforcement authorities to EU-originating data transferred to US-based companies under the Safe Harbour scheme. As the Commission observed, all companies involved in PRISM that grants access to US authorities to data stored and processed in the US, appeared to be Safe Harbour certified. This made the Safe Harbour scheme 'one of the conduits through which access [was] given to US intelligence authorities to collecting personal data initially processed in the EU.'[78] The Commission recognised that limitations to data protection rules

---

[71] ibid, Annex III.

[72] ibid, Art 1.

[73] For an analysis, see *inter alia* S Kierkegaard Mercado, 'Safe Harbor Agreement—Boon or Bane' (2005) 1 *Shidler Journal of Law Commerce and Technology* 1; C Kuner, 'Beyond Safe Harbor: European Data Protection Law and Electronic Commerce' (2001) 35 *International Law* 79; G Pearce and N Platten, 'Orchestrating Transatlantic Approaches to Personal Data Protection: A European Perspective' (1999) 22 *Fordham International Law Journal* 2024; J Reidenberg, 'E-Commerce and Trans-Atlantic Privacy' (2002) 38 *Houston Law Review* 717; A Charlesworth, 'Clash of the Data Titans—US and EU Data Privacy Regulation' (2000) 6 *European Public Law* 253; P Blume, 'Transborder Data Flow: Is There a Solution in Sight' (2000) 8 *International Journal of Law and Information Technology* 65; R Schriver, 'You Cheated, You Lied: The Safe Harbor Agreement and Its Enforcement by the Federal Trade Commission' (2002) 70 *Fordham Law Review* 277.

[74] Communication from the Commission to the European Parliament and the Council on the Functioning of the Safe Harbour from the Perspective of EU Citizens and Companies Established in the EU, Brussels, 27.11.2013, COM(2013) 847 final, 6.

[75] ibid, p 7.

[76] ibid, p 8.

[77] ibid, pp 9–13.

[78] ibid, p 16.

were permitted under the Safe Harbour on grounds of national security,[79] but it was dubious whether 'the large-scale collection and processing of personal information under US surveillance programmes' was 'necessary and proportionate to meet the interests of national security.'[80] According to the Commission, 'the reach of these surveillance programmes, combined with the unequal treatment of EU citizens', brought into question 'the level of protection afforded by the Safe Harbour arrangement. The personal data of EU citizens sent to the US under the Safe Harbour may be accessed and further processed by US authorities in a way incompatible with the grounds on which the data was originally collected in the EU and the purposes for which it was transferred to the US.'[81]

In this respect, the Commission reiterated that it had the authority under the Data Protection Directive and under Article 3 of the Safe Harbour adequacy decision to suspend or revoke the Safe Harbour if the scheme no longer provides an adequate level of protection. Against this background, the Commission had to consider three available policy options: maintain the status quo; strengthen the Safe Harbour scheme; or suspend or revoke the Safe Harbour decision.[82] Taking the view that the revocation of Safe Harbour 'would adversely affect the interests of member companies in the EU and in the US', the Commission concluded that the scheme should be strengthened to address both its structural shortcomings and the operation of the national security exception.[83]

III. THE *SCHREMS* JUDGMENT

A. Factual Background

The *Schrems* case arose from the proceedings between Mr Maximillian Schrems, an Austrian national residing in Austria, and the Irish Data Protection Commissioner ('the Commissioner'). Mr Schrems, who had been a subscriber to the social network Facebook since 2008, lodged a complaint with the Commissioner in June 2013, by which he asked the latter to exercise his statutory powers by prohibiting Facebook Ireland from transferring his personal data to the US. Mr Schrems's complaint was based on the fact that any person residing in the EU who wishes to use Facebook is required to conclude, at the time of his registration, a contract with Facebook Ireland, a subsidiary of Facebook Inc., which is itself established in the US. Some or all of the personal data of Facebook Ireland's users who reside in the European Union is transferred to servers belonging to Facebook Inc located in the US, where it undergoes processing. In his complaint Mr Schrems referred

---

[79] See Commission Decision 2000/520/EC, Annex I.
[80] Communication from the Commission, n 52 above, p 4.
[81] ibid.
[82] ibid.
[83] ibid.

to the revelations made by Edward Snowden concerning the activities of the US intelligence services, and in particular the PRISM programme, under which the NSA obtained access to mass data stored on servers in the United States owned or controlled by a range of companies active in the internet and technology field, such as Facebook USA. In this regard, he contended that the law and practice in force in the US did not ensure adequate protection of the personal data held in its territory against the surveillance activities that were engaged in there by the public authorities. The Commissioner rejected Mr Schrems' complaint as 'frivolous or vexatious' on the basis that it was unsustainable in law.

Mr Schrems brought an action before the Irish High Court challenging the Commissioner's decision. The High Court found that the mass and undifferentiated accessing of personal data was contrary to the principle of proportionality and the fundamental rights to privacy and to inviolability of the dwelling, protected by the Irish Constitution.[84] However, the High Court considered that this case concerned the implementation of EU law and in particular it raised the issue of the legality of the Safe Harbour regime, established by Decision 2000/520 in the light of Articles 7 and 8 of the EUCFR.[85] In this respect, the High Court decided to stay the proceedings and refer two preliminary questions to the Court asking whether National Data Protection Authorities (NDPAs) were bound by the Commission's Safe Harbour adequacy decision or whether they could conduct their own investigation of the matter in the light of factual developments that arose after the publication of this decision.

B. The Opinion of the Advocate General

Advocate General Bot delivered his Opinion on the case on 23 September 2015.[86] He commenced his analysis by stating that there were two aspects in the case at issue. The first concerned the powers of NDPAs to investigate complaints concerning transfers of personal data to a third country where it was alleged that this did not guarantee an adequate level of protection despite of a Commission's finding to the contrary. The second concerned the suspension of data transfers to the US under the Safe Harbour regime in light of Articles 7 and 8 EUCFR on the basis that this did not provide adequate protection.

Regarding the first issue, in his Opinion the AG disagreed with the Commission that the allocation of powers between this and the NDPAs made the Commission solely responsible for decisions of finding, suspension or repeal of adequacy decisions, while the NDPAs' role was merely to apply the relevant legislation and

---

[84] Case C-362/13 *Maximillian Schrems v Data Protection Commissioner*, 6 October 2015, unreported, para 30.

[85] ibid, para 35.

[86] Opinion of Advocate General Bot delivered on 23 September 2015 in Case C-362/13 *Maximillian Schrems v Data Protection Commissioner*, 6 October 2015, unreported.

held that the existence of an adequacy decision adopted by the Commission on the basis of Article 25(6) of the Data Protection Directive could not eliminate the NDPAs' powers under Article 28.[87] The AG employed a series of arguments to justify this position. First, he invoked the independence and the importance of the role played by NDPAs as guardians of the fundamental rights to privacy and data protection under Article 8(3) EUCFR.[88] In this respect, he called for a broad interpretation of the powers of NDPAs under Article 28 of the Data Protection Directive,[89] noting that if supervisory authorities were absolutely bound by decisions adopted by the Commission, that would inevitably limit their total independence.[90] Moreover, the AG opined that Article 25 of the Data Protection Directive establishes a shared competence of the Commission and the Member States to make a finding of whether a third country ensures an adequate level of protection[91] and does not attribute exclusive powers to the Commission on the issue.[92] The purpose of the Commission's adequacy decision was, therefore, to authorise transfers and not to prevent citizens from making complaints to NDPAs[93] and the latter from investigating these when they are faced with allegations of infringement of fundamental rights.[94] Furthermore, the AG also stated that there should be no 'irrebuttable presumption' that the transfer of data to a third country under the Commission's adequacy decision complies with fundamental rights;[95] on the contrary, where 'systemic deficiencies' are found in the third country in question, the Member States must be able to take the measures necessary to safeguard the fundamental rights protected by Articles 7 and 8 EUCFR.[96] Finally, the AG agreed with the Parliament that it is the EU legislature that decided what powers were to devolve to the NDPAs, and the implementing power conferred on the Commission in Article 25(6) of the Data Protection Directive could not affect these.[97] The AG therefore concluded that NDPAs 'must be able to carry out their investigations and, where appropriate, suspend the transfer of data' to the US irrespective of the conditions laid down in Decision 2000/520.[98]

Taking the view that the 'mass, indiscriminate surveillance'[99] carried out in the USA 'is inherently disproportionate and constitutes an unwarranted interference with the rights guaranteed by Articles 7 and 8 of the Charter',[100] AG Bot invited the Court to invalidate on its own motion the Commission's adequacy decision

---

[87] ibid, para 61.
[88] ibid, paras 57–74.
[89] ibid, para 79.
[90] ibid, para 73.
[91] ibid, para 86.
[92] ibid, para 89.
[93] ibid, para 92.
[94] ibid, para 93.
[95] ibid, para 104.
[96] ibid, para 105.
[97] ibid, para 116.
[98] ibid, para 118.
[99] ibid, para 200.
[100] ibid.

and suspend data transfers to the US. The AG based this conclusion on two main arguments: the national security limitations in Decision 2000/520 were not limited to what is strictly necessary to achieve the objectives referred to;[101] and, Decision 2000/520 did not contain appropriate guarantees—including measures of judicial redress[102]—for preventing mass and generalised access to the transferred data.[103]

C. The Judgment of the Court

Less than one month after the AG's Opinion, on 6 October 2015, the Court issued its judgment in a Grand Chamber formation. In a rather short analysis, it agreed with the AG on both points: it held that NDPAs have the power to investigate complaints lodged by individuals regarding transfers of data to third countries where the Commission has adopted an adequacy decision and declared the Safe Harbour adequacy decision invalid.

Insofar as the powers of the NDPAs were concerned, the CJEU noted that NDPAs must be able to examine, with complete independence, whether transfers of data to third countries comply with fundamental rights and the requirements of the Data Protection Directive.[104] The Court clarified how NDPAs should proceed in doing so, employing an a fortiori *Foto-Frost*[105] argument that would enable it to have the final saying in a question of validity. According to this, following *Foto-Frost,* national courts are entitled to consider the validity of an EU act, but they do not have the power to declare such an act invalid themselves; *a fortiori*, NDPAs can examine complaints on the compatibility of a Commission's adequacy decision with fundamental rights, but they are not entitled to declare that decision invalid themselves.[106] The CJEU distinguished two potential outcomes when NDPAs are asked to examine a complaint lodged by an individual regarding the transfer of his data to third countries: if the NDPA comes to the conclusion that it is unfounded and therefore rejects it, the individual can challenge this decision before the national courts—as Mr Schrems did—and the latter must stay the proceedings and make a reference to the Court for a preliminary ruling on validity.[107] If the NDPA considers, however, that the individual's claim is well-founded, it must engage in legal proceedings before the national courts in order for them to make a reference for a preliminary ruling on the validity of the measure.[108]

On the basis of this pronouncement and in order to give the referring national court a full answer, the CJEU decided to examine the validity of the Commission's

---

[101] ibid, para 197.
[102] ibid, paras 204–06 and 211–13.
[103] ibid, para 202.
[104] *Schrems*, n 84 above, para 57.
[105] Case 314/419 *Foto-Frost v Hauptzollamt Lübeck-Ost* [1985] ECR 4199.
[106] *Schrems*, n 84 above, para 62.
[107] ibid, para 64.
[108] ibid, para 65.

adequacy decision 2000/520.[109] Having explained that adequacy requires a level of protection of personal data in third countries 'essentially equivalent' to the one guaranteed within the EU,[110] the Court held that the Commission is obliged to check periodically whether such an adequacy finding is 'still factually and legally justified',[111] taking into account the circumstances that have arisen after that decision's adoption.[112] It then went on to discuss Articles 1 and 3 of Decision 2000/520. It observed that the derogation to the Safe Harbour principles on the basis of 'national security, public interest, or law enforcement requirements' constituted an interference with the fundamental right to privacy of the persons whose personal data is transferred from the EU to the US.[113] The CJEU reiterated its finding in *Digital Rights Ireland*[114] that legislation is

> not limited to what is strictly necessary where it authorises, on a generalised basis, storage of all the personal data of all the persons whose data has been transferred from the European Union to the United States without any differentiation, limitation or exception being made in the light of the objective pursued and without an objective criterion being laid down by which to determine the limits of the access of the public authorities to the data, and of its subsequent use, for purposes which are specific, strictly restricted and capable of justifying the interference which both access to that data and its use entail.[115]

In particular, the Court found that legislation permitting the public authorities to have access on a generalised basis to the content of electronic communications compromises the essence of the fundamental right to privacy established in Article 7 EUCFR.[116] Likewise, legislation not providing for any possibility for an individual to pursue legal remedies in order to have access to personal data relating to him, or to obtain the rectification or erasure of such data affects the essence of the fundamental right to effective judicial protection enshrined in Article 47 EUCFR.[117] Consequently, the CJEU declared Article 1 of Decision 2000/520 invalid, on the basis that it failed to comply with the requirements laid down in Article 25 (6) of the Data Protection Directive, read in the light of the Charter.[118] The Court also held that Article 3 of Decision 2000/520 was problematic because it denied the NDPAs the powers granted by Article 28 of the Data Protection Directive to investigate complaints brought forward by individuals.[119] In this respect, the CJEU held that the Commission had exceeded its implementing powers under

---

[109] ibid, para 67.
[110] ibid, para 73.
[111] ibid, para 76.
[112] ibid, para 77.
[113] ibid, paras 86–87.
[114] Joined Cases C 293/12 and C 594/12 *Digital Rights Ireland Ltd v Minister for Communications, Marine and Natural Resources* [2014] ECR I-238.
[115] ibid, para 93.
[116] ibid, para 94.
[117] ibid, para 95.
[118] ibid, para 98.
[119] ibid, para 102.

Article 25(6) of the Data Protection Directive,[120] and declared Article 3 of Decision 2000/520 also invalid.[121] Taking the view that the invalidity of Articles 1 and 3 of Decision 2000/520 affected the validity of the Decision in its entirety,[122] the Court annulled the Commission's Safe Harbour adequacy decision.

IV. INTERNET DATA SURVEILLANCE AND THE RIGHTS TO PRIVACY AND DATA PROTECTION

A. The Fundamental Rights Involved

The CJEU in *Schrems* considered that two fundamental rights were interfered with: the right to privacy under Article 8 EUCFR and the right to effective judicial protection under Article 47 EUCFR. In contrast to *Digital Rights Ireland*, the fundamental right to data protection enshrined in Article 8 EUCFR was absent from the Court's analysis. Indeed, the CJEU referred only three times to the fundamental right to data protection in its judgment: in paragraph 72, where the Court pointed out that the adequacy requirement under Article 25(6) of the Data Protection Directive 'implements the express obligation laid down in Article 8(1) of the Charter to protect personal data'; in paragraph 91 where it reiterated its pronouncement in *Digital Rights Ireland* that EU legislation involving interference with the fundamental rights guaranteed by Articles 7 and 8 EUCFR must

> lay down clear and precise rules governing the scope and application of a measure and imposing minimum safeguards, so that the persons whose personal data is concerned have sufficient guarantees enabling their data to be effectively protected against the risk of abuse and against any unlawful access and use of that data. The need for such safeguards is all the greater where personal data is subjected to automatic processing and where there is a significant risk of unlawful access to that data

and in paragraph 92, where it recalled that the protection of the fundamental right to privacy at EU level requires derogations and limitations in relation to the protection of personal data to apply only in so far as is strictly necessary.

While it is not disputable that US online surveillance interferes with the fundamental right to privacy, it is regrettable that the CJEU did not discuss the fundamental right to data protection. Indeed, AG Bot in his Opinion did so. In particular, he held that

> any form of processing of personal data is covered by Article 8 of the Charter and constitutes an interference with the right to the protection of such data. The access enjoyed by the United States intelligence services to the transferred data therefore also constitutes an interference with the fundamental right to protection of personal data guaranteed in Article 8 of the Charter, since such access constitutes a processing of that data.[123]

---

[120] ibid, para 103.
[121] ibid, para 104.
[122] ibid, para 105.
[123] Opinion of AG Bot, n 86 above, para 170.

This assertion that follows the Court's approach in *Digital Rights Ireland* is problematic. It has been emphasised elsewhere in this book, that processing of the data itself should not be considered as an interference with the fundamental right to data protection. An interference with this right should be ascertained on the fact that certain type of processing of personal data indeed interferes with one or more data protection principles. Mass electronic surveillance, based on the systematic government access to private-sector data[124] challenges once again the purpose limitation principle. As explained above, 'purpose limitation', which requires that personal data must be collected for specified, explicit and legitimate purposes and should not be further processed in a way incompatible with the initial purposes,[125] embodies the values of transparency, foreseeability in data processing and accountability of data controllers in order to mitigate the inherent power asymmetries in data protection law between data subjects and data controllers and is, thus, another expression of the right to informational self-determination.[126] Indeed, as the Commission noted, the personal data that EU citizens transferred to companies such as Facebook in order to be able to use their respective services are accessed by the US authorities in a way incompatible with the grounds on which the data were originally collected for: completely unrelated commercial purposes.[127] Furthermore, as the AG pointed out in his Opinion, EU citizens who are Facebook users are not aware that 'their personal data will be generally accessible to the United States security agencies'.[128] Such deviation of the purpose limitation principle leads to the 'function creep' problem: data can be accessed by different bodies and further processed in order to pursue different objectives from the ones for which they were initially collected, just because they are readily available and the relevant technology exists.[129] By leaving the right to data protection altogether outside its analysis in *Schrems*, the Court missed an opportunity to clarify whether the purpose limitation principle still has a meaning or whether it is dead letter in the Internet era of mass electronic surveillance.

There are also further data protection principles interfered with by the US Internet surveillance. These are the principle of proportionality in the sense of the vast quantity of Internet data retained, the protection of sensitive data, the control by an independent supervisory authority under the requirements of Article 8(3) EUCFR and data security, as analysed by the CJEU in *Digital Rights Ireland*. Furthermore, the fact that data subjects did not have any due process rights to request

---

[124] See F Cate, J Dempsey and I Rubinstein, 'Systematic government access to private-sector data' (2012) 2 (4) *International Data Privacy Law* 195.

[125] Data Protection Directive, Art 6(1)(b); CoE Convention for the Protection of Individuals with regard to Automatic Processing of Personal Data, European Treaty Series No 108, Art 5(b).

[126] M Tzanou, 'Data Protection as a Fundamental Right next to Privacy? "Reconstructing" a Not so New Right' (2013) 3 *International Data Privacy Law* 88, 91.

[127] See Communication from the Commission, n 52 above, p 4.

[128] Opinion of AG Bot, n 86 above, para 172.

[129] M Tzanou, 'The EU as an emerging "Surveillance Society": The function creep case study and challenges to privacy and data protection' (2010) 4 *Vienna Journal on International Constitutional Law* 407.

access, rectification (and erasure) of their personal data under the US surveillance programmes, constituted an interference with the relevant requirements of Article 8(2) EUCFR. This was raised by the CJEU, but it was considered an issue falling within Article 47 EUCFR and not Article 8(2) EUCFR, even if as the Court expressly mentioned such remedies were required to allow the individual 'to have access to personal data relating to him, or to obtain the rectification or erasure of such data.'[130] It seems, therefore, that an issue of demarcation between procedural data protection rights under Article 8(2) EUCFR and Article 47 EUCFR emerged in *Schrems*.

B. Transnational Data Transfers and 'Adequacy' of Protection: Extraterritorial Application of EU Fundamental Rights

Global trade has brought with it an 'information explosion', where personal data are considered 'crucial raw materials of the global economy'.[131] As a result, cross-border data flows have grown massively in volume and complexity.[132] There are a number of risks associated with transborder data transfers,[133] which have prompted governments around the world to regulate them in order to protect the fundamental rights to data protection and privacy of individuals and to ensure their own 'informational sovereignty'.[134] As mentioned above, among the systems adopted worldwide to regulate transborder data flows, the EU's adequacy requirement under the Data Protection Directive—that is further strengthened in the General Data Protection Regulation[135]—has been characterised as 'gunboat diplomacy'[136] that has prompted many countries to change their data protection rules—or indeed introduce new ones—in order to be able to receive data transfers from the EU.[137]

The Court took the opportunity in *Schrems* to clarify the adequacy criterion. While noting that there was no definition provided in law of the concept of an adequate level of protection,[138] the CJEU observed that adequacy does not require a level of protection 'identical to that guaranteed in the EU legal order',

---

[130] *Schrems*, n 84 above, para 95.

[131] Kuner, *Transborder Data Flows and Data Privacy Law* (Oxford: Oxford University Press 2013) 1.

[132] Schwartz, 'Managing Global Data Privacy: Cross- Border Information Flows in a Networked Environment' (2009), http://theprivacyprojects.org/wp-content/uploads/2009/08/The-Privacy-Projects-Paul-Schwartz-Global-Data-Flows-20093.pdf, 4.

[133] Kuner, n 131 above, pp 103–06.

[134] ibid, p 28.

[135] Regulation (EU) 2016/679 of the European Parliament and of the Council of 27 April 2016 on the protection of natural persons with regard to the processing of personal data and on the free movement of such data, and repealing Directive 95/46/EC (General Data Protection Regulation) [2016] OJ L119/1.

[136] Papakonstantinou and de Hert, n 67 above, p 901.

[137] See M Birnhack, 'The EU data protection directive: an engine of a global regime' (2008) 24 *Computer Law & Security Report* 508.

[138] *Schrems*, n 84 above, para 70.

but nevertheless protection of fundamental rights and freedoms that is 'essentially equivalent' to that of the EU.[139] This requires an assessment of the content of the applicable domestic and international law rules in the third country as well as the practice designed to ensure compliance with those rules. The 'essentially equivalent' criterion shows that the Court is trying to bring external legal systems as close as possible to the EU's internal data protection legal framework[140] in order to ensure that domestic data protection rules are not circumvented by transfers of personal data from the EU to third countries.[141]

This means that the CJEU is taking a stricter approach to international data transfers than the one adopted 13 years earlier in *Lindqvist*.[142] In that case, the Court stated that one cannot presume that transfers of data to third countries under EU law were intended to cover situations such as where an individual loads data on an Internet page, thus making them accessible to persons in third countries.[143] This pragmatic approach adopted by the Court seemed to be based on a consideration of the potential consequences of a contrary decision, which could 'effectively make the entire Internet subject to EU data protection law'.[144] Such an approach appears to be significantly restricted in recent case law and replaced by a more privacy-proactive approach that brings the Internet under EU data protection law. This line of jurisprudence started in *Google Spain*[145] where the Court held that, in certain circumstances, Internet search engines are required under EU law to delist links to individuals from their results. Admittedly the data protection issues raised in *Schrems* are significantly different from the ones that arose in *Lindqvist*, but faced with mass surveillance the Court seems to be moving towards a more stringent approach, in accordance with its role as the constitutional court preserving the rule of law in the EU legal order.

There is a second element that differentiates *Schrems* from *Lindqvist*. Since the latter was decided, data protection has been recognised as a fundamental right in the EUCFR alongside the right to privacy. This means that transborder data flows should be regarded now as part of the EU institutions' fundamental rights protective duty.[146] In this respect, the Court stated that individuals cannot be deprived of their fundamental rights by the transfer of their data to third countries.[147] A valid argument can be made, therefore, in favour of the extraterritorial application of

---

[139] ibid, para 73.
[140] S Peers, 'The party's over: EU data protection law after the Schrems Safe Harbour judgment', posted on 7 October 2015, http://eulawanalysis.blogspot.co.uk/2015/10/the-partys-over-eu-data-protection-law.html.
[141] *Schrems*, n 84 above, para 73.
[142] Case C-101/01 *Criminal proceedings against Bodil Lindqvist* [2003] I-12971.
[143] ibid, para 68.
[144] Kuner, n 131 above, p 12.
[145] C-131/12 *Google Spain SL, Google Inc v Agencia Española de Protección de Datos and Mario Costeja González* [2014] ECR I-000 (nyr), para 97.
[146] See Kuner, n 131 above, pp 129–33.
[147] *Schrems*, n 84 above, para 58.

EU data protection standards.[148] The judgment of the Court in *Schrems* confirmed this. The Court adopted a broader application of its fundamental rights law to cover data processing in the US.[149] However, it did so in a cautious way: it dealt with the problems of the Commission's adequacy decision, rather than directly challenging the US legislation.

The new powers of NDPAs to investigate complaints of individuals regarding the adequacy of data protection provided in third countries, as confirmed in *Schrems,* can be seen as an additional safeguard concerning the application of these fundamental rights outside the EU's territory. The final decision, however, on whether a third country does not ensure adequate protection is left to the CJEU as NDPAs do not have the power to invalidate a Commission's adequacy decision, but merely to investigate complaints and—if they consider them well-founded—initiate proceedings before national courts, which must then make a preliminary reference to the CJEU. The European Court thus retained for itself the role of the ultimate adjudicator of the adequacy of the protection of fundamental rights outside the EU.

V. A SUBSTANTIVE FUNDAMENTAL RIGHTS' ASSESSMENT OF INTERNET DATA SURVEILLANCE

A. Internet Data Surveillance and the Right to Privacy

i. Interference

It should be mentioned at the outset that neither the AG nor the CJEU engaged in any fact-finding, in accordance with the rules and limitations of the preliminary reference procedure.[150] The AG based his reasoning on the facts determined by the referring Irish High Court[151] and the CJEU endorsed the Commission's findings regarding the US secret surveillance measures and the lack of remedies and safeguards.[152]

---

[148] C Kuner, 'Extraterritoriality and regulation of international data transfers in EU data protection law' (2015) 5 (4) *International Data Privacy Law* 235; M Taylor, 'The EU's human right obligations in relation to its data protection laws with extraterritorial effect' (2015) 5 (4) *International Data Privacy Law* 246.

[149] M Tzanou, 'European Union Regulation of Transatlantic Data Transfers and Online Surveillance' (2016) *Human Rights Law Review* (forthcoming).

[150] See D Bender, 'Having mishandled Safe Harbor, will the CJEU do better with Privacy Shield? A US perspective' (2016) *International Data Privacy Law* Advance Access published May 13, 3; R Epstein, 'The ECJ's Fatal Imbalance: Its cavalier treatment of national security issues poses serious risk to public safety and sound commercial practices' (2016) 12 (2) *European Constitutional Law Review* 330.

[151] See AG Opinion, n 86 above, para 35.

[152] See *Schrems*, n 84 above, para 90.

According to long-established case law, an interference with the fundamental right to privacy is established irrespective of whether the information in question relating to private life is 'sensitive' or 'whether the persons concerned have suffered any adverse consequences on account of that interference.'[153] This means that there are no standing requirements for the admissibility of secret surveillance claims under EU law.[154]

Such an approach should be contrasted from the one adopted by the European Court of Human Rights (ECtHR) regarding admissibility of complaints in secret surveillance cases. The Court has repeatedly held that the Convention does not provide for an *actio popularis* and the ECtHR does not normally review the law and practice *in abstracto*.[155] Therefore, in order to be able to lodge an application an individual was required to show that he was 'directly affected' by the measure complained of.[156] The ECtHR recognised, however, that this might prove problematic in cases of secret surveillance. In *Klass v Germany* the Court held that an individual might, under certain conditions, claim to be the victim of a violation occasioned by the mere existence of secret measures or of legislation permitting secret measures, without having to allege that such measures had been in fact applied to him.[157] In *Kennedy*[158] and *Zakharov*,[159] the ECtHR held that secret surveillance cases will be reviewed under two conditions: first, legislation can be challenged when the applicant is considered to be 'potentially at risk' of being subjected to such measures; secondly, the Court will consider the availability of remedies at the national level and adjust the degree of scrutiny depending on the effectiveness of such remedies.[160] Where the domestic system does not afford an effective remedy to the person who suspects that he was subjected to secret surveillance, 'the menace of surveillance' can constitute an interference with Article 8 ECHR. In such instances, the ECtHR opined that there is a greater need for scrutiny by the Court and, thus, an exception to the rule, which denies individuals the right to challenge a law *in abstracto*, is justified.

A strict standing condition for challenging surveillance measures targeting non-US nationals exists in the US since the US Supreme Court held in *Clapper v Amnesty International*[161] that neither individuals nor organisations have standing to bring a lawsuit under section 702 because they cannot know whether they have been subject to surveillance or not.

---

[153] ibid, para 87; *Digital Rights Ireland*, n 114 above, para 33 and Joined Cases C-465/00, C-138/01 and C-139/01 *Österreichischer Rundfunk and Others* [2003] ECR I-4989, para 75.

[154] Tzanou, n 149 above.

[155] See *N.C. v Italy* ECHR Reports 2002-X at para 56; and *Centre for Legal Resources on behalf of Valentin Câmpeanu v Romania* ECHR Reports 2014 at para 101.

[156] Ibid.

[157] *Klass and Others v Germany*, 6 September 1978, Series A No. 28 at para 34.

[158] *Kennedy v the United Kingdom*, Application No. 26839/05, 18 May 2010.

[159] *Zakharov v Russia*, Application No. 47143/06, 4 December 2015.

[160] Ibid.

[161] *Clapper v Amnesty International USA*, 133 S. Ct. 1138 (2013).

ii. The Essence of the Fundamental Rights to Privacy and Effective Judicial Protection

The broad scope of the US surveillance programmes, which grant access on a generalised basis not only to communications metadata—as was the case with the Data Retention Directive—but to the actual content of electronic communications, was found to breach the essence of the right to privacy. Furthermore, the US legislation does not provide EU citizens with sufficient guarantees and effective legal remedies to exercise their data access, rectification and erasure rights. On the one hand, the remedies available under the Safe Harbour scheme—the private dispute resolution mechanisms and the procedures before the FTC—did not cover complaints on fundamental rights questions as they were limited to unfair or deceptive acts and practices in commerce and could not deal with the US authorities access to the data held by the companies.[162] On the other hand, as seen in detail in Chapter 4, the US privacy regime is not as protective as the EU one, and there are serious limitations regarding the rights of non-US and US citizens to challenge surveillance measures in the US due to the strict standing requirements. This lack of legal remedies was considered by the Court to violate the essence of the fundamental right to effective judicial protection guaranteed by Article 47 EUCFR.

The CJEU's analysis on the essence of the Charter fundamental rights raises again a number of issues. First, one might wonder why the Court did not assess in detail the proportionality of US mass surveillance measures and the other requirements under Article 52(1) EUCFR and instead just held that the essence of the fundamental rights to privacy and effective judicial review had been affected. One possible explanation for this could be that the interference in *Schrems* was deemed to be so serious as to touch the essence of fundamental rights and, therefore, the CJEU considered that a discussion of proportionality was simply not needed.[163] In this respect, the Court demonstrated that the essence of fundamental rights under the Charter does not have a mere 'symbolic' significance, as some commentators have suggested.[164]

Nevertheless, the lack of depth of the CJEU's analysis of the essence of fundamental rights is particularly disturbing.[165] Is the essence of the fundamental right to privacy always affected by access to the content of the communications? Or is it the combined effect of mass data retention and access to the content that touches upon the essence of privacy? What about access to the content that is targeted?

---

[162] *Schrems*, n 84 above, para 89.
[163] M Scheinin, 'Towards evidence-based discussion on surveillance: A Rejoinder to Richard A. Epstein' (2016) 12 (2) *European Constitutional Law Review* 341, 343.
[164] F Boehm and MD Cole, 'Data retention after the Judgement of the Court of Justice of the European Union', Munster/Luxembourg, 30 June 2014, www.janalbrecht.eu/fileadmin/material/Dokumente/Boehm_Cole_-_Data_Retention_Study_-_June_2014.pd, 90.
[165] Tzanou, n 149 above.

Would this violate the essence of privacy? *Schrems* and *Digital Rights Ireland* did not shed much light on these questions. In addition, it should be recalled once again that the line drawn between content and metadata presents in many respects an artificial—and even dangerous—analysis of what constitutes the essence of the fundamental right to privacy. This is not the least because a distinction between the two is extremely problematic.[166] However, there might be another possible explanation for the Court's essence analysis in *Schrems*. This has to do with the extraterritorial application of EU fundamental rights. As seen above, the Court, indeed, confirmed in *Schrems* the application of the fundamental rights to privacy and effective judicial protection outside the EU territorial boundaries, but it might be the case that it has opted to limit this to the 'essence' of these fundamental rights only.[167] Nevertheless, given that the CJEU, unlike the ECtHR, is not a specialised human rights court, it is very regrettable that it did not engage in a more thorough discussion of the essence of fundamental rights drawing inspiration from a comparative perspective[168] and from national and supranational Courts that have assessed the issue,[169] such as the ECtHR[170] and the German Constitutional Court.[171]

iii. Provided for by Law

The CJEU held that the Safe Harbour adequacy decision did not contain

> any finding regarding the existence, in the United States, of rules adopted by the State intended to limit any interference with the fundamental rights of the persons whose data is transferred from the European Union to the United States, interference which the State entities of that country would be authorised to engage in when they pursue legitimate objectives, such as national security,[172]

but did not discuss the 'provided for by law' requirement in detail. This is regrettable, given the total lack of transparency of PRISM and upstream surveillance, which operated for a considerable period, as secret programmes in practice, if not

---

[166]   Scheinin, n 163 above, p 342.

[167]   See Kuner, n 148 above, pp 242–43.

[168]   See B Shima, 'EU Fundamental Rights and Member State Action After Lisbon: Putting the ECJ's Case Law in its Context' (2015) 38 (4) *Fordham International Law Journal*, 1095, 1111.

[169]   See L Besselink, 'General Report. The Protection of Fundamental Rights Post-Lisbon: The Interaction Between the Charter of Fundamental Rights of the European Union, the European Convention on Human Rights and National Constitutions' (XXV FIDE Congress, Tallinn, 30 May–2 June 2012), 47.

[170]   The ECtHR case law on the right to privacy should have been taken into account all the more because the EU is legally obliged to accede to the ECHR and, pursuant to Art 52(3) EUCFR, in so far as the Charter contains rights which correspond to rights guaranteed by the ECHR, the meaning and scope of those rights shall be the same as those laid down by the Convention and the Explanations relating to the Charter confirm that 'Article 7 corresponds to Article 8 ECHR'. See Explanations relating to the Charter of Fundamental Rights, OJ [2007] C303/17.

[171]   For a discussion of the case law of the German Constitutional Court, see R Alexy, *A Theory of Constitutional Rights* (Oxford, Oxford University Press, 2002) 192–96.

[172]   *Schrems*, n 84 above, para 88.

in law. As discussed above, the legal basis of these programmes, section 702 allowed US authorities to seek access to information, including the content of Internet communications, by targeting a non-US person 'reasonably believed to be located outside the United States'. Foreign surveillance is authorised without showing a probable cause or any other standard to believe that the individuals are properly targeted; what is required is merely that 'a significant purpose of the acquisition is to obtain foreign intelligence information'.[173] This requirement makes the US surveillance programmes inherently discriminatory on grounds of nationality. As a report presented before the European Parliament noted:

> According to the leaked 'targeting procedures' (dated 2009) of FAA known Americans [are eliminated] from being inadvertently targeted by section 702. Analysts may only proceed to access 'content data' under the 702 power if there is more than a 50% likelihood the target is not American and located outside the US, because the Fourth Amendment was held not to apply ... This shows that the 'probable cause' requirement for evidence of a 50% likelihood of criminality was converted into a *50% probability of nationality*.[174]

In practice, the operation of the programmes was obscured and only brought to light and made known in the EU by the Snowden revelations. Arguably, the US programmes' foreignness requirement is to an extent understandable in the context of national security, but the law targeting the Internet communication of individuals—even non-US—cannot operate in limbo. The ECtHR has repeatedly held in this respect that the law must be accessible to the person concerned and foreseeable as to its effects.[175] While the ECtHR has accepted that 'foreseeability' in the context of secret surveillance cannot be the same as in other fields, the risks of arbitrariness of the powers vested in the executive are higher, therefore surveillance rules must be clear and detailed, and citizens must be given adequate indication as to the circumstances in which public authorities can resort to such measures.[176] It is arguable that these requirements were met under the US secret online surveillance measures, since EU citizens became aware of them only after the Snowden revelations.

iv. Objective of General Interest Recognised by the Union

This seems a fairly easy requirement to satisfy, since the CJEU has repeatedly held that the fight against international terrorism and against serious crime are indeed objectives of general interest recognised by the EU. Nevertheless, while the CJEU did not discuss this requirement in *Schrems*, the AG found that the Safe Harbour

---

[173] PCLOB Report, n 12 above.

[174] C Bowden, 'The US Surveillance Programmes and Their Impact on EU Citizens' Fundamental Rights' (2013) Directorate General for Internal Policies, European Parliament, Policy Department C: Citizens' Rights and Constitutional Affairs, Note, 23–24. Emphasis added.

[175] See among others *Rotaru v Romania* ECHR 2000-V, para 52; and *S and Marper v the United Kingdom* [2008] ECHR 1581, para 95.

[176] See *Rotaru*, para 55; *Zakharov*, n 159 above, para 229.

adequacy decision did 'not pursue an objective of general interest defined with sufficient precision'[177] because Annex I to this provided that adherence to the Safe Harbour principles may be limited by

> statute, government regulation, or case-law that create conflicting obligations or explicit authorisations, provided that, in exercising any such authorisation, an organisation can demonstrate that its non-compliance with the Principles is limited to the extent necessary to meet the overriding legitimate interests furthered by such authorisation,

but without defining such 'legitimate interests'.[178] According to the AG, this could lead to uncertainty as to the—potentially very wide—scope of that derogation from the application of the Safe Harbour principles.[179]

v. Proportionality

The CJEU reiterated in *Schrems* that legislation authorising on a generalised basis storage of all the personal data of all the persons whose data has been transferred from the European Union to the US without any differentiation, limitation or exception being made in the light of the objective pursued and without an objective criterion being laid down by which to determine the limits of the access of the public authorities to the data, and of its subsequent use, for purposes which are specific, strictly restricted and capable of justifying the interference which both access to that data and its use entail, was not limited to what is strictly necessary.[180] This means that, as already held in *Digital Rights Ireland*, the retention and storage of the data by companies in order for them to be made available to law enforcement and intelligence authorities is already problematic from the point of fundamental rights, even if the authorities do not access in fact the data relating to every individual. The CJEU, however, did not discuss the issues of necessity, appropriateness, effectiveness and proportionality *stricto sensu* any further.

B. Internet Data Surveillance and the Fundamental Right to Data Protection

As discussed above, while the CJEU mentioned Article 8 EUCFR, and in particular, Article 8(3) EUCFR in the first part of its analysis concerning the investigatory powers of NDPAs, it referred to this fundamental right in the second part of its analysis regarding the validity of the Safe Harbour adequacy decision only twice: in paragraph 72, where it pointed out that the adequacy requirement under Article 25(6) 'implements the express obligation laid down in Article 8(1) EUCFR', and in paragraph 92, where the Court repeated its pronouncement in *Digital Rights*

---

[177] AG Opinion, n 86 above, para 181.
[178] ibid, para 178.
[179] ibid, para 179.
[180] *Schrems*, n 84 above, para 93.

Ireland that the protection of the fundamental right to privacy at EU level requires derogations and limitations in relation to the protection of personal data to apply only in so far as is strictly necessary. However, the substantive fundamental rights analysis in *Schrems* took place only on the basis of Articles 7 and 47 EUCFR, with no further mention of the right to data protection. As seen above, the US authorities' Internet data surveillance interferes with a number of data protection principles, such as purpose limitation, data minimisation, data subjects' due process rights, control by an independent authority and potentially data security. It is, therefore, unclear why the CJEU omitted from its substantive analysis the fundamental right to data protection. A possible explanation for the absence of data protection could be that the CJEU considered that the interference with privacy affected the very essence of this right that data protection did not need to be mentioned. Such an approach is problematic for a number of reasons. First, it does not fit well with the Court's analysis in *Digital Rights Ireland* that involved a separate discussion of both these fundamental rights. Secondly, it implies that data protection is a second-class right, that even if in fact it is interfered with, very serious interferences to privacy matter more—at least outside the borders of the EU. Thirdly and more importantly, the absence of data protection and its principles makes the implementation of and compliance with the *Schrems* judgment difficult. What steps exactly do US authorities have to take in order to make Internet surveillance compatible with EU fundamental rights? Would it be enough not to access the content of Internet communications? Arguably, the guidelines laid down in *Digital Rights Ireland* apply in this case as well, even if it involves surveillance outside the EU borders. This approach was followed by AG Mengozzi in his Opinion on the draft EU–Canada PNR Agreement.[181] To an extent, it is understandable that the Court in *Schrems* avoided providing prescriptive conditions on how surveillance should be undertaken, given that this case referred to another legal order, but the inclusion of Article 8 EUCFR could have made the judgment more complete, clearer and compliance with this potentially easier. Finally, the CJEU's analysis on Article 47 EUCFR and judicial redress is somewhat confusing. More particularly, the Court held that 'legislation not providing for any possibility for an individual to pursue legal remedies in order to have access to personal data relating to him, or to obtain the rectification or erasure of such data'[182] compromises the essence of Article 47 EUCFR. While this pronouncement is understandable, regarding legal remedies, it is unclear why the data subject's rights to access, rectification and erasure fall within Article 47 EUCFR, and not within Article 8(2) EUCFR that expressly mentions them.

---

[181] Opinion of AG Mengozzi in Opinion 1/15, delivered on 8 September 2016.
[182] Schrems, n 84 above, para 95.

VI. TRANSATLANTIC DATA FLOWS AFTER *SCHREMS*

A. The Consequences of the *Schrems* Judgment

The annulment of the Commission's Safe Harbour adequacy decision had important practical consequences, on the one hand, for commercial data transfers to the US and the everyday operations of Internet giants, and, on the other hand, for the access of law enforcement authorities to commercial data in order to fight terrorism. There are, therefore, two pertinent questions that need to be answered after the Court's judgment in *Schrems*. What happens to transatlantic data transfers now? And, under which conditions can the US authorities (still) access EU citizens' data held by private companies in a manner that means that they do not violate fundamental EU rights? The two questions seem inextricably linked to each other given that the CJEU invalidated the Safe Harbour scheme on the ground that US mass electronic surveillance did not respect the essence of EU fundamental rights.

Insofar as transatlantic data flows are concerned, the first obvious ramification of the invalidation of the Commission's adequacy decision is that Safe Harbour can no longer serve as a legal basis for data transfers to the US.[183] In this respect, a number of possible short and longer-term solutions are available at different levels: individual-initiated, private-sector initiated, technological solutions and legislative solutions.[184] Article 26(1) of the Data Protection Directive provides that data can be transferred to third countries even when those do not ensure an adequate level of protection, a) on the basis of the consent of the data subject; b) where the transfer is necessary for the performance of a contract between the data subject and the controller or the implementation of pre-contractual measures taken in response to the data subject's request; c) where the transfer is necessary for the conclusion or performance of a contract concluded in the interest of the data subject between the controller and a third party; or d) where the transfer is necessary or legally required on important public interest grounds or for the establishment, exercise or defence of legal claims.[185] Individuals based in the EU could use one of these provisions in order to continue to use the services of US-based Internet companies. A second set of solutions could be private-sector initiated: US undertakings collecting and processing data of EU citizens could store this data solely in Europe in order to prevent them from being accessed by US authorities. It should be recalled that this solution was adopted by SWIFT in the wake of the revelations that the US had established a secret Terrorist Financing Tracking Programme (TFTP), under which the US Department of Treasury in

---

[183]   See Article 29 WP Statement, 16 October 2015.

[184]   See Communication from the Commission to the European Parliament and the Council on the Transfer of Personal Data from the EU to the United States of America under Directive 95/46/EC following the Judgment by the Court of Justice in Case C-362/14 (*Schrems*), COM(2015) 566 final, 6.11.2015.

[185]   ibid, pp 10–11.

collaboration with the CIA collected and analysed for counter-terrorism purposes huge amounts of data from SWIFT's database.Another possibility for companies comes under Article 26(2) of the Data Protection Directive. According to this, Member States may authorise a transfer to a third country that does not ensure an adequate level of protection, 'where the controller adduces adequate safeguards' under either the so-called 'Standard Contractual Clauses' ('SCCs') approved by the Commission or the 'ad hoc' clauses drafted by the undertakings and approved by the relevant DPA.[186] Data may be transferred between the different entities of a multinational corporate group through Binding Corporate Rules ('BCRs').[187] Finally, technological solutions, such as the encryption of personal data originating from the EU do not seem to offer effective protection from US surveillance.[188] The most comprehensive solution is a Commission adequacy decision providing the legal basis for data transfers to the US on the basis of a new privacy transfer scheme. Adequacy can be asserted only if the new data transfer regime complies with the requirements that the Court set out in *Schrems*: no generalised access of the US authorities to the content of the data, sufficient safeguards and effective judicial mechanisms for the data subjects, and no circumscription of the NDPAs' powers.[189]

B. Privacy Shield

On 2 February 2016, the Commission announced that a political agreement was reached on a new framework for transatlantic data flows, the EU–US Privacy Shield, which would replace the annulled Safe Harbour system.[190] On 29 February 2016, the Commission published a draft Privacy Shield adequacy decision.[191] Both the Article 29 WP and the EDPS expressed concerns about several aspects of the draft decision and requested further clarifications.[192] Following further negotiations, the EU–US Privacy Shield was finally adopted on 12 July 2016.[193] The new framework is constituted by the Commission's adequacy decision,[194] the

---

[186] Kuner, n 131 above, p 43.

[187] Communication from the Commission, n 184 above, pp 5–7.

[188] Donohue, n 13 above, pp 200–02.

[189] See Article 29 WP Statement on the consequences of the *Schrems* judgment, 3 February 2016; Article 29 WP Working Document 01/2016 on the justification of interferences with the fundamental rights to privacy and data protection through surveillance measures when transferring personal data (European Essential Guarantees), WP237, 13 April 2016.

[190] See http://europa.eu/rapid/press-release_IP-16-216_en.htm?locale=en.

[191] See http://ec.europa.eu/justice/data-protection/files/privacy-shield-adequacy-decision_en.pdf.

[192] Article 29 WP Opinion 01/2016 on the EU–US Privacy Shield draft adequacy decision, WP 238, 13 April 2016; EDPS Opinion 4/2016 on the EU–US Privacy Shield draft adequacy decision, 30 May 2016.

[193] See http://europa.eu/rapid/press-release_IP-16-2461_en.htm.

[194] Commission Implementing Decision of 12.7.2016 pursuant to Directive 95/46/EC of the European Parliament and of the Council on the adequacy of the protection provided by the EU–US Privacy Shield, Brussels, 12.7.2016, C(2016) 4176 final.

US Department of Commerce Privacy Shield Principles (Annex II) and the US Government's official representations and commitments on the enforcement of the arrangement (Annexes I and III to VII).[195]

Similar to its predecessor, Privacy Shield is based on a system of self-certification by which US organisations commit to a set of privacy principles.[196] The system is administered and monitored by the US Department of Commerce.[197] However, unlike Safe Harbour that contained a general derogation on national security and law enforcement grounds, the Privacy Shield decision includes a section on the 'access and use of personal data transferred under the EU–US Privacy Shield by US public authorities'.[198] In this, the Commission concludes that 'there are rules in place in the United States designed to limit any interference for national security purposes with the fundamental rights of the persons whose personal data are transferred from the EU to the US to what is strictly necessary to achieve the legitimate objective in question.'[199] This conclusion is based on the representations and assurances provided by the Office of the Director of National Surveillance (ODNI) (Annex VI), the US Department of Justice (Annex VII) and the US Secretary of State (Annex III), which describe the limitations, oversight and opportunities for judicial redress under the US surveillance programmes. In particular, the Commission employed four main arguments arising from these letters to reach its adequacy conclusion. First, US surveillance prioritises targeted rather than bulk collection of personal data (this captures the essence of the principles of necessity and proportionality, according to the Commission).[200] Secondly, the US intelligence community is subject to 'various review and oversight mechanisms that fall within the three branches of the State.' Thirdly, there are three main avenues of redress available under US law to EU data subjects. Fourthly, a new oversight mechanism for national security interference, the Privacy Shield Ombudsperson, is created under the Privacy Shield.

---

[195] Annexes to the Commission Implementing Decision pursuant to Directive 95/46/EC of the European Parliament and of the Council on the adequacy of the protection provided by the EU–US Privacy Shield, Brussels, 12.7.2016, C(2016) 4176 final. The Annexes include the following: Annex I, a letter from the US Secretary of Commerce, and a letter from the International Trade Administration (ITA) of the Department of Commerce; Annex II, the EU-US Privacy Shield Framework Principles; Annex III, a letter from the US Secretary of State and accompanying memorandum describing the State Department's commitment to establish a Privacy Shield Ombudsperson for submission of inquiries regarding US intelligence practices; Annex IV, a letter from the FTC describing its enforcement of the Privacy Shield; Annex V, a letter from the Department of Transportation; Annex VI, two letters prepared by the Office of the Director of National Intelligence (ODNI) regarding safeguards and limitations applicable to US national security authorities; and Annex VII, a letter prepared by the US Department of Justice regarding safeguards and limitations on US Government access for law enforcement and public interest purposes.

[196] See Annex II. The following principles are included in the Privacy Shield: Notice; Data Integrity and Purpose Limitation; Choice; Security; Access; Recourse, Enforcement and Liability; and, Accountability for Onward Transfer.

[197] Privacy Shield adequacy decision, n 194 above, Recitals 30–37.

[198] ibid, section 3.

[199] ibid, Recital 88.

[200] ibid, Recital 76.

i. Access and Use of the Data by US Authorities for National Security Purposes

According to the Privacy Shield adequacy decision, the limitations prescribing the activities of the US intelligence authorities are found in 'two central legal instruments'[201]: Executive Order 12333[202] and Presidential Policy Directive 28 (PPD-28).[203] Executive Order 12333 regulates the goals, duties and responsibilities of US intelligence activities and PPD-28 introduces certain limitations for 'signals intelligence' operations. In particular, PPD-28, which is binding to US intelligence authorities, provides that: a) the collection of signals intelligence must be based on statute or Presidential authorisation, and must be undertaken in accordance with the US Constitution (in particular the Fourth Amendment) and US law; b) all persons should be treated with dignity and respect, regardless of their nationality or wherever they might reside; c) all persons have legitimate privacy interests in the handling of their personal information; d) privacy and civil liberties shall be integral considerations in the planning of US signals intelligence activities; and, e) US signals intelligence activities must include appropriate safeguards for the personal information of all individuals, regardless of their nationality or where they might reside.

According to the ODNI representations, intelligence collection should be 'as tailored as feasible' and the US Intelligence Community prioritises the availability of other information and appropriate and feasible alternatives over bulk collection.[204] Bulk collection of signals intelligence is defined as collection that 'due to technical or operational considerations', is acquired without the use of discriminants.[205] The US Intelligence Community must collect bulk signals intelligence in certain circumstances in order to identify 'new or emerging threats' and 'other vital national security information that is often hidden within the large and complex system of modern global communications'.[206] In this regard, PPD-28 provides that signals intelligence collected in bulk can only be used for six purposes: detecting and countering certain activities of foreign powers; counter-terrorism; counter-proliferation; cybersecurity; detecting and countering threats to US or allied armed forces; and combatting transnational criminal threats, including sanctions evasion. The Privacy Shield decision notes that even where the Intelligence Community cannot use specific identifiers to target collection, it will seek to narrow the collection 'as much as possible' by applying 'filters and other technical tools to focus the collection on those facilities that are likely to contain communications

---

[201]   ibid, Recital 68.

[202]   Executive Order 12333, United States Intelligence Activities, Federal Register Vol 40, No 235 (8.12.1981).

[203]   Presidential Policy Directive/PPD-28 Signals Intelligence Activities, 17 January 2014.

[204]   Privacy Shield adequacy decision, n 194 above, Recital 71 and Annex VI, p 79.

[205]   'Discriminant' refers to the identifier and selection terms associated with a specific target, such as the target's email address or phone number.

[206]   Privacy Shield adequacy decision, n 194 above, Recital 72 and Annex VI, p 79.

of foreign intelligence value'.[207] According to the Commission, this makes bulk collection 'targeted' in two ways: it relates to specific foreign intelligence objectives and focuses collection on communications that have such a nexus.[208] The ODNI also assures that filters and other technical tools are used to make the collection 'as precise as possible' and to ensure that the amount of 'non-pertinent information' collected is minimised.[209] In this respect, the Commission concludes that the US Intelligence Community 'does not engage in arbitrary and indiscriminate surveillance of anyone, including ordinary European citizens' and access requests under FISA 'only concern a relatively small number of targets when compared to the overall flow of data on the Internet.'[210]

Regarding data security, storage and dissemination of the collected information, the ODNI representations provide that these are subject to FISC-approved 'minimisation procedures'. 'Minimisation procedures' are defined in the PCLOB report as a set of

> specific procedures that are reasonably designed in light of the purpose and technique of the particular surveillance to minimise the acquisition and retention, and prohibit the dissemination, of non-publicly available information concerning unconsenting United States persons consistent with the need of the United States to obtain, produce, and disseminate foreign intelligence information.[211]

This suggests that 'minimisation procedures' under the FISA refer to the safeguards excluding US persons from being targeted for foreign intelligence information and is, therefore, different from the concept of 'data minimisation'[212] that embeds the proportionality principle in the processing of personal data. There are certain protections under the minimisation procedures that apply to non-US persons as well;[213] these include the storage of communications in databases with strict access controls limited to intelligence personnel 'who have been trained in the privacy-protective minimisation procedures and who have been specifically approved for that access in order to carry out their authorised functions',[214] their dissemination only if there is 'a valid foreign intelligence or law enforcement purpose'[215] and their retention for a maximum of five years.[216] But it is inaccurate to state that bulk collection is accompanied by 'additional safeguards to minimise the amount of data collected and subsequent access',[217] as the Commission does in its adequacy decision. In this respect, it is unclear what the Commission is referring

---

[207] ibid, Recital 73 and Annex VI, p 79.
[208] ibid, Recital 73.
[209] ibid.
[210] ibid, Recital 82.
[211] PCLOB Report, n 12 above, p 50.
[212] The principle of 'data minimisation' is mentioned in the GDPR, see Recital 156 and Art 5(1)(c).
[213] Annex VI, p. 87.
[214] Ibid.
[215] Ibid.
[216] Privacy Shield adequacy decision, n 194 above, Recital 86.
[217] Ibid, Recital 89.

to when it notes that 'minimum safeguards' must be imposed by legislation interfering with Articles 7 and 8 EUCFR in order to comply with the *Schrems* judgment.[218] What is certain is that the fundamental right to privacy and the fundamental right to data protection and its fair information principles cannot be reduced to 'minimum safeguards'.

The adequacy decision and the accompanying letter from the ODNI go to great lengths to assure that US intelligence collection is 'as tailored as feasible' and prioritises targeted over bulk collection of personal data.[219] Indeed, the ODNI argues that bulk collection is neither 'mass' nor 'indiscriminate'[220] and insists that US intelligence agencies 'do not have the legal authority, the resources, the technical capability or the desire to intercept all of the world's communications. Those agencies are not reading the emails of everyone in the United States, or of everyone in the world.'[221] Even if we accept that the US authorities engage only in targeted surveillance, the CJEU held in *Digital Rights Ireland* that the mere retention of private-sector data for the purpose of making it available to national authorities interferes with Articles 7 and 8 EUCFR[222] and might have a chilling effect on the use by subscribers of platforms of communication, such as Facebook and, consequently, on their exercise of freedom of expression guaranteed by Article 11 EUCFR.[223] When faced with surveillance, individuals cannot know when they are targeted; nevertheless, the possibility of being the object of surveillance has an effect on the way they behave.[224]

Furthermore, there is little reference in the Privacy Shield adequacy decision to the fact that the US authorities access the content of the personal data that was deemed to violate the essence of the right to privacy in *Schrems*. In this respect, the Commission appears convinced that the representations provided by the US, including the assurance that US signals intelligence activities touch only a fraction of the communications traversing the Internet, 'exclude that there would be access "on a generalised basis" to the content of electronic communications.'[225] The argument, therefore, seems to be that the US authorities indeed access the content of communications, but that they do so not 'on a generalised basis', but only through targeted surveillance. This complies with *Schrems* only if we accept that the CJEU's pronouncement on the essence of the right to privacy is cumulative and requires both retention of the content of communications and access in a generalised way. Moreover, there are significant exceptions to the principle

---

[218] Ibid, Recital 90.

[219] Privacy Shield adequacy decision, n 194 above, Recital 71.

[220] Annex VI, p 95.

[221] Annex VI, p 93.

[222] *Digital Rights Ireland*, n 114 above, para 29.

[223] ibid, para 28. See also Report of the Special Rapporteur on the promotion and protection of the right to freedom of opinion and expression, A/HRC/29/32, www.ohchr.org/EN/Issues/Freedom Opinion/Pages/CallForSubmission.aspx, para 11.

[224] P Birnstil et al, 'Privacy-preserving surveillance: an interdisciplinary approach' (2015) 5 (4) *International Data Privacy Law* 298.

[225] Privacy Shield adequacy decision, n 194 above, Recital 90.

of prioritising 'targeted surveillance.' PPD-28 allows for the bulk collection of signals intelligence to be used for six purposes, including counter-terrorism, when deemed necessary in order to identify 'new or emerging threats' and other 'vital national security information hidden in global communications.' Both these reasons and the six purposes appear too wide to accept that bulk collection is only 'exceptionally' authorised.[226]

ii. Oversight and Redress

According to the adequacy decision, the US intelligence community is subject to various review and oversight mechanisms that fall within the three branches of the state. These include internal and external bodies within the executive branch, a number of Congressional Committees, as well as judicial supervision with respect to activities under the FISA, from courts such as the FISC.[227] First, within the executive branch, 'multiple oversight layers have been put in place in this respect, including civil liberties or privacy officers, Inspector Generals, the PCLOB, and the President's Intelligence Oversight Board.'[228] Second, the US Congress and in particular, the House and Senate Intelligence and Judiciary Committees, have oversight responsibilities regarding signals intelligence.[229] Third, the adequacy decision provides that US intelligence activities are reviewed and authorised by the FISC, whose decisions can be challenged before the Foreign Intelligence Court of Review (FISCR)[230] and, ultimately, the Supreme Court of the United States.[231] Individuals with expertise in national security and civil liberties may serve as *amicus curiae* to assist the FISC with applications that 'present a novel or significant interpretation of the law'.[232]

The avenues of redress depend on the complaint individuals want to raise: interference under FISA; unlawful, intentional access to personal data by government officials; and access to information under Freedom of Information Act (FOIA).[233] Under FISA, individuals can bring a 'civil cause of action for money damages against the US when information about them has been unlawfully and wilfully used or disclosed'; 'sue US government officials in their personal capacity ("under colour of law") for money damages'; and 'challenge the legality of surveillance and seek to suppress the information' if the US Government 'intends to use or disclose

---

[226] See Recital 89 and Article 29 WP Opinion 01/2016, n 192 above, p 38.
[227] ibid, Recital 92.
[228] ibid, Recital 95.
[229] ibid, Recital 102. The USA Freedom Act of 2015 provides that the US Government must disclose to the Congress (and the public) each year the number of FISA orders and directives sought and received, as well as estimates of the number of US and non-US persons targeted by surveillance, among others. See USA Freedom Act of 2015, Pub L No 114-23, s 602(a) and Recital 104.
[230] See s 103 FISA (50 USC § 1803 (b)).
[231] Privacy Shield adequacy decision, n 194 above, Recital 105.
[232] ibid, Recital 106.
[233] ibid, Recital 111.

any information obtained or derived from electronic surveillance against the individual in judicial or administrative proceedings in the United States.'[234] Finally, individuals can make a FOIA to seek access to existing federal agency records, including where these contain their personal data.[235] However, information held by national agencies and information concerning law enforcement investigations may be excluded from FOIA requests.[236]

Insofar as Article 47 EUCFR and the right to effective judicial protection is concerned, the Commission itself notes in its adequacy decision that the avenues of redress provided to EU citizens do not cover all the legal bases that US intelligence authorities may use and the individuals opportunities to challenge FISA are very limited due to the strict standing requirements.[237] As seen in Chapter 4, the Judicial Redress Act[238] does not sufficiently address these concerns as it does not apply to national security.[239]

iii. The Privacy Shield Ombudsperson Mechanism

The creation of the Ombudsperson Mechanism with the important function of receiving and responding to individual complaints should be welcomed as the main addition of Privacy Shield. Individuals are able to access the Privacy Shield Ombudsperson without having to demonstrate that their personal data has in fact been accessed by the US Government through signals intelligence activities,[240] and the Ombudsperson, who carries out his functions independently from Instructions by the US Intelligence Community, is able to rely on the US oversight and review mechanisms. According to the Commission, the Ombudsperson Mechanism guarantees 'independent oversight and individual redress'; his cooperation with other oversight bodies 'ensures access to the necessary expertise'; and, 'the mechanism reflects a commitment from the US Government as a whole to address and resolve complaint from EU individuals.'[241] The Commission is, therefore, satisfied that 'there are adequate and effective guarantees against abuse'[242] and on the basis of this concluded that the US 'ensures effective legal protection against interferences by its intelligence authorities with the fundamental rights of the persons whose data are transferred from the Union to the United States under the EU–US Privacy Shield.'[243]

This conclusion, however, is debatable. Given that the individual redress avenues provided under Privacy Shield are insufficient to satisfy the right to judicial

---

[234] ibid, Recital 112.
[235] ibid, Recital 114.
[236] ibid.
[237] ibid, Recital 115.
[238] HR 1428 Judicial Redress Act of 2015, 24 February 2016.
[239] Article 29 WP Opinion 01/2016, n 192 above, p 43.
[240] Privacy Shield adequacy decision, n 194 above, Recital 119.
[241] ibid, Recital 118.
[242] ibid, Recital 122.
[243] ibid, Recital 123.

redress guaranteed in Article 47 EUCFR, it should be considered whether the Ombudsperson Mechanism can be seen as effective legal redress under this Article. It should be observed that there are several limitations to the function of the Privacy Shield Ombudsperson. First, the procedure for accessing the Ombudsperson is not as straightforward as lodging a complaint before NDPAs. Individuals have to submit their requests initially to the Member States' bodies competent for the oversight of national security services and, eventually, a centralised EU individual complaint handling body that will channel them to the Privacy Shield Ombudsperson if they are deemed 'complete'.[244] In terms of the outcome of the Ombudsperson's investigation, the Ombudsperson will provide a response to the submitting EU individual complaint handling body—who will then communicate with the individual—confirming (i) that the complaint has been properly investigated, and (ii) that the US law has been complied with, or, in the event of non-compliance, such non-compliance has been remedied.[245] However, the Ombudsperson will neither confirm nor deny whether the individual has been the target of surveillance, nor will the Ombudsperson confirm the specific remedy that was applied.[246] Moreover, Annex III stipulates that commitments in the Ombudsperson's Memorandum will not apply to general claims that the EU–US Privacy Shield is inconsistent with EU data protection requirements.[247] Finally, concerns have been raised by the Article 29 Working Party and the EDPS about the independence of the Ombudsperson. It should be recalled that independence is particularly important for such administrative authorities in order to ensure the impartiality of their decisions.[248] While, the the Representations assure that the 'Privacy Shield Ombudsperson will be independent from, and thus free from instructions by, the US Intelligence Community',[249] the fact remains that the Ombudsperson is an Under-Secretary in the State Department. In the light of the above, it is difficult to conclude that the Privacy Shield Ombudsperson Mechanism can provide effective judicial redress in the context of Article 47 EUCFR[250] or independent supervision in the context of Article 8(3) EUCFR.

Overall, it is not clear that Privacy Shield complies with *Schrems*. Despite the assurances of targeted surveillance, bulk collection of communications data, including content data is allowed. The redress avenues enshrined in the scheme, including the creation of the Ombudsperson Mechanism do not seem to satisfy Article 47 EUCFR. Therefore, it is extremely uncertain that data transferred to US companies under Privacy Shield are adequately protected against intelligence surveillance. The adoption of a transatlantic privacy and data protection framework

---

[244] Annex III, p 53.
[245] ibid, p 54.
[246] ibid.
[247] ibid.
[248] Article 29 WP Opinion 01/2016, n 192 above, pp 46–47.
[249] Privacy Shield adequacy decision, n 194 above, Recital 121.
[250] Article 29 WP Opinion 01/2016, n 192 above, pp 49–50; EDPS Opinion n 192 above, p 8.

that also ensures the transparency and accountability of transnational counter-terrorism operations could be a possible solution to this problem. Regrettably, the 'Umbrella' Agreement does not apply to intelligence agencies operations and raises serious concerns as to its compatibility with EU fundamental rights.[251] Thus, the best option would be the accession of the US to the Council of Europe Convention 108 and its Additional Protocol.[252] These contain a comprehensive framework of data protection safeguards and some enforcement mechanisms and are open to accession by non-Member States.[253]

---

[251] See Ch 4.

[252] Council of Europe Additional Protocol to the Convention for the Protection of Individuals with regard to Automatic Processing of Personal Data regarding supervisory authorities and transborder data flows, Strasbourg, 8.11.2001.

[253] Greenleaf, n 67 above, p 82.

7

Conclusions

I. THE FUNDAMENTAL RIGHT TO DATA PROTECTION RECONSTRUCTED

THE FIRST CHAPTER of this book examined the normative added value of the fundamental right to data protection in the EU legal order. It explored the current theories about this right and concluded that three important limitations that this has faced since its emergence in the EU constitutional order impair it from functioning as a fully fledged fundamental right with a normative value of its own: its *interconnectivity* with privacy, its *linking* with secondary legislation, and the *elusiveness* of its content.

The first limitation arises from its relationship with the right to privacy. Privacy and data protection have been inextricably intertwined for several reasons: their scope overlaps to the extent that they both refer to the concept of 'control over personal information', privacy is an aim that data protection pursues and the two rights have been frequently associated in legislative instruments. For instance, Article 1(1) of the Data Protection Directive provides that Member States must 'protect the fundamental rights and freedoms of natural persons, and in particular their right to privacy with respect to the processing of personal data.' This interconnectivity between the two rights has prompted some scholars[1] to argue that data protection operates as a transparency tool that permits certain processing, while privacy as the opacity tool, against which permissible limitations should be judged. In its initial case law following the entry into force of the Lisbon Treaty that made the EU Charter of Fundamental Rights binding, the CJEU considered that the two rights could not be dissociated, and were to be seen together as 'the right to respect for private life with regard to the processing of personal data, recognised by Articles 7 and 8 of the Charter'.[2] This association of the two rights prevents the right to data protection from having a normative significance on its own, since all permissible limitations are reviewed either on the basis of the right to privacy or through the combination of this right to the seemingly insufficient data protection.

---

[1] P De Hert and S Gutwirth, 'Privacy, Data Protection and Law Enforcement. Opacity of the Individual and Transparency of Power', in Erik Claes et al (eds), *Privacy and the Criminal Law* (Antwerpen, Intersentia, 2006) 61.

[2] Joined Cases C-92/09 and C-93/09 *Volker und Markus Schecke GbR* (C-92/09), *Hartmut Eifert* (C-93/09) *v Land Hessen* (CJEU (GC), 9 November 2010), para 52.

The second limitation that data protection faces in its operation as a fully fledged fundamental right concerns its relationship with secondary legislation. Data protection was regulated in different secondary EU law instruments long before its elevation to the status of a fundamental right. Data protection legislation has been subject to review and amendment by the EU institutions, and the recent adoption of the General Data Protection Regulation and the Data Protection Directive are significant instruments for the modernisation of this legislation in order to be able to respond to the challenges that arise from new technologies, the Internet and the modern techniques of processing Big Data. However, if the fundamental right to data protection enshrined in Article 8 EUCFR is made dependent on secondary legislation to the extent that its content has to be assessed on the basis of this, this right cannot have a normative value. Such linking is all the more dangerous, because subsequent amendments of secondary data protection legislation affecting the standard of protection offered may have an impact on the fundamental right to data protection.

Thirdly, data protection is limited from operating as a fully fledged fundamental right because of the uncertainty that surrounds the actual content of this right. Two pertinent questions arise in this respect: first, is the right to data protection confined in paragraph 1 of Article 8 EUCFR, which contains the general recognition that 'everyone has the right to the protection of personal data concerning him or her', or should all the three paragraphs of this article be taken into account in order to establish an interference with this right? Secondly, is the content of the fundamental right to data protection determined only by the six elements explicitly included in paragraphs 2 and 3 of Article 8 EUCFR (principle of fair processing, purpose specification principle, legitimate basis laid down by the law, right to access, right to rectification and independent supervision), or can it be argued that further data protection principles not expressly mentioned in this article can be part of this right?

This book developed a theory on data protection that reconstructed this fundamental right on the basis of three conditions. The first condition requires that the fundamental right to data protection has an 'autonomous content' of its own, which is independent from secondary legislation. The second condition provides that data protection should be balanced against opposing rights or other interests as such, not through the proxy of privacy. The third condition stipulates that data protection as a fundamental right should be able to function both positively and negatively, in that it should be able to both regulate and prohibit power.

The first condition, which requires that the fundamental right to data protection has an 'autonomous content' of its own, arises from the supremacy of the Charter and the rights enshrined therein in the hierarchy of EU norms. The fundamental right to data protection is autonomous of secondary data protection legislation, and this legislation and its subsequent amendments are reviewable on the basis of this right. However, it was clarified that such autonomous content does not bar courts from drawing inspiration from secondary legislative instruments to assist them with the interpretation of technical concepts such as 'personal data' or 'processing' or the meaning of different data protection principles enshrined in Article 8 EUCFR, in accordance with the relevant provision of Article 52(7) EUCFR, which points to the Explanations of the Charter that mention the Data Protection Directive. In this regard, I argue that the content of the fundamental right to data protection is not necessarily confined to the six principles expressly listed in Article 8 EUCFR; further fair information principles inspired from various sources of national, international and supranational law can be part of Article 8 EUCFR. This is consistent with the fact that the article itself stipulates the principle of fair processing, which incorporates further data protection requirements, such as transparency and accountability of processing. Such an interpretation was confirmed by the CJEU in *Digital Rights Ireland*,[3] where the Court held that data security, a principle which is not expressly mentioned in Article 8 EUCFR, indeed forms part of this fundamental right. What should be cautioned, however, is that the content of the fundamental right to data protection should be autonomous, and, thus, independent from secondary law. The book also argued that the right to data protection is to be found in Article 8 EUCFR taken as a whole, reading together paragraphs 1, 2 and 3 of this Article, and not only on the basis of paragraph 1. If the right is to be found in the whole Article 8 EUCFR, this means that processing of personal data in accordance with paragraphs 2 and 3 does not constitute an interference with this fundamental right. It is only counter-intuitive to consider that any processing of personal data interferes with the fundamental right to data protection and as the data surveillance case studies have shown, this also presents an extremely superficial and even erroneous analysis.

The second condition that data protection has to satisfy in order to operate as a fundamental right with a value of its own requires that this should be balanced against opposing rights or other interests as such, not through the proxy of privacy. Any potential interference with the right to data protection should be determined on the basis of the data protection principles themselves, with the application of the principle of proportionality, without the need to recourse to the right to privacy. Determining disproportionate processing on the basis of the right to privacy, and not of the specific data protection principle that this goes against, is not only an unnecessary circumvention of the existing EU constitutional law that renders the right to data protection virtually useless, but it is also erroneous and dangerous, because there could be instances of disproportionate processing of personal data that hardly constitute disproportionate interferences with the right to privacy. Such an approach, furthermore, accepts that an interference with data protection does not necessarily imply an interference with privacy and vice-versa

---

[3] Joined Cases C-293/12 and C-594/12 *Digital Rights Ireland Ltd v Minister for Communications, Marine and Natural Resources* [2014] ECR I-238.

and, thus, avoids the fallacies committed by Advocate General Cruz Villalón in his Opinion in *Digital Rights Ireland*.[4] The two rights are autonomous to each other and should operate in this way.

The third condition requires that data protection as a fundamental right should be able to function both positively and negatively. This requires recognition that data protection has an essential core that cannot be submitted to further restrictions, in accordance with Article 52(1) EUCFR. By recognising that data protection has an essential core, this right is able to prohibit power as well as regulate it—it can, therefore, perform the function of a fundamental right with an intrinsic normative value. Determining what constitutes the essence of the right to data protection is not an easy task. Recent case law has provided some guidance, but the issue still remains—rightly—vague. The Court spoke of the essence of the right to data protection in *Digital Rights Ireland*,[5] connecting it to 'certain principles of data protection and data security'. In this respect, it should be cautioned that the essence of the fundamental right to data protection—or any fundamental right— should not operate as a 'floor',[6] offering merely minimum standards of protection. The essence of data protection would be what needs to be protected, so that the final values that this right pursues, and in particular dignity, are safeguarded. The essence of this right should play a role when an 'aggravated' interference based on processing that goes against a multitude of data protection principles occurs. It was explained that, for instance, the processing of data of the whole population, carried out for different purposes from those for which the data were initially collected, for a long period of time, and that can lead to profiling and discrimination based on 'predetermined criteria and scenarios'[7] developed by algorithms, could touch on the essence of the fundamental right to data protection, since it interferes *cumulatively* with different data protection principles, and challenges the dignity of individuals.

Thus reconstructed to satisfy these three conditions, there is no reason why data protection cannot operate as a *bona fide* fundamental right and have a normative significance. Before this right is examined in the context of data surveillance, it is worth summarising the Court's case law on the right to data protection as this emerged in Chapter 2. Before the constitutional entrenchment of data protection as a fundamental right in the Charter, the Court in *Österreichischer Rundfunk*[8] and *Lindqvist*[9] dissociated the application of EU data protection legislation from internal market objectives. Since the entry into force of the Lisbon Treaty, its

---

[4] Opinion of AG Cruz Villalón in Joined Cases C-293/12 and C-594/12 *Digital Rights Ireland Ltd v Minister for Communications, Marine and Natural Resources, Minister for Justice, Equality and Law Reform, Commissioner of the Garda Síochána, Ireland, The Attorney General and Kärntner Landesregierung, Michael Seitlinger, Christof Tschohl and others*, delivered on 12 September 2013.

[5] *Digital Rights Ireland*, n 3 above, para 40.

[6] See F Fabbrini, *Fundamental Rights in Europe—Challenges and Transformations in Comparative Perspective* (Oxford, Oxford University Press, 2014) 37.

[7] Opinion of AG Mengozzi in Opinion 1/15, delivered on 8 September 2016, para 261.

[8] Joined Cases C-465/00, C-138/01 and C-139/01, *Österreichischer Rundfunk* [2003] ECR I-4989.

[9] Case C-101/01 *Bodil Lindqvist* [2003] ECR I-12971.

case law on the fundamental right to data protection has evolved progressively, with the analysis identifying three stages of maturity. At the first stage, the Court could not dissociate data protection from privacy, and assessed the permissibility of limitations on what I call the '*Schecke* formula' of viewing the two rights together. In this respect, the Court felt compelled to often repeat in its case law the close connection between data protection and privacy. At the second stage, the Court started to slowly distinguish between the two rights, but it did so in a somewhat confusing way, struggling with the relevant terminology. At the third stage, the case law of the CJEU not only proves that the Court can now see the two rights separately, but it also demonstrates how the permissible limitations to these rights should be assessed. Although the Court is, therefore, to be praised for reaching maturity in its case law concerning the right to data protection, some questions regarding the content and essence of this right have been left unanswered. These concern mainly the Court's insistence to read the fundamental right to data protection only in paragraph 1 of Article 8 EUCFR and to consider, therefore, that any processing of personal data constitutes an interference with this right.

II. DATA SURVEILLANCE AND THE FUNDAMENTAL RIGHT TO DATA PROTECTION

The analysis of the four case studies on communications metadata (Chapter 3), travel data (Chapter 4), financial data (Chapter 5) and Internet data (Chapter 6) surveillance in Part II of the book reveals a number of common trends as to the *why*, the *how* and the *what for* of data surveillance. Data surveillance measures, whatever their focus, have *similar purposes*; are made possible through the (compelled) *cooperation of private actors*; they collect a significant *volume* of data; that are further processed and analysed in a *probabilistic* manner.

As emerged from all the cases discussed, fighting terrorism is one of the main purposes of surveillance. Some measures had further purposes, such as the fight against serious crime (Data Retention Directive), the prevention of transnational crime (PNR) and the acquisition of foreign intelligence (PRISM and UPSTREAM surveillance). Furthermore, data surveillance is undertaken through the cooperation of private actors that collect the data in the first place. Electronic communications' metadata retention was based on the collection of such information by communications service providers; PNR data are collected by airline companies; financial data are extracted from the SWIFT database that provides financial messaging services; and information on Internet communications and activities has been obtained by the US authorities from leading Internet companies. In all the four case of data surveillance examined, the personal data are granted to the private actors by individuals for completely unrelated purposes, such as billing purposes (metadata retention); in order to book a flight (PNR); to transfer money (TFTP); and to use the services provided by Internet companies, such as Facebook and Google (PRISM). The volume of data collected and targeted under the four examined surveillance cases is extensive. They all concern a generalised, mass retention of the electronic communications and Internet communications of virtually every individual that uses the respective services of communications providers, airlines and SWIFT. This retention is often not based on evidence of suspicion, but is undertaken pre-emptively in a probabilistic manner to uncover 'risky' individuals on the basis of algorithm processing and analysis of 'terrorist patterns'.

Data surveillance poses serious challenges to the fundamental rights to privacy and data protection. These should be approached by assessing the potential interference with the two rights separately, as the Court rightly did in *Digital Rights Ireland*. Metadata retention, such as that prescribed in the Data Retention Directive, the TFTP and Internet surveillance programmes, such as PRISM and UPSTREAM collection interfere with the confidentiality of electronic and financial communications and, therefore, the right to privacy. It was argued that PNR is a different story, since most of the data retained in this case, albeit personal, are hardly private. Nevertheless, it was submitted that all the four data surveillance programmes examined in Part II interfere with the fundamental right to data protection as this was reconstructed in Chapter 1. The section below brings together the conclusions drawn from the substantive analysis of the four case studies and explains the steps that should be taken in order to assess the permissibility of the interference with this fundamental right.

III. COUNTER-TERRORISM DATA SURVEILLANCE AND PERMISSIBLE LIMITATIONS TO THE FUNDAMENTAL RIGHT TO DATA PROTECTION

The analysis of permissible limitations should follow Article 52(1) EUCFR, which provides that any limitation of a right of the Charter should be provided for by law; meet objectives of general interest recognised by the Union or the need to protect the rights and freedoms of others; be necessary; be subject to the principle of proportionality; and respect the essence of the right. Before I turn to these conditions, an initial comment should be made about the CJEU's approach to data protection. Taking into account the importance of fighting terrorism, the Court should be praised for not following a 'reductionist' approach[10] to data protection (and privacy) through the adoption of strict standing conditions, that require some degree of 'harm' to allow the challenging of data surveillance measures. In addition, the CJEU has adopted a strict standard of judicial review of surveillance considering the seriousness of the interference this poses to data protection and privacy.

First, it must be established that data surveillance programmes pose an interference to the fundamental right to data protection. The mere processing of

---

[10] See L Floridi, 'The ontological interpretation of informational privacy' (2005) 7 *Ethics and Information Technology* 185, 194.

personal data is not enough to establish such an interference. All three paragraphs of Article 8 EUCFR should be taken into account and processing that does not comply with them, because it goes against certain fair information principles should be considered to interfere with Article 8 EUCFR. The fair information principles interfered with should be mentioned expressly in the analysis in order for this to be able to proceed to assess their permissibility. It was concluded from the four surveillance cases analysed that these interfere with the purpose limitation principle, the data minimisation principle, the data security principle, in many cases the data are retained for longer periods than necessary, many measures do not provide for adequate due process rights for data subjects or these rights—if provided—are substantially watered down in the protection they offer, and finally some of these measures do not guarantee control by an independent supervisory authority, thus failing to comply with the requirements laid down by the CJEU in *Commission v Hungary*.[11]

Having established that there is an interference with the fundamental right to data protection, it should be examined whether this is 'provided for by law'. In this respect, the measure must be foreseeable and accessible to individuals who should also be made aware of the potential access of public authorities to the data they grant to private actors in order to receive a service, such as to book a flight or transfer money or send an e-mail or a text message or browse the Internet. Surveillance programmes that have operated secretly for years and were revealed by media articles or whistle-blowers, such as TFTP and PRISM, do not satisfy this requirement.

Fighting terrorism and crime are considered objectives of general interest recognised by the Union and, therefore, there are a few difficulties for data surveillance measures to meet this requirement. It should be noted, however, that indiscriminate, mass data surveillance should not be undertaken for purposes such as border control management, as it was seen in the EU–US PNR case.

Assessing the necessity of a data surveillance measure requires an examination of the appropriateness of such a measure, its effectiveness to fight terrorism and an assessment whether this is the least restrictive measure that could be adopted in order to attain this objective. The data surveillance case studies examined were considered in general appropriate to fight terrorism. However, their effectiveness is far from proven, as robust empirical evidence as to their efficacy is not available. This is highly problematic, given that data surveillance is extremely broad in its scope and targets the whole population without providing for any exception for individuals that do not have any link to terrorism or serious crime. The broad reach of metadata surveillance as well as the fact that the Data Retention Directive did not determine the conditions of access to the data and did not make the retention period subject to any differentiation depending on the usefulness of the data retained were considered to violate the necessity requirement in *Digital Rights*

---

[11] Case C-288/12 *Commission v Hungary* (CJEU (GC), 8 April 2014).

Ireland. Data surveillance measures should include robust provisions guaranteeing data security, the irreversible destruction of the data at the end of the data retention period and control by an independent authority. Even so, it is argued that data surveillance as such interferes disproportionately with the purpose limitation principle. Indeed, using data that individuals provided to private actors for totally unrelated commercial purposes empties this principle of its very content. The fact that the data surveillance measures provide the legal basis for the purpose deviation does not change this conclusion. It is crucial, therefore, that the courts and in particular the CJEU address this issue and decide whether the purpose limitation principle still has a meaning in the era of Big Data surveillance. Finally, data surveillance as a whole should be examined under the scope of proportionality *stricto sensu* to assess its advantages and the risks it engenders in a democratic society.[12]

Finally, data surveillance measures cannot compromise the essence of the fundamental right to data protection. The CJEU has demonstrated in *Schrems* that essence of fundamental rights does not only have a symbolic value, but this can indeed play a decisive role on the invalidation of a data surveillance measure on the basis of its incompatibility with the fundamental rights at stake. What constitutes the essence of the right to data protection, however, is still unclear and vague. While this is not *per se* problematic, this book argued that the essence of this right cannot be confined to a 'floor' concept of safeguarding of certain minimum data protection and data security safeguards, as *Digital Rights Ireland* suggested. Such an approach would imply that Article 8 EUCFR can function only as a transparency tool that channels power, and not as a fully fledged fundamental right that can prohibit power.

IV. THE NORMATIVE VALUE OF THE FUNDAMENTAL RIGHT TO DATA PROTECTION IN COUNTER-TERRORISM SURVEILLANCE

Having discussed the different case studies, we should go back to the core question of this book: does data protection have a normative added value as a fundamental right? First, it should be observed that the fundamental right to data protection is neither obsolete next to privacy, nor does it serve as the *lex specialis* of privacy. The scope of the two rights may overlap to an extent, but it is different, as the PNR case demonstrated. Moreover, data protection pursues multifarious values that go beyond privacy. But even if data surveillance raises both privacy and data protection issues, as was seen in the context of metadata, financial and Internet data surveillance, the fundamental right to data protection does not lose its added value. The two rights can co-exist and operate independently next to each other

---

[12] See Opinion of Advocate General Saugmandsgaard Øe in Joined Cases C-203/15 and C-698/15 *Tele2 Sverige v Post- och telestyrelsen* and *Secretary of State for the Home Department v Tom Watson, Peter Brice, Geoffrey Lewis*, delivered on 19 July 2016, para 262.

to provide the individual with the most effective protective framework against counter-terrorism surveillance. The fundamental right to data protection does not threaten privacy and there is no hierarchy between the two rights.

The value of data protection is not limited to the fact that it indeed adds something to privacy, as the PNR case showed. The fundamental right to data protection has a *legal* and *practical* significance of its own. In legal terms, data protection is instrumental in ensuring informational self-determination, autonomy, non-discrimination and ultimately human dignity. Furthermore, as reconstructed in Chapter 1, data protection can stand as a bulwark against counter-terrorism data surveillance and the probabilistic processing of personal data. But data protection also has a *practical* significance. The right's *procedural nature* expressed through the various information principles makes its demands clearly articulated for legislators, law enforcement and intelligence authorities, private actors whose compelled assistance is crucial for the carrying out of data surveillance, individuals and courts. The fair information principles provide specific guidance on the permissibility of processing and in this respect they should be used by legislators when they lay down counter-terrorism legislation. Law enforcement and intelligence authorities can use these principles as guidance when they conduct surveillance activities. Private actors are also bound by the fundamental right to data protection and have certain obligations as 'processors' of personal data. The constitutional entrenchment of data protection as a fundamental right in the EU has made this right more visible to the data subjects that often feel powerless in front of the modern means of surveillance. Finally, the reconstructed fundamental right to data protection is valuable for courts that are called upon to assess *ex post* the compliance of surveillance measures in the light of this fundamental right.

The discussion contained in this book would be incomplete if it did not concern itself with the question of whether counter-terrorism data surveillance can be—at all—compatible with fundamental rights. All the data surveillance measures examined in this book were found to interfere seriously with the fundamental rights to privacy and data protection. The only way that data surveillance can be made compatible with fundamental rights in order to pursue the legitimate objective of fighting terrorism is through its compliance with different data protection principles and requirements. These demand that:

— personal data are collected and processed on the basis of objective reasons that justify their usefulness in fighting terrorism, and the mass, indiscriminate collection of data of all the people without any differentiation just because they are readily available is not acceptable (data minimisation principle);

— there are measures in place ensuring data security and the protection of information from unauthorised access (data security principle);

— the conditions of access and use of personal data are clearly defined on the basis of objective criteria;

— data subjects have the right to know about the potential further purposes of the processing of their personal data and they can exercise effectively their rights to access, rectification and erasure as well as having avenues of effective judicial redress; and

— the processing of the personal data collected and, in particular, its use by counter-terrorism authorities is subject to independent control.

Data protection principles, therefore, are the only way forward for the compatibility of data surveillance with fundamental rights. The challenge for legislators is now to design such measures that respect the fundamental rights to privacy and data protection and do not deprive them of their very essence. Regulating data surveillance on the basis of the fundamental right to data protection and its fair information principles would be a first step towards this direction. But the reconstructed right to data protection does not only serve in regulating permissible data surveillance; it can altogether prohibit this if it compromises its ultimate values.

This book has studied the value of the right to data protection in the most difficult context: counter-terrorism data surveillance. The study of other instances of processing is work left for the future; nevertheless, it is hoped that the reader will have obtained important insights about this right's capabilities that are transferrable to further different contexts of processing.

Bibliography

BOOKS AND JOURNAL ARTICLES

Abel, W and Schafer, B, 'The German Constitutional Court on the Right in Confidentiality and Integrity of Information Technology Systems—a Case Report on BVerfG, NJW 2008 822' (2009) 6 *SCRIPT-ed* 106.

Alexy, R, 'Discourse Theory and Fundamental Rights' in Agustín José Menéndez and Erik Oddvar Eriksen (ed) *Arguing Fundamental Rights* (Dordrecht, Springer, 2006), 15.

—, *A Theory of Constitutional Rights* (Oxford, Oxford University Press, 2009).

Alston, P, 'Conjuring up New Human Rights: A Proposal for Quality Control' (1984) 78 *American Journal of International Law* 607.

—, P, 'Making Space for New Human Rights: The Case of the Right to Development' (1988) 1 *Harvard Human Rights Year Book* 3.

Arendt, H, *The Human Condition* (Chicago, University of Chicago Press, 1998).

AuBuchon, M, 'Comment: Choosing How Safe Is Enough: Increased Antiterrorist Federal Activity and Its Effect on the General Public and the Airport/airline Industry' (1999) 64 *Journal of Air Law & Commerce* 891.

Bagley, A, 'Don't Be Evil: The Fourth Amendment in the Age of Google, National Security, and Digital Papers and Effects' (2011) 21 *Alberta Law Journal of Science & Technology* 153.

Bailey, J, 'From Public to Private: The Development of the Concept of the "Private"' (2002) 69 *Social Research: An International Quarterly* 15.

Baker, E, 'Flying While Arab—Racial Profiling and Air Travel Security' (2002) 67 *Journal of Air Law & Commerce* 1375.

Bannon, A, 'Romania retrenches on data retention' (2010) 24(2) *International Review of Law, Computers and Technology* 145.

Beaney, W, 'The Right to Privacy and American Law' (1996) 31 *Law & Contemporary Problems* 253.

Bedley, D, 'A Look at the Proposed Electronic Communications Privacy Act Amendments Act of 2011: Where is Smart Grid Technology, and How Does Inevitable Discovery Apply?' (2012) 36 *Nova Law Review* 521.

Bender, D, 'Having mishandled Safe Harbor, will the CJEU do better with Privacy Shield? A US perspective' (2016) *International Data Privacy Law* 117.

Bennet, CJ and Raab, C, *The Governance of Privacy: Policy Instruments in a Global Perspective*, 2nd edn (Boston MA, MIT Press, 2006).

Bergkamp, L, 'EU Data Protection Policy—The Privacy Fallacy: Adverse Effects of Europe's Data Protection Policy in an Information-Driven Economy' (2002) 18 *Computer Law and Security* 31.

Bernal, P, *Internet Privacy Rights—Rights to Protect Autonomy* (Cambridge, Cambridge University Press, 2014).

Besselink, L, 'General Report. The Protection of Fundamental Rights Post-Lisbon: The Interaction Between the Charter of Fundamental Rights of the European Union, the European Convention on Human Rights and National Constitutions' (XXV FIDE Congress, Tallinn, 30 May–2 June 2012).

BeVier, L, 'Information About Individuals in the Hands of Government: Some Reflections on Mechanisms for Privacy Protection' (1995) 4 *William and Mary Bill of Rights Journal* 455.

Bezanson, RP, 'The Right to Privacy Revisited: Privacy, News, and Social Change, 1890–1990' (1992) 80 *California Law Review* 1133.

Bignami, F, 'European Versus American Liberty: A Comparative Privacy Analysis of Antiterrorism Data Mining' (2007) 48 *Boston College Law Review* 609.

—, 'Privacy and Law Enforcement in the European Union: The Data Retention Directive' (2007) 8 *Chicago Journal of International Law* 233.

—, 'The Case for Tolerant Constitutional Patriotism: The Right to Privacy Before the European Courts' (2008) 41 *Cornell International Law Journal*, 211.

—, 'The US legal system on data protection in the field of law enforcement. Safeguards, rights and remedies for EU citizens', Study for the LIBE Committee, PE 519.215, European Union, Brussels, 2015.

Birnhack, M, 'The EU data protection directive: an engine of a global regime' (2008) 24 *Computer Law & Security Report* 508.

Birnstil, P, Bretthauer, S, Greiner, S and Krempel, E, 'Privacy-preserving surveillance: an interdisciplinary approach' (2015) 5 (4) *International Data Privacy Law* 298.

Birrer, F, 'Data mining to combat terrorism and the roots of privacy concerns' (2005) 7 *Ethics and Information Technology* 211.

Bloustein, EJ, 'Privacy as an Aspect of Human Dignity: An Answer to Dean Prosser' (1964) 39 *New York Law Review* 962.

Blume, P, 'Transborder Data Flow: Is There a Solution in Sight' (2000) 8 *International Journal of Law and Information Technology* 65.

Bobek, M, 'Joined Cases C-92 & 93/09, Volker und Markus Schecke GbR and Hartmut Eifert, Judgment of the Court of Justice (Grand Chamber) of 9 November 2010' (2011) 48 (6) *Common Market Law Review* 2005.

Boehm, F, *Information Sharing and Data Protection in the Area of Freedom, Security and Justice: Towards Harmonised Data Protection Principles for Information Exchange at EU-level* (Springer, 2012).

Boehm, F and Cole, MD, Data retention after the Judgement of the Court of Justice of the European Union. Munster/Luxembourg, 30 June 2014, www.janalbrecht.eu/fileadmin/material/Dokumente/Boehm_Cole_-_Data_Retention_Study_-_June_2014.pd.

Bok, S, *Secrets: On the Ethics of Concealment and Revelation* (New York, Vintage Books 1989).

Botta, M and Viola de Azevedo Cunha, M, 'La Protezione dei dati personali nelle relazioni tra UE e USA, Le Negoziazioni sul trasferimento dei dati PNR' (2010) XXVI *Il Diritto dell' Informazione e dell'Informatica* 315.

Bowden, C, 'The US Surveillance Programmes and Their Impact on EU Citizens' Fundamental Rights' (2013) Directorate General for Internal Policies, European Parliament, Policy Department C: Citizens' Rights and Constitutional Affairs, Note.

Breckenridge, AC, *The Right to Privacy*, (Lincoln NB, University of Nebraska Press, 1970).

Brenner, S, 'Constitutional Rights and New Technologies in the United States' in R Leenes, BJ Koops and P De Hert (eds), *Constitutional Rights and new technologies: A comparative Study* (TMC Asser Press, Distributed by Cambridge University Press, 2008) 225.

Breyer, P, 'Telecommunications Data Retention and Human Rights: The Compatibility of Blanket Traffic Data Retention with the ECHR' (2005) 11 *European Law Journal* 365.

Brouwer, E, *Digital Borders and Real Rights: Effective Remedies for Third-Country Nationals in the Schengen Information System* (The Netherlands, Brill, 2008).

—, 'Ignoring Dissent and Legality—The EU's proposal to share the personal information of all passengers', CEPS 2011.

Brown, I and Korff, D, 'Terrorism and the Proportionality of Internet Surveillance', (2009) 6 *European Journal of Criminology* 119.

Brown, I, 'Communications Data Retention in an Evolving Internet', (2010) 19 *International Journal of Law and Information Technology* 95.

Burkert, H, 'Towards a New Generation of Data Protection Legislation' in S Gutwirth et al (eds), *Reinventing Data Protection?* (New York, Springer, 2009) 335.

Busser de, E, *Data Protection in EU and US criminal cooperation: A substantive law approach to the EU internal and transatlantic cooperation in criminal matters between judicial and law enforcement authorities* (Antwerpen, Maklu Publishers, 2009).

—, 'EU Data Protection in Transatlantic Cooperation in Criminal Matters: Will the EU Be Serving Its Citizens an American Meal?' (2010) 6 *Utrecht Law Review* 86.

Buttarelli, G, 'What Future for the Data Retention Directive', EU Council Working Party on data protection and information exchange (DAPIX—DATA PROTECTION), Discussion on the Commission Evaluation report, 4 May, 2011.

—, 'EU–US "Umbrella Agreement"—Presentation of EDPS Preliminary Opinion 1/2016 before Civil Liberties, Justice and Home Affairs Committee (LIBE) of the European Parliament', 15 February 2016, https://secure.edps.europa.eu/ EDPSWEB/webdav/site/mySite/shared/Documents/EDPS/Publications/Speeches/ 2016/16-02-15_Umbrella_Agreement_LIBE_EN.pdf.

Bygrave, L, 'Where Have All the Judges Gone? Reflections on Judicial Involvement in Developing Data Protection Law' (2000) *Privacy Law & Policy Reporter* 11.

—, 'The Place of Privacy in Data Protection Law' (2001) 24 *University of New South Wales Law Journal* 277.

—, *Data Protection Law approaching its rationale logic and limits* (The Hague, Kluwer Law International, 2002).

—, 'Privacy and data protection in an international perspective' (2010) 56 *Scandinavian Studies in Law*, 165.

—, *Data Privacy Law—An International Perspective* (Oxford, Oxford University Press, 2013).

Bygrave, L and Schartum, D, 'Consent, Proportionality and Collective Power' in S Gutwirth et al (eds), *Reinventing Data Protection?* (New York, Springer, 2009) 157.

Cate, F, 'Government Data Mining: The Need for a Legal Framework' (2008) 43 *Harvard Civil Rights—Civil Liberties Law Review* 435.

Cate, F and Cate, B, 'The Supreme Court and information privacy' (2012) 2 (4) *International Data Privacy Law* 255.

Cate, F, Dempsey, J, and Rubinstein, I, 'Systematic government access to private-sector data' (2012) 2 (4) *International Data Privacy Law* 195.

Chandrasekhar, C, 'Flying While Brown: Federal Civil Rights Remedies to Post-9/11 Airline Racial Profiling of South Asians' (2003)10 *Asian Law Journal* 215.

Charlesworth, A, 'Clash of the Data Titans—US and EU Data Privacy Regulation' (2000) 6 *European Public Law* 253.

Chertoff, M, 'A Tool We Need to Stop the Next Airliner Plot', *Washington Post*, 29 August 2006.

Clarke, R, 'Introduction to Dataveillance and Information Privacy, and Definitions of Terms' (1988) 31 (5) *Communications of ACM* 498.

—, 'The Digital Persona and Its Application to Surveillance' (1994) 10 *The Information Society* 77.

Classen, CD, Joined Cases C-465/00, C-138/01 & C-139/01, Österreichischer Rundfunk, Judgment of 20 May 2003, Full Court, [2003] ECR I-4989 (2004) 41 *Common Market Law Review* 1377.

Cohen, J, 'Examined Lives: Informational Privacy and the Subject as Object' (2000) 52 *Stanford Law Review* 1373.

Coudray, L, '*Bodil Lindqvist* case note' (2004) 41 *Common Market Law Review*, 1361.

Crandall, R, 'Security for the Future: Let's Get Our Airlines Flying', 2001 Airline Security and Economic Symposium (2002) 67 *Journal of Air Law & Commerce* 9.

Cremona, M, 'EU External Action in the JHA Domain: A legal perspective' EUI Working Papers LAW 2008/24.

—, 'Justice and Home Affairs in a Globalised World: Ambitions and Reality in the Tale of the EU-US SWIFT Agreement', Austrian Academy of Sciences, Institute for European Integration Research, Working Paper No 04/2011, March 2011.

—, Risk in 'Three Dimensions: The EU–US Agreement on the Processing and Transfer of Financial Messaging Data' in H Micklitz and T Tridimas (eds), *Risk and EU law* (Cheltenham, Edward Elgar, 2015), 69.

Currie, D, 'Positive and Negative Constitutional Rights' (1996) 53 *University of Chicago Law Review* 864.

Delany, H and Carolan, E, *The Right to Privacy : A Doctrinal and Comparative Analysis* (Dublin, Thompson Round Hall, 2008) 4.

Dempsey, J and Flint, L, 'Commercial Data and National Security' (2004) 72 *The George Washington Law Review* 1459.

DeSimone, C, 'Pitting Karlsruhe Against Luxembourg? German Data Protection and the Contested Implementation of the EU Data Retention Directive' (2010) 11 *German Law Journal* 291.

Donke, WVD et al, 'The Politics and Policy of Data Protection: Experiences, Lessons, Reflections and Perspective' (1996) 62 *International Review of Administrative Science* 459.

Donohue, L, 'Anti-terrorist Finance in the United Kingdom and United States' (2006) 27 *Michigan Journal of International Law* 303.

—, 'Section 702 and the Collection of International Telephone and Internet Content' (2015) 38 *Harvard Journal of Law & Public Policy* 117.

Dougan, M, 'The Treaty of Lisbon 2007: Winning Minds, Not Hearts' (2008) 45 *Common Market Law Review* 617.

Doyle, C, 'Privacy: An Overview of the Electronic Communications Privacy Act' (2012) Congressional Research Service 7-5700.

Dummer, S, 'COMMENT: Secure Flight and Dataveillance, A New Type of Civil Liberties Erosion: Stripping Your Rights When You Don't Even Know It' (2006) 75 *Mississippi Law Journal* 583.

Dupré, C, 'Human Dignity in Europe: A Foundational Constitutional Principle', (2013) 19 (2) *European Public Law*, 319.

Edwards, L, 'Taking the "Personal" Out of Personal Data: Durant v FSA and Its Impact on the Legal Regulation of CCTV' (2004) 1 *SCRIPT-ED* 341.

Eger, J, 'Emerging Restrictions on Transnational Data Flows: Privacy Protections or Non- Tariff Barriers?' (1978) 10 *Law and Policy in International Business* 1065.

Ehlers, D and Becker, U, (eds), *European Fundamental Rights and Freedoms* (De Gruyter, 2007).

Epstein, R, 'The ECJ's Fatal Imbalance: Its cavalier treatment of national security issues poses serious risk to public safety and sound commercial practices' (2016) 12 (2) *European Constitutional Law Review* 330.

Etzioni, A, *The Limits of Privacy* (New York, Basic Books, 1999).

EU Network of Independent Experts on Fundamental Rights, Commentary of the EU Charter of Fundamental Rights, 2006.

—, 'Ethnic Profiling', CFR-CDF Opinion 4/2006, December 2006.

Expert Group on Fundamental Rights, *Affirming Fundamental Rights in the European Union: Time to Act* (Brussels: European Commission, 1999).

Exten, SE, 'Major Developments in Financial Privacy Law 2006: The SWIFT Database Incident, and Updates to the Gramm-Leach-Bliley and Fair Credit Reporting Acts' (2008) 3 *Journal of Law & Policy of the Information Society* 649.

Fabbrini, F, *Fundamental Rights in Europe- Challenges and Transformations in Comparative Perspective* (Oxford, Oxford University Press, 2014).

—, 'Human Rights in the Digital Age: The European Court of Justice Ruling in the Data Retention Case and its Lessons for Privacy and Surveillance in the U.S.' (2015) 28 *Harvard Human Rights Journal* 65.

Fahey, E, 'Law and Governance as Checks and Balances in Transatlantic Security: Rights, Redress, and Remedies in EU–US Passenger Name Records and the Terrorist Finance Tracking Program' (2013) *Yearbook of European Law* 1.

—, 'On the Use of Law in Transatlantic Relations: Legal Dialogues between the EU and US' (2014) 20 (3) *European Law Journal* 368.

Fahey, E and Curtin, D, *Transatlantic Community of Law: Legal Perspectives on the Relationship between the EU and US Legal Orders* (Cambridge, Cambridge University Press, 2014).

Fishman, W, 'Introduction to Transborder Data Flows' (1980) 16 *Stanford Journal of International Law* 3.

Flaherty, D, *Protecting Privacy in Surveillance Societies: The Federal Republic of Germany, Sweden, France, Canada and the United States* (Chapel Hill, University of North Carolina Press, 1989).

Floridi, L, 'The ontological interpretation of informational privacy' (2005) 7 *Ethics and Information Technology* 185.

—, 'Four challenges for a theory of informational privacy' (2006) 8 *Ethics and Information Technology* 109.

Frantziou, E, 'The Horizontal Effect of the Charter of Fundamental Rights of the EU: Rediscovering the Reasons for Horizontality' (2015) 21 (5) *European Law Journal* 657.

Fried, C, 'Privacy' (1968) 77 *Yale Law Journal* 475.

—, *An Anatomy of Values Problems of Personal and Social Choice* (Cambridge MA, Harvard University Press, 1970).

Gavison, R, 'Privacy and the Limits of Law' (1979) 89 *Yale Law Journal* 421.

Gellman, B and Poitras, L, 'U.S., British intelligence mining data from nine U.S. Internet companies in broad secret program', *Washington Post*, 7 June 2013, www.washingtonpost.com/investigations/us-intelligence-mining-data-from-nine-us-internet-companies-in-broad-secret-program/2013/06/06/3a0c0da8-cebf-11e2-8845-d970ccb04497_story.html.

Gellman, B, et al., 'Bank Records Secretly Tapped', *The Washington Post*, 23 June 2006.

Godkin, E, 'The Rights of the Citizen-IV-To His Own Reputation' (1890) 8 *Scribner's Magazine* 58.

Goede de, M, 'The SWIFT affair and the global politics of European security' (2012) 50 (2) *Journal of Common Market Studies* 214.

Goemans, C and Dumortier, J, 'Enforcement Issues—Mandatory Retention of Traffic Data in the EU: Possible Impact on Privacy and On-line Anonymity' in C Nicoll, J Prins and M van Dellen (eds), *Digital Anonymity and the Law* (The Hague, Asser Press ITeR, 2003) 161.

Gómez-Arostegui, T, 'Defining Private Life Under the European Convention on Human Rights by Referring to Reasonable Expectations' (2005) 35 *California Western International Law Journal* 153.

González Fuster, G, 'Balancing intellectual property against data protection: a new right's wavering weight' (2012) *Revista de Internet, Derecho y Politica* 34.

—, *The Emergence of Personal Data Protection as a Fundamental Right of the EU* (Cham, Springer, 2014).

González Fuster, G, De Hert, P and Gutwirth, S, 'SWIFT and the Vulnerability of Transatlantic Data Transfers' (2008) 22(1) *International Review of Law, Computers & Technology* 194.

González Fuster, G, De Hert, P and Gutwirth, S, 'The Law-Security Nexus in Europe: State-of the-art report' (2008) *INEX*.

Gotlieb, A, Dalfen, C and Katz, K, 'The Transborder Transfer of Information by Communications and Computer Systems: Issues and Approaches to Guiding Principles', (1974) 68 *American Journal of International Law* 227.

Granger, MP and Irion, K, 'The Court of Justice and the Data Retention Directive in Digital Rights Ireland: telling off the EU legislator and teaching a lesson in privacy and data protection' (2014) 39 (6) *European Law Review* 835.

Greenleaf, G, 'The influence of European data privacy standards outside Europe: implications for globalization of Convention 108' (2012) 2 (2) *International Data Privacy Law* 68.

Greenwald, G and McAskill, E, 'NSA Prism program taps in to user data of Apple, Google and others', *The Guardian*, 7 June 2013, www.theguardian.com/world/2013/jun/06/us-tech-giants-nsa-data.

Greenwald, G, McAskill, E and Poitras, L, 'Edward Snowden: the whistleblower behind the NSA surveillance revelations', *The Guardian*, 9 June 2013, www.theguardian.com/world/2013/jun/09/edward-snowden-nsa-whistleblower-surveillance.

Groussot, X, 'Music Production in Spain (Promusicae) v Telefónica de España SAU—Rock the KaZaA: Another Clash of Fundamental Rights' (2008) 45 *Common Market Law Review* 1745.

Gstrein, O, 'The cascade of decaying information: putting the "right to be forgotten" in perspective', (2015) 21 (2) *Computer and Telecommunications Law Review* 40.

Guild, E, 'Inquiry into the EU–US Passenger Name Record Agreement', CEPS, Policy Brief No 125, March 2007.

Guild, E and Brouwer, E, 'The political life of data: the ECJ decision on the PNR Agreement between the EU and the US', CEPS Policy Brief No 109, July 2006.

Guild, E and Carrera, S, 'The Political and Judicial Life of Metadata: Digital Rights Ireland and the Trail of the Data Retention Directive', CEPS Paper in Liberty and Security No 65 (May 2014) (Policy Paper).

Gutwirth, S, *Privacy and the Information Age* (Oxford, Rowman & Littlefield, 2002).

Gutwirth S and Hilderbrandt, M, 'Some Caveats on Profiling' in S Gutwirth, Y Roullet and PD Hert (eds), *Data Protection in a Profiled World* (Dordrecht, Springer, 2010) 31.

Habermas, J, *The Structural Transformation of the Public Sphere—An Inquiry into a Category of Bourgeois Society* (Cambridge, Polity Press, 1992).

Hahn, R, 'The Economics of Airline Safety and Security: An Analysis of the White House Commission's Recommendations' (1997) 20 *Harvard Journal of Law & Public Policy* 791.

Harris, E, 'Tradeoffs in Personal Data Privacy: A Swedish Church Lady, Austrian Public Radio Employees and Transatlantic Air Carriers Show That Europe Does Not Have the Answers' (2007) 22 *American University International Law Review* 745.

Hasbrouck, E, 'What's in a Passenger Name Record?', https://hasbrouck.org/articles/PNR.html.

Herlin-Karnell, E, 'Annotation of Ireland v Parliament and Council' (2009) 46 *Common Market Law Review* 1667.

Hert de, P, 'The Case of Anonymity In Western Political Philosophy—Benjamin Constant's Refutation of Republican And Utilitarian Arguments Against Anonymity' in C Nicoll et al (eds), *Digital Anonymity And The Law: Tensions and Dimensions* (Asser Press, 2003) 47.

Hert de, P and de Schutter, B, 'International Transfers of Data in the Field of JHA: The Lessons of Europol, PNR and Swift' in B Martenczuk and S Van Thiel (eds), *Justice, Liberty, Security: New Challenges for EU External Relations* (Brussels, VUBRESS, Brussels University Press, 2008) 303.

Hert de, P and Gutwirth, S, Privacy, 'Data Protection and Law Enforcement. Opacity of the Individual and Transparency of Power' in E Claes et al (eds), *Privacy and the Criminal Law* (Antwerpen, Intersentia, 2006) 61.

Hert de, P and Gutwirth, S, 'Data Protection in the Case Law of Strasbourg and Luxemburg: Constitutionalisation in Action' in S Gutwirth et al (eds), *Reinventing Data Protection?* (New York, Springer, 2009).

Hijmans, H, *The European Union as Guardian of Internet Privacy: The Story of Art 16 TFEU* (Springer, 2016).

Hins, W, Case C-73/07 Satakunnan Markkinapörssi and Satamedia, Judgment of 16 December 2008, not yet reported (2010) 47 *Common Market Law Review*, 215.

Hixson, RF, *Privacy in a Public Society: Human Rights in Conflict* (New York, Oxford University Press, 1987).

Hondius, FW, *Emerging Data Protection in Europe* (New York, American Elsevier, 1975).

—, 'Data Law in Europe' (1980) 16 *Stanford Journal of International Law* 87.

Hoofnagle, C, 'Big Brother's Little Helpers: How ChoicePoint and Other Commercial Data Brokers Collect, Process, and Package Your Data for Law Enforcement' (2004) 29 *N.C.J. Int'l L. & Com. Reg.* 595.

Hummer, W, 'Die SWIFT-Affaire US-Terrorismusbekämpfung Versus Datenschutz' (2011) 49 *Archiv des Völkerrechts* 203.

Hunt, C, 'Conceptualizing Privacy and Elucidating its Importance: Foundational Considerations for the Development of Canada's Fledgling Privacy Tort' (2011) 37 (1) *Queen's Law Journal* 167.

Hunt, C, 'From Right to Wrong: Grounding a "right" to Privacy in the "Wrongs" of Tort' (2015) 52 (3) *Alberta Law Review* 635.

Hustinx, P, European Data Protection Supervisor, Speaking points to Joint Meeting of LIBE and ECON Committees on EU-US interim agreement following the entry into force of the new SWIFT architecture, European Parliament, Brussels, 3 September 2009.

Iglesias Sánchez, S, 'The Court and the Charter: The impact of the entry into force of the Lisbon Treaty on the ECJ's approach to fundamental rights' (2012) 49 *Common Market Law Review* 1565.

Inness, JC, *Privacy, Intimacy and Isolation* (Oxford, Oxford University Press, 1996).

Jonas, J and Harper, J, 'Effective Counterterrorism and the limited role of predictive data mining', CATO Report, 2006.

Jones, C and Hayes, B, 'The EU Data Retention Directive: a case study in the legitimacy and effectiveness of EU counter-terrorism policy', SECILE—Securing Europe through Counter-Terrorism—Impact, Legitimacy & Effectiveness, www.statewatch.org/news/2013/dec/secile-data-retention-directive-in-europe-a-case-study.pdf, D2.4.

Kaifa-Gbanti, M, 'Surveillance Models in the Security State & Fair Criminal Trial', (2010) *Nomiki Vivliothiki* 43.

Kaiser, AB, 'German Federal Constitutional Court: German data retention provisions unconstitutional in their present form, Decision of 2 March 2010, NJW 2010, p. 833' (2010) 6 (3) *European Constitutional Law Review* 503.

Kalven, H, 'Privacy in Tort Law- Were Warren and Brandeis Wrong?'(1966) 31 *Law and Contemporary Problems* 326.

Kaufmann, M, *Ethnic Profiling and Counter-terrorism: Examples of European Practice and Possible Repercussions* (Münster, LIT Verlag, 2010).

Kerr, O, 'The Fourth Amendment and New Technologies: Constitutional Myths and the Case for Caution', (2004) 102 *Michigan Law Review* 801.

—, 'The Case for the Third-Party Doctrine', (2009) 107 *Michigan Law Review* 561.

Kett-Straub, G, 'Data Screening of Muslim Sleepers Unconstitutional' (2006) 7 *German Law Journal* 967.

Kielsgard, MD, 'A human rights approach to counter-terrorism' (2006) 36 (2) *California Western International Law Journal* 249.

Kierkegaard Mercado, S, 'Safe Harbor Agreement—Boon or Bane' (2005) 1 *Shidler Journal of Law Commerce and Technology* 1.

Kite, LA, 'Red Flagging Civil Liberties and Due Process Rights of Airline Passengers: Will a Redesigned CAPPS II System Meet the Constitutional Challenge' (2004) 61 *Washington & Lee Law Review* 1385.

Kleiner, Y, 'Racial Profiling in the Name of National Security: Protecting Minority Travelers' Civil Liberties in the Age of Terrorism' (2010) 30 *British Columbia Third World Law Journal* 103.

Kokott, J and Sobotta, C, 'The distinction between privacy and data protection in the jurisprudence of the CJEU and the ECtHR' (2013) *International Data Privacy Law* 22.

Konstadinides, T, 'Destroying democracy on the ground of defending it? The Data Retention Directive, the surveillance state and our constitutional ecosystem' (2011) 36 *European Law Review* 722.

—, 'Wavering between Centres of Gravity: Comment on Ireland v Parliament and Council' (2010) 35 *European Law Review* 88.

Koops, BJ, 'Law, Technology, and Shifting Power Relations' (2010) 25 *Berkeley Tech Law Journal* 973.

Korff, D, Note on the EU-US Umbrella Data Protection Agreement, Fundamental Rights European Experts Group (FREE), 14 October 2015, www.statewatch.org/news/2015/oct/eu-usa-umbrella-freegroup-Korff-Note.pdf.

Kosta, E, 'The Way to Luxembourg: National Court Decisions on the Compatibility of the Data Retention Directive with the Rights to Privacy and Data Protection' (2013) 10 (3) *SCRIPTed* 339.

—, *Consent in European Data Protection Law* (Leiden-Boston, Martinus Nijhoff Publisher, 2013).

Kosta, E and Valcke, P, 'Retaining the Data Retention Directive' (2006) 22 *Computer Law & Security Report* 370.

Kudrna, J, 'Human rights—real of just formal rights? Example of the (un)constitutionality of data retention in the Czech Republic' (2012) 19 (4) *Jurisprudence* 1289.

Kühling, J and Heitzer, S, 'Returning through the national back door? The future of data retention after the ECJ judgment on Directive 2006/24 in the UK and elsewhere' (2015) *European Law Review* 263.

Kuner, C, 'A "Super-right" to Data Protection? The Irish Facebook Case & the Future of EU Data Transfer Regulation', LSE Media Policy Project Blog, http://blogs.lse.ac.uk/mediapolicyproject/2014/06/24/a-super-right-to-data-protection-the-irish-facebook-case-the-future-of-eu-data-transfer-regulation/.

—, 'Beyond Safe Harbor: European Data Protection Law and Electronic Commerce' (2001) 35 *International Law* 79.

—, 'An International Legal Framework for Data Protection: Issues and Prospects' (2009) 25 *Computer Law and Security Review* 307.

—, *Transborder Data Flows and Data Privacy Law* (Oxford, Oxford University Press, 2013).

—, 'Extraterritoriality and regulation of international data transfers in EU data protection law' (2015) 5 (4) *International Data Privacy Law* 235.

Kuner, C, Cate, F, Millard, C and Svantesson, DJ, 'Let's not kill all the privacy laws (and lawyers)' (2011) 1 *International Data Privacy Law* 209.

Lenaerts, K, 'Exploring the Limits of the EU Charter of Fundamental Rights' (2012) 8 *European Constitutional Law Review* 375.

Lessig, L, 'Privacy As Property' (2002) 69 *Social Research: An International Quarterly* 247.

Levi, M and Wall, D, 'Technologies, Security and Privacy in the post 9/11 European Information Society' (2004) 31 *Journal of Law and Society* 194.

Lichtblau, E and Risen, J, 'Bank Data Is Sifted by U.S. in Secret to Block Terror', *The New York Times*, 23 June 2006.

Lichtblau, E, Risen, J and Mazzetti, M, 'Reported Drop in Surveillance Spurred a Law', *New York Times*, 11 August 2007, www.nytimes.com/2007/08/11/washington/11nsa.html.

Lynskey, O, 'The Data Retention Directive is incompatible with the rights to privacy and data protection and is invalid in its entirety: *Digital Rights Ireland*. Joined Cases C-293 & 594/12, Digital Rights Ireland Ltd and Seitlinger and others, Judgment of the Court of Justice (Grand Chamber) of 8 April 2014', (2014) 51 (6) *Common Market Law Review* 1789.

—, *The Foundations of EU Data Protection Law* (Oxford, Oxford University Press, 2016).

Lyon, D, *Surveillance Society—Monitoring Everyday Life* (Buckingham, Open University Press, 2001).

Markou, C, 'The Cyprus and other EU court rulings on data retention: The Directive as a privacy bomb' (2012) 28 *Computer Law & Security Review* 468.

Marx, M, 'The EP Committee Rejects the Proposal for an European Passenger Name Record System (PNR)' (European Area of Freedom Security & Justice, 1 May 2013) http://free-group.eu/2013/05/01/the-ep-committee-rejects-the-proposal-for-an-european-passanger-name-record-system-pnr/#_ftn5.

McCarthy, JT, *The rights of publicity and privacy* (Thomson West, 1987).

Mendes De Leon, P, 'The Fight Against Terrorism Through Aviation: Data Protection Versus Data Production' (2006) 31 *Air & Space Law* 320.

Mendez, F and Mendez, M, 'Comparing Privacy Regimes: Federal Theory and the Politics of Privacy Regulation in the European Union and the United States' (2009) 40 *Publius: The Journal of Federalism* 617.

Mendez, M, 'Passenger Name Record Agreement—European Court of Justice' (2007) 3 *European Constitutional Law Review* 127.

Meyer, J and Miller, G, 'U.S. Secretly Tracks Global Bank Data', *Los Angeles Times*, 23 June 2006.

Miller, AR, *The Assault on Privacy: Computer, Data Banks, and Dossier*, (Ann Arbor, University of Michigan Press, 1973).

Mitsilegas, V, *EU Criminal Law* (Oxford, Hart Publishing, 2009).

Mitsilegas, V and Baldaccini, A, 'Interdependence of the various initiatives and legislative proposals in the fields of Counter-terrorism and police co-operation at the European level', Briefing Note requested by the European Parliament's LIBE Committee, October 2007

Moeckli, D, 'Discriminatory Profiles: Law Enforcement After 9/11 and 7/7' (2005) 5 *European Human Rights Law Review* 517.

—, 'Terrorist Profiling and the Importance of a Proactive Approach to Human Rights Protection' (2006), https://a1papers.ssrn.com/sol3/papers.cfm?abstract_id=952163.

—, *Human Rights and Non-Discrimination in the 'War on Terror'* (Oxford, Oxford University Press, 2008).

Molek, P, 'Czech Constitutional Court—Unconstitutionality of the Czech implementation of the Data Retention Directive; Decision of 22 March 2011, PI. ÚS 24/10' (2012) 8 *European Constitutional Law Review* 338.

Monar, J, 'Editorial Comment: The Rejection of the EU-US TFTP Interim Agreement by the European Parliament: A Historic Vote and Its Implications' (2010) 15 *European Foreign Affairs Review* 143.

Moore, AD, *Privacy Rights: Moral and Legal Foundations* (Philadelphia PA, The Pennsylvania State University Press, 2010).

—, 'Privacy, speech, and values: what we have no business knowing' (2016) 18 *Ethics & Information Technology* 41.

Moreham, NA, 'Privacy in Public Places' (2006) 65 (3) *Cambridge Law Journal* 606.

Müller, F and Richter, T, 'Report on the Bundesverfassungsgericht's (Federal Constitutional Court) Jurisprudence in 2005/2006' (2008) 9 *German Law Journal* 161.

Murphy, C, 'Fundamental rights and security: the difficult position of the European judiciary' (2010) 16 *European Public Law* 289.

—, 'Romanian Constitutional Court, Decision No 1258 of 8 October 2009 Regarding the Unconstitutionality Exception of the Provisions of Law No 298/2008 Regarding the

Retention of the Data Generated or Processed by the Public Electronic Communications Service Providers, as Well as for the Modification of Law No 506/2004 Regarding the Personal Data Processing and Protection of Private Life in the Field of Electronic Communication Area' (2010) 47 *Common Market Law Review* 933.

—, *EU Counter-Terrorism Law: Pre-Emption and the Rule of Law* (Oxford, Hart Publishing, 2012).

Murphy, RS, 'Property Rights in Personal Information: An Economic Defence of Privacy' (1996) 84 *Georgetown Law Journal* 2381.

Newman, AL, *Protectors of Privacy: Regulating Personal Data in the Global Economy* (Ithaca, Cornell University Press, 2008).

Nissenbaum, H, 'Protecting Privacy in an Information Age: The Problem of Privacy in Public' (1998) 17 *Law and Philosophy* 559.

Nouwt, S, 'Towards a Common European Approach to Data Protection: A Critical Analysis of Data Protection Perspectives of the Council of Europe and the European Union' in S Gutwirth et al (eds), *Reinventing Data Protection?* (New York, Springer, 2009) 275.

Ntouvas, I, 'Air Passenger Data Transfer to the USA: The Decision of the ECJ and Latest Developments' (2007) 16 *International Journal of Law and Information Technology* 73.

Office of Legal Policy, US Department of Justice 22 June 2004, http://kyl.senate.gov/legis_center/subdocs/062204_brand.pdf.

Ojanen, T, 'Terrorist Profiling: Human Rights Concerns' (2010) 3 *Critical Studies on Terrorism* 295.

—, 'Privacy Is More Than Just a Seven-Letter Word: The Court of Justice of the European Union Sets Constitutional Limits on Mass Surveillance. Court of Justice of the European Union, Decision of 8 April 2014 in Joined Cases C-293/12 and C-594/12, Digital Rights Ireland and Seitlinger and Others' (2014) 10 *European Constitutional Law Review* 528.

—, 'Making the Essence of Fundamental Rights Real: The Court of Justice of the European Union Clarifies the Structure of Fundamental Rights under the Charter' (2016) 12 (2) *European Constitutional Law Review* 318.

Ozcan, M and Yilmaz, F, 'Pendulum Swings in Between Civil Rights and Security: EU Policies Against Terrorism in the Light of the PNR Case' (2008) *Ysak Year Book of International Policy & Law* 51.

Papakonstantinou, V and de Hert, P, 'The PNR Agreement and Transatlantic Anti-Terrorism Co-operation: No Firm Human Rights Framework on Either Side of the Atlantic' (2009) 46 *Common Market Law Review* 885.

Parker, RB, 'A Definition of Privacy' (1974) 27 *Rutgers Law Review* 275.

Patton, C, 'No Man's Land: The EU–US Passenger Name Record Agreement and What It Means for the European Union's Pillar Structure' (2008) 40 *George Washington International Law Review* 527.

Pearce, G and Platten, N, 'Orchestrating Transatlantic Approaches to Personal Data Protection: A European Perspective' (1999) 22 *Fordham International Law Journal* 2024.

Peers, S, 'The party's over: EU data protection law after the Schrems Safe Harbour judgment', 7 October 2015, http://eulawanalysis.blogspot.co.uk/2015/10/the-partys-over-eu-data-protection-law.html.

Pell, S, 'Systematic government access to private-sector data in the United States' (2012) 2 (4) *International Data Privacy Law* 245.

Petkova, B, 'The Safeguards of Privacy Federalism' (2016) 20 (2) *Lewis & Clark Law Review* 595.

Polcak, R, 'Aims, Methods and Achievements in European Data Protection' (2009) 23 *International Review of Law Computers and Technology* 179.

Posner, RA, *The Economics of Justice* (Boston MA, Harvard University Press, 1983).

—, *Economic Analysis of Law*, 5th edn (New York, Aspen, 1998).

Post, RC, 'Three Concepts of Privacy' (2000) 89 *Georgetown Law Journal*, 2087.

Raab, CD and Bennett, CJ, 'Taking the Measure of Privacy: Can Data Protection Be Evaluated?' (1996) 62 *International Review of Administrative Sciences* 535.

Rachels, J, 'Why Privacy is Important' (1975) 4 (4) *Philosophy & Public Affairs* 323.

Ramasastry, A, 'Lost in Translation—Data Mining, National Security and the Adverse Inference Problem' (2006) 22 *Santa Clara Computer & High Technology Law Journal* 757.

Rasmussen, R, 'Is International Travel Per Se Suspicion of Terrorism? The Dispute Between the United States and European Union over Passenger Name Record Data Transfers' (2009) 26 *Wisconsin International Law Journal* 551.

Rauhofer, J, 'Just Because You're Paranoid, Doesn't Mean They're Not After You: Legislative Developments in Relation to the Mandatory Retention of Communications Data in the European Union' (2006) *Script-ED* 322.

Rauhofer, J and MacSithigh, D, 'The data retention directive never existed' (2014) 11 *Script-ED* 122.

Ravich, T, 'Is Airline Passenger Profiling Necessary?' (2007) 62 *University of Miami Law Review* 1.

Raviv, E, 'Homing In: Technology's Place in Fourth Amendment Jurisprudence' (2015) 28 (2) *Harvard Journal of Law & Technology* 593.

Rees, W, *Transatlantic Counter-Terrorism Cooperation: The New Imperative* (London, Routledge, 2006).

Regan, PM, *Legislating Privacy: Technology, Social Values, and Public Policy* (Chapel Hill, University of North Carolina Press, 1995).

Reidenberg, J, 'E-Commerce and Trans-Atlantic Privacy' (2002) 38 *Houston Law Review* 717.

Reiman, JH, 'Privacy, Intimacy, and Personhood' (1976) 6 *Philosophy and Public Affairs* 26.

Rhee, J, 'Comment, Rational And Constitutional Approaches To Airline Safety In The Face Of Terrorist Threats' (2000) 49 *Depaul Law Review* 847.

Rijpma, J and Gilmore, G, 'Joined Cases C-317/04 and C-318/04, European Parliament v Council and Commission, Judgment of the Grand Chamber of 30 May 2006, [2006] ECR I-4721' (2007) 44 *Common Market Law Review* 1081.

Ripoll Servent, A and MacKenzie, A, 'The European Parliament as a Norm Taker? EU-US Relations after the SWIFT Agreement' (2012) 17 *European Foreign Affairs Review* 71.

Risen, J and Lichtblau, E, 'Bush Lets US Spy on Callers Without Courts', *New York Times*, 16 December 2005, www.nytimes.com/2005/12/16/politics/bush-lets-us-spy-on-callers-without-courts.html.

Roberts, A, 'Privacy, Data Retention and Domination: *Digital Rights Ireland Ltd v Minister for Communications* (2015) 78 (3) *Modern Law Review* 522.

Rodotà, S, 'Data Protection as a Fundamental Right' in S Gutwirth et al (eds), *Reinventing Data Protection?* (New York, Springer, 2009) 77.

Rodriguez-Ruiz, B, 'Protecting the secrecy of telecommunications: a comparative study of the European Convention on Human Rights, Germany and United States' (PhD thesis, European University Institute 1995).

Roos, M, 'Definition of the Problem: The Impossibility of Compliance with Both European Union and United States Law' (2005) 14 *Transnational Law & Contemporary Problems* 1137.

Rosen, J, 'Continental Divide: Americans See Privacy as a Protection of Liberty, Europeans as a Protection of Dignity. Will One Conception Trump the Other—or Are Both Destined to Perish?' (2004) *Legal Affairs*, https://legalaffairs.org/issues/September-October-2004/review_rosen_sepoct04.msp.

Rousseau, JJ, 'Du contrat social' (1762), in *Oeuvres completes de Jean-Jacques Rousseau*, eds B Gagnebin and M Raymond (Paris, Gallimard (Pleiade), 1964), Book 1, ch VIII, 365.

Rouvroy, A and Poullet, Y, 'The Right to Informational Self-Determination and the Value of Self-Development: Reassessing the Importance of Privacy for Democracy?', in S Gutwirth et al (eds), *Reinventing Data Protection?* (New York, Springer, 2009).

Rowland, D, 'Data Retention and the War Against Terrorism—A Considered and Proportionate Response?' (2004) 3 *The Journal of Information, Law and Technology*.

Salbu, S, 'The European Union Data Privacy Directive and International Relations' (2002) 35 *Vanderbilt Journal of Transnational Law* 655.

Santolli, J, 'Note: The Terrorist Finance Tracking Program: Illuminating the Shortcomings of the European Union's Antiquated Data Privacy Directive' (2008) 40 *The George Washington International Law Review* 553.

Sartor, G, 'Privacy, Reputation, and Trust: Some Implications For Data Protection', European University Institute, EUI Working Papers, Law No 2006/04/

—, 'Providers' liabilities in the new EU Data Protection Regulation: A threat to Internet freedoms?' (2013) 3 (1) *International Data Privacy Law* 3

Scandamis, N, Sigalas, F and Stratakis, S, 'Rival Freedoms in Terms of Security: The Case of Data Protection and the Criterion of Connexity', (2007) CEPS, CHALLENGE, Research Paper No 7.

Scannell, B, 'TSA Cannot Be Trusted' *USA Today*, 27 September 2004.

Scheinin, M, 'Towards evidence-based discussion on surveillance: A Rejoinder to Richard A. Epstein' (2016) 12 (2) *European Constitutional Law Review* 341.

Scheinin, M and Vermeulen, M, 'Detection Technologies, Terrorism, Ethics and Human Rights', European Commission, Seventh Framework Programme.

Schneier, B, 'An Easy Path for Terrorists', *Boston Globe*, 24 August 2004.

Schriver, R, 'You Cheated, You Lied: The Safe Harbor Agreement and Its Enforcement by the Federal Trade Commission' (2002) 70 *Fordham Law Review* 2777.

Schutter de, O and Ringelheim, J, 'Ethnic Profiling: A Rising Challenge for European Human Rights Law' (2008) 71 *Modern Law Review* 358.

Schutze, R, 'Three "Bills of Rights" for the European Union' (2011) 30 *Yearbook of European Law* 131.

Schwartz, P, 'Privacy and Participation: Personal Information and Public Sector Regulation in the United States' (1995) 80 *Iowa Law Review* 553.

Schwartz, P and Peifer, KN, 'Prosser's Privacy and the German Right of Personality: Are Four Torts Better than One Unitary Concept?', (2010) 98 *California Law Review* 1925.

Schwartz, P and Reidenberg, J, *Data Privacy Law: A Study of United States Data Protection* (Charlottesville, Michie Law Publishers, 1996).

Seifert, J, 'Data mining and Homeland Security: An Overview', Library of Congress, Washington DC Congressional Research Service, 2007.

Serrano, V, 'Comment: The European Court of Justice's Decision to Annul the Agreement Between the United States and European Community Regarding the Transfer of Personal Name Record Data, Its Effects, and Recommendations for a New Solution' (2007) 13 *ILSA Journal of International & Comparative Law* 453.

Shaffer, G, 'Globalization and Social Protection: The Impact of EU and International Rules in the Ratcheting up of US Data Privacy Standards' (2000) 25 *Yale Journal of International Law* 1.

Shea, C, 'A Need for Swift Change: The Struggle Between the European Union's Desire for Privacy in International Financial Transactions and the United States' Need for Security from Terrorists as Evidenced by the Swift Scandal' (2008) 8 *Journal of High Technology Law* 143.

Shetterly, D, 'Starving the Terrorists of Funding: How the United States Treasury Is Fighting the War on Terror' (2006) 18 *Regent University Law Review* 327.

Shima, B, 'EU Fundamental Rights and Member State Action After Lisbon: Putting the ECJ's Case Law in its Context' (2015) 38 (4) *Fordham International Law Journal* 1095.

Shoenberger, A, 'Privacy Wars: EU Versus US: Scattered Skirmishes, Storm Clouds Ahead' (2007) 17 *Indiana International & Comparative Law Review* 375.

Shrader, J, 'Secrets Hurt: How SWIFT Shook Up Congress, the European Union, and the US Banking Industry' (2007) 11 *North Carolina Banking Institute* 397.

Simitis, S, 'Datenschutzrecht' in Hans Meyer and Michael Stolleis (eds), *Hessisches Staats- und Verwaltungsrecht* 2nd edn (1986) 111.

—, 'Reviewing Privacy in an Information Society' (1987) 135 *University of Pennsylvania Law Review* 707.

—, New Developments in National and International Data Protection Law in Recent Developments in J Dumortier (ed), *Data Privacy Law: Belgium's Data Protection Bill and the European Draft Directive* (1992) 1.

—, 'Privacy– An Endless Debate?' (2010) 98 *California Law Review* 1989.

Simpson, G, 'Treasury Tracks Financial Data In Secret Program', *The Wall Street Journal*, 23 June 2006.

Slobogin, C, *Privacy at Risk: The New Government Surveillance and the Fourth Amendment* (Chicago IL, University of Chicago Press, 2007).

Slobogin, C and Schumacher, J, 'Reasonable Expectations of Privacy and Autonomy in Fourth Amendment Cases: An Empirical Look at Understandings Recognized and Permitted by Society' (1993) 42 *Duke Law Journal* 727.

Solove, D, 'Privacy and Power: Computer Databases and Metaphors for Information Privacy' (2001) 53 *Stanford Law Review* 1393

—, 'Digital Dossiers and the Dissipation of Fourth Amendment Privacy' (2002) 75 *Southern California Law Review* 1083.

—, 'The Origins and Growth of Information Privacy Law' (2003) 748 *PLI/PAT* 29.

—, 'A Brief History of Information Privacy Law', (2006) *Proskauer on Privacy*, GWU Law School Public Law Research Paper No 215.

—, 'A Taxonomy of Privacy' (2006) 154 *University of Pennsylvania Law Review* 477.

—, *Understanding Privacy* (Cambridge MA, Harvard University Press, 2008).

—, 'Data Mining and the Security-Liberty Debate' (2008) 74 *University of Chicago Law Review* 343.

Solove, D and Schwartz, P, *Information Privacy Law* (Wolters Kluwer Law & Business, 2009).

Spaventa, E, 'The horizontal application of fundamental rights as general principles of Union Law', in A Arnull, C Barnard, M Dougan and E Spaventa (eds.) *A constitutional order of states: essays in honour of Alan Dashwood* (Oxford, Hart Publishing, 2011).

Spina, A, 'Risk Regulation of Big Data: Has the Time Arrived for a Paradigm Shift in EU Data Protection Law? (2014) 5 (2) *European Journal of Risk Regulation* 248.

Steinbock, D, 'Data Matching, Data Mining, and Due Process' (2005) 40 *Georgia Law Review* 82.

Swire, P, 'The Second Wave of Global Privacy Protection: Symposium Introduction' (2013) 74 (6) *Ohio State Law Journal* 841.

Taipale, KA, 'Data Mining and Domestic Security: Connecting the Dots to Make Sense of Data' (2003) 5 *Columbia Science & Technology Law Review* 1.

Taylor, M, 'The EU Data Retention Directive' (2006) 22 *Computer Law & Security Review* 309.

Taylor, M, 'The EU's human right obligations in relation to its data protection laws with extraterritorial effect' (2015) 5 (4) *International Data Privacy Law* 246.

Terwangne, CD, 'Is a Global Data Protection Regulatory Model Possible?' in S Gutwirth et al (eds), *Reinventing Data Protection?* (New York, Springer, 2009).

Thai, J, 'Is Data Mining Ever a Search Under Justice Stevens's Fourth Amendment?' (2006) 74 *Fordham Law Review* 1731.

Thoukidides, 'Pericle's Funeral Oration from the Peloponnesian War' (Book 2.34-46). English translation, http://hrlibrary.umn.edu/education/thucydides.html.

Tourkochoriti, I, 'The Transatlantic Flow of Data and the National Security Exception in the European Data Privacy Regulation: In Search for Legal Protection Against Surveillance' (2014) 36 (2) *University of Pennsylvania Journal of International Law* 459.

Tracol, X, 'Legislative genesis and judicial death of a directive: The European Court of Justice invalidated the data retention directive (2006/24/EC) thereby creating a sustained period of legal uncertainty about the validity of national laws which enacted it' (2014) 30 (6) *Computer Law & Security Review* 751.

Trubow, G and Hudson, D, 'The Right to Financial Privacy Act of 1978: New Protection from Federal Intrusion' (1979) 12 *John Marshall Journal of Practice & Procedure* 487.

Tsiftsoglou, A and Flogaitis, S, 'Transposing the Data Retention Directive in Greece: Lessons from Karlsruhe' paper presented at the 4th International Conference of Information Law, *Values and Freedoms in Modern Information Law & Ethics*, Thessaloniki, 21 May 2011.

Tukdi, I, 'Transatlantic Turbulence: The Passenger Name Record Conflict' (2008) 45 *Houston Law Review* 587.

Tzanou, M, 'Case-note on Joined Cases C-402/05 P & C-415/05 P Yassin Abdullah Kadi & Al Barakaat International Foundation v Council of the European Union & Commission of the European Communities' (2009) *German Law Journal*, 121.

—, 'Balancing Fundamental Rights: United in Diversity? Some Reflections on the Recent Case Law of the European Court of Justice on Data Protection' (2010) 6 *Croatian Yearbook of European Law and Policy* 53.

—, 'Data Protection in EU Law: An Analysis of the EU Legal Framework and the ECJ Jurisprudence' in C Akrivopoulou and A Psygkas (eds), *Personal Data Privacy And Protection In A Surveillance Era: Technologies and practices*, (Hershey PA, IGI Global, 2011) 273.

—, 'Data protection as a fundamental right next to privacy? "Reconstructing" a not so new right' (2013) 3 (2) *International Data Privacy Law* 88.

—, 'Is Data Protection the Same as Privacy? An Analysis of Telecommunications' Metadata Retention Measures' (2013) *Journal of Internet Law* 21

—, 'Data Protection in EU Law after Lisbon: Challenges, Developments, and Limitations' in M Gupta (ed), *Handbook of Research on Emerging Developments in Data Privacy* (Hershey PA, IGI Global, 2014) 24.

—, 'The War Against Terror and Transatlantic Information Sharing: Spillovers of Privacy or Spillovers of Security?' (2015) 31 (80) *Utrecht Journal of International and European Law* 87.

—, 'European Union Regulation of Transatlantic Data Transfers and Online Surveillance', *Human Rights Law Review* (forthcoming).

Vainio, N and Miettinen, S, 'Telecommunications data retention after *Digital Rights Ireland*: legislative and judicial reactions in the Member States' (2015) 23 *International Journal of Law and Information Technology* 290.

Viola de Azevedo Cunha, M, Marin, L and Sartor, G, 'Peer-to-Peer Privacy Violations and ISP Liability: Privacy Violations in the User-Generated Web' (2012) 2 *International Data Privacy Law* 50.

Vries de, K, Bellanova, R, De Hert, P and Gutwirth, S, 'The German Constitutional Court judgement on data retention: Proportionality overrides unlimited surveillance (Doesn't it?)' in Gutwirth, S et al (eds), *Computers, Privacy and Data Protection: an Element of Choice* (Heidelberg, Springer, 2011), 3.

Wacks, R, *Privacy: A Very Short Introduction* (Oxford: Oxford University Press, 2010).

Walker, C and Akdeniz, Y, 'Anti-terrorism Laws and Data Retention: War Is Over?' (2003) 54 *Northern Ireland Legal Quarterly* 159.

Warren, SD and Brandeis, LD, 'Right to Privacy' (1890) 4 *Harvard Law Review* 193.

Westin, A, *Privacy and Freedom* (London, The Bodley Head Ltd, 1970).

Whitman, J, 'Two Western Cultures of Privacy: Dignity Versus Liberty' (2003) 113 *Yale Law Journal* 1151.

Witte de, B, 'Too Much Constitutional Law in the European Union's Foreign Relations?' in M Cremona and B de Witte (eds), *EU Foreign Relations Law: Constitutional Fundamentals* (Oxford, Hart Publishing, 2008) 3.

Witten, I and Frank, E, *Data Mining* (San Francisco CA, Morgan Kaufmann, 2000).

Wright, D and Kreissl, R, 'European responses to the Snowden revelations: A discussion paper', December 2013, *Increasing Resilience in Surveillance Societies* (IRISS), http://irissproject.eu/wp-content/uploads/2013/12/IRISS_European-responses-to-the-Snowden-revelations_18-Dec-2013_Final.pdf.

Yano, M, 'Come Fly the (Unfriendly) Skies: Negotiating Passenger Name Record Agreements Between the United States and European Union' (2010) 5 *Journal of Law and Policy for the Information Society* 479.

Zöller, V, 'Liberty Dies by Inches: German Counter-Terrorism Measures and Human Rights' (2004) 5 *German Law Journal* 469.

Zucca, L, *Constitutional Dilemmas: Conflicts of Fundamental Legal Rights in Europe and the USA* (Oxford, Oxford University Press, 2008).

REPORTS AND OTHER DOCUMENTS

European Union

Commission

Communication on the global approach to transfers of Passenger Name Record (PNR) data to third countries, COM(2010) 492 final.

Communication from the Commission to the European Parliament and the Council, A European terrorist finance tracking system: available options, Brussels, 13 July 2011, COM(2011) 429 final.

Communication from the Commission to the European Parliament and the Council, 'Rebuilding Trust in EU–US Data Flows', 27 November 2013 COM(2013) 846 final.

Communication from the Commission to the European Parliament and the Council on the Functioning of the Safe Harbour from the Perspective of EU Citizens and Companies Established in the EU, Brussels, 27 November 2013, COM(2013) 847 final.

Communication from the Commission to the European Parliament and the Council on the Transfer of Personal Data from the EU to the United States of America under Directive 95/46/EC following the Judgment by the Court of Justice in Case C-362/14 (*Schrems*), COM(2015) 566 final, 6 November 2015.

Communication from the Commission to the European Parliament and the Council, Transatlantic Data Flows: Restoring Trust through Strong Safeguards, COM(2016) 117 final, 29 February 2016.

Proposal for a directive on the retention of data processed in connection with the provision of public electronic communication services and amending Directive 2002/58/ EC, 21 September, 2005.

Proposal for a Council Framework Decision on the use of Passenger Name Record (PNR) for law enforcement purposes COM(2007) 654 final.

Proposal for a Council Decision on the conclusion of the Agreement between the European Union and the United States of America on the processing and transfer of Financial Messaging Data from the European Union to the United States for purposes of the Terrorist Finance Tracking Program, COM(2009/0703 final)-NLE 2009/0190/.

Proposition de Recommandation du Conseil Autorisant l'ouverture de Negociations en vue d'un Accord entre l'Union Europeene et les Etats- Unis d'Amerique sur la protection des donnees personnelles lors de leur transfert et de leur traitement a des fins de prevention, d' investigation, de detection ou de poursuite d'actes criminels y compris le terrorism, dans le cadre de la Cooperation Policiaire et Judiciaire en matiere penale COM(2010) 252/2.

Proposal for a Directive of the European Parliament and of the Council on the use of Passenger Name Record data for the prevention, detection, investigation and prosecution of terrorist offences and serious crime COM(2011) 32 final.

Proposal for a Council Decision on the conclusion of the Agreement between the United States of America and the European Union on the use and transfer of Passenger Name Records to the United States Department of Homeland Security, COM(2011) 807 final.

Proposal for a Council Decision on the signing, on behalf of the European Union, of an Agreement between the United States of America and the European Union on the protection of personal information relating to the prevention, investigation, detection, and prosecution of criminal offences, COM (2016) 238 final, 29 April 2016.

Commission Staff Working Document, Report on the second joint review of the implementation of the Agreement between the European Union and the United States of America on the processing and transfer of Financial Messaging data from the European Union to the United States for the purposes of the Terrorist Finance Tracking Programme, October 2012, Brussels, 14.12.2012, SWD(2012) 454 final.

Commission Staff Working Paper, Joint Review of the Implementation by the US Bureau of Customs and Border Protection of the Undertakings set out in Commission Decision 2004/535/EC of 14 May 2004, Washington, 20–21 September 2005, COM (2005) final, 12 December 2005.

Commission Staff Working Paper, Report on the joint review of the implementation of the Agreement between the European Union and the United States of America on the processing and transfer of Financial Messaging data from the European Union to the United States for the purposes of the Terrorist Finance Tracking Programme 17–18 February 2011, Brussels, 30 March 2011, SEC(2011) 438 final.

Staff Working Document, Joint Review Report of the implementation of the Agreement between the European Union and the United States of America on the processing and transfer of Financial Messaging Data from the European Union to the United States for the purposes of the Terrorist Finance Tracking Program, Brussels, 11 August 2014, COM(2014) 513 final.

Recommendation from the Commission to the Council to authorize the opening of negotiations for an agreement between the EU and the USA to make available to the US Treasury Department financial payment messaging data to prevent and combat terrorism and terrorist financing, Brussels, 24 March 2010, SEC (2010) 315 final.

Report on the Joint Review of the implementation of the Agreement between the European Union and the United States of America on the processing and transfer of Passenger Name Record (PNR) data by air carriers to the United States Department of Homeland Security (DHS) 8–9 February 2010, 7 April 2010.

Report from the Commission to the Council and the European Parliament, Evaluation report on the Data Retention Directive (Directive 2006/24/EC) COM(2011) 225 final, 18 April 2011.

Commission Legal Service, Note for the Attention of Mr Stefano Manservisi Director General, DG HOME, Subject: Draft Agreement on the Use of Passenger Name Records (PNR) between the EU and the United States, SJ1 (2011) 603245, 18 May 2011.

Commission, Statistics on requests for data under the directive for 2008–2012, http://ec.europa.eu/dgs/home-affairs/what-we-do/policies/police-cooperation/data-retention/docs/statistics_on_requests_for_data_under_the_data_retention_directive_en.pdf.

Commission, First report on the implementation of the Data Protection Directive (95/46/EC) (Data Protection), COM(2003) 265.

Commission Memo, Frequently asked questions: The EU–US agreement on the transfer of Passenger Name Record (PNR) data, 27 November 2013, available at http://europa.eu/rapid/press-release_MEMO-13-1054_en.htm.

European Commission/US Customs Talks on PNR transmission, Brussels, 17/18 February 2003, Joint Statement, http://ec.europa.eu/transport/air_portal/security/doc/prn_joint_declaration_en.pdf.

Joint Report from the Commission and the US Treasury Department regarding the value of TFTP Provided Data pursuant to Article 6(6) of the Agreement between the European Union and the United States of America on the processing and transfer of Financial Messaging Data from the European Union to the United States for the purposes of the Terrorist Finance Tracking Program, Brussels, 27 November 2013, COM(2013) 843 final.

Press release announcing the designation of Judge Jean-Louis Bruguière as the SWIFT/TFTP 'eminent European person' IP/08/400, 7 March 2008, http://europa.eu/rapid/pressReleasesAction.do?reference=IP/08/400&format=HTML&aged=0&language=en&guiLanguage=en.

European Parliament

European Parliament Resolution on transfer of personal data by airlines in the case of transatlantic flights, 13 March 2003, P5_TA(2003)0097.

European Parliament Resolution on the draft Commission decision noting the adequate level of protection provided for personal data contained in the Passenger Name Records (PNRs) transferred to the US Bureau of Customs and Border Protection (2004/2011(INI)), P5_TA(2004)0245.

European Parliament Resolution on the interception of bank transfer data from the SWIFT system by the US secret services (P6_TA-PROV(2006)0317).

European Parliament Resolution on SWIFT, the PNR agreement and the transatlantic dialogue on these issues P6_TA(2007)0039.

European Parliament Resolution of 12 July 2007 on the PNR agreement with the United States of America P6_TA-PROV(2007)0347.

European Parliament Resolution of 20 November 2008 on the proposal for a Council framework decision on the use of Passenger Name Record (PNR) for law enforcement purposes P6_TA(2008)0561.

European Parliament Resolution of 17 September 2009 on the envisaged international agreement to make available to the United States Treasury Department financial payment messaging data to prevent and combat terrorism and terrorist financing, P7_TA(2009)0016.

European Parliament Resolution of 11 February 2010 on the proposal for a Council decision on the conclusion of the Agreement between the European Union and the United States of America on the processing and transfer of Financial Messaging Data from the European Union to the United States for purposes of the Terrorist Finance Tracking Programme (05305/1/2010 REV 1—C7-0004/2010—2009/0190(NLE)) P7_TA(2010)0029.

European Parliament Resolution of 5 May 2010 on the Recommendation from the Commission to the Council to authorise the opening of negotiations for an agreement between the European Union and the United States of America to make available to the United States Treasury Department financial messaging data to prevent and combat terrorism and terrorist financing P7_TA-PROV(2010)0143.

European Parliament Resolution of 5 May 2010 on the launch of negotiations for Passenger Name Record (PNR) agreements with the United States, Australia and Canada, P7_TA(2010)0144.

European Parliament Resolution of 8 July 2010 on the draft Council decision on the conclusion of the Agreement between the European Union and the United States of America on the processing and transfer of Financial Messaging Data from the European Union to the United States for the purposes of the Terrorist Finance Tracking Program (11222/1/2010/REV 1 and COR 1—C7-0158/2010—2010/0178(NLE)) P7_TA(2010)0279.

European Parliament Resolution of 12 March 2014 on the US NSA surveillance programme, surveillance bodies in various Member States and their impact on EU citizens' fundamental rights and on transatlantic cooperation in Justice and Home Affairs (2013/2188(INI)), P7_TA(2014)0230.

European Parliament Recommendation to the Council on the negotiations for an agreement with the United States of America on the use of passenger name records (PNR) data to prevent and combat terrorism and transnational crime, including organised crime (2006/2193(INI)), P6_TA(2006)0354.

LIBE Committee Recommendation on the draft Council decision on the conclusion of the Agreement between the European Union and the United States of America on the processing and transfer of Financial Messaging Data from the European Union to the

United States for the purposes of the Terrorist Finance Tracking Program (11222/1/2010/ REV 1 and COR 1—C7-0158/2010—2010/0178(NLE)) A7-0224/2010, Rapporteur: Alexander Alvaro.

LIBE Committee Recommendation on the proposal for a Council decision on the conclusion of the Agreement between the European Union and the United States of America on the processing and transfer of Financial Messaging Data from the European Union to the United States for purposes of the Terrorist Finance Tracking Program (05305/1/2010REV—C7-0004/2010—2009/0190(NLE)).

Committee on Civil Liberties, Justice and Home Affairs, Report of the European Parliament on the initiative by the French Republic, Ireland, the Kingdom of Sweden and the United Kingdom for a Draft Framework Decision on the retention of data processed and stored in connection with the provision of publicly available electronic communications services or data on public communications networks for the purpose of prevention, investigation, detection and prosecution of crime and criminal offences including terrorism (8958/2004–C6-0198/2004–2004/0813(CNS)) (31 May 2005), Rapporteur: Alexander Nuno Alvaro, A6-0174/2005 final.

Committee on Civil Liberties, Justice and Home Affairs, Report with a proposal for a European Parliament Recommendation to the Council on the Negotiations for an Agreement with the United States of America on the use of Passenger Name Records (PNR) data to prevent and combat terrorism and transnational crime, including organised crime, 19 July 2006, (2006/2193(INI).

European Parliament Debates, Monday, 9 July 2007, Strasbourg, www.europarl.europa.eu/ sides/getDoc.do?pubRef=-//EP//TEXT+CRE+20070709+ITEM-018+DOC+XML+V0// EN&language=EN.

Summary of the meeting of the European Parliament Committee on Civil Liberties, Justice and Home Affairs, held in Brussels on 10 April 2014, document 8940/14, 11 April 2014, http://register.consilium.europa.eu/doc/srv?l=EN&f=ST%208940%202014%20INIT.

Press release, 'EU Passenger Name Record (PNR) directive: An overview', www. europarl.europa.eu/news/en/news-room/20150123BKG12902/EU-Passenger-Name-Record-(PNR)-directive-an-overview.

Press release, 'EU Passenger Name Record (PNR): Civil Liberties Committee backs EP/ Council deal', www.europarl.europa.eu/news/en/news-room/20151207IPR06435/EU-Passenger-Name-Record-(PNR)-Civil-Liberties-Committee-backs-EPCouncil-deal.

Press release, 'Civil Liberties Committee green light for air passenger data deal with the US', www.europarl.europa.eu/pdfs/news/expert/infopress/20120326IPR41838/20120326 IPR41838_en.pdf.

European Council

Cologne European Council, 3-4 June 1999, Conclusions of the Presidency, Annex IV— European Council Decision on the drawing up of a Charter of Fundamental Rights of the European Union.

Conclusions of the Special Meeting of the European Council of 30 August 2014, EUCO 163/14 CO EUR 11 CONCL 4.

European Council, Declaration on Combating Terrorism, 25 March 2004.

European Council, The Stockholm Programme—An Open and Secure Europe Serving and Protecting Citizens, [2010] OJ C-115/1.

Council Notice concerning the denunciation of the Agreement between the European Community and the United States of America on the processing and transfer of PNR data by air carriers to the United States Department of Homeland Security, Bureau of Customs and Border Protection, OJ C219/1 of 12 September 2006.

Council of the European Union, Negotiating directives for negotiations between the European Union and the United States of Am5rica for an international agreement to make available to the United States Treasury Department financial payment messaging data to prevent and combat terrorism and terrorist financing.

Council of the European Union, Reports by the High Level Contact Group (HLCG) on information sharing and privacy and personal data protection, 9831/08 JAI 275 DATAPROTECT 31 USA.

Council of the European Union, Statements, Council doc 5777/06 ADD 1 (10 February 2006).

Press release, 'EU-US Agreement on the Transfer of Financial Messaging Data for purposes of the Terrorist Finance Tracking Programme', Brussels, 9 February 2010 6265/10 (Presse 23).

Article 29 Working Party

Opinion 6/2002 on Transmission of Passenger Manifest Information and other data from airlines to the United States.

Opinion 2/2004 on the adequate protection of personal data contained in the PNR of air passengers to be transferred to the US' Bureau of Customs and Border Protection (US CBP).

Opinion 9/2004 on a Draft Framework Decision on the storage of data processed and retained for the purpose of providing electronic public communications services or data available in public communications networks with a view to the prevention, investigation, detection and prosecution of criminal acts, including terrorism. (Proposal presented by France, Ireland, Sweden and Great Britain (Council Doc 8958/04—28 April, 2004)).

Opinion 4/2005 on the proposal for a Directive of the European Parliament and of the Council on the retention of data processed in connection with the provision of public electronic communication services and amending Directive 2002/58/EC (COM(2005)438 Final of 21.09.2005).

Opinion 113/2005 on the Proposal for a Directive of the European Parliament and of the Council on the Retention of Data Processed in Connection with the Provision of Public Electronic Communication Services and Amending Directive 2002/58/EC (COM(2005)438 final of 21.09.2005), 21 October 2005.

Opinion 3/2006 on the Directive 2006/XX/EC of the European Parliament and of the Council on the retention of data processed in connection with the provision of public electronic communication services and amending Directive 2002/58/EC, as adopted by the Council on 21 February 2006.

Opinion 5/2006 on the ruling by the European Court of Justice of 30 May 2006 in Joined Cases C-317/04 and C-318/04 on the transmission of Passenger Name Records to the United States.

Opinion 10/2006 on the Processing of Personal Data by the Society for Worldwide Interbank Financial Telecommunication (SWIFT).

Opinion 4/2007 on the concept of personal data.

Opinion 5/2007 on the Follow-up Agreement between the European Union and the United States of America on the processing and transfer of Passenger Name Record (PNR) data by air carriers to the United States Department of Homeland Security concluded in July 2007.

Opinion 10/2011 on the proposal for a Directive of the European Parliament and of the Council on the use of Passenger Name Record data for the prevention, detection, investigation and prosecution of terrorist offences and serious crime.

Opinion 01/2016 on the EU–US Privacy Shield draft adequacy decision, WP 238, 13 April 2016.

Article 29 Working Party, Working Party on Police and Justice, Joint Opinion on the Proposal for a Council Framework Decision on the Use of Passenger Name Record (PNR) for Law Enforcement Purposes, Presented by the Commission on 6 November 2007.

Recommendation 4/99 on the inclusion of the fundamental right to data protection in the European catalogue of fundamental rights.

Report 01/2010 on the second joint enforcement action: Compliance at national level of Telecom Providers and ISPs with the obligations required from national traffic data retention legislation on the legal basis of Articles 6 and 9 of the e-Privacy Directive 2002/58/EC and the Data Retention Directive 2006/24/EC amending the e-Privacy Directive, WP 172, 13 July 2010.

Working Document 'Privacy on the Internet—An Integrated EU Approach to on-line data protection', 5063/00/EN/FINAL, 21 November 2000.

Working Document 01/2016 on the justification of interferences with the fundamental rights to privacy and data protection through surveillance measures when transferring personal data (European Essential Guarantees), WP237, 13 April 2016.

Transfers of personal data to third countries: Applying Articles 25 and 26 of the EU Data Protection Directive, 24 July 1998.

Article 29 Working Party & Working Party on Police and Justice, Press Release 'EU–US TFTP Agreement not in line with privacy legislation: European Data Protection Authorities not satisfied with safeguards in EU–US financial transactions agreement', Brussels, 28 June 2010.

Letter to the LIBE Committee of the European Parliament, 6 January 2012, Ref. Ares(2012)15841-06/01/2012.

Statement, 16 October 2015.

Statement on the consequences of the *Schrems* judgment, 3 February 2016.

European Data Protection Supervisor

European Data Protection Supervisor, Press release, 'PNR: EDPS First Reaction to the Court of Justice Judgment' (2006).

Opinion of the European Data Protection Supervisor on the proposal for a Directive of the European Parliament and of the Council on the retention of data processed in connection with the provision of public electronic communication services and amending Directive 2002/58/EC (COM(2005) 438 final), [2005] OJ 298/1.

Opinion on the Evaluation Report from the Commission to the Council and the European Parliament on the Data Retention Directive (Directive 2006/24/EC), 31 May 2011.

Opinion on the role of the European Central Bank in the SWIFT case, 1 February 2007.

Opinion on the draft Proposal for a Council Framework Decision on the use of Passenger Name Record (PNR) data for law enforcement purposes [2008] OJ C110/1.

Opinion on the Final Report by the EU–US High Level Contact Group on Information Sharing and Privacy and personal data protection, 11 November 2008.

Opinion on the Proposal for a Council Decision on the conclusion of the Agreement between the European Union and the United States of America on the processing and transfer of financial messaging data from the European Union to the United States for purposes of the Terrorist Finance Tracking Program (TFTP II), 22 June 2010.

Opinion on the Proposal for a Directive of the European Parliament and of the Council on the use of Passenger Name Record data for the prevention, detection, investigation and prosecution of terrorist offences and serious crime, Brussels, 25 May 2011.

Opinion on the Proposal for a Council Decision on the conclusion of the Agreement between the United States of America and the European Union on the use and transfer of Passenger Name Records to the United States Department of Homeland Security, 9 December 2011.

Opinion 1/2016, Preliminary Opinion on the agreement between the United States of America and the European Union on the protection of personal information relating to the prevention, investigation, detection and prosecution of criminal offences, 12 February 2016.

Opinion 4/2016 on the EU–US Privacy Shield draft adequacy decision, 30 May 2016.

EU Agency of Fundamental Rights

FRA Annual report 2014, Information society, privacy and data protection, http://fra.europa.eu/sites/default/files/fra_uploads/information_society_chapter_fra-annual-report-2014_en.pdf.

Fundamental Rights Agency (FRA) Report 2016, Chapter 5: Information society, privacy and data protection, http://fra.europa.eu/sites/default/files/fra_uploads/fra-2016-frr-chapter-5-data-protection_en.pdf.

Opinion on the Proposal for a Council Framework Decision on the Use of Passenger Name Record (PNR) Data for Law Enforcement Purposes (2008), http://fra.europa.eu/fraWebsite/attachments/FRA_opinion_PNR_en.pdf.

'Towards more effective policing understanding and preventing discriminatory ethnic profiling: A Guide', October 2010, http://fra.europa.eu/sites/default/files/fra_uploads/1133-Guide-ethnic-profiling_EN.pdf.

Belgium

Belgium Privacy Commission, Opinion No 37/2006 of 27 September 2006 on the Transfer of Personal Data by the CSLR SWIFT by virtue of UST (OFAC) Subpoenas.

Belgium Privacy Commission, Decision of 9 December 2008, Control and Recommendation Procedure initiated with respect to the Company SWIFT SCRL.

United Kingdom

House of Lords European Union Committee, 'After Madrid: The EU's response to terrorism', 5th Report of Session 2004–05.

—, 'The EU/US Passenger Name Record (PNR) Agreement', 21st Report of Session 2006–07.
—, 'The Passenger Name Record (PNR) Framework Decision' 15th Report of Session 2007–08.
House of Lords, Select Committee on the Constitution, 'Surveillance: Citizens and the State', 2nd Report of Session 2008–09.
UK Information Commissioner, 'The Legal Framework: An Analysis of the "Constitutional" European Approach to Issues of data protection law', Study Project.

United Nations

Report of the Special Rapporteur on the promotion and protection of Human Rights and Fundamental Freedoms while Countering Terrorism, A/HRC/4/26, 29 January 2007.
Report of the Special Rapporteur on the promotion and protection of the right to freedom of opinion and expression, A/HRC/29/32, http://www.ohchr.org/EN/Issues/FreedomOpinion/Pages/CallForSubmission.aspx.
Report of the United Nations High Commissioner for Human Rights (Human Rights Council) on the right to privacy in the digital age, 30 June 2014, A/HRC/27/37.

United States of America

Authorization for Specified Electronic Surveillance Activities During a Limited Period to Detect and Prevent Acts of Terrorism Within the United States, Oct. 4, 2001, cited in Office Of The Inspector Gen, Nat'l Sec Agency Cent Sec Serv, Working Draft ST-09-0002, 1, 7–8, 11, 15 (2009).
DNI Announces the Declassification of the Existence of Collection Activities Authorized by President George W. Bush Shortly After the Attacks of September 11, 2001 (Dec.21,2013),http://icontherecord.tumblr.com/post/70683717031/dni-announces-the-declassification-of-the.
Hearing Before the Committee on Finance, US Senate 'Financial War on Terrorism: New Money Trails Present Fresh Challenges', 107th Cong, 2002.
Hearing before the United States Senate Judiciary Committee, Subcommittee on Terrorism, Technology and Homeland Security: 'Tools to Fight Terrorism: Subpoena Authority and Pretrial Detention of Terrorists' Testimony of Rachel Brand, Principal Deputy Assistant Attorney General.
House Select Committee on Homeland Security: Subcommittee on Econ Sec, Infrastructure Prot & Cybersecurity Hearing on Air Passenger Pre-Screening, 109th Cong (June 29, 2005).
National Transportation Safety Board, Aircraft Accident Report in-flight breakup over the Atlantic Ocean Trans World Airlines Flight 800 Boeing 747-131, 17 July 1996, www.ntsb.gov/doclib/reports/2000/AAR0003.pdf.
Press release, 'Secretary Napolitano Announces Major Aviation Security Milestone, DHS performs 100 percent watchlist matching for domestic flights', 7 June 2010, www.tsa.gov/press/releases/2010/0607.shtm.
Press release, 'TSA's Secure Flight Program Enters Next Public Phase', www.tsa.gov/press/releases/2009/0812.shtm.

Privacy and Civil Liberties Oversight Board (PCLOB), Report on the Surveillance Program Operated Pursuant to Section 702 of the Foreign Intelligence Surveillance Act, 2 July 2014, www.pclob.gov/Library/702-Report-2.pdf.

Statement of Rajesh De, General Counsel, NSA at the Privacy and Civil Liberties Oversight Board: Public Hearing Regarding the Surveillance Program Operated Pursuant to Section 702 of the Foreign Intelligence Surveillance Act 26, 19 March 2014.

Technology and Privacy Advisory Committee, US Department of Defence, Safeguarding Privacy in the fight against terrorism, TAPAC Report, March 2004.

Unclassified Report on the President's Surveillance Program, Prepared by the Office of Inspectors General of the Department of Defence, Department of Justice, Central Intelligence Agency, National Security Agency and the Office of the Director of National Intelligence, 2009.

United States General Accounting Office, Report to Congressional Committees, Aviation Security 'Computer-Assisted Passenger Pre-screening System faces significant Implementation Challenges', GAO Report, February 2004, www.gao.gov/new.items/d04385.pdf.

United States General Accounting Office, Report to the ranking minority member, Subcommittee on Financial Management, The Budget, and International Security, Committee on governmental affairs, US Senate, 'Data Mining—Federal Efforts cover a wide range of uses', May 2004.

United States Government Accountability Office, Testimony before the Committee on Commerce, Science, and Transportation, US Senate, Aviation Security, 'Significant Management Challenges May Adversely Affect Implementation of the Transportation Security Administration's Secure Flight Program', GAO Report, 9 February 2006, at www.gao.gov/new.items/d06374t.pdf.

United States National Commission for Terrorist Attacks, 'The Aviation Security System and the 9/11 Attacks', Staff Statement No. 3.

US Department of Homeland Security, Privacy Office, 'A Report concerning Passenger Name Record Information derived from flights between the US and the European Union', 18 December 2008, www.dhs.gov/xlibrary/assets/privacy/privacy_pnr_report_20081218.pdf.

US Department of the Treasury, Terrorist Financing Tracking Program: Fact Sheet, 23.06.2006, www.treasury.gov/press-center/press-releases/Pages/js4340.aspx.

US Government Accountability Office, Terrorist Watch List Screening Efforts to Help Reduce Adverse Effects on the Public, September 2006, www.gao.gov/new.items/d061031.pdf.

White House Commission on Aviation Safety and Security, Final Report to President Clinton, 1997, www.fas.org/irp/threat/212fin~1.html.

Miscellaneous

ACLU, 'Why the "Registered Traveler" Program Will Not Make Airline Passengers Any Safer', www.aclu.org/other/why-registered-traveler-program-will-not-make-airline-passengers-any-safer?redirect=why-registered-traveler-program-will-not-make-airline-passengers-any-safer.

Addendum to the Final Report by EU–US High Level Contact Group on information sharing and privacy and personal data protection, Report and Agreed Text from the High Level Contact Group of 28 October 2009.

Address of Frits Bolkestein to European Parliament Committees on Citizens' Freedoms and Rights, Justice and Home Affairs and Legal Affairs and the Internal Market, EU/US talks on transfers of airline passengers' personal data SPEECH/03/613 of 16 December 2003.

Arbeitskreis Vorratsdatenspeicherung (Working Group on Data Retention), *amicus curiae* brief www.vorratsdatenspeicherung.de/images/data_retention_brief_08-04-2008.pdf.

Deutsche Welle, 'US Accesses European Bank Data under Controversial SWIFT Agreement'.

Electronic Privacy Information Centre, 'Spotlight on Surveillance: Secure Flight Should Remain Grounded Until Security and Privacy Problems Are Resolved', https://epic.org/privacy/airtravel/secureflight.html.

EPIC Alert, www.epic.org/alert/epic_alert_23.03.html.

EPIC Statement on Judicial Redress Act of 2015, S 1600, 12 January 2006, https://epic.org/foia/eu-us-data-transfer/EPIC-Ltr-S1600.pdf.

EPIC, The Privacy Act 1974 (2015), https://epic.org/privacy/1974act/.

EU Business, 'EU-US spying row stokes concern over anti-terror campaign', 26 October 2013, www.eubusiness.com/news-eu/us-intelligence.r38.

'EU executive plans no new data retention law', www.reuters.com/article/us-eu-data-telecommunications-idUSKBN0M82CO20150312.

European Data Protection Authorities, Opinion on the transfer of Passengers' data to the United States, 17.6.2003.

Europol Activities in Relation to the TFTP Agreement, Information Note to the European Parliament 1 August 2010–1 April 2011, The Hague, 8 April 2011, File no 2566-566.

FATF, 9 Special Recommendations on terrorist financing, www.fatf-gafi.org/pages/0,2987, en_32250379_32235720_1_1_1_1_1,00.html; www.oecd.org/document/18/0,3746,en_ 2649_34255_1815186_1_1_1_1,00.html; www.oecd.org/document/18/0,3746,en_2649_ 34255_1815186_1_1_1_1,00.html.

Joint Industry Statement on Data Retention Directive, http://www.gsmeurope.org/documents/Joint_Industry_Statement_on_DRD.PDF.

Memo, 'Frequently Asked Questions: The Data Retention Directive', 8 April 2014, http://europa.eu/rapid/press-release_MEMO-14-269_en.htm.

OECD Guidelines on the Protection of Privacy and Transborder Flows of Personal Data.

Open Rights Group, Data retention in the EU following the CJEU ruling- updated April 2015, www.openrightsgroup.org/assets/files/legal/Data_Retention_status_table_updated_ April_2015_uploaded_finalwithadditions.pdf.

Open Society, 'Justice Initiative, Ethnic Profiling in the European Union: Pervasive, Ineffective, and discriminatory', www.opensocietyfoundations.org/sites/default/files/ profiling_20090526.pdf.

Press Information by European Information Society Institute (in Slovak), www.eisionline. org/index.php/sk/projekty%E2%80%90m/ochrana%E2%80%90sukromia/75%E2%80 %90ussr%E2%80%90pozastavil%E2%80%90sledovanie.

Press Information by European Information Society Institute (in Slovak), www.eisionline. org/index.php/sk/projekty%E2%80%90m/ochrana%E2%80%90sukromia/75%E2%80 %90ussr%E2%80%90pozastavil%E2%80%90sledovanie.

Press release No 54/14, 'The Court of Justice declares the Directive to be invalid', 8 April 2014, http://curia.europa.eu/jcms/upload/docs/application/pdf/2014-04/cp140054en. pdf.

Press release, 'EU–US Negotiations on an agreement to protect personal information exchanged in the context of fighting crime and terrorism', http://europa.eu/rapid/pressReleasesAction.do?reference=MEMO/11/203.

Press release, 'SWIFT Board approves messaging re-architecture', www.swift.com/about_swift/legal/compliance/statements_on_compliance/swift_board_approves_messaging_re_architecture/index.page.

Press release, 'SWIFT completes transparency improvements and obtains registration for Safe Harbor', www.swift.com/about_swift/legal/compliance/statements_on_compliance/swift_completes_transparency_improvements_and_files_for_safe_harbor/index.page.

'Privacy and Transborder Flows of Personal Data' (23 September 1980).

Privacy International, Memorandum of laws concerning the legality of data retention with regard to the rights guaranteed by the European Convention on Human Rights, 10 October 2003.

Privacy International, Memorandum of laws concerning the legality of data retention with regard to the rights guaranteed by the European Convention on Human Rights, 10 October 2003.

Report on the Inspection of Europol's Implementation of the TFTP Agreement, Conducted in November 2010 by the Europol Joint Supervisory Body, JSB Europol inspection report 11–07, Brussels, 1 March 2011.

Reports by the High Level Contact Group (HLCG) on information sharing and privacy and personal data protection, Brussels, 23 November 2009, 15851/09, JAI 822 DATAPROTECT 74 USA 102.

Second Report on the Processing of EU-Originating Personal Data by the US Treasury Department for Counter-terrorism purposes, TFTP, Judge Jean-Louis Bruguière, www.statewatch.org/news/2010/aug/eu-usa-swift-2nd-bruguiere-report.pdf.

Speech of Commissioner Avramopoulos at the LIBE Committee in the European Parliament, 3 December 2014, http://europa.eu/rapid/press-release_SPEECH-14-2351_en.htm.

Statement by Commissioner Věra Jourová on the signature of the Judicial Redress Act by President Obama, http://europa.eu/rapid/press-release_STATEMENT-16-401_en.htm.

Statement by EU Commissioner Věra Jourová on the finalisation of the EU-US negotiations on the data protection 'Umbrella Agreement', http://europa.eu/rapid/press-release_STATEMENT-15-5610_en.htm.

Statewatch, 'Slovakian data retention law faces challenge before Constitutional Court', http://database.statewatch.org/article.asp?aid=31892.

Summary of the First Annual Report on the Processing of EU Originating Personal Data by the United States Treasury Department For Counter Terrorism Purposes, Terrorist Finance Tracking Programme, Judge Jean-Louis Bruguière, www.statewatch.org/news/2011/apr/eu-usa-tftp-swift-1st-report-2008-judge-bruguiere.pdf.

US Homeland Security Secretary Michael Chertoff's Address before the Civil Liberties Committee of the European Parliament, Brussels 14 May 2007.

Working Party on Information Security and Privacy, 'The Evolving Privacy Landscape: 30 Years after the OECD Privacy Guidelines', OECD Digital Economy Paper, 30 April 2011, www.oecd.org/officialdocuments/displaydocumentpdf/?cote=dsti/iccp/reg(2010)6/final&doclanguage=en.

World Summit on the Information Society in its Declaration of Principles ('Declaration of Principles—Building the Information Society: a global challenge in the new Millennium', Document WSIS-03/GENEVA/DOC/4-E, Geneva, 12 December 2003).

Index